CAREER OPPORTUNITIES IN THE ARMED FORCES

C. J. HENDERSON

AND

JACK DOLPHIN

Checkmark Books®

An imprint of Facts On File, Inc.

Career Opportunities in the Armed Forces

Checkmark Books
An imprint of Facts On File, Inc.
132 West 31st Street
New York NY 10001

Library of Congress Cataloging-in-Publication Data

Henderson, C. J.
  Career opportunities in the armed forces / C.J. Henderson and Jack Dolphin.
    p. cm.
  ISBN 0-8160-4624-7 (HC) — ISBN 0-8160-4625-5 (PB)
  1. United States—Armed Forces—Job descriptions. 2. United States—Armed Forces—Occupational specialties.
3. United States —Armed Forces—Vocational guidance. I. Dolphin, Jack. II. Title.
UB337.H45 2003
355'.0023'73—dc21

Cover design by Nora Wertz

Printed in the United States of America

VB Hermitage 10 9 8 7 6 5 4 3 2 1

This book is printed on acid-free paper.

CONTENTS

FOREWORD

The armed services constantly beckon from your television, with recruiting slogans such as "Join the Navy and see the world," "Be all you can be," or "We're looking for a few good men." These slogans promise a lot. I have been on active duty, and in the reserves, since the Vietnam War, and the military delivers on these promises. I have been to many places in the world and had many adventures that I would never have experienced had it not been for my service in the armed forces.

These advantages come not only to the person who joins the military but to his or her children as well. Before joining up, I was a military dependent for 22 years, and I can tell you from personal experience that military "brats" get the best education and an exposure to the world that are unsurpassed even by those who attend exclusive prep schools. A representative list of those military dependents who have gone on to fame and fortune include singer Christina Aguilera, *Roots* and *Star Trek* star LeVar Burton, singer John Dever, actress Faye Dunaway, movie star Robert Duvall (his father was an admiral; he served in Korea), actor Michael J. Fox (his father was in the Canadian army), TV personality Kathie Lee Gifford, *Star Wars*'s Mark Hamill, actor and singer Kris Kristofferson (his father was a general and he was an army helicopter pilot), musician Jim Morrison (of The Doors), Tamara and Tia Mowry (stars of the TV series *Sister, Sister*), professional basketball player Shaquille O'Neal, actress Priscilla Presley (who was also the wife of army sergeant Elvis Presley), actress Victoria Principal, performer Lionel Ritchie, comedians Dick and Tommy Smothers (their father died on the Bataan Death March), actress Sharon Tate, actor Blair Underwood, action star Bruce Willis, and actor James Woods. For all of these successful individuals, being the children of military parents certainly did not hinder their careers and probably helped them. Military brats are usually gregarious and outgoing, the result of lives spent constantly moving to new states and countries and making new friends.

The military is obviously not for everyone, but if you're even thinking about a career in the military, this book is an excellent resource to make sure that you are pointed in the right direction. The different services and different occupational specialties can be as different as night and day, and it is important when joining up that you pursue a career path that meets your interests and talents.

Your commitment to the military does not have to be for life. Service in the military can be for differing periods of time. Some choose to join just for three years, learn a useful trade, and then enter the civilian job market with those skills. The military is well aware that it is a training ground for industry, and this tactic is fully accepted. The military is funded by taxpayers, and one of the advantages received by the country for their tax dollars is the training of the youth of our country. However, do not be surprised if, at the end of your first tour, the military tempts you with all sorts of bonus plans to try to get you to stay in!

Entering the military opens up the opportunity not only for military schooling, but for civilian schooling as well. You can attend college and graduate school while you are on active duty and get it paid for by the military. In addition, there are corresponding programs for reserves, and of course the G.I. bill applies to veterans. As mentioned above, educational opportunites also exist for children, especially when you are serving overseas. All of the celebrities mentioned above attended special overseas schools for dependents in places as diverse as Japan and Germany, and I was fortunate enough to attend high school for four years in England.

Of course, there also exists the opportunity to stay in the military for a career, and there are two ways to do that. One way is to remain on active duty for 20 or more years, in which case you will begin to draw a pension immediately on the day of your retirement. Another method is to remain in the reserves when you leave active duty, and if you stay in for 20 or more years (combined active and reserve service), then you begin to draw a pension when you reach age 60. This is the method I chose. I joined the military 31 years ago and have served in a combination of active duty and reserve positions during that time.

A lot of people still harbor the misconception that soldiers all live together in open barracks, as if it were still World War II. It's not your dad's military anymore. The following scene from the Goldie Hawn film *Private Benjamin* (1980) might be funny, but it is also indicative of the changes that have occurred in the military over the years:

Judy Benjamin: I think they sent me to the wrong place.
Capt. Lewis (amused): Uh-huh.
Judy Benjamin: See, I did join the army, but I joined a "different" army. I joined the one with the condos and the private rooms.

Actually, while Goldie Hawn did not find any condos in basic training, life in the military, once you have reached your permanent job, can be very pleasant. There is base housing, and if that isn't sufficient, you can get a tax-free housing allowance to help you pay for your apartment, or buy a house. During my parents' 20-year active duty military career, they bought and sold houses on an average of once every two years.

There is also a massive support system in place, not only for the soldier, sailor, or airman or airwoman, but also for the person's entire family. Schools for the kids, as well as sports teams, family centers, and group activities, are available. There are also offices tasked with planning and supporting leisure activities, whether it is discount tickets for Disneyland or ski trips to Switzerland. In addition, the commissary provides a great place to save money on groceries, and the PX (Post Exchange) delivers clothes and electronic equipment at rock-bottom prices.

Aside from the obvious financial advantages of serving in the military, however, and the great opportunities for travel, perhaps the most important facet is the camaraderie engendered among people in the same unit. You make friends you will keep for the rest of your life, and especially when you are deployed, you have a great time with your comrades every day.

All right, you say, this is all very well, but you are leaving out a very important little fact—I might get killed! After all, it's the military, and don't they do things like get shot at by Afghans and Iraqis and Koreans, and just about everyone else on the planet? Fortunately, it's really not the bloodbath you would think. In fact, if automobile and life insurance casualty rates are any indication, you've got a better longevity rate in the military than you do as a civilian.

That's fine as long as I'm stateside, you say, but what happens when I get into the war? Well, even there, you are more likely to sustain a basketball injury than get shot. Only 378 people—.075 percent—of the 500,000 Americans serving in the Persian Gulf War lost their lives. This means that not even one in every 1,000 Americans fighting in Operation Desert Storm was killed. A group of 500,000 average Americans who were not in the war actually would have a higher death rate. And of those 378, only 147 were combat deaths; the other 145 were non-combat-related deaths, such as auto accidents.

The same could be said of those who were injured during the Gulf War. It should come as no surprise that many people became ill or were injured in the Gulf, considering the large number of troops involved, and the quickness in which they were deployed to a foreign environment. Most of the injuries in the Gulf were attributed to troops who were out of shape. During the war, U.S. Central Command medically evacuated about 8,000 military persons, but only about 1,000 of those evacuations were combat-related. The other 7,000 people were evacuated for such non-combat-related maladies as sports injuries, auto accidents, psychological problems, and pregnancies (not all of which were preexisting pregnancies, but that's another story).

Another misconception that many people have about the military is that everyone is a war fighter. Nothing could be further from the truth. The proportion of support troops dwarfs the number of combat positions. Positions covered in the book are as diverse as electrician, chemist, computer programmer, geoscientist, surveyor, medical laboratory technician, registered nurse, social worker, graphic designer, interpreter, and auto mechanic. Practically any occupation you can envision has a counterpart in the military. Whether you just want to learn the trade and then go into the civilian sector or spend a career in the military, you can find the type of job that you want in the armed services.

I have examined *Career Opportunities in the Armed Forces* in detail, and the amount of information included on each occupational specialty is amazing. This is definitely a must-read for anyone considering joining the military.

—Robert R. Davenport, Lieutenant Colonel,
U.S. Army (Reserve)

Robert Davenport holds an MFA in screenwriting from UCLA, an MBA from Harvard Business School, and a law degree from St. John's Law School. He is a member of the bar in both California and New York, and a graduate of the Army Command and General Staff College. He has served with honors in both the Navy and Army JAG Corps and is presently a lieutenant colonel in the U.S. Army Reserve.

HOW TO USE THIS BOOK

The military of the United States of America is the greatest fighting force the world has ever known. At this stage in history it is unparalleled in its domination of all tactical and combative theaters of operation. From time to time it has its problems politically, and though a short while ago it was said to be able to fight two major campaigns simultaneously, today there are worries about its ability to sustain even one major ground and air conflict. But movements are already under way to strengthen the armed services and return them to their former glory.

For those who are considering joining a branch of the American military, weighing risk is certainly a consideration. History has proven that it's possible for the U.S. military to be caught off guard. On December 7, 1941, the Japanese surprised the navy at Pearl Harbor, and on September 11, 2001, it was bankers and investors who were cruelly murdered by enemy forces. In addition the U.S. military has sustained casualties in all the major conflicts throughout its existence. But today's armed forces are not the cannon fodder of ancient history. Indeed, there are scores of careers to be found within the military which allow one the opportunity to serve one's country without unreasonably risking life or limb. And, these are excellent positions which prepare the young men and women who do their patriotic duty for careers in the civilian world after their tours of duty come to an end.

Indeed, some of you may be considering a lifelong commitment to the military. Like becoming a doctor or a police officer, the decision to protect one's country and its citizens, to put one's own life on the line in defense of not only home and family, but of the American Constitution and democratic form of government, is an honorable, and even noble, one. These are the ultimate service careers.

One does not sign up to become a general, however. As much as one might desire to enlist in the air force or navy with the goal of ending up as one of the Joint Chiefs of Staff, things do not automatically work that way. Unless one attends an ROTC program in order to enter the armed forces as an officer, one enters on the bottom rung and must work up from there.

Privates are the trainees of the army. As a private works, studies, and trains hard, with determination he or she can advance to corporal, then on through the various degrees of sergeant, and then through the officer ranks until he or she reaches general. And then, of course, there are varying degrees of general.

But, what does a private do in the army? As stated above, the armed forces have plenty of varied jobs for their members. And, the military will be happy to find a spot for those who enlist without any idea of what they want to do. Thus, the purpose of this book becomes clear.

When entering a recruiting office, a person needs to know exactly what he or she wants to do once he or she becomes a soldier, sailor or flier. Most people assume that all branches of the armed services need cooks, doctors, barbers, supply managers, and so on. But, what many people don't realize is that every branch of the armed services has its own divers, pilots, and truck drivers as well. There are numerous positions available within the military: air traffic controllers, engineers, mechanics, electricians, nurses, and even grief counselors are needed to work hand-in-hand with those who drive tanks, man the artillery, and sling rifles over their shoulders.

Whether one wishes to make the military their home, or to use it as a stepping stone toward a good job in the civilian world, this book outlines scores of careers available within the armed forces. It outlines the duties of each position and discusses which branches offer it. The various entries will also give you:

Alternate Titles

This section will outline the various titles the same position might be known by, especially in the civilian world. Although the duties of these jobs might be remarkably similar, they can have quite different names.

Prerequisites

This section gives a brief snapshot of the experience and/or training *civilian* employers are looking for in an entry-level employee (the military does not expect most newcomers to arrive with more than a high school diploma). The important part of this section is the "rank" listing. This tells one whether or not one needs to be an officer to hold this or that position within the armed forces. If the career is really the one you want, but you need to be an officer to get it, then you might want to consider signing on in a program wherein the military pays for your college degree. You'll have to serve extra years, but you'll have your college paid for, go in at an officer's pay, and be guaranteed the training you want.

Career Ladder

The career ladder illustrates possible career paths for each job *after* one has left the military. Within the military, all advancement is the same—from rank to rank. Outside the armed forces, however, advancement may occur in different manners.

Position Description

These sections begin with a look at the career being described as it exists *within the military*. This area will cover the duties of enlisted personnel within the career, outlining their duties and what they will be responsible for as soldiers.

This section is followed by a discussion of how this career translates to a similar position in the outside world. Obviously some of these translations will be smooth. Cooks and air traffic controllers do essentially the same work in and out of the military. Others, however, such as combat positions, or those in engineering, do not translate so readily, and need extra information to illustrate how one would move from a military to civilian position within the same career.

Salary Range

Salaries within the military do not differ by occupation. They differ by rank. Helicopter piloting majors are not paid the same as helicopter piloting captains. For military pay ranges, see the pay scales below. Use the Military Rank and Grade table to find the pay grade for different ranks and salary can be calculated according to number of years in service. Salary ranges listed with the entries are those one will find in the civilian world. These ranges are as accurate and up-to-date as possible. Earnings, of course, often depend on the location of the job, the size and prestige of the employing company, as well as the experience, training, responsibilities, and education of the worker.

Employment Prospects

These sections give ratings, ranging from excellent, good, fair to poor, of the outlook for finding an opening in a given field over the next five to 10 years. Interestingly, there are very few excellent ratings due to the current downturn of the economy, but there are also very few poor ratings as well. This is because careers to be found within the military are "bread and butter" jobs. Power plant operators, printing specialists, X ray technicians—these are not jobs that go out of demand.

The Prospects sections will outline what parts of the country are likely to hold the most positions as well as what segments of the particular field are expected to have more available jobs than others.

MILITARY RANK AND GRADE

Grade	Rank				
Service	Navy	Army	Air Force	Marine Corps	Coast Guard
01	Ensign (ENS)	2nd Lieutenant (2LT)	2nd Lieutenant (2d Lt)	2nd Lieutenant (2ndLt)	Ensign (ENS)
02	Lieutenant Junior Grade (LTJG)	1st Lieutenant (1LT)	1st Lieutenant (1st Lt)	1st Lieutenant (1stLt)	Lieutenant Junior Grade (LTJG)
03	Lieutenant (LT)	Captain (CPT)	Captain (Capt)	Captain (Capt)	Lieutenant (LT)
04	Lieutenant Commander (LCDR)	Major (MAJ)	Major (Maj)	Major (Maj)	Lieutenant Commander (LCDR)
05	Commander (CDR)	Lieutenant Colonel (LTC)	Lieutenant Colonel (Lt Col)	Lieutenant Colonel (LtCol)	Commander (CDR)
06	Captain (CAPT)	Colonel (COL)	Colonel (Col)	Colonel (Col)	Captain (CAPT)
07	Rear Admiral (Lower Half) (RADM)(L)	Brigadier General (BGEN)	Brigadier General (Brig Gen)	Brigadier General (BrigGen)	Rear Admiral (Lower Half) (RADM)(L)
08	Rear Admiral (Upper Half) (RADM)(U)	Major General (MGEN)	Major General (Maj Gen)	Major General (MajGen)	Rear Admiral (Upper Half) (RADM)(U)
09	Vice Admiral (VADM)	Lieutenant General (LGEN)	Lieutenant General (Lt Gen)	Lieutenant General (LtGen)	Vice Admiral (VADM)
10	Admiral (ADM)	General (GEN)	General (Gen)	General (Gen)	Admiral (ADM)
11*	Fleet Admiral (FADM)	General of the Army (GA)	NA	NA	NA
12*		Chairman of the Joint Chiefs of Staff			

* They are not used unless those pay grades are authorized for additional pay (ie., CNO, Chairman JCS, wartime, etc.). So, a typical four-star general is an O10.

MILITARY RANK AND GRADE

Grade	Rank			
Service	Navy	Army	Marine Corps	Coast Guard
W1		Warrant Officer-1 (WO1)		
W2	Chief Warrant Officer-2 (CWO-2)	Warrant Officer-2 (CW2)	Chief Warrant Officer 2 (CWO2)	Chief Warrant Officer 2 (CWO2)
W3	Chief Warrant Officer-3 (CWO-3)	Warrant Officer-3 (CW3)	Chief Warrant Officer 3 (CWO3)	Chief Warrant Officer 3 (CWO3)
W4	Chief Warrant Officer-4 (CWO-4)	Chief Warrant Officer-4 (CW4) "Chief"	Chief Warrant Officer 4 (CWO4)	Chief Warrant Officer 4 (CWO4)

Service	Navy	Army	Air Force	Marine Corps	Coast Guard
E1	Seaman Recruit (SR)	Private E-1 (PV1)	Airman Basic (AB)	Private (Pvt)	Seaman Recruit (SR)
E2	Seaman Apprentice (SA)	Private E-2 (PV2)	Airman (Am)	Private First Class (PFC)	Seaman Apprentice (SA)
E3	Seaman (SN)	Private First Class (PFC)	Airman First Class (A1C)	Lance Corporal (LCpl)	Seaman (SN)
E4	Petty Officer 3rd Class (PO3) "Third Class"	Specialist 4 OR Corporal (SPC/CPL)	Sergeant (SGT) OR Senior Airman (SrA)	Corporal (Cpl)	Petty Officer 3rd Class (PO3) "Third Class"
E5	Petty Officer 2nd Class (PO2) "Second Class"	Sergeant (SGT)	Staff Sergeant (SSgt)	Sergeant (Sgt)	Petty Officer 2nd Class (PO2) "Second Class"
E6	Petty Officer 1st Class (PO1) "First Class"	Staff Sergeant (SSG)	Technical Sergeant (TSgt)	Staff Sergeant (SSgt)	Petty Officer 1st Class (PO1) "First Class"
E7	Chief Petty Officer (CPO) "Chief"	Sergeant First Class (SFC)	Master Sergeant (MSgt) OR First Sergeant (E-7)	Gunnery Sergeant (GySgt)	Chief Petty Officer (CPO) "Chief"
E8	Senior Chief Petty Officer (SCPO) "Senior Chief"	Master Sergeant (MSG) OR First Sergeant (1SG)	Senior Master Sergeant (SMSgt) OR First Sergeant (E-8)	First Sergeant (1st Sgt) OR Master Sergeant (MSgt)	Senior Chief Petty Officer (SCPO) "Senior Chief"
E9	Fleet (or Command) Master Chief Petty Officer OR Master Chief Petty Officer (MCPO)	Sergeant Major (SMAJ) OR Command Sergeant Major (CSM)	Chief Master Sergeant (SMSgt) OR First Sergeant (E-9)	Sergeant Major (SgtMaj) OR Master Gunnery Sergeant (MGySgt)	Command Enlisted Advisor OR Master Chief Petty Officer (MCPO)
E10*	Master Chief Petty Officer of the Navy (MCPON)	Sergeant Major of the Army (SMA)	Chief Master Sergeant of the Air Force (CMSAF)	Sergeant Major of the Marine Corps (SgtMajMC)	Master Chief Petty Officer of the Coast Guard (MCPO-CG)

* "Pay grade E10 is used here to reflect Master Chief Petty Officer of the Navy serving in certain billets for which additional pay is authorized"

Note: O=Officer E=Enlisted W=Warrant Officers

BASIC PAY

Effective: January 1, 2002

PAY GRADE	UNDER 2	OVER 2	OVER 3	OVER 4	OVER 6	OVER 8	OVER 10	OVER 12	OVER 14	OVER 16	OVER 18	OVER 20	OVER 22	OVER 24	OVER 26
						CUMULATIVE YEARS OF SERVICE 5/									
O-10 1/ & 2/												11,601.90	11,659.20	11,901.30	12,324.00
O-9 1/ & 2/												10,147.50	10,293.60	10,504.80	10,873.80
O-8 2/	7,180.20	7,415.40	7,571.10	7,614.90	7,809.30	8,135.10	8,210.70	8,519.70	8,608.50	8,874.30	9,259.50	9,614.70			
O-7 2/	5,966.40	6,371.70	6,418.20	6,657.90	6,840.30	7,051.20	7,261.80	7,472.70	8,135.10	8,694.90	8,694.90				8,738.70
O-6 2/	4,422.00	4,857.90	5,176.80	5,196.60		5,418.90	5,448.60		5,628.60	6,305.70	6,627.00	6,948.30	7,131.00	7,316.10	7,675.20
O-5 2/	3,537.00	4,152.60	4,440.30	4,494.30	4,673.10		4,813.50	5,073.30	5,413.50	5,755.80	5,919.00	6,079.80	6,262.80		
O-4 2/	3,023.70	3,681.90	3,927.60	3,982.50	4,210.50	4,395.90	4,696.20	4,930.20	5,092.50	5,255.70	5,310.60				
O-3 2/	2,796.60	3,170.40	3,421.80	3,698.70	3,875.70	4,070.10	4,232.40	4,441.20	4,549.50						
O-2 2/	2,416.20	2,751.90	3,169.50	3,276.30	3,344.10										
O-1 2/	2,097.60	2,183.10	2,638.50												
O-3E 2/ & 3/				3,698.70	3,875.70	4,070.10	4,232.40	4,441.20	4,617.00	4,717.50	4,855.20				
O-2E 2/ & 3/				3,276.30	3,344.10	3,450.30	3,630.00	3,768.90	3,872.40						
O-1E 2/ & 3/				2,638.50	2,818.20	2,922.30	3,028.50	3,133.20	3,276.30						
W-5 2/												4,965.60	5,136.00	5,307.00	5,478.60
W-4 2/	2,889.60	3,108.60	3,198.00	3,285.90	3,437.10	3,586.50	3,737.70	3,885.30	4,038.00	4,184.40	4,334.40	4,480.80	4,632.60	4,782.00	4,935.30
W-3 2/	2,638.80	2,862.00	2,898.90	2,936.10	3,017.40	3,152.40	3,330.90	3,439.50	3,558.30	3,693.90	3,828.60	3,963.60	4,098.30	4,233.30	4,368.90
W-2 2/	2,321.40	2,454.00	2,569.80	2,654.10	2,726.40	2,875.20	2,984.40	3,093.90	3,200.40	3,318.00	3,438.90	3,559.80	3,680.10	3,801.30	
W-1 2/	2,049.90	2,217.60	2,330.10	2,402.70	2,511.90	2,624.70	2,737.80	2,850.00	2,963.70	3,077.10	3,189.90	3,275.10			
E-9 2/ & 4/							3,423.90	3,501.30	3,599.40	3,714.60	3,830.40	3,944.10	4,098.30	4,251.30	4,467.00
E-8						2,858.10	2,940.60	3,017.70	3,110.10	3,210.30	3,314.70	3,420.30	3,573.00	3,724.80	3,937.80
E-7 2/	1,986.90	2,169.00	2,251.50	2,332.50	2,417.40	2,562.90	2,645.10	2,726.40	2,808.00	2,892.60	2,975.10	3,057.30	3,200.40	3,292.80	3,526.80
E-6 2/	1,701.00	1,870.80	1,953.60	2,033.70	2,117.40	2,254.50	2,337.30	2,417.40	2,499.30	2,558.10	2,602.80				
E-5 2/	1,561.50	1,665.30	1,745.70	1,828.50	1,912.80	2,030.10	2,110.20	2,193.30							
E-4 2/	1,443.60	1,517.70	1,599.60	1,680.30	1,752.30										
E-3 2/	1,303.50	1,385.40	1,468.50												
E-2 2/	1,239.30														
E-1 (+4mos.)	1,105.50														
E-1 (<4mos.)	1,022.70														
Cadets / Midshipmen	734.10														

NOTES:

1. While serving as JCS/Vice JCS, CNO, CMC, Army/Air Force CS, basic pay is $13,598.10 (see note 2).
2. Basic pay for an O-7 to O-10 is limited by Level III of the Executive Schedule, which is $11,516.70. Basic pay for O-6 and below is limited by Level V of the Executive Schedule, which is $10,133.40.
3. Applicable to O-1 to O-3 with at least four years and one day of active duty as a warrant and/or enlisted member.
4. For the MCPO of the Navy, CMSgt of the AF, Sergeant Major of the Army or Marine Corps, basic pay is $5,382.90. Combat Zone Tax Exclusion for O-1 and above is based on this basic pay rate plus HFP/IDP.
5. If there is no amount under cumulative years of service, the amount immediately to the left applies.

ALLOWANCES

BASIC ALLOWANCE FOR HOUSING

PAY GRADE	BAH-II (with dependent)	BAH-II (without dependent)	BAH Differential	BAH Partial
O-10	1,205.70	979.80	238.80	50.70
O-9	1,205.70	979.80	238.80	50.70
O-8	1,205.70	979.80	238.80	50.70
O-7	1,205.70	979.80	238.80	50.70
O-6	1,085.40	898.80	197.70	39.60
O-5	1,046.40	865.50	191.10	33.00
O-4	922.20	801.90	126.90	26.70
O-3	762.90	642.90	126.60	22.20
O-2	651.30	510.00	149.70	17.70
O-1	582.60	429.60	162.00	13.20
O-3E	819.90	694.20	133.20	22.20
O-2E	739.80	589.80	159.00	17.70
O-1E	683.70	507.60	186.30	13.20
W-5	890.40	814.80	79.50	25.20
W-4	816.30	723.60	97.80	25.20
W-3	748.20	608.40	147.60	20.70
W-2	687.90	539.70	156.00	15.90
W-1	594.90	452.40	150.60	13.80
E-9	783.30	594.30	199.50	18.60
E-8	722.40	545.70	186.60	15.30
E-7	670.50	465.90	216.30	12.00
E-6	619.80	421.80	208.80	9.90
E-5	557.40	389.10	177.60	8.70
E-4	484.20	338.40	153.90	8.10
E-3	450.90	332.10	125.70	7.80
E-2	429.60	269.70	168.90	7.20
E-1	429.60	240.60	199.50	6.90

PERSONAL MONEY ALLOWANCE

Pay Grade/Position	Annual Amount	Monthly Amount
Chairman/Vice Chairman JCS	4,000.00	333.33
General/Vice Admiral	2,200.00	183.33
Senior Member of the Military Staff Committee of the United Nations	2,200.00 plus 500.00	225.00
Lieutenant General/Vice Admiral	500.00	41.67
While Serving as Senior Enlisted Member of a Military Service (MCPO — Navy/Coast Guard, Sgt Major — Army/Marine Corps or CMSgt — Air Force)	2,000.00	166.67

BASIC ALLOWANCES FOR SUBSISTENCE

Officers: 166.37 per month

Enlisted:

Rations in kind are not available — 166.37 per month

Standard rate — 241.67 per month

FAMILY SEPARATION ALLOWANCE

All Grades — 100.00

For specific requirement for these pays and other allowances not included in this table, go to the Web at http://www.dtic.mil/comptroller/fmr/07a/index.html

For station allowances, see the Joint Travel Regulation, Volume 1

CLOTHING ALLOWANCES

Cash Clothing Replacement Allowances — Enlisted Only (Effective October 1, 2001)

TYPE	Army Male	Army Female	Navy Male	Navy Female	Air Force Male	Air Force Female	Marine Corps Male	Marine Corps Female
Basic	280.80	338.40	291.60	342.00	205.20	230.40	219.60	248.40
Standard	403.20	482.40	414.00	486.00	291.60	331.20	313.20	356.40
Special	0.00	0.00	594.00	730.80	0.00	0.00	0.00	0.00

Civilian Clothing Allowance — Enlisted and Officers (Effective 1, 2001)

Permanent Duty		Temporary Duty	
Initial	811.42	At least 15 days in 30-day period	270.49
Replacement	270.49	At least 30 days in 36-month period	540.98

SPECIAL/INCENTIVE PAY

HAZARDOUS DUTY INCENTIVE PAY FOR FLYING — AIR WEAPONS CONTROLLERS 1/

CUMULATIVE YEARS OF SERVICE AS AN AIR WEAPONS CONTROLLER 1/

PAY GRADE	2 or LESS	OVER 2	OVER 3	OVER 4	OVER 6	OVER 8	OVER 12	OVER 14	OVER 18	OVER 20	OVER 22	OVER 24	OVER 25
O-7 & Above	200.00												150.00
O-6	225.00	250.00	300.00	325.00	350.00					300.00	250.00		225.00
O-5	200.00	250.00	300.00	325.00	350.00					300.00	250.00		225.00
O-4	175.00	225.00	275.00	300.00	350.00					300.00	250.00		225.00
O-3	150.00	156.00	188.00	206.00	350.00					275.00	250.00	225.00	200.00
O-2	150.00	156.00	188.00	206.00	250.00	300.00	350.00		275.00	245.00	210.00	200.00	180.00
O-1	150.00	156.00	188.00	206.00	250.00	250.00		245.00			210.00	180.00	150.00
W-5	200.00	225.00	275.00	300.00	300.00					276.00	250.00	225.00	200.00
W-4	200.00	225.00	275.00	300.00	325.00					276.00	250.00	225.00	200.00
W-3	175.00	225.00	275.00	300.00	325.00						250.00	225.00	200.00
W-2	150.00	200.00	250.00	275.00	325.00					275.00	250.00	225.00	200.00
W-1	150.00			175.00	325.00					275.00	250.00	225.00	200.00
E-9	200.00	225.00	250.00	275.00	300.00					275.00	230.00	200.00	
E-8	200.00	225.00	250.00	275.00	300.00					265.00	230.00	200.00	
E-7	175.00	200.00	225.00	250.00	275.00					265.00	230.00	200.00	
E-6	156.00	175.00	200.00	225.00	250.00		300.00			265.00	200.00	200.00	150.00
E-5	150.00	156.00	175.00	188.00	200.00		300.00			225.00	200.00	175.00	
E-4 & Below	150.00	156.00	175.00	188.00	200.00		250.00			175.00	150.00		

Note: If there is no amount under cumulative years of experience, the amount immediately to the left applies.

DIVING PAY

OFFICERS	ENLISTED
240 Max.	340 Max.

See DoDFMR, Volume 7A, Chapter 11, Tables 11-1 through 11-8 for specific rates.

Imminent Danger
Hostile Fire Pay
All Grades
150.00 per month

HAZARDOUS DUTY INCENTIVE PAY FOR FLYING — CREWMEMBER (Except for AWACS)

PAY GRADE	0-10	0-9	0-8	0-7	0-6	0-5	0-4	0-3	0-2	0-1	W-5	W-4	W-3	W-2	W-1
Amount	150.00	150.00	150.00	150.00	250.00	250.00	225.00	175.00	150.00	150.00	250.00	250.00	175.00	150.00	150.00

PAY GRADE	E-9, E-8, and E-7	E-6	E-5	E-4	E-3, E-2, and E-1
Amount	240.00	215.00	190.00	165.00	150.00

MONTHLY AVIATION CAREER INCENTIVE PAY RATES 1/, 2/, 3/, and 4/

PAY GRADE	UNDER 2	OVER 2	OVER 3	OVER 4	OVER 6	OVER 14	OVER 22	OVER 23	OVER 24	OVER 25
All Officers	125.00	156.00	188.00	206.00	650.00	840.00	585.00	495.00	385.00	250.00

1. A rated officer in pay grade 0-7 may not be paid incentive pay at a rate greater than $200 per month.
2. A rated officer in pay grade 0-8 or above may not be paid incentive pay at a rate greater than $206 per month.
3. A rated officer in pay grade 0-6 may not be paid incentive pay after completion of 25 years of aviation service.
4. A rated warrant officer with over 22, 23, 24, or 25 years of aviation service, will continue to receive the rate prescribed for officers with over 14 years of aviation service.

HDIP FOR PARACHUTE, FLIGHT DECK, DEMOLITION, EXPERIMENTAL STRESS, AND OTHERS

All Grades — 150.00 per month (except for a member who qualifies for HALO pay, which is 225.00 per month)

HARDSHIP DUTY LOCATION PAY (MONTHLY AMOUNTS)

HDP-M — 150 (Enlisted and Officers)
HDP-L(DA) — 50 to 150 (Enlisted and Officers)
HDP-L(CP) — (Enlisted Only) (E-7 to E-9 — 22.50), (E-6 — 20.00), (E-5 — 16.00), (E-4 — 13.00), (E-3 — 9.00), (E-2 & E1 — 8.00)

For specific requirement for these pays, go to the Web at http://www.dtic.mil/comptroller/fmr/07a/index.html

SPECIAL PAY/BONUSES (Dental, Medical, Pharmacy, Optometry, and Veterinary Officers)

VARIABLE SPECIAL PAY — DENTAL OFFICERS

PAY GRADE	UNDER 3	3 & OVER	8 & OVER	10 & OVER	12 & OVER	14 & OVER	18 & OVER	22 & OVER
Intern	250.00							
Thru O-6		583.33			833.33	750.00	666.67	
Above O-6	583.33		1,000.00					

SPECIAL PAY — DENTAL OFFICERS (Annual Amount)

All Grades	######

ADDITIONAL SPECIAL PAY — DENTAL OFFICERS (Annual Amount)

All Grades	4,000.00	6,000.00	15,000.00

BOARD-CERTIFIED SPECIAL PAY — DENTAL OFFICERS

	Under 10	10 & OVER	12 & OVER	14 & OVER	18 & OVER	22 & OVER
All Grades	208.33	291.66	333.33	416.66	500.00	

DENTAL OFFICER MULTIYEAR RETENTION BONUS (DOMRB)

	2-Year Agreement	3-Year Agreement	4-Year Agreement
Level 1	4,000.00	8,000.00	14,000.00
Level 2	3,000.00	6,000.00	12,000.00

MEDICAL OFFICER MULTIYEAR SPECIAL PAY

	2-Year Agreement	3-Year Agreement	4-Year Agreement
Level 1	9,000.00	10,000.00	14,000.00
Level 2	8,000.00	9,000.00	10,000.00
Level 3	6,000.00	7,000.00	8,000.00

VARIABLE SPECIAL PAY — MEDICAL OFFICERS

PAY GRADE	UNDER 6	6 & OVER	8 & OVER	10 & OVER	12 & OVER	14 & OVER	18 & OVER	22 & OVER
Intern	100.00							
Thru O-6	416.66	1,000.00	958.33	916.67	833.33	750.00	666.67	583.33
Above O-6	583.33							

BOARD-CERTIFIED SPECIAL PAY — MEDICAL OFFICERS

	Under 10	10 & OVER	12 & OVER	14 & OVER	18 & OVER	22 & OVER
All Grades	208.33	291.66	333.33	416.66	500.00	

DIPLOMATE/BOARD-CERTIFIED SPECIAL PAY — Non-Health-Care Physician, Veterinarians, and Psychologists

	Under 10	10 & OVER	12 & OVER	14 & OVER	18 & OVER	22 & OVER
All Grades	166.66	208.33	250.00	333.33	416.66	

SPECIAL PAY — Pharmacy Officers (Annual Amounts)

PAY GRADE	UNDER 3	3 & OVER	6 & OVER	8 & OVER	12 & OVER	14 & OVER	18 & OVER	22 & OVER
All Grades	3,000.00	7,000.00		12,000.00	10,000.00	9,000.00	8,000.00	

ADDITIONAL SPECIAL PAY — Veterinary Officers (Annual Amounts)

PAY GRADE	UNDER 10	10 & OVER	12 & OVER	14 & OVER	18 & OVER
All Grades	2,000.00	2,500.00	3,000.00	4,000.00	5,000.00

Nurses Incentive Special Pay (CRNA)
All Grades — $6,000.00 (Annual Amount)

Nurses Accession Bonus (Annual Amount)
All Grades — $5,000.00

SPECIAL PAY (Physicians) — Reserve Medical Officers on Active Duty for less than One Year (Monthly Amount)
All Grades — $450.00

Additional Special Pay — Medical Officers (Annual Amount)
All Grades — $15,000

Incentive Special Pay — Medical Officers (Annual Amount)
All Grades — $36,000

Accession Bonus — Pharmacy Officers (Annual Amount)
All Grades — $30,000

Accession Bonus — Dental Officers (Annual Amount)
All Grades — $30,000

Retention Special Pay — Optometry Officers (Annual Amount)
All Grades — $6,000

Special Pay — Pharmacy, Optometry, and Veterinary Officers (Monthly Amount)
All Grades — $100.00

For specific requirements, for these pay bonuses, go to the Web at http://www.dtic.mil/comptroller/fmr/07a/index.html

SUBMARINE PAY [1/] & [2/]

CUMULATIVE YEARS OF SERVICE

PAY GRADE	2 or LESS	OVER 2	OVER 3	OVER 4	OVER 6	OVER 8	OVER 10	OVER 12	OVER 14	OVER 16	OVER 18	OVER 22	OVER 26
O-10	355.00												
O-9	355.00												
O-8	355.00												
O-7	355.00									540.00	535.00	410.00	355.00
O-6	595.00												
O-5	595.00				595.00								
O-4	365.00			405.00	595.00								
O-3	355.00			390.00	595.00								
O-2	235.00						355.00						
O-1	175.00						355.00						
W-5	235.00	310.00		355.00									
W-4	235.00	310.00		355.00									
W-3	235.00	310.00		355.00									
W-2	235.00	310.00		355.00									
W-1	235.00	310.00		355.00									
E-9	225.00			270.00	295.00	310.00	315.00	330.00	345.00	355.00			
E-8	225.00			250.00	270.00	295.00	310.00	315.00	330.00		345.00		
E-7	225.00			250.00	255.00	265.00	275.00	295.00	310.00				
E-6	155.00	170.00	175.00	215.00	230.00	245.00	255.00	265.00					
E-5	140.00	155.00		175.00	190.00	195.00							
E-4	80.00	95.00	100.00	170.00	175.00								
E-3	80.00	90.00	95.00		140.00								
E-2	75.00	90.00											
E-1	75.00												

NOTES:

1. If there is no amount under cumulative years of service, the amount immediately to the left applies.

2. Under Public Law 107-107, section 617, the secretary of the navy is authorized to prescribe the monthly rates of submarine-duty incentive pay up to $1,000 per month. The rates reflected in this table will be updated when the secretary of the navy prescribes the new rates authorized by this statute.

Effective: October 1, 2001

MONTHLY CAREER SEA PAY — (NAVY AND MARINE CORPS MEMBERS)

PAY GRADE	1 or LESS	OVER 1	OVER 2	OVER 3	OVER 4	OVER 5	OVER 6	OVER 7	OVER 8	OVER 9	OVER 10	OVER 11	OVER 12	OVER 13	OVER 14	OVER 16	OVER 18	OVER 20
							CUMULATIVE YEARS OF SEA DUTY[1]											
O-6	100.00			315.00	320.00		335.00	360.00	370.00	395.00	405.00	420.00	435.00		455.00	475.00	500.00	535.00
O-5	100.00			315.00				320.00	345.00	350.00	365.00	370.00			400.00	420.00	440.00	475.00
O-4	100.00			260.00	265.00		285.00	300.00	310.00		315.00		335.00		380.00	395.00	405.00	420.00
O-3	100.00			210.00	225.00	260.00	265.00	275.00	285.00	300.00	315.00		335.00		365.00	380.00	395.00	405.00
O-2	100.00			210.00	225.00	260.00	265.00	275.00	285.00	300.00	315.00		335.00		350.00	365.00	380.00	395.00
O-1	100.00			210.00	225.00	260.00	265.00	275.00	285.00	300.00	315.00		335.00		350.00	365.00	380.00	395.00
W-5	210.00				240.00		435.00				490.00	525.00	560.00		630.00		700.00	
W-4	210.00				240.00	405.00	435.00				490.00	525.00	560.00		630.00		700.00	
W-3	210.00				240.00	380.00	395.00	400.00		435.00	490.00	525.00	560.00		595.00		630.00	
W-2	210.00				240.00	365.00	370.00		380.00	435.00	475.00	525.00	560.00					
W-1	180.00		195.00	210.00	240.00	245.00	280.00	350.00	380.00	420.00	455.00		475.00		505.00	525.00		
E-9	135.00		160.00	305.00	320.00	350.00		375.00	490.00	500.00		510.00	520.00	550.00	575.00	620.00		
E-8	135.00		160.00	305.00	320.00	350.00		375.00	490.00	500.00		510.00	520.00	550.00	575.00	600.00	620.00	
E-7	135.00		160.00	305.00	320.00	350.00		375.00	490.00	500.00		510.00	520.00	550.00	575.00	600.00		
E-6	135.00		160.00	280.00	300.00	315.00	325.00	350.00	450.00	460.00	465.00		480.00	495.00	510.00	525.00	550.00	
E-5	70.00	80.00	160.00	280.00	300.00	315.00	325.00	350.00	450.00									
E-4	70.00	80.00	160.00	280.00	290.00				390.00									
E-3	50.00	60.00	100.00															
E-2	50.00	60.00	75.00															
E-1	50.00																	

NOTES:
1. If there is no amount under cumulative years of service, the amount immediately to the left applies.

MONTHLY CAREER SEA PAY — (ARMY AND AIR FORCE CORPS MEMBERS)

PAY GRADE	1 or LESS	OVER 1	OVER 2	OVER 3	OVER 4	OVER 5	OVER 6	OVER 7	OVER 8	OVER 9	OVER 10	OVER 11	OVER 12	OVER 13	OVER 14	OVER 16	OVER 18	OVER 20
							CUMULATIVE YEARS OF SEA DUTY[1]											
O-6				225.00	230.00		240.00	255.00	265.00	280.00	290.00	300.00	310.00		325.00	340.00	355.00	380.00
O-5				225.00				230.00	245.00	250.00	260.00	265.00			285.00	300.00	315.00	340.00
O-4				185.00	190.00	200.00	205.00	215.00	220.00		225.00		240.00		270.00	280.00	290.00	300.00
O-3				150.00	160.00	185.00	190.00	195.00	205.00	215.00	225.00		240.00		260.00	270.00	280.00	290.00
O-2				150.00	160.00	185.00	190.00	195.00	205.00	215.00	225.00		240.00		250.00	260.00	270.00	280.00
O-1				150.00	160.00	185.00	190.00	195.00	205.00	215.00	225.00		240.00		250.00	260.00	270.00	280.00
W-4 & W-5	150.00				170.00		310.00			310.00	350.00		400.00		450.00		500.00	
W-3	150.00				170.00	270.00	280.00	285.00	290.00	310.00	350.00	375.00	400.00		425.00		450.00	
W-2	150.00				170.00	260.00	265.00		270.00	310.00	340.00	375.00	375.00		400.00			
W-1	130.00	135.00	140.00	150.00	170.00	175.00	200.00	250.00	270.00	300.00	325.00		340.00		360.00	375.00		
E-9	100.00		120.00	175.00	190.00	350.00		375.00	390.00	400.00		410.00	420.00	450.00	475.00	520.00		
E-8	100.00		120.00	175.00	190.00	350.00		375.00	390.00	400.00		410.00	420.00	450.00	475.00	500.00	520.00	
E-7	100.00		120.00	175.00	190.00	350.00		375.00	390.00	400.00		410.00	420.00	450.00	475.00	500.00		
E-6	100.00		120.00	150.00	170.00	315.00	325.00	350.00	365.00				380.00	395.00	410.00	425.00	450.00	
E-5	50.00	60.00	120.00	150.00	170.00	315.00	325.00	350.00	365.00									
E-4	50.00	60.00	120.00	150.00	160.00													

NOTES:
1. If there is no amount under cumulative years of service, the amount immediately to the left applies.

DRILL PAY

COMMISSIONED OFFICERS [1] & [2]

PAY GRADE	CUMULATIVE YEARS OF SERVICE														
	UNDER 2	OVER 2	OVER 3	OVER 4	OVER 6	OVER 8	OVER 10	OVER 12	OVER 14	OVER 16	OVER 18	OVER 20	OVER 22	OVER 24	OVER 26
O-7	5,966.40	6,371.70		6,418.20	6,657.90	6,840.30	7,051.20	7,261.80	7,472.70	8,135.10	8,694.90				8,738.70
1 drill	198.88	212.39		213.94	221.93	228.01	235.04	242.06	249.09	271.17	289.83				291.29
4 drills	795.52	849.56		855.76	887.72	912.04	940.16	968.24	996.36	1084.68	1159.32				1165.16
O-6	4,422.00	4,857.90	5,176.80		5,196.60	5,418.90	5,448.60		5,628.60	6,305.70	6,627.00	6,948.30	7,131.00	7,316.10	7,675.20
1 drill	147.40	161.93	172.56		173.22	180.63	181.62		187.62	210.19	220.90	231.61	237.70	243.87	255.84
4 drills	589.60	647.72	690.24		692.88	722.52	726.48		750.48	840.76	883.60	926.44	950.80	975.48	1023.36
O-5	3,537.00	4,152.60	4,440.30	4,494.30	4,673.10		4,813.50	5,073.30	5,413.50	5,755.80	5,919.00	6,079.80	6,262.80		
1 drill	117.90	138.42	148.01	149.81	155.77		160.45	169.11	180.45	191.86	197.30	202.66	208.76		
4 drills	471.60	553.68	592.04	599.24	623.08		641.80	676.44	721.80	767.44	789.20	810.64	835.04		
O-4	3,023.70	3,681.90	3,927.60	3,982.50	4,210.50	4,395.90	4,696.20	4,930.20	5,092.50	5,255.70	5,310.60				
1 drill	100.79	122.73	130.92	132.75	140.35	146.53	156.54	164.34	169.75	175.19	177.02				
4 drills	403.16	490.92	523.68	531.00	561.40	586.12	626.16	657.36	679.00	700.76	708.08				
O-3	2,796.60	3,170.40	3,421.80	3,698.70	3,875.70	4,070.10	4,232.40	4,441.20	4,549.50						
1 drill	93.22	105.68	114.06	123.29	129.19	135.67	141.08	148.04	151.65						
4 drills	372.88	422.72	456.24	493.16	516.76	542.68	564.32	592.16	606.60						
O-2	2,416.20	2,751.90	3,169.50	3,276.30	3,344.10										
1 drill	80.54	91.73	105.65	109.21	111.47										
4 drills	322.16	366.92	422.60	436.84	445.88										
O-1	2,097.60	2,183.10	2,638.50	2,638.50											
1 drill	69.92	72.77	87.95	87.95											
4 drills	279.68	291.08	351.80	351.80											
COMMISSIONED OFFICERS WITH AT LEAST FOUR YEARS AND A DAY OF ACTIVE DUTY SERVICE AS AN ENLISTED MEMBER AND/OR (Includes Reserve Commissioned Officers With At Least 1,460 Points When Paid From Reserve Appropriations)															
O-3E				3,698.70	3,875.70	4,070.10	4,232.40	4,441.20	4,617.00	4,717.50	4,855.20				
1 drill				123.29	129.19	135.67	141.08	148.04	153.90	157.25	161.84				
4 drills				493.16	516.76	542.68	564.32	592.16	615.60	629.00	647.36				
O-2E				3,276.30	3,450.30	3,630.00	3,768.90	3,872.40							
1 drill				109.21	115.01	121.00	125.63	129.08							
4 drills				436.84	460.04	484.00	502.52	516.32							
O-1E				2,638.50	2,818.20	2,922.30	3,028.50	3,133.20	3,276.30						
1 drill				87.95	93.94	97.41	100.95	104.44	109.21						
4 drills				351.80	375.76	389.64	403.80	417.76	436.84						
WARRANT OFFICERS															
W-5												4,965.60	5,136.00	5,307.00	5,478.60
1 drill												165.52	171.20	176.90	182.62
4 drills												662.08	684.80	707.60	730.48
W-4	2,889.60	3,108.60	3,198.00	3,285.90	3,437.10	3,586.50	3,737.70	3,885.30	4,038.00	4,184.40	4,334.40	4,480.80	4,632.60	4,782.00	4,935.30
1 drill	96.32	103.62	106.60	109.53	114.57	119.55	124.59	129.51	134.60	139.48	144.48	149.36	154.42	159.40	164.51
4 drills	385.28	414.48	426.40	438.12	458.28	478.20	498.36	518.04	538.40	557.92	577.92	597.44	617.68	637.60	658.04
W-3	2,638.80	2,862.00		2,898.90	3,017.40	3,152.40	3,330.90	3,439.50	3,558.30	3,693.90	3,828.60	3,963.60	4,098.30	4,233.30	4,368.90
1 drill	87.96	95.40		96.63	100.58	105.08	111.03	114.65	118.61	123.13	127.62	132.12	136.61	141.11	145.63
4 drills	351.84	381.60		386.52	402.32	420.32	444.12	458.60	474.44	492.52	510.48	528.48	546.44	564.44	582.52

Notes:

1. The monthly basic pay is on the same line as the pay grade. One drill is at least three hours of training, and four drills is normally for one weekend training (eight hours Saturdays and eight hours Sunday).

2. If there is not amount under cumulative years of service, the amount immediately to the left applies.

DRILL PAY (Continued)

WARRANT OFFICERS

PAY GRADE	UNDER 2	OVER 2	OVER 3	OVER 4	OVER 6	OVER 8	OVER 10	OVER 12	OVER 14	OVER 16	OVER 18	OVER 20	OVER 22	OVER 24	OVER 26
W-2	2,321.40	2,454.00	2569.80	2,654.10	2,726.40	2,875.20	2,984.40	3,093.90	3,200.40	3,318.00	3,438.90	3,559.80	3,680.10	3,801.30	
1 drill	77.38	81.80	85.66	88.47	90.88	95.84	99.48	103.13	106.68	110.60	114.63	118.66	122.67	126.71	
4 drills	309.52	327.20	342.64	353.88	363.52	383.36	397.92	412.52	426.72	442.40	458.52	474.64	490.68	506.84	
W-1	2049.90	2,217.60	2,330.10	2,402.70	2,511.90	2,624.70	2,737.80	2,850.00	2,963.70	3,077.10	3,189.90	3,275.10			
1 drill	68.33	73.92	77.67	80.09	83.73	87.49	91.26	95.00	98.79	102.57	106.33	109.17			
4 drills	273.32	295.68	310.68	320.36	334.92	349.96	365.04	380.00	395.16	410.28	425.32	436.68			

ENLISTED MEMBERS

PAY GRADE	UNDER 2	OVER 2	OVER 3	OVER 4	OVER 6	OVER 8	OVER 10	OVER 12	OVER 14	OVER 16	OVER 18	OVER 20	OVER 22	OVER 24	OVER 26
E-9							3,423.90	3,501.30	3,599.40	3,714.60	3,830.40	3,944.10	4,098.30	4,251.30	4,467.00
1 drill							114.13	116.71	119.98	123.82	127.68	131.47	136.61	141.71	148.90
4 drills							456.52	466.84	479.92	495.28	510.72	525.88	546.44	566.84	595.60
E-8						2,858.10	2,940.60	3,017.70	3,110.10	3,210.30	3,314.70	3,420.30	3,573.00	3,724.80	3,937.80
1 drill						95.27	98.02	100.59	103.67	107.01	110.49	114.01	119.10	124.16	131.26
4 drills						381.08	392.08	402.36	414.68	428.04	441.96	456.04	476.40	496.64	525.04
E-7	1,986.90	2,169.00	2,251.50	2,332.50	2,417.40	2,562.90	2,645.10	2,726.40	2,808.00	2,892.60	2,975.10	3,057.30	3,200.40	3,292.80	3,526.80
1 drill	66.23	72.30	75.05	77.75	80.58	85.43	88.17	90.88	93.60	96.42	99.17	101.91	106.68	109.76	117.56
4 drills	264.92	289.20	300.20	311.00	322.32	341.72	352.68	363.52	374.40	385.68	396.68	407.64	426.72	439.04	470.24
E-6	1,701.00	1,870.80	1,953.60	2,033.70	2,117.40	2,254.50	2,337.30	2,417.40	2,499.30	2,558.10	2,602.80				
1 drill	56.70	62.36	65.12	67.79	70.58	75.15	77.91	80.58	83.31	85.27	86.76				
4 drills	226.80	249.44	260.48	271.16	282.32	300.60	311.64	322.32	333.24	341.08	347.04				
E-5	1,561.50	1,665.30	1,745.70	1,828.50	1,912.80	2,030.10	2,110.20	2,193.30							
1 drill	52.05	55.51	58.19	60.95	63.76	67.67	70.34	73.11							
4 drills	208.20	222.04	232.76	243.80	255.04	270.68	281.36	292.44							
E-4	1,443.60	1,517.70	1,599.60	1,680.30	1,752.30										
1 drill	48.12	50.59	53.32	56.01	58.41										
4 drills	192.48	202.36	213.28	224.04	233.64										
E-3	1,303.50	1,385.40	1,468.50												
1 drill	43.45	46.18	48.95												
4 drills	173.80	184.72	195.80												
E-2	1,239.30														
1 drill	41.31														
4 drills	165.24														
E-1 (4+mos.)	1,105.50														
1 drill	36.85														
4 drills	147.40														
E-1 (<4mos.)	1,022.70														
1 drill	34.09														
4 drills	136.36														

Advancement Prospects

Here the career ladder is expanded to explain in more detail how one progresses from entry level to the top of any given field in the civilian workplace. This is not a "tips" section (try to be cooperative, be as helpful in the workplace as possible, don't try to see how little you can do). The assumption is that once a person makes it through basic training and has spent a number of years within the service, these kinds of suggestions should be completely unnecessary. Life in the armed forces prepares most people thoroughly for the workplaces of the outside world. Thus, here we have merely listed the career path from trainee on upward.

Education and Training

This section begins with the training one will receive from the military in a particular career. Outside of medical positions, nearly all jobs skills held within the armed forces are taught to new soldiers by soldiers on military installations. You do not need to bring any previous experience. For most jobs, you do not even need to come with a college education. The military will teach you everything you need to know.

The second part of this section lists the minimum training necessary for the same job in the outside world. Many positions which call for years of training or college degrees, or both, can be obtained just as easily by having learned and performed them previously in the military. This second section will give one an idea of when this is true, what employers are looking for in the way of previous education and experience, and also what state and federal licenses (if any) are needed for a particular career in the outside world.

Experience, Skills, and Personality Traits

This section lists what types of previous experience (or experiences) can be helpful in a career. It also goes into what types of personal skills, hobbies, or interests might be useful. It highlights the fact that if one has a certain set of interests, then he or she might be suitable for a particular career.

Unions and Associations

This section offers other sources for career information and assistance once one leaves the military. Unions and trade associations often offer valuable help in obtaining career guidance, support, personal contact, and further training. They can often lead one to such things as grants and scholarships for further education, seminars that can quickly help upgrade military skills to civilian ones as well as valuable information on how easily armed forces service will translate into a civilian career.

INDUSTRY OUTLOOK

Why a career in the armed forces? What reasons could one have for joining the military? Isn't it dangerous? What could one learn there? How's that going to prepare me for life? Isn't it really all just a big waste?

Absolutely not.

Despite the United States military's efforts to improve its image, many people still have an extremely limited idea of what the military is actually all about. Much of popular culture and the nightly news have fostered the impression that abusive indoctrination, bad food, and fighting and dying for one's country is all the air force, army, navy, coast guard, or marines have to offer. Social and political changes of the past 20 years have left most people without much common knowledge of how the military operates and what it has to offer the average person. How does one receive training? What jobs never see frontline action? How many years can one stay in the armed forces? When can one retire or return to the civilian world with their accumulated skills to seek a new career? *Career Opportunities in the Armed Forces* is designed to answer these questions and many, many others.

The military isn't just a job and it's not just an adventure, either. For the men and women who sign on, it becomes a complete way of life. The military claims a person, body and soul, for a number of years, and provides all of life's necessities during that period. For the young man or woman ready to leave home, it can be an appealing package. For some willing individuals it can be become their home for life, offering good pay, good food, warm beds, challenging work, and so on.

For those interested in launching careers beyond the armed forces, however, the military holds far more possibilities than one might expect. Many people think of military training as learning to shoot little guns, then maybe learning to shoot bigger guns or other activities with an emphasis on combat and defense. But the massive, and increasingly sophisticated, support arms of the various services—administration, communications, transportation, health care, and many others—far outweigh the combat troops they service. And, unlike the job of the combat soldier, these support positions translate directly into training that the outside world finds immensely valuable.

Learning to fly a jumbo jet, managing a computer network, or becoming a Civil Engineer gives a person readily bankable skills they can utilize easily in any state in the union or in any other country around the world. And these are, of course, just a few of the scores of useful and prof-

itable high-tech careers for which one might receive training in the modern armed forces.

"But," the question arises, "will I really get the military career I want?" The honest answer is that the armed forces try their level best to get everyone into the slot they request. The military is not just looking for bodies. They need willing, capable personnel to fill scores of different types of jobs, and like any other employer, they're eager to match the right person to the right position.

The two main factors that go into the job assignment decision are, first, the recruit's scores on the military tests administered to indicate special talents or abilities, and, second, the specific needs of the branch of the armed forces they wish to join at the time they wish to join.

But what does this really mean? If you want to be a pilot you'll be told that every effort will be made just to convince you to sign up and then you'll be dumped in the infantry—right? Wrong. Right now all branches of the armed forces are experiencing major personnel shortages. Every single branch of the American military has fallen drastically short of their recruitment goals since the late 1990s. Last year (2001) every branch fell at least 20,000 slots short. According to the U.S. Census Bureau Statistical Abstract of the U.S.A., total enlistments for all branches dropped by 181,000 in the years from 1990 to 1997. What other industry is actively looking for in excess of 100,000 workers? In other words, the military is a buyer's market right now. If you have the aptitude for the job you want, your chances are as good as possible that you'll get it.

But, what job is it that you want? And, are you thinking of going in to the military as a lifelong career, or only as a stepping stone to a career in the civilian world? This is the first big question anyone considering the armed forces must ask themselves.

Each plan has its advantages, but they are highly personal ones. What looks like a positive to one individual will seem like a drawback to another. To some, a home where someone cleans their clothes and cooks for them, pays for their college tuition, their haircuts, their rent, and so on, can look like a great deal. For others, having someone else hold so much control of their lives can seem like a nightmare.

The military is like any other aspect of life. Some people let their jobs take control of them, and others take control of their jobs. The type of person you are will determine how you approach any future career. Some people will be entry-level personnel forever. Others will advance to become generals and CEOs. In reality, what becomes of a person entering the armed forces is up to them, the same way it is any field of endeavor.

When considering a career in the military it's important to focus on both how long you want to sign up for (enlisting as an active-duty soldier requires a commitment of two to six years. Enlistment cash bonuses are available with certain jobs), and what you want to do within the service. Signing one's life away to the army or another branch of the service sounds scary in some ways, but the decision is similar to the one you might make choosing a college to prepare for a career. If you choose wrong, the same amount of time is wasted. The only difference is, the military pays its soldiers to sign up and be trained for a career, while colleges make the students pay.

Once you know exactly how many years of your life you want to dedicate to the service, and you know exactly what career you want, the next thing you must ask yourself is, do you want to go in as an enlisted soldier or as an officer.

Certain positions can only be held by officers and certain other positions cannot be held by officers. Anyone who wants an enlisted position has few worries beyond signing on and working to meet their goal. Those who want to be an officer, however, have other things to consider.

Becoming an officer requires education beyond high school. For some, the rising cost of tuition can be hard to manage, but the military's Tuition Assistance Program pays for 75 percent of the cost of tuition (or expenses up to a maximum of $187.50 per semester hour credit and a personal maximum of $3,500 per fiscal year per student). This program is the same for active duty members in each military service. Selected military reserve and National Guard units also offer a Tuition Assistance Program, although the benefits may vary from the active duty program.

The Montgomery GI Bill offers up to $28,800 in tuition in return for a three-year commitment on active duty. One can use the GI Bill for college degree programs but also for certificate programs, flight training, apprenticeship/on-the-job training, correspondence courses, and other programs.

There are also the military's College Fund Programs which provide any eligible serviceman or woman up to $50,000 toward their college tuition when combined with the Montgomery GI Bill upon honorable discharge. One does need to qualify for these additional funds, true, but in 1997 alone more than 23,000 young veterans made use of the military's College Fund programs. To qualify one must sign up for active duty for two, three, or four years, enroll in the Montgomery GI Bill, score above a 50 on the Armed Services Vocational Aptitude Battery (ASVAB) and have no prior service in the military. The army, navy, marine corps and coast guard programs are administered much the same. The air force maintains the Community College of the Air Force, an accredited two-year college open only to enlisted men and women in the U.S. Air Force.

For those who've completed college but are weighed down by debt, the military offers Loan Repayment Programs. In the active duty army, soldiers can qualify to have their loan repaid at the rate of one-third of the loan for each year of active duty served (maximum loan repayment is $65,000). The army even helps soldiers pay off student loans (provided they attended schools on an approved Perkins, Stafford, or other Department of Education Guaranteed Student Loan).

In the active duty navy and air force, a $10,000 Loan Repayment Program is available. It requires that one have no prior military service, a high school diploma, and a loan guaranteed under the Higher Education Act of 1965. One must also qualify for Navy Nuclear Field or another designated critical rating as defined by the navy among other restrictions.

One can also go to college and train to be an officer at the same time, through the Reserve Officer Training Corps (ROTC). ROTC is a curriculum of elective leadership and military courses you take while enrolled in college. Not every campus offers an ROTC program, but considering that enlisting in ROTC can qualify one for up to $60,000 in scholarships, it isn't a terrible thing to look into, especially considering that to enroll in ROTC all one really needs is to be accepted or enrolled in a participating college or university, between the ages of 17 and 21, and a U.S. citizen.

Officer Candidate School is another way to become an officer in the army, navy, air force, marine corps, or coast guard. Candidates attend Officer Basic Training and then go through some 10 to 14 weeks of rigorous training. Admission immediately after graduation is possible in all branches but the army (the army expects candidates to serve an enlisted term first).

Other options include the service academies, such as the U.S. Military Academy at West Point, New York, one of the country's top universities, a competitive environment that has produced some of the nation's finest leaders. Many graduates of West Point go on to success in the military and in big corporations.

West Point applicants must be between the ages of 17 and 23 as of July 1 of the year they're admitted, U.S. citizens, single, not married, not pregnant or with any legal obligation to support a child, in excellent academic standing and rank in high school class, and a recipient of strong scores on either the ACT or SAT. The other service academies, all with similar requirements, are the U.S. Naval Academy in Annapolis, Maryland; the U.S. Air Force Academy in Colorado Springs, Colorado; and the U.S. Coast Guard Academy in New London, Connecticut.

There are also Direct Commission Officers, degreed professionals with specialized training who join the military as high-ranking officers. Direct Commission Officers can be part of the Judge Advocate General Corps, the Army Chaplain Corps, and the Army Medical Corps.

The military also has a network of more than 300 schools with more than 10,000 courses to train its members. Some 60 percent of these courses are certified for college credit by the American Council on Education, which means one can earn college credits for being trained to learn a marketable skill. Also, there are the Servicemember Opportunity Colleges, a group of more than 1,400 colleges and universities that agree to transfer credits among themselves for military members and their families. Whether one is stationed in Key West, Florida or San Diego, California, they can continue their college studies via SOC, either in the classroom, at a distance by computer, or by mail.

Military personnel can also take the College-Level Examination Program (CLEP) series (general exams like Mathematics or subject exams like Western Civilization), the DANTES Subject Standardized Tests (DSST), or the well-known Regents examination series. Passing the test gets one the credits involved, usually three credits per subject exam.

So, you know what career you would want to pursue, and whether you would want to enter the service as an enlisted soldier or an officer. You have figured out all the details of whether you would go to college before entering the service, or during, how it would be paid for, and what skills you would have when it was all over. You know whether or not you want the military to be your life, or only a stepping stone to a fruitful civilian life. Is there anything else to consider?

There certainly is. At this point one must think long and hard about exactly what joining the armed forces means. It means that one can end up living anywhere in the world—anywhere. The American military maintains bases around the world, in Germany, the Philippines, Turkey, Alaska—everywhere. There is also the very real possibility that one can be sent into combat, or into a combat area. Chaplains and cooks and computer tech support people in the military do get killed. Of course, people die before their time in the civilian world every minute of every day as well. Considering the grim facts of 9/11, it seems safe to say that we are all combatants these days.

Still, these are things that one must consider, just as one must consider every step in life. Military careers offer wide-open opportunities for promotion and progressive responsibility for both the enlisted and the officer. Early promotions seem more or less predictable. To be promoted beyond a certain point, however, means one's intellectual, moral, and leadership qualities have been recognized. That said, it must be added that advancement in the military is usually far more dependable than in the civilian world. Career military members are also attracted by the impressive array of benefits and the job security offered by the armed forces as well as their excellent education opportunities.

Still, if one only wants to sign up long enough to get his or her college education and career training, that's fine with the military as well. The modern, technologically sophisti-

cated military needs to attract smart, intelligent recruits. To do this, they offer a wide variety of programs that help recruits earn college credit, attend college while in the service, and/or provide cash for college tuition. They also make certain these programs are portable, so that a duty station change won't interrupt one's progress toward their degree (in 1999 alone, over 30,000 college degrees were earned by members of the active duty military through the off-duty, voluntary education program). The military knows people join so they can afford college. Practically every pilot working for an American airline has a military background.

Once one has put in his or her time, the military honors their commitments. Certainly they will entice people they find outstanding to stay, the way any business will. But, their contracts are binding, and those who want to head for the civilian world are free to do so. And, usually their time in the armed forces helps skip them, if not to the front of the job application line, certainly a number of steps ahead of the general population.

Employers know veterans can be counted upon to lead within a team setting, an ability that is often rare and always valuable. In the military, high school graduates become "can do" individuals in short order—just the type of employees on whom employers know they can rely. Military personnel bring values to their civilian jobs like service before self, honor, commitment, respect, loyalty, and the quest for excellence. These days, these are qualities all too rare in the workplace. Smart employers know they need leaders—and quite often they look for them in the military veteran.

Young service members get far more responsibility for property and people than they could anywhere else. Looking for a job in transportation? Imagine listing the ability to drive a 70-ton tank on your résumé. What hospital is going to turn down the nurse who can maintain a field hospital? What computer systems center is going to hesitate to consider the young person who already has years of experience analyzing satellite information in the nerve center of an air base?

Employers know veterans have been trained well to do their jobs (they also know that 92 percent of all military jobs today involve computers, either desktop computers, computer workstations, mainframes, or minicomputers). A large part of that training centers around learning how to focus on the job at hand. As a physical therapist evaluating a patient, a technician repairing an electronic instrument, or an air cargo specialist unloading freight, the habit of mission focus is universal. This "habit" usually lasts a lifetime, and employers know it.

The military veterans coming to them for a job may not yet have the exact skills the employer requires, but that doesn't matter. The employer knows they can be trained. An honorable discharge is proof positive that one has done well in the largest job training system in the world, that they know not only how to take orders, but how to give them, and analyze them, as well.

There are drawbacks to joining the service, of course, as there are drawbacks to everything in life. But, it must be said that for many, military careers are both interesting and challenging. Military service constantly places one in new environments, new jobs, and new situations. And for many, one of the newest things they will be introduced to is the concept of "Service Before Self."

The ideals of the modern military go back thousands of years. Every successful fighting force has been built around the same foundation—duty, honor, respect, and loyalty. These principles are only words to most of us in the civilian world. We know what they mean only in the abstract. The men and women of the military, however, do more than simply learn to identify these values, they practice them and embrace them until finally they become the reasons they do what they do.

Military personnel are not simply civilians with uniforms and weapons. They are an elite segment of society, transformed at an early age into the defenders of their country. They are given responsibilities their friends back home can scarcely imagine. Their "nine-to-five" lives are spent becoming warriors, champions, and leaders.

Young men and women in the military make lifelong friends, and develop desirable work skills as well as positive, winning attitudes. They are given tremendous opportunities to further their education, and they gain valuable experience mastering military careers which will serve them in good stead when they decide to leave the service. Indeed, for literally millions of young men and women over the nearly three hundred years of our country's history, being a part of the American armed forces has been the proudest part of their lives.

Over the centuries, many have died for that privilege, it's true. But they died protecting their country, their families, and their ideals. And, while the possibility of dying is a consideration, most servicepeople don't die in action. Most have never seen combat. Even in wartime, most members of the military are far from the action.

In the end, a career in the modern American armed forces must be weighed against considerations such as stability of lifestyle vs. the possibility of reassignment to another state or country, the loss of certain freedoms vs. having to provide everything for one's life by one's self. Getting a job with the navy isn't like getting one with McDonald's—you can't quit and go home when you're fed up, and telling off your boss can land you in the stockade.

The military life is not for everyone. Regimentation, respecting authority, becoming an authority figure oneself, even the wearing of a uniform or having to maintain a service haircut can be too much for some people. But, for those who find the idea appealing, like millions before you, a career in the armed forces could be the answer you've been looking for. Only *you* can decide.

ADMINISTRATION
AND MANAGEMENT

COMMUNICATIONS MANAGER

CAREER PROFILE

Duties: Develop rules and procedures for sending and receiving communications; direct personnel who operate computer systems and electronic telecommunications and satellite communications equipment; develop ways to track and ensure security of communications; direct maintenance and repair personnel; develop communications centers budgets

Alternate Title(s): Communications Supervisor; Station Manager; Operations Managers; Communications Superintendent

Availability: Army, Navy, Marine Corps, Coast Guard

Military Salary: See How to Use This Book

Civilian Salary: $37,180

Civilian Employment Prospects: Good

Civilian Advancement Prospects: Good

Prerequisites:

　Rank—Officer

　Education and Training—Four-year college degree, preferably in engineering, mathematics, computer science, or a related field

　Experience—Any training and work experience obtained in the armed services

　Special Skills and Personality Traits—Organizational skills; leadership qualities; the ability to motivate employees and maintain high morale; able to deal with different situations and a diverse work force; good communication and interpersonal skills; an interest in working with computers, radios, and electronic equipment

CAREER LADDER

```
┌─────────────────────────────────┐
│   Manager or Superintendent     │
└─────────────────────────────────┘

┌─────────────────────────────────┐
│ Assistant Manager or Superintendent │
└─────────────────────────────────┘

┌─────────────────────────────────┐
│      Management Trainee         │
│  or Lower Echelon Supervisor    │
└─────────────────────────────────┘
```

Position Description

Instantaneous communication among air, sea, and land forces is crucial to any sort of military operation. The communications networks run by the armed services are among the largest and most complex in operation today. Communications Managers plan and direct the operation of these vast military communication systems. They also manage personnel in communications centers and relay stations.

　Military communications managers usually work in communications centers on land or aboard ships. They are charged with keeping channels open under all circumstances, including inclement weather and battle situations. Communications Managers are often responsible for relaying orders and crucial information in a precise and timely manner. They organize staff and delegate assignments to see that all aspects of the communication center are manned. They coordinate the maintenance and repair of existing equipment and the installation and integration of new technologies. Like other managers they oversee the budgets and staffing for their division and see to it that all record-keeping and clerical duties are attended to. Communications Managers also insure that correct procedures and protocols are followed so that no sensitive information is compromised. It can be a stressful and demanding job.

In civilian life Communications Managers work for those firms involved with telephone and telegraph communications, radio and television broadcasting, and the ever-expanding field of satellite communications. Their duties are quite similar to those performed by their military counterparts. They may also (depending on their specialty) be called station managers, operations managers, or communications superintendents.

Civilian Salaries

Although, in general, blue-collar worker supervisors earned a median wage of just $37,180 in 1998, the average earned by workers with similar positions in the telecommunications industry were generally higher. In some cases, the difference was significant totaling as much as 20 percent higher. Those who made the jump to white-collar management positions could more than double that figure.

The table below shows median hourly earnings of the largest occupations in telecommunications in 2000.

	Telephone occupation	All communications industries
General and operations managers	$38.88	$29.41
First-line supervisors/ managers of non-retail sales workers	22.86	23.54
First-line supervisors/ managers of office and administrative support workers	22.56	17.51

Civilian Employment Prospects

The telecommunications industry provided 1,042,000 wage and salary jobs in 1998. Most jobs were concentrated in telephone communications, which employed 1,007,000 workers. The two remaining sectors of the telecommunications industry—telegraph and other message communications and communications services, not elsewhere classified—provided 35,000 jobs in 1998.

Civilian Advancement Prospects

Although, overall job growth in telecommunications is projected to be lower than in all industries (12 percent vs. 15 percent), the prospects for most management personnel are somewhat better, particularly in the areas of marketing and computer and information systems.

Employment in 2000			
Occupation	Number	Percent	Change 2000–2010
Management, business, and financial occupations	235	20.2	15.0
Marketing and sales managers	11	1.0	30.6
Computer and information systems managers	9	0.7	48.0
General and operations managers	23	1.9	12.1
Human resources managers	10	0.8	8.9

Education and Training

Military job training can consist of as little as 12 weeks of classroom instruction up to as many as 32. The length of training will vary depending on the desired specialty. Course content typically includes such material as communications theory and security, communications-electronics management, satellite communications, including tactical ground terminals, electronic principles, technologies and systems, plus tactical combat communications systems. There will be, of course, much more in the way of further training that occurs on the job or through advanced courses.

A high school diploma is often the minimum educational requirement to become a manager in many industries. Workers generally receive training in human resources, computer software, and management before they advance to these positions. Although many with only high school diplomas still rise through the ranks, employers increasingly seek applicants with post-secondary technical degrees. In high-technology industries, such as telecommunications, employers will often be looking for a B.A. or B.S. degree or at least some kind of technical school training. The larger companies usually offer better opportunities for promotion to blue-collar worker supervisor positions than their smaller counterparts.

In some telecommunications companies, a degree in business or engineering, combined, of course, with in-house training, is needed to advance upward from supervisor to a higher level such as department head or production manager.

Although most employers require a minimum of a high school diploma, a bachelor's degree will usually be desired. Continuing education is important for those in technological fields for those who fail to keep up with the rapid changes in technology risk obsolescence (which brings on layoffs or a likelihood of being passed over for advancement). For example, due to the rapid introduction of new technologies and services, the telephone industry is among the most rapidly changing in the economy. For managers, increased knowledge of both computer hardware and software is of paramount importance. Telecommunications industry employers now look for employees with skills, abilities, and knowledge in such areas as: computer programming and software design; voice telephone technology, known as telephony; laser and fiber-optic technology; wireless technology; data compression skills; and sales ability enhanced by interpersonal skills and a knowledge of telecommunications terminology.

Experience, Special Skills, and Personality Traits

Employers look for experience, job knowledge, organizational skills, and leadership qualities. They will also emphasize the ability to motivate employees, maintain high morale, and command respect, which gives former military personnel a decided advantage. An applicant with a solid background who can deal with different situations and a diverse workforce will be highly prized. Communication and interpersonal skills are also extremely important attributes in this occupation. It is helpful to have an interest in working with computers, radios, and electronic equipment as well as an interest in technical work.

Unions and Associations

Communications Managers may apply their skills to a remarkable variety of industries. Candidates should seek out associations in the field of their choice for specific information. Supervisors are usually considered management and thus tend to be ineligible for union membership. Some organizations helpful to managers in general include the American Management Association and the National Management Association.

FINANCIAL AND ACCOUNTING MANAGER

CAREER PROFILE

Duties: Advise management on all fiscal matters; develop ways to track financial transactions; prepare and examine financial records and reports; set policies for the use of military funds; direct the activities of finance and accounting staff and the preparation of budgets and financial forecasts

Alternate Title(s): Cash Manager; Controller; Chief Financial Officer; Accountant; Pension Consultant; Insurance Consultant; Portfolio Manager; Budget Officer; Credit Analyst; Auditor; Loan Officer; Real Estate Adviser; Securities Analyst or Underwriter; Insurance Risk Manager; Treasurer

Availability: All branches

Military Salary: See How to Use This Book

Civilian Salary: $27,680 to $319,200

Civilian Employment Prospects: Good

Civilian Advancement Prospects: Good

Prerequisites:
  Rank—Officer
  Education and Training—Bachelor's degree minimum; postgraduate degree may be required for advancement; additional specialized education and training may be required.
  Experience—Any experience managing money or in business management; related experience in the service
  Special Skills and Personality Traits—Interest in working with numbers and statistics; detail-oriented; precise; conscientious; well-organized; aptitude for planning and directing the work of others
  Licensure/Certification—Certified Public Accountant, Certified Management Accountant required; additional certifications may be required in some fields; optional certification

CAREER LADDER

Chief Financial Officer

Controller

Accountant or Financial Manager

Cash Manager

Position Description

Together, all branches of the military spend billions of dollars every year. These funds must be carefully managed and put to their best use. Financial and Accounting Managers direct and manage the financial affairs of the military. They also advise commanders on financial and accounting matters.

Outside the military, all businesses, government agencies, and corporations must have Financial and Accounting Managers to prepare financial reports and direct investment activities. They must also implement cash management strategies as well as the long-term goals of their organization. Their duties increase greatly as their position titles increase in importance. For instance, a chief financial officer (CFO) will oversee all financial and accounting functions for an organization as well as formulate and administer its overall financial plans and policies. Somewhat further down the ladder are controllers who direct the preparation of financial reports (summaries and predictions of an organization's financial position—income statements, balance sheets, and analysis of future earnings or expenses). Controllers must also prepare those reports required by regulatory agencies and oversee such departments as accounting, auditing, and budget.

Treasurers and finance officers direct a company's financial objectives and budgets. They invest funds and manage the associated risks as well as raise capital in support of a firm's expansion. They are also heavily involved with mergers and acquisitions. Cash managers control cash receipts and disbursements flow. Risk and insurance managers handle programs created with companies to minimize risks and losses as well as managing the firm's insurance budget. Credit managers watch over credit rating criteria, determine credit ceilings, and monitor the collections of past due accounts.

Financial institutions (banks, S&Ls, credit unions, and mortgage and finance companies) employ Financial Managers to oversee such functions as lending, trusts, mortgages, and investments, or programs like sales, operations, or electronic financial services. These Managers, often considered executives, wear many hats. They may be required to solicit business, authorize loans or direct the investment of funds. They may also be in charge of hiring personnel, approving loans and lines of credit, working within the community to attract business, assisting customers with account problems, etc.

Financial Managers must be experts within their own fields, of course. Government Managers must be up on all the latest developments in the government appropriations and budgeting processes, whereas health care Financial Managers must be knowledgeable about issues surrounding health-care financing. They must all be aware of special tax laws and regulations that affect their specific industry.

Technology has greatly reduced the amount of time it takes to produce financial reports. Thus Managers now work more as data analyzers, handing off ideas to senior managers on how to maximize profits. They need to keep abreast of the latest computer technology in order to increase the efficiency of their firm's financial operations. They are also playing a larger role these days in mergers as well as global expansion and financing.

Financial Managers are almost always quartered in comfortable surroundings. They generally are supplied with their organization's idea of state-of-the-art computer systems and information services. They do work a longer than average week—often as much as 50 to 60 hours per week. They also must attend seminars and meetings of financial and economic associations. Often they must travel (visiting subsidiary firms, meeting new or potential customers, etc.).

Civilian Salaries

The average yearly salary for Financial Managers was $55,070 in 1998. Those in the middle 50 percent earned between $38,240 and $83,800. The lowest 10 percent brought in less than $27,680, while the top 10 percent garnered in excess of $118,950. A sample of yearly earnings averages for Financial Managers in 1997 are as follows:

Security brokers and dealers	$95,100
Computer and data processing	$63,200
Management and public relations	$62,800
Local government	$48,700
Commercial banks	$45,800
Savings institutions	$41,800

The Robert Half International survey for 1999 showed that earning for assistant controllers and treasurers varied from $42,700 to $84,000 in the smallest to the largest companies. Corporate controllers brought in between $47,500 and $141,000. Chief financial officers and treasurers captured between $65,000 to $319,200. Those with a graduate degree or Certified Public Accountant or Certified Management Accountant designation could count on an additional 10 percent above the norm for their occupation.

In 1999 the Treasury Management Association conducted a compensation survey. The salaries presented below show the average total compensation for the occupation including bonuses and deferred compensation.

Vice president of finance	$165,400
Chief financial officer	$150,100
Treasurer	$129,800
Controller	$109,700
Assistant treasurer	$96,500
Director treasury/finance	$93,200
Assistant controller	$75,900
Senior analyst	$63,000
Cash manager	$56,600
Analyst	$45,500

As is to be expected, large companies often pay more than small ones. Salary levels also vary by the type of industry and location. Many Financial Managers outside of government receive additional compensation such as bonuses and deferred compensation (often in the form of stock options). These may also vary substantially from firm to firm according to the type of industry and location.

Civilian Employment Prospects

Financial Managers held roughly 693,000 jobs in 1998. Although these positions exist in practically every type of industry, more than a third of these were to be found in services industries (business, health, social, and management services). Three in 10 were employed by financial institutions (banks, savings institutions, finance companies, credit unions, insurance companies, securities dealers, and real estate firms).

For Financial Managers with the right credentials the future looks excellent. Such credentials would be expertise in accounting and finance, strong computer skills, knowledge of international finance, and well-honed communication skills. Loss of jobs due to mergers, acquisitions, and corporate downsizing should continue to be offset by economic growth and the ever-increasing need for financial expertise through 2008.

The banking industry will most likely continue to reduce the number of its Financial Managers due to consolidation. However, the securities and commodities industry are expected to hire more Financial Managers to handle increasingly complex financial transactions and manage investments. Risk managers (those who assess risks for insurance and investment purposes) are expected to be in especially high demand. The industry may see the hiring of Financial Managers on a temporary basis to see companies through short-term periods of emergency or to offer suggestions for boosting profits.

Many companies are expected to begin contracting out their accounting and financial operations. Also, with computer technology reducing both the time and staff required to produce financial reports, forecasting earnings, profits and costs (as well as generating ideas and creative ways to increase profitability) will become the major roles of corporate Financial Managers during the next 10 years. Those Financial Managers thoroughly familiar with the appropriate software and applications needed for these duties will be in high demand.

Civilian Advancement Prospects

Those with a bachelor's degree in finance, accounting, or some other related field will have the minimum academic preparation to break into the field. Many employers, however, are looking for a master's degree, as well as candidates with a strong analytical background. There is expected to be a continuing need for more skilled Financial Managers, which will, of course, spur employment growth. Those who continue their education should find advancement opportunities to remain healthy.

It must be noted that Financial Managers are being hired more often on a temporary basis. These short-term hires are brought in to advise senior managers. This means that the better-prepared, more diversified prospective employee will have the greater chance at sustained job offers. Indeed, one must consider that some firms contract out all accounting and financial functions to companies that provide these ser-

vices. Self-employment should be considered an option for the future.

Education and Training

Outside the military, a four-year college degree in accounting, finance, or a related field is necessary to even begin in this field. Indeed, some specialties require a master's degree in business administration or recognition as a Certified Public Accountant or Certified Management Accountant.

Military training consists of two to 16 weeks of classroom instruction depending on the specialty for which one is being trained. This training covers such areas as the duties of Financial and Accounting Managers, management techniques, including budget preparation and review, military accounting, personnel management and payroll procedures as well as statistical analysis and fiscal planning.

Experience (especially within the field of bank branch managers) can often be more important than formal education. Banks often fill branch manager positions by promoting from within. But, continuing education is vital for Financial Managers as global trade grows more complex and federal and state laws and regulations continue to change practically overnight. Many companies encourage their employees to take graduate courses or attend conferences related to their specialty.

Financial management, banking, and credit union associations sponsor training programs (often in cooperation with universities and graduate schools). Although these programs often call for extensive at-home preparation, most companies will pay all or part of the costs for those who successfully complete courses. Even though experience and ability are often emphasized for promotion, advancement opportunities can often be enhanced by such studies.

Special Requirements

Financial Managers can also enhance their chances for advancement by attaining professional certification. The Association for Investment Management and Research has the Chartered Financial Analyst designation for those who meet their requirements. The National Association of Credit Management, through a combination of experience and examinations, confers the titles of Credit Business Associate, Credit Business Fellow and Certified Credit Executive. The Treasury Management Association gives the Certified Cash Manager credential and the Certified Treasury Executive designation to those who meet their requirements. The Association of Government Accountants will grant the Certified Government Financial Manager certification to those with the appropriate experience and training. Then, of course, for those managers who specialize in accounting, there are the Certified Public Accountant (CPA) or Certified Management Accountant (CMA) designations.

Experience, Special Skills, and Personality Traits

Since Financial Managers usually don't work with merely their own department, but interact with many departments throughout their companies, a broad overview of their business is critical. Financial Managers are also finding interpersonal skills increasingly important. More and more often these positions involve managing people as well as solving problems as part of a team. Superb communication skills are needed for explaining complex financial data.

This position calls for creative thinkers and problem solvers who can apply their analytical skills to business problems. They must have knowledge of international finance due to the nation's expanding interdependence on the global economy. Indeed, the correct foreign language skills could mean greatly expanded duties and rewards.

Experienced Financial Managers who thoroughly understand the operations of the various departments within their company are on the fast track to top management positions. Financial Managers with the proper experience often make the ultimate move to starting their own consulting firms.

Unions and Associations

Several organizations serve Financial and Accounting Managers. They include the American Bankers Association, the Financial Management Association International, the Financial Executives Institute, the National Association of Credit Management, the Association for Financial Professionals, the Association for Investment Management and Research, and the Association for Government Accountants. Each one offers a range of opportunities for networking, continuing education, and professional advancement. Some also offer certifications.

FOOD SERVICE MANAGER

CAREER PROFILE

Duties: Oversee the preparation of food at mess halls and officers' dining halls; calculate food budgets; hire staff and purchase equipment needed for serving halls, kitchens, and meat-cutting plants; maintain standards for food preparation and storage as well as the nutritional and sanitary standards at all food service facilities

Alternate Title(s): Resource Manager; Nutritional Planner; Kitchen Managers (Hotels, Restaurants and Cafeterias)

Availability: All branches

Military Salary: See How to Use This Book

Civilian Salary: $14,430 to $45,520

Civilian Employment Prospects: Good

Civilian Advancement Prospects: Good

Prerequisites:

Rank—Officer

Education and Training—Bachelor's degree in food service management or related field preferred but not required; additional classroom instruction; on-the-job training

Experience—Experience serving or preparing food; business experience helpful

Special Skills and Personality Traits—Interest in food service management, food preparation, nutrition, and business administration; well-organized; strong interpersonal skills; detail-oriented; able to direct the work of others and handle multiple tasks simultaneously

Licensure/Certification—Voluntary certification

CAREER LADDER

Owner/Manager

Food Service Manager

Assistant Manager

Position Description

Food Service Managers select and price menu items. They must make certain that food and other supplies are used efficiently and keep records to that effect. Not only must they sct a high standard in food preparation and service, they are also responsible for administrative and human resource tasks, like finding new ways to recruit fresh employees as well as ways to retain experienced workers. In most restaurants and institutional food service facilities, the management team consists of a general manager, one or more assistant managers, and a chief chef. The chief chef's duties are to operate the kitchen while the assistant managers maintain the dining room and other areas.

The task of selecting successful menu items varies from establishment to establishment. Some rarely change their menu while others make frequent alterations. When selecting items, managers must take into account the likely number of customers and the past popularity of dishes. They must consider the issue of unserved food left over from prior meals that should not be wasted, the need for variety, and seasonal changes in the availability of foods. They must also analyze recipes to determine food, labor, overhead costs, and to assign prices to various dishes. Menus must be developed far enough in advance that supplies can be ordered and received in time.

Managers must estimate food consumption every day, then place orders with suppliers, and schedule deliveries of fresh food and beverages per their calculations. They must check each delivery, and evaluate the quality of meats, poultry, fish, fruits, vegetables, and baked goods. Managers must meet with restaurant suppliers' sales representatives to place orders replenishing stocks of tableware, linens, paper, cleaning supplies, cooking utensils, and furniture and fixtures. They also arrange for equipment maintenance and repairs and coordinate a variety of services such as pest control and garbage removal.

A restaurant's quality depends almost solely on its Manager's ability to interview, hire, and, when necessary, fire employees. They must explain an establishment's policies and practices to new employees and oversee any necessary training. Managers must schedule their employees' work hours, coordinating the entire staff to make certain there are enough workers present to cover peak dining periods. Managers must be prepared to fill in for employees who are unable to work. They may also need to help with cooking, clearing tables, or other tasks.

In supervising the kitchen and dining room, Managers often oversee all food preparation and cooking. They must examine dishes for both their quality and the size of the portions. They also investigate and resolve customers' complaints. They must supervise the cleaning of the kitchen and dining areas as well as the washing of tableware, kitchen utensils, and equipment so as to maintain company or government sanitation standards. Managers must also observe their employees and patrons continually to make certain health and safety standards as well as local liquor regulations are strictly followed.

In large establishments most administrative responsibilities are delegated to a bookkeeper. Managers in most smaller establishments, such as fast-food restaurants, must keep records of employees' wages, prepare payroll, and fill out paperwork in compliance with licensing laws and reporting requirements of tax, wage, and hour; unemployment compensation; and Social Security laws. They must maintain supply and equipment purchase records and make certain that suppliers' accounts are paid on time. Managers in full-service establishments must also record the number, type, and cost of items sold to evaluate and discontinue dishes that may be unpopular or less profitable.

To help in these paperwork duties, as well as to minimize food costs and spoilage, many Managers use inventory-tracking software to compare the record of daily sales with a record of present inventory. In some cases, when supplies run low additional inventory can be ordered directly from the supplier using the computer. Computers also allow restaurant and Food Service Managers to more efficiently keep track of employee schedules and pay.

Managers arrive first and leave last. At the end of each day or each shift they must tally the cash and charge receipts received and balance them against the record of sales. Then they are usually responsible for either depositing those receipts at the bank or securing them in a safe place. At closing, the manager is responsible for checking that all equipment (ovens, grills, lights, etc.) have been shut down, locking the doors, and turning on alarm systems.

Civilian Salaries

Median earnings for Food Service Managers were $26,700 in 1998. The middle 50 percent earned between $19,820 and $34,690. The lowest paid 10 percent earned $14,430 or less. The highest paid 10 percent earned over $45,520. Median annual earnings in the industries employing the largest number of Food Service Managers in 1997 were as follows:

Hotels and motels	$28,600
Eateries and taverns	$25,000
Elementary and secondary schools	$21,300

It should be noted that as well as the usual benefits one expects at any job, Food Service Managers can reasonably expect to receive free meals as well as the opportunity for additional training depending on their length of service.

Civilian Employment Prospects

Restaurant and Food Service Managers held roughly 520,000 jobs in 1998. Most were salaried, but close to one in six was self-employed. Most Food Service Managers work in restaurants or for contract institutional food service companies, while a smaller number are employed by educational institutions; hospitals; nursing and personal care facilities; and civic, social, and fraternal organizations. Although job opportunities are located throughout every part of the country, it must be noted that larger cities, most especially tourist areas, provide far more opportunities for full-service dining positions.

Civilian Advancement Prospects

Food Service Manager positions are expected to increase about as fast as the average for all occupations through 2008. Also, the need to replace managers who transfer to other occupations or stop working should create many additional job openings. Chances to fill these openings will favor those with a bachelor's or associate degree in restaurant and institutional food service management.

As the population, personal incomes, and leisure time grow, so will the demands on the food service industry. Also, Manager jobs will increase as schools, hospitals, and other businesses contract out more of their food services to institutional food service companies. Food Service Manager jobs are expected to grow in many of these other industries, but this expansion of opportunities will slow down, as contracting out becomes more popular. However, growth in the elderly population should result in more Food Service Manager jobs in nursing homes and other health-care institutions such as residential-care and assisted-living facilities.

It should be noted that job opportunities will be better for salaried rather than self-employed Managers. New eateries these days are more usually opened by national chains rather than being independently owned and operated. Since this trend is expected to continue, most restaurant managers will be employed by larger companies to run establishments in the future.

A willingness to relocate is usually necessary for advancement to higher positions with more responsibility. Managers typically advance to larger establishments or regional management positions within restaurant chains. Some eventually open their own eating and drinking establishments. Others transfer to hotel management positions because their restaurant management experience provides a good background for food and beverage manager jobs in hotels and resorts.

Also, Manager's positions in eating and drinking establishments are not very sensitive to changes in economic conditions. These workers are rarely let go during economic downturns. But competition among restaurants is always intense, and often restaurants do not survive.

Education and Training

Job training consists of three to four months of classroom instruction. Courses usually include such subjects as food service operations and management, resource and hotel management, and nutritional meal planning. Most management trainees are recruited from two- and four-year college hospitality management programs. People with degrees in restaurant and institutional food service management are often preferred as managers by food service and restaurant chains. But, it must be noted that employers quite often hire graduates with degrees in other fields who can demonstrate the proper interest and aptitude for food service management. Some Manager positions, especially those within self-service and fast-food chains, are filled by promoting experienced food and beverage preparation and service workers. Workers demonstrating potential for handling increased responsibility can move up the ladder to assistant manager or management trainee jobs.

A bachelor's degree in restaurant and food service management is strongly recommended as preparation for a career in this occupation. In 1998, more than 150 colleges and universities offered four-year programs in restaurant, hotel, or institutional food service management. There are also over 800 junior colleges, technical institutes, etc., offering programs in these fields that lead to either an associate degree or some other form of formal certification. Two- and four-year programs both provide instruction in the same range of subjects. Classes in nutrition and food planning and preparation are accompanied by courses in accounting, business law and management, and computer science. On-the-job internships are possible.

Through both classroom and on-the-job training, prospective Managers gather instruction and work experience. Beyond their degrees, Managers must be versed in their particular company's policies and procedures (personnel management, record keeping, report preparation, computer systems, etc.). It can take six months to a year before prospective Managers can receive their first permanent assignment as an assistant manager.

Special Requirements

Although certainly not a requirement for employment or even advancement in the occupation, voluntary certification as a Foodservice Management Professional (FMP) confers a measure of professional achievement for restaurant and food service managers that provides recognition of professional competence. This can be quite helpful for the manager who skips college and acquires their skills mainly on the job. The FMP designation is awarded by the Educational Foundation of the National Restaurant Association to those who: 1) reach a qualifying score on a written exam; 2) complete a required course series covering a range of food service management topics; and 3) meet their standards of work experience within the field.

Experience, Special Skills, and Personality Traits

Employers search for qualities such as self-discipline, initiative, and leadership in their Managers. Managers must be able to focus on details. They must be problem solvers with excellent communication skills for dealing with customers, suppliers, and their staff. Managers must display a neat and clean appearance because of their face-to-face dealings with the public. The long hours and high stress levels make good health an important factor.

Unions and Associations

Two organizations for Food Service Managers are The Educational Foundation of the National Restaurant Association, which offers Foodservice Management Professional certification, and The Council on Hotel, Restaurant, and Institutional Education. Both provide opportunities for networking, education, and keeping up with trends in the industry.

INTERNATIONAL RELATIONS OFFICER

CAREER PROFILE

Duties: Collect and report information about the military forces of foreign countries; hold meetings with foreign military and government officials; analyze political, social, and economic matters in foreign countries; project foreign political trends; advise commanders about situations in foreign countries

Alternate Title(s): Foreign Service Officer; Political Scientist; University Instructor; Corporate Overseas Adviser

Availability: Army, Navy, Air Force, Marines

Military Salary: See How to Use This Book

Civilian Salary: $20,600 to $80,640

Civilian Employment Prospects: Good

Civilian Advancement Prospects: Good

Prerequisites:

    Rank—Officer

    Education and Training—Bachelor's degree required; postgraduate degrees may be required for advancement.

    Experience—Any managerial experience or experience in communications or negotiation; on-the-job training; additional experience may be required by field.

    Special Skills and Personality Traits—Excellent communication skills; interest in data collection and analysis; comfortable living and working in a foreign country; strong interpersonal skills; analytical; focused; highly motivated; enjoy solving problems

CAREER LADDER

```
┌─────────────────────────────────┐
│      Foreign Service Officer      │
│      or University Professor      │
└─────────────────────────────────┘

┌─────────────────────────────────┐
│   Junior Officer or Instructor    │
└─────────────────────────────────┘

┌─────────────────────────────────┐
│       Trainee or Lecturer         │
└─────────────────────────────────┘
```

Position Description

International Relations Officers (IROs) are sent to every corner of the globe to serve the diplomatic needs of the United States in the country's embassies, consulates, and other diplomatic missions. This title applies to an enormous number of career options, from administrators to anthropologists.

Traditionally, International Relations Officers in military service could expect to be assigned to any type of job, in any part of the world on a moment's notice. Data on the military strengths and weaknesses of both friendly and unfriendly countries is crucial to national defense. IROs collect, analyze, and report information about other nations to be used for military planning.

One of the primary avenues open to IROs, once they leave military service, is to continue their work as civilian employees of the government, working for the State Department, accepting civilian posts in one of the United States embassies around the world. These days the Foreign Service seeks candidates interested in more than political science. The service now looks for people who can manage programs and personnel to meet new and emerging needs, making discipline an organizational skill learned in the military useful. These might include science and technology goals such as the global fight against diseases such as AIDS, efforts to save the environment, or antinarcotics efforts. Today the Foreign Service actively recruits professionals such as anthropologists, geographers, historians, political scientists, and sociologists.

The State Department has an increasing need for candidates with training and experience in administration and management. Applicants must select a "Functional Area of Specialization," or, "cone" when applying to take the written examination. The Foreign Service cones are Administrative, Consular, Economic, Political, and Public Diplomacy.

An extremely brief summation of the duties of these cones is as follows:

Administrative Officers manage the property, financial, and human resources that keep diplomatic and consular missions functioning. These officers interact with every section and every agency at a mission. They serve as manager of the post's human and material resources and as advisers to the head of their agency or mission. They must establish and maintain contact with officials at all levels in both the local and national governments, other diplomatic missions, banks, airlines, and local business organizations.

Consular Officers issue visas to foreign applicants, monitor migration issues, and provide both emergency and nonemergency services to American citizens residing or traveling abroad. Their duties cover such chores as recording the birth of an American citizen abroad and issuing a consular report that serves as proof of citizenship, issuing a passport if one expires or is lost or stolen, distributing federal benefits checks such as social security or pension, and issuing issue U.S. voting registration materials, tax forms, and so on. They must learn the laws and regulations of their mission's host country, develop the skills to be able to combat fraud, and stay current with new technologies. Consular work combines an incredible range of skills. Consular officers are quite often the only U.S. officials with whom foreign nationals or U.S. citizens come into contact in other lands. They are in every sense ambassadors to the countries where they are located.

Economic Officers concentrate on issues such as money and banking, trade and commerce, communication and transportation, economic development, and government finance, reporting significant developments to the State Department. They must deal with environmental, scientific, and technology matters such as ocean fisheries, cooperation in space, acid rain, global warming, population, health, biodiversity, and intellectual property rights. These officers must be alert to the promotion of U.S. national interests and intervene with foreign governments and multilateral organizations when circumstances warrant.

Economic Officers are expected to be knowledgeable in all aspects of economics and in how economic systems work, in policy issues that are important in an eco-

nomic context, in how the U.S. economy and U.S. government function, and in host country commercial practices and opportunities. They must understand the culture of the host country and be conversant in its language in order to see the world through its eyes. This may also involve trade within the country. Economic Officers stationed abroad are both information gatherers and analysts, informing Washington agencies of important developments and their implications.

Political Officers follow political events within the host country and report significant developments to the State Department. These officers are alert to the promotion of U.S. national interests in many areas, and intervene with foreign governments and entities when circumstances warrant. Political officers must know the people and customs of the host country, travel widely within that country, and be able to speak the local language. They must be able to sift through all those who offer information and be able to recognize those few who can actually provide accurate advance information. Political officers must also assist visiting U.S. officials by making certain that every aspect of their visit from reservations to all the details of their meetings and social events are planned, coordinated, and executed.

Public Diplomacy Officers must keep open the lines of communication between the U.S. and the host country. The overall management of a mission's public diplomacy program is in their hands. They are charged with explaining and defending the content of U.S. foreign policy as well as providing foreign nationals with an understanding of the social and cultural context of U.S. foreign policy. They accomplish this by providing their host country contacts with a complete picture of American values, beliefs, and principles—not only those which help fashion U.S. domestic political policy but foreign policy as well.

Other civilian opportunities for IROs vary by area of interest or expertise and include positions as university professors, cultural anthropologists, archaeologists, geographers, historians, economists, political scientists, sociologists, psychologists, urban and regional planners, and consultants for corporations doing business overseas.

Civilian Salaries

The standard operating procedure for determining entry level salaries for Foreign Service Officer Career Candidates is:

1. General entry for all candidates without a college degree — FP 6, Step 1 — $30,719
2. Candidates who have a bachelor's degree in any field — FP 6, Step 5 — $34,575

3. Candidates who have   FP 5, Step 5 $38,675
   a master's, a law degree,
   or both
4. Candidates with a doctorate FP 5, Step 7 $41,030
   or a master's degree in law

Within each grade, additional steps may be added based on the candidate's years of professional experience. FP-6 salary range is $30,719 to $45,112. FP-5 salary range is $34,362 to $50,462. All salaries are annual rates based on January 2001 schedule.

Average annual income of social scientists (excluding economists, psychologists, and urban and regional planners) were $38,990 in 1998. The middle 50 percent earned between $28,950 and $56,550 a year. The lowest 10 percent earned less than $21,530 and the highest 10 percent earned in excess of $80,640 a year. The average annual income of all other social scientists in 1997 were:

| Federal government | $53,700 |
| State government | $37,300 |

Social scientists with a bachelor's degree and no experience could start within the federal government at between $20,600 or $25,500 a year in 1999. Those with an M.A. could start at $31,200 and those with a Ph.D. at $37,700. Those with both experience and an advanced degree could begin at more than $45,200.

Civilian Employment Prospects

The State Department's Foreign Service employs approximately 11,000 civilians worldwide. They fill approximately 500 foreign service officer positions annually and expect this trend to continue through 2004.

Social scientists held about 50,000 jobs in 1998. Many worked as researchers, administrators, and counselors for a wide range of employers, including federal, state, and local governments, educational institutions, social service agencies, research and testing services, and management consulting firms. Other employers include international organizations, associations, museums, and historical societies.

Many additional individuals with training in a social science discipline teach in colleges and universities, and in secondary and elementary schools. The proportion of social scientists that teach varies by specialty—for example, the academic world usually is a more important source of jobs for graduates in history than for graduates in the other fields of study.

Civilian Advancement Prospects

Overall employment of social scientists is expected to grow about as fast as the average for all occupations through 2008. Prospects are best for those with advanced degrees, and usually are better in disciplines such as soci-

ology and geography, which offer more opportunities in nonacademic settings.

Government agencies, social service organizations, marketing, research and consulting firms, and a wide range of businesses seek social science graduates, although often in jobs with titles unrelated to their academic discipline. Social scientists will face stiff competition for academic positions. However, the growing importance and popularity of social science subjects in secondary schools is strengthening the demand for social science teachers at that level.

Candidates seeking positions as social scientists can expect to encounter competition in many areas of social science. Some social science graduates, however, will find good employment opportunities in areas outside traditional social science, often in related jobs that require good research, communication, and quantitative skills.

Education and Training

Job training for International Relations Officers is provided in some specialties. Training length varies by entry requirements and specialty area. Training also occurs on the job, but course content typically includes:

- Political and cultural awareness
- Development of foreign area expertise
- Organization and functions of diplomatic missions

Educational attainment of social scientists is among the highest of all occupations. The Ph.D. or equivalent degree is a minimum requirement for most positions in colleges and universities and is important for advancement to many top level nonacademic research and administrative posts. Graduates with master's degrees in applied specialties usually have better professional opportunities outside of colleges and universities, although the situation varies by field. Graduates with a master's degree in a social science qualify for teaching positions in junior colleges. Bachelor's degree holders have limited opportunities and in most social science occupations do not qualify for "professional" positions. The bachelor's degree does, however, provide a suitable background for many different kinds of entry-level jobs, such as research assistant, administrative aide, or management or sales trainee. With the addition of sufficient education courses, social science graduates also can qualify for teaching positions in secondary and elementary schools.

Training in statistics and mathematics is essential for many social scientists. Mathematical and quantitative research methods are increasingly used in geography, political science, and other fields. The ability to use computers for research purposes is mandatory in most disciplines.

Experience, Special Skills, and Personality Traits

Depending on their jobs, International Relations Officers and social scientists may need a wide range of personal characteristics. Because they constantly seek new information about people, things, and ideas, intellectual curiosity and creativity are fundamental personal traits. The ability to think logically and methodically is important to a political scientist comparing, for example, the merits of various forms of government. Objectivity, open-mindedness, and systematic work habits are important in all kinds of social science research. Perseverance is essential for an anthropologist, who might spend years accumulating artifacts from an ancient civilization. Excellent written and oral communication skills are essential for all these professionals.

Helpful fields of study include political science, history, and international affairs. Helpful attributes include:

- Ability to express ideas clearly and concisely
- Interest in collecting and analyzing data
- Interest in living and working in a foreign country
- Interest in working closely with people
- Resourcefulness, initiative, and leadership, as well as organizational and negotiating skills

Good consular officers must be resourceful and know how to prioritize, as well as how to make available technical and personnel resources to cover the workload. In many cases, professional-level foreign language skill is required in order to interview clients or to speak in public. An ability to read documents in the local language is always beneficial. Knowledge of one's locale and the ability to quickly analyze and report on situations within or outside the office are essential.

Unions and Associations

One organization that serves International Relations Officers and related fields is the National Association of Schools of Public Affairs and Administration.

MANAGEMENT ANALYST

CAREER PROFILE

Duties: Minimize waste and inefficiency; suggest ways to better organize, staff, and manage military activities; measure workloads; design manual or computerized systems to satisfy information needs; design organizations for new or existing offices as well as rules or procedures for work activities or information flow; gather data for studies by conducting interviews and reviewing records; write reports and give briefings on findings

Alternate Title(s): Consultant; Management Consultant

Availability: All branches

Military Salary: See How to Use This Book

Civilian Salary: $38,900 to $266,700

Civilian Employment Prospects: Good

Civilian Advancement Prospects: Good

Prerequisites:

Rank—Officer

Education and Training—Bachelor's degree minimum; master's degree often required; on-the-job training

Experience—Business or administration experience; on-the-job training; five years professional experience for consultants

Special Skills and Personality Traits—Expert knowledge of management, operations research, business or public administration; interest in solving problems; well-organized; detail-oriented; strong analytical skills; excellent oral and written communication skills; good judgment; time management skills; creativity

Licensure/Certification—Optional

CAREER LADDER

```
┌─────────────────────────────┐
│         Consultant          │
└─────────────────────────────┘

┌─────────────────────────────┐
│      Management Analyst     │
└─────────────────────────────┘

┌─────────────────────────────┐
│           Manager           │
└─────────────────────────────┘
```

Position Description

The nation's firms are increasingly relying on Management Analysts to help them remain competitive. Management Analysts, also called management consultants, look for ways to improve a business's structure, efficiency, and profits. Military Management Analysts refine operational procedures, overhaul organizational structures, and keep the various departments and branches of the service running smoothly. They must analyze performance and implement changes. In the civilian world, Management Analysts are found in consulting firms, hospitals, universities, government agencies, or manufacturing firms. Some Analysts specialize in a specific industry while others specialize by type of business function, such as human resources or information systems, records management analysis or systems management analysis.

Government Analysts differ from their business counterparts, who tend to specialize by type of agency. An Analyst's duties vary from employer to employer and from project to project. Some projects require a team of consultants, each specializing in one area. Some require consultants to work independently with a firm's managers. No matter what the case, however, Analysts still always perform the same basic functions: collect, review, and analyze information so they can make recommendations to management.

Consultants may be called in for a variety of reasons. Often times firms are simply too small to cover every necessity, needing a consultant's particular expertise for a project—to determine what resources will be required, what problems may be encountered if they pursue a particular opportunity, etc.

Management analysis is a field that requires a great deal of self-motivation and discipline due to the minimal supervision nature of the job. The ability to work in teams is also becoming a more important attribute in the field as consulting teams become more common.

After obtaining an assignment or contract, Management Analysts first define the nature and extent of the problem. During this phase, they analyze relevant data, which may include annual revenues, employment, or expenditures, and interview managers and employees while observing their operations. The Analyst or consultant then develops solutions to the problem. In the course of preparing their recommendations, they take into account the nature of the organization, the relationship it has with others in that industry, and its internal organization and culture. Insight into the problem is often gained by building and solving mathematical models.

Once they have decided on a course of action, consultants report their findings and recommendations, usually in writing, although oral presentations are also common. Management Analysts will sometimes be asked to stay on the job to oversee the implementation of their recommendations.

Consultants quite often split their workweek between their own offices and on-site visits with various clients. In either situation, they generally work at least 40 hours a week. Overtime often goes uncompensated. And, while it is true that self-employed analysts can set their own hours and even work from home, their income depends on maintaining their existing client base while steadily expanding it. Even salaried Analysts must work to keep their employer's clients and to help secure new ones.

Civilian Salaries

The average annual earnings of Management Analysts in 1998 were $49,470. The middle 50 percent earned between $39,420 and $72,690. The lowest 10 percent earned less than $31,800. The highest 10 percent earned in excess of $88,470. Average annual earnings in the industries employing the largest numbers of management analysts and consultants in 1997 were as follows:

Management and public relations	$57,200
Federal government	$56,400
Local government, except education and hospitals	$47,500
Computer and data processing services	$47,500
State government, except education and hospitals	$39,600

The Association of Management Consulting Firms 1998 survey showed that earnings (including bonuses, profit sharing, etc.) for research associates in member firms averaged $38,900; entry level consultants, $50,500; management consultants, $69,700; senior consultants, $96,800; junior partners, $151,100; and senior partners, $266,700.

Salaried consultants can count on common benefits (health and life insurance, retirement plans, vacation and sick leave) as well as other benefits such as profit sharing or bonuses. Travel expenses will almost always be reimbursed.

Civilian Employment Prospects

In 1998 consultants held roughly 350,000 positions throughout the country. Most of these jobs were to be found in large metropolitan areas. Slightly more than half of these positions were self-created. The majority of the remaining positions were to be found in financial and management consulting firms and in federal, state, and local governments.

Although employment in this field is expected to grow at a rapid rate, competition for these jobs is expected to be fierce. The pool of prospective applicants is expected to be quite large. First, workers can join the field from diverse educational backgrounds, making the choice of candidates for employers quite large. Second, the very nature of the work, combined with its high earnings potential, draws many to the field. Those with a graduate degree, previous experience, or a talent for salesmanship and public relations can expect to be hired first.

Employment of Management Analysts is expected to grow faster than the average for all occupations through 2008. Large firms (especially those with international expertise) should do nicely as well as smaller consulting firms that learn to specialize, picking fields such as biotechnology, health care, human resources, engineering, or telecommunications.

Much of this growth has been forced by the recent upsurge in competition from international and domestic markets. This has forced American companies to learn to use their available resources more efficiently. For this reason the use of outside consultants has grown as they are brought in to help reduce costs, streamline operations, and develop marketing strategies. This trend can only continue to grow as more and more businesses downsize their operations.

Companies have also begun to rely on analysts to organize and evaluate their restructuring efforts, international expansions, and to help them step further into the technological era. Technical backgrounds, such as engineering or biotechnology, especially those that come with an M.A. in business administration will be highly sought after.

Civilian Advancement Prospects

With more experience Management Analysts will generally be given complete responsibility for specific projects. This may include managing a staff as well as their own hours. As they progress, Analysts will often find their duties expanded to the supervision of a large staff and even outside recruitment of new clients. This can lead to partnerships or other advancements for those with exceptional skills. Management Analysts at this level of expertise are in an excellent position to open their own consulting firm.

Relatively low start-up costs for such ventures make them an attractive option. Self-employed Analysts also can greatly reduce their overhead by sharing office space, administrative help, etc. with other self-employed consultants or small consulting firms. It must be noted that many small consulting firms fail each year. Those considering such a move would be cautioned not to do so before honing their organizational and marketing skills first.

Education and Training

Military job training, depending on the field of specialization, consists of a month and a half to two and a half months of classroom instruction. This will usually contain such courses as methods of statistical analysis, internal review and analysis techniques, management engineering techniques, and systems analysis procedures among others.

Entry-level educational requirements vary widely in this field. Private industry tends to require a master's degree in business administration plus a minimum of five years experience in the field wherein a consultant is required. Government agencies tend to need only a bachelor's degree and often times no pertinent work experience (at least for entry-level positions).

Because of the many different areas consultants can be brought in to analyze, a wide variety of educational backgrounds can prove appropriate for this occupation. Most academic programs in business and management are good starting points as well as computer and information sciences or engineering. Those seeking entry into the field of consult-

ing will need years of practical work experience. This could be in management, human resources, inventory control, etc. Consultants also need to constantly stay abreast of current developments in their specialty through attending conferences and reading the latest journals.

Special Requirements

The Institute of Management Consultants, a division of the Council of Consulting Organizations, Inc., offers the Certified Management Consultant (CMC) designation to those who pass their examination and meet their set minimum levels of education and experience. This type of certification is by no means mandatory, but it can give one a competitive advantage in a job market growing increasingly competitive.

Experience, Special Skills, and Personality Traits

Highly desirable skills and traits for consultants are a thorough knowledge of management, operations research, business, or public administration. Management Analysts should have an interest in solving problems and collecting and analyzing data, as well as excellent analytical skills and strong oral and written communication skills. Good judgment and time management are always a plus. So is the ability to think creatively. A candidate for such positions should have a background of study that includes management, operations research, business, or public administration.

Unions and Associations

Organizations for Management Analysts include The Association of Management Consulting Firms and The Institute of Management Consultants. They offer opportunities for networking, career advancement, education, and certification.

PREVENTIVE MAINTENANCE ANALYST

CAREER PROFILE

Duties: Prepare charts and reports on maintenance activities; review maintenance schedules and notify mechanics about the types of service needed; calculate how many mechanics and spare parts are needed to maintain equipment; compare schedules to records of maintenance work actually performed; operate computers and calculators to enter or retrieve maintenance data

Alternate Title(s): Management Analyst; Manager; Computer Systems Analyst; Operations Research Analyst; Economists and Financial Analyst

Availability: All branches

Military Salary: See How to Use This Book

Civilian Salary: $31,800 to $266,700

Civilian Employment Prospects: Good

Civilian Advancement Prospects: Good

Prerequisites:

Rank—Enlisted

Education and Training—Bachelor's degree minimum; master's degree may be required for advancement in some areas; three to five months classroom training

Experience—Several years experience in management or a specific field

Special Skills and Personality Traits—Thorough knowledge of general mathematics and algebra; interest in working with numbers and statistics; detail-oriented; well-organized; able to apply mathematical formulas to practical uses; good computer skills

Licensure/Certification—Optional

CAREER LADDER

Senior Analyst/Consultant

Staff Analyst/Consultant

Trainee

Position Description

Regular maintenance extends the lifetimes of military equipment. Preventive Maintenance Analysts promote equipment maintenance. They create maintenance schedules then notify mechanics when they are needed and where. They coordinate the repair and use of vehicles and equipment and make sure that required parts and tools and other inventory are available. Often they must prioritize repairs based on the needs of their branch of the military and its current objectives. They also take steps to increase effi-

ciency and implement procedures that decrease wear and tear on vehicles and equipment, and conduct all maintenance on or under budget. Preventive Maintenance Analysts may also be responsible for controlling costs and keeping expenses down.

Preventive Maintenance Analysts can translate their skills directly into the civilian world by taking similar positions with companies that utilize vehicle fleets or large amounts of equipment. These might include airlines, buslines, car rental agencies, and construction companies. With additional training and experience, they might turn their military skills toward a more corporate environment, where efficiency and forward thinking are increasingly valuable.

In an effort to constantly prepare for new challenges, corporations increasingly rely on Management Analysts to help them remain competitive. Management consultants look for ways to improve an organization's structure, efficiency, and profits. Modern companies are constantly bringing such consultants on board to help improve their systems of control or to help reorganize their corporate structure and eliminate duplicate or nonessential jobs. Consultants of this type can work for firms with thousands of employees, or they can set up their own firms with themselves as sole employee. Management analysis firms of all sizes seem to prosper. Some will specialize in a specific field, others in a particular industry. The work of these firms will vary with each client or employer. Some projects will require entire teams, each member specializing in one area. Some will require those involved to work independently with the client's managers. Always consultants will gather and study information in order to make their recommendations.

Many firms hire temporary consultants because it is simply cost-effective. Creating space in an organization for employees who are only needed on occasion is considered a payroll burden in today's "lean" marketplace. After taking on a client, a management analyst must first determine exactly what the client's problem is and how widespread it is throughout the client's organization. They will have to review all relevant data (annual revenues, employment records and histories, expenditures, etc.) and then both interview employees and observe them at their posts. The consultant then must create plausible solutions to the client's problem. Once a solution has been decided upon, consultants report their findings and recommendations to the client. At times consultants will be asked to stay on to oversee the implementation of their suggestions.

Consultants do most of their work on-site at the client's base of operations, thus they must expect to not only be out of the office much of the time, but to also have to be ready for a great deal of travel. Their workweek will be at least 40 hours in length and will often be accompanied by more than a little uncompensated overtime. This can lead to a great deal of stress (especially since their "outsider" status will offer them little protection from an executive facing a large problem or a tight schedule).

Civilian Salaries

Average yearly earnings of management analysts in 1998 were $49,470. The middle 50 percent earned between $39,420 and $72,690. The lowest 10 percent earned under $31,800 and the highest 10 percent earned over $88,470. Average yearly earnings in the industries employing the largest numbers of management analysts and consultants in 1997 were:

Management and public relations	$57,200
Federal government	$56,400
Local government, except education and hospitals	$47,500
Computer and data processing services	$47,500
State government, except education and hospitals	$39,600

In 1998 the Association of Management Consulting Firms conducted a survey which showed the following yearly earnings averages:

Entry level consultants	$50,500
Management consultants	$69,700
Senior consultants	$96,800
Junior partners	$151,100
Senior partners	$266,700

Standard benefits, including health and life insurance, retirement planning, vacation days, sick leave, profit sharing, and so on can be expected by salaried management consultants. Considering the amount of travel in their work, they can also expect their travel expenses to be reimbursed. Self-employed consultants, of course, will have to provide their own workplaces, benefits, and salaries.

Civilian Employment Prospects

Civilian Preventive Maintenance Analysts can be found in all levels of government agencies, as well as airlines, large transportation firms, and firms with large numbers of machines. Those with military training as analysts can branch out into such fields as managers, computer systems analysts, operations research analysts, economists, and financial analysts.

Faster than average employment growth is predicted in these fields, but intense competition is expected for those positions which will be available. In 1988 just under 350,000 jobs were held by preventive management analysts. The highest concentration may be found in or around large metropolitan areas. Fifty-five percent of these were self-employed. The majority of the remaining 45 percent were to be found in financial and management consulting firms as well as in local, state, and the federal governments. The majority of those attached to the federal government were found in the Department of Defense.

Civilian Advancement Prospects

Management analysts in consulting firms may rise to senior positions. Experienced consultants will often be placed in charge of projects, at which point they will make their own hours. Senior consultants will manage sections of their own firm and work to bring in new business.

Because business start-up costs are exceedingly low, more than half of all management analysts are self-employed. Some share office space, assistants, and other expenditures with other self-employed consultants and thus reduce their overhead.

Since consultants come from diverse educational backgrounds, the pool of applicants prospective employers can select from is often overstocked. This means that despite projections of rapid growth in this field, keen competition is expected for jobs as management analysts. Also, this career is sought by many due to the independent and challenging nature of the work, along with its potential for high salaries.

Employment in this field will grow, however, as private firms and government continue to increase their dependence on outside expertise. The highest job growth is projected for both those with international expertise as well as small, niche consulting firms that specialize in specific areas (biotechnology, health care, human resources, engineering, telecommunications, etc.).

As the world's marketplaces have become more competitive, firms have needed to reduce costs, streamline operations, and develop marketing strategies. This process is not only the current standard but the trend for future business, as well, making it likely that more opportunities will be created for consultants.

Education and Training

Job training consists of one to three months of classroom instruction. Training will cover the basics such as, equipment maintenance management concepts, accounting procedures, statistical reporting methods, and parts and supply inventory control procedures. Available positions will go first to those with a graduate degree, industry expertise, and/or a talent for salesmanship and public relations.

Private industry looks for those with a master's degree in business administration or a related discipline as well as at least five years experience in the consultation field they plan to pursue. Government positions are usually filled by those with a bachelor's degree and no pertinent work experience (entry-level positions only).

Those fields of study that provide a suitable educational background for this work are academic programs in business and management, as well as computer and information sciences and engineering. Also, those wishing to enter this field should have several years of experience in management, human resources, inventory control, or some other specialty.

As firms increasingly rely on technology, there will be more demand for consultants with technical backgrounds, such as engineering or biotechnology, particularly when combined with a master's degree in business administration. Consultants will also be in greater demand in the public sector, as federal, state, and local agencies are expected to seek ways to become more efficient.

Finally, consultants routinely attend conferences to keep informed on current developments in their field.

Special Requirements

The Institute of Management Consultants, a division of the Council of Consulting Organizations, Inc., offers the Certified Management Consultant (CMC) designation to those who pass an examination and meet minimum levels of education and experience. Certification is not mandatory for a consultant's position, but it may give a job seeker a competitive advantage.

Experience, Special Skills, and Personality Traits

Most firms require a master's degree and at least five years of specialized experience. Normal color vision is required to read and interpret maintenance charts and graphs in some specialties. Other specialties may require good public speaking skills.

Consultants often work with minimal supervision, so they should be self-motivated and disciplined. They should also possess analytical skills, the ability to get along with a wide range of people as well as strong oral and written communication skills. Good judgment, time management skills, and creativity are other highly desirable qualities as is the ability to work in teams.

Unions and Associations

Information on obtaining positions within the federal government may be obtained from the Office of Personnel Management through a telephone-based system. Consult your telephone directory under U.S. Government for a local number or call (912) 757-3000; TDD (912) 744-2299. Also check: http://www.usajobs.opm.gov. The Association of Management Consulting Firms and The Institute of Management Consultants are two organizations that offer networking opportunities, continuing education, certification, and other services to analysts and consultants.

SUPPLY AND WAREHOUSING MANAGER

CAREER PROFILE

Duties: Analyze the demand for supplies and forecast future needs; direct personnel who receive inventory; manage the inspection of inventory; store and issue supplies and equipment; direct the preparation of reports and records; evaluate bids and proposals submitted by potential suppliers; study ways to use space and distribute supplies efficiently

Alternate Title(s): Purchasing Agent; Purchasing Professional; Warehouse Manager; Operations Manager; Wholesale Sales Representative; Retail Salesperson; Sales Engineer; Sales Manager

Availability: All branches

Military Salary: See How to Use This Book

Civilian Salary: $22,290 to $86,740

Civilian Employment Prospects: Fair

Civilian Advancement Prospects: Fair

Prerequisites:

Rank—Officer

Education and Training—Bachelor's or master's degree in business, economics; technical training in engineering or one of the applied sciences

Experience—Any training and work experience obtained in the Armed Services or Job Corps

Special Skills and Personality Traits—Interest in planning and directing the work of others; computer literacy (including word processing and spreadsheet software); ability to analyze technical data in suppliers' proposals; good communication skills; strong negotiation skills; excellent math ability; knowledge of supply chain management; ability to perform financial analyses

CAREER LADDER

```
┌─────────────────────────────────────┐
│     Supply or Warehouse Manager      │
└─────────────────────────────────────┘

┌─────────────────────────────────────┐
│         Assistant Supply             │
│       or Warehouse Manager           │
└─────────────────────────────────────┘

┌─────────────────────────────────────┐
│    Experienced Purchasing Agent      │
└─────────────────────────────────────┘
```

Position Description

The military requires great quantities of supplies. Not only during times of war, but every day multiple tons of food, fuel, medicine, ammunition, etc., must be ordered, stored, and distributed. In the military, these duties are overseen by Supply and Warehousing Managers whose job it is to not only arrange and schedule the distribution of these items worldwide, but also manage the personnel beneath them who order, receive, store, account for, and issue said equipment and supplies.

In the civilian world such Managers work for storage companies, manufacturers, hospitals, schools, and government agencies. Their job is to obtain the best possible merchandise at the lowest possible price for their employers. In some cases, rather than making these purchases for a company or organization, some managers buy items strictly for resale.

To perform this job successfully, purchasing managers, buyers, and purchasing agents study sales records and inventory levels of current stock, identify foreign and domestic suppliers, and keep abreast of changes affecting both the supply of and demand for products and materials for which they are responsible. They evaluate suppliers based upon price, quality, service support, availability, reliability, and selection. They must review catalogs, industry periodicals, directories, trade journals, and Internet sites, research the reputation and history of suppliers, and advertise anticipated purchase actions in order to solicit bids. They will inspect goods and services during meetings, trade shows, conferences, and visits to suppliers. They are also responsible for assessing a supplier's production and distribution capabilities and discussing other technical and business considerations that influence the purchasing decision.

Purchasing professionals can also be employed to acquire product materials, intermediate goods, machines, supplies, services, and other materials used in the production of a final product. The production process can be slowed or even halted if the right supplies are not on hand when needed. To be effective, purchasing professionals must have a working technical knowledge of the goods or services to be purchased.

Purchasing agents are involved at most stages of product development because of their ability to forecast the cost of parts or materials, its availability, and its suitability for its intended purpose. They also can help avoid potential problems with the supply of materials.

On the other hand, wholesale purchasing agents buy goods directly from manufacturers or other wholesale firms for resale. In retail firms, buyers purchase goods from wholesale firms or directly from manufacturers for resale to the public. Buyers largely determine which products their establishment will sell. This means they must be able to accurately predict what will sell. They must stay informed of the latest trends, follow newspaper ads and other media to check competitors' sales activities and watch general economic conditions to anticipate consumer buying patterns.

These days computers handle the more routine tasks of this job. They are used to obtain instant and accurate product and price listings, to track inventory levels, process routine orders, and help determine when to make purchases. Computers also maintain lists of bidders and offers, record the history of supplier performance, and issue purchase orders. This, of course, frees purchasers to concentrate more on the analytical aspects of their profession.

Purchasing agents usually work more than the standard 40-hour week because of special sales, conferences, or production deadlines. This can be especially true prior to holiday seasons. The job also brings excessive pressure on those in the field because wholesale and retail stores are so competitive; buyers need physical stamina to keep up with the fast-paced nature of their work. There can also be travel involved, often at least several days a month, sometimes even outside the United States.

Civilian Salaries

Average yearly earnings of purchasing professionals—the most likely civilian equivalent for military Supply and Warehousing Managers—were $41,830 in 1998. The middle 50 percent earned between $29,930 and $63,520 a year. The lowest 10 percent earned less than $22,290 and the highest 10 percent earned more than $86,740 a year. Average yearly earnings in the industries employing the largest number of purchasing managers in 1997 were as follows:

Electrical goods	$39,300
Professional and commercial equipment	$37,700
Machinery, equipment, and supplies	$36,400
Department stores	$35,500
Grocery stores	$25,900

The average yearly earnings for purchasers, except wholesale, retail, and farm products were $38,040 in 1998. The middle 50 percent earned between $29,660 and $49,660 a year. The lowest 10 percent earned less than $23,960 and the highest 10 percent earned more than $74,050 a year. Average yearly earnings in the industries employing the largest number of purchasing agents, except wholesale, retail, and farm products in 1997 were as follows:

Federal government	$47,200
Aircraft and parts	$41,100
Electronic components and accessories	$36,600
Local government, except education and hospitals	$35,300
Hospitals	$29,300

Purchasing professionals receive equal benefits packages to their coworkers, including vacations, sick leave, life and health insurance, and pensions. Buyers can also earn bonuses based on their performance and may also receive discounts on merchandise bought from the employer.

Civilian Employment Prospects

Prospects for entering this field are fair. Computerization, while making this job easier in many ways, has reduced the demand for lower-level buyers. In 1998, about one-half of all Supply and Warehousing Managers and purchasing professionals were employed in wholesale trade or manufacturing establishments such as distribution centers or factories. Another one-fifth worked in retail trade establishments such as grocery or department stores. The remainder worked mostly in service establishments or different levels of government. A small number were self-employed. They held roughly 550,000 jobs.

Civilian Advancement Prospects

Employment for Supply and Warehousing Managers and purchasing professionals is expected to grow more slowly than average through the year 2008. Computers have eliminated many of the low-level jobs traditionally associated with this field. Also, limited sourcing and long-term contracting have allowed companies to negotiate with fewer suppliers less frequently. This means most job openings will result from the need to replace workers who transfer to other occupations or leave the labor force.

Also, mergers and acquisitions have forced the consolidation of buying departments, which eliminates jobs. On top of this, many organizations are eliminating their buying departments from geographic markets and centralizing them, eliminating even more positions.

Those with a bachelor's degree in business should have the best chance of obtaining a buyer's job in wholesale or retail trade or within government. A bachelor's degree combined with industry experience and knowledge of a technical field will be an advantage for those interested in working for a manufacturing or industrial company. Government agencies and larger companies usually require a master's degree in business or public administration for top-level purchasing positions.

Qualified applicants usually begin as trainees, purchasing clerks, expediters, junior buyers, or assistant buyers. Retail and wholesale firms prefer to hire applicants who are familiar with the merchandise they sell as well as with wholesaling and retailing practices. Some retail firms promote qualified employees to assistant buyer positions; others recruit and train college graduates as assistant buyers.

With experience, buyers may advance by moving to a department that manages a larger volume or by becoming a merchandise manager. Others may go to work in sales for a manufacturer or wholesaler. They may also become an assistant purchasing manager before advancing to purchasing manager, supply manager, or director of materials management.

Education and Training

Large firms tend to prefer applicants with a bachelor's or master's degree in business, economics, or technical training such as engineering or one of the applied sciences.

Job training consists of a half month to four months of classroom instruction. Course content typically includes such subjects as warehousing and storage procedures, handling and packaging procedures, administrative procedures, field supply management and planning for future supply needs.

Of course, new employees must learn the specifics of their firm's business. Training periods vary, with most lasting one to five years. In wholesale and retail establishments, most trainees begin by selling merchandise, supervising sales workers, checking invoices on material received, and keeping track of stock on hand. As they progress, retail trainees are given increased buying-related responsibilities. In manufacturing, new purchasers often spend a considerable amount of time learning about company operations and purchasing practices as well as about commodities, prices, suppliers, and markets.

The recognized marks of experience and professional competence for this profession are the designations Accredited Purchasing Practitioner (A.P.P.) and Certified Purchasing Manager (C.P.M.), conferred by the National Association of Purchasing Management, and Certified Purchasing Professional (C.P.P.), conferred by the American Purchasing Society.

In federal, state, and local government, the indications of professional competence are Certified Professional Public Buyer (C.P.P.B.) and Certified Public Purchasing Officer (C.P.P.O.), conferred by the National Institute of Governmental Purchasing.

Please note that continuing education is essential for advancement. Many purchasing professionals participate in seminars offered by professional societies and take college courses in purchasing.

Experience, Special Skills, and Personality Traits

Good fields of study include business administration, inventory management, and operations research. Someone planning to enter this field should show an interest in planning and directing the work of others as well as the ability to express ideas clearly and concisely.

Purchasers must be computer literate, including knowledge of word processing and spreadsheet software. They must have the ability to analyze technical data in suppliers' proposals; good communication, negotiation, and math skills; knowledge of supply chain management; and the ability to perform financial analyses.

They must be good planners and decision-makers and have an interest in merchandising. Anticipating consumer preferences and ensuring that goods are in stock when they are needed require resourcefulness, good judgment, and self-confidence. They must be risk-takers who make decisions quickly. Marketing skills and the ability to identify products that will sell are also very important, as is leadership ability because buyers spend a large portion of their time supervising assistant buyers and dealing with manufacturers' representatives and store executives.

Unions and Associations

The National Association of Purchasing Management and Certified Purchasing Professional (C.P.P.), the Accredited Purchasing Practitioner (A.P.P.) and Certified Purchasing Manager (C.P.M.), are designated marks of experience and professional competence which are conferred by the American Purchasing Society. In federal, state, and local government, the indications of professional competence are Certified Professional Public Buyer (C.P.P.B.) and Certified Public Purchasing Officer (C.P.P.O.), conferred by the National Institute of Governmental Purchasing.

For further information about education, training, and/or certification for purchasing careers contact the American Purchasing Society, the National Association of Purchasing Management, the National Institute of Governmental Purchasing, Inc., and the Federal Acquisition Institute.

COMBAT

ARTILLERY CREW MEMBER

CAREER PROFILE

Duties: Determine target locations; set up and load artillery weapons; prepare ammunition; fire artillery weapons; clean and maintain artillery weapons; drive trucks and self-propelled artillery

Alternate Title(s): None

Availability: Army, Navy, Marines, Coast Guard

Military Salary: See How to Use This Book

Civilian Salary: Varies by industry

Civilian Employment Prospects: Fair

Civilian Advancement Prospects: Fair

Prerequisites:
  Rank—Enlisted
  Education and Training—None required
  Experience—None required
  Special Skills and Personality Traits—The ability to think and remain calm under stress; able to work as a member of a team; capable of performing a wide variety of duties; an interest in cannon and rocket operations; physical stamina and normal color vision

CAREER LADDER

```
┌─────────────────────────────┐
│         Supervisor          │
└─────────────────────────────┘

┌─────────────────────────────┐
│           Worker            │
└─────────────────────────────┘
```

Position Description

Those who think all wars will be fought from the sky in the future may be surprised to find that such policies are already being seriously rethought due to the fact they are extremely cost prohibitive. This means that the Artillery Corps will not soon be replaced. Artillery is a term that covers all weapons that fire large shells or missiles. Today's military uses artillery to support infantry and tank units in combat. Artillery is also used to protect land and sea forces from air attack. Artillery crew members position, direct, and fire artillery guns, cannons, howitzers, missiles, and rockets to destroy enemy positions and aircraft.

Artillery Crew Members generally specialize by type of artillery. In the army and marines they work outdoors when on land maneuvers. Some work in sheltered fire control stations. In the navy and coast guard they mainly work below deck. In all branches of the service, artillery crew members determine target location using computers or manual calculations. They set up and load artillery weapons, prepare ammunition, fuses, and powder for firing and fire artillery weapons according to instructions from artillery officers. They also clean and maintain artillery weapons and drive both trucks and self-propelled artillery.

Due to the combat nature of this occupation, it is open only to men. Like many combat positions, the job of artillery crew member has no real equivalent in the civilian world. However, the close teamwork, discipline, and leadership experiences it provides are helpful in many civilian jobs.

The only direct application of the talents learned in this occupation in the civilian world are in the world of fireworks displays. Those with experience not only with the positioning and firing of artillery, but also with the setting up of fuses and powder charges will have an advantage when such jobs come available. This is a small, clannish field, however, and not many openings exist.

More likely is the translating of such skills into jobs calling for the handling of large vehicles, including those that pull other large vehicles. These include long distance hauling, driving cement trucks or construction site dump trucks, heavy-duty tow trucks reserved for towing buses, and tow trucks for other large vehicles like those used at airports for positioning jets. Construction projects requiring the use of explosives may also offer opportunities to those proven to be able to handle crews working with dangerous materials.

Civilian Salaries

Civilian salaries will vary widely by industry. Once an Artillery Crew Member has chosen a field to pursue, he may contact related organizations for salary information or consult general career resources for that field.

Civilian Employment Prospects

Employment prospects for Artillery Crew Members will vary widely by industry. Since the skills gained in the military may be applied to a wide number of fields, artillery crew members stand a fair chance of finding employment since they can choose to look in areas offering the most openings.

Civilian Advancement Prospects

Most civilian opportunities open to Artillery Crew Members tend to be blue-collar jobs, offering little chance for direct advancement. Some workers may move into supervisory positions. In some fields workers may advance by starting their own business or becoming an independent contractor.

Education and Training

In the military, those interested in this career receive two and a half to three and a half months of classroom instruction, depending on specialty, and field training under simulated combat conditions. Classes usually include courses such as the methods of computing target locations, ammunition-handling techniques, gun, missile, and rocket system operations and artillery tactics.

Further training occurs on the job and through advanced courses. The army, navy, and Marine Corps offer certified apprenticeship programs for one specialty in this occupation.

Experience, Special Skills, and Personality Traits

This is an arduous position. Artillery Crew Members must have great physical stamina to perform strenuous activities for long periods without rest. It is also imperative that they have normal color vision. This is necessary for the identification of color-coded ammunition and to read maps and charts.

Also important are the abilities to think and remain calm under stress, to work as a member of a team and to perform a wide variety of duties calmly under pressure. An interest in cannon and rocket operations also helps.

Unions and Associations

There are no unions or associations specifically for Artillery Crew Members. Helpful organizations may exist for various civilian industries an Artillery Crew Member may choose to enter after service.

COMBAT ENGINEER

CAREER PROFILE

Duties: Construct trails, roads, and field fortifications; erect floating or prefabricated bridges; lay and clear mine fields, place and detonate explosives; erect camouflage and other protective barriers; load, unload, and move supplies and equipment; construct airfields; participate in combat operations as infantrymen

Alternate Title(s): None

Availability: Army, Navy, Marine Corps

Military Salary: See How to Use This Book

Civilian Salary: Varies by industry

Civilian Employment Prospects: Fair

Civilian Advancement Prospects: Fair

Prerequisites:

   Rank—Enlisted

   Education and Training—None required

   Experience—Any training and work experience obtained in the Armed Services or Job Corps

   Special Skills and Personality Traits—A preference for working outdoors; agility; balance; physical strength; the ability to swim; the ability to use hand and power tools and to think and remain calm under stress

CAREER LADDER

Varies by industry

Position Description

Combat troops are essential to any military campaign, but they are helpless without support. When rapid travel across difficult terrain or swift-flowing rivers is needed, it is the Combat Engineer who is called in with his combination of combat ability and building skill to make certain the advance continues.

Working in all manners of conditions and on all manner of terrain, Combat Engineers construct trails, roads, and field fortifications, such as shelters, bunkers, and gun emplacements. They also erect floating or prefabricated bridges, lay and clear mine fields and booby traps, place and detonate explosives as needed, and erect camouflage and other protective barriers for artillery and troop positions. They also load, unload, and move supplies and equipment, using planes, helicopters, trucks, and amphibious vehicles. They construct airfields and perform ground traffic control

duties. Then, when all the building is done, instead of sitting back and watching others move ahead, they turn in their tools, grab their weapons, and participate in the coming combat as infantrymen.

Because Combat Engineers must be prepared to support operations anywhere in the world, they work and train for long hours under every kind of extreme weather condition and in all manners of climates available. Combat Engineers work, eat, and sleep outdoors during training exercises as they would in real combat situations. Most of the time, Combat Engineers are assigned to military bases.

The job of Combat Engineer has no direct equivalent in civilian life. However, experience as a Combat Engineer is related to occupations in several civilian fields. These include the logging, mining, construction, shipping, and landscaping industries. Civilians in these jobs are called forestry aides, loggers, blasters, and construction workers.

Civilian Salaries

In 2000, the average hourly wage for forest, conservation, and logging occupations were as follows:

Log graders and scalers	$13.07
Fallers	$12.33
Logging equipment operators	$12.07
Forest and conservation workers	$8.97

Earnings of logging workers vary by size of establishment and by geographic area. Workers in larger establishments earn more than those in smaller ones. Forest and conservation workers who work for state and local governments and large private firms generally enjoy more generous benefits than workers in smaller firms.

In 2000, the average hourly wage for construction laborers in the largest industries employing construction laborers were as follows:

Nonresidential building construction	$11.85
Miscellaneous special trade contractors	$11.71
Concrete work	$11.27
Heavy construction, except highway	$10.90
Residential building construction	$10.62

Earnings for construction laborers can be reduced by poor weather or by downturns in construction activity, which sometimes result in layoffs.

Civilian Employment Prospects

Experience as a Combat Engineer may lead to a wide variety of opportunities in the civilian workforce, according to a worker's personal interests, personality, and skills.

In 2000, forest, conservation, and logging workers held just under 90,000 jobs, distributed among the following occupations:

Logging equipment operators	47,000
Forest and conservation workers	21,000
Fallers	13,000
Log graders and scalers	8,000

Workers in these physically demanding, hazardous occupations spend all their time outdoors, sometimes in poor weather and often in isolated areas. A few lumber camps in Alaska house workers in bunkhouses or company towns. Workers in sparsely populated western states commute long distances between their homes and logging sites. In the more densely populated eastern and southern states, commuting distances are much shorter. The jobs of forest and conservation workers generally are much less hazardous. It may be necessary for some forestry aides or forest workers to walk long distances through densely wooded areas to do their work.

Most wage and salary fallers and logging equipment operators are employed in the logging camps and logging contractors industry, although some work in sawmills and planing mills. Employment of log graders and scalers is largely concentrated in sawmills and planing mills. Although logging operations are found in most states, the Southeast employs about 37 percent of all logging workers, followed by the Northwest, which employs 30 percent.

About 40 percent of the wage and salary forest and conservation workers are employed by companies that operate timber tracts, tree farms, or forest nurseries, or by establishments that supply forestry services. Some of those employed in forestry services work on a contract basis for the U.S. Department of Agriculture's Forest Service. Of the remainder, about 4,300 work for state governments, and 1,900 work for local governments. A small number work in sawmills and planing mills. Although forest and conservation workers are located in every state, employment is concentrated in the West and Southeast where many national and private forests and parks are located.

Through 2010, opportunities for forest, conservation, and logging workers are expected to decline slightly. Slower-than-average employment growth is also expected for forest and conservation workers.

Weather conditions often halt logging operations during the muddy spring and cold winter months. In addition, logging operations must relocate when timber harvesting in a particular area has been completed. During prolonged periods of inactivity, some workers stay on the job to maintain or repair logging machinery and equipment.

In 2000, construction laborers held just over 790,000 jobs. They worked throughout the country, but are concentrated in metropolitan areas. Almost all construction laborers work in the construction industry. Nearly 40 percent work for special trade contractors. In 2000, fewer than 10 percent worked part time. Most laborers do physically demanding work. They generally work eight-hour shifts, although longer shifts are common. They also may work only during certain seasons, when the weather permits construction activity.

Through 2010, opportunities for construction laborers are expected to grow about as fast as the average for all occupations due to the numerous openings arising each year from laborers who leave the occupation. Opportunities will be best for well-trained workers willing to relocate to different worksites.

Civilian Advancement Prospects

Experience working at a nursery or as a laborer can be useful in obtaining a job as a forest or conservation worker. Manual labor jobs can often lead to those involving the operation of expensive, sometimes complicated, machinery and other equipment. Familiarization with logging operations can also lead to jobs such as log handling equipment operator.

Experience in many construction laborer jobs may allow some workers to advance to positions such as supervisor or construction superintendent. A few become independent contractors.

Education and Training

In the military, job training for Combat Engineers is mainly provided on the job, usually consisting of such construction projects as basic construction methods, bridge building, road maintenance and repair, rough carpentry and rigging, and the use of hand and power tools. The marine corps offers a six-week course in basic combat engineering skills. Combat training in infantry skills is also provided to combat engineers.

Most forest, conservation, and logging workers develop skills through on-the-job training as well, with instruction coming primarily from experienced workers. Many state forestry or logging associations provide training sessions for fallers, whose job duties require more skill and experience than other positions on the logging team. Training programs for loggers are becoming common in many states. Such programs generally include some type of classroom or field training in a number of areas—some lead to logger certification.

Experience in other occupations can expedite entry into some logging occupations. Little formal education is usually required for most forest, conservation, and logging occupations. Many secondary schools, including vocational and technical schools, and some community colleges offer courses or a two-year degree in general forestry, wildlife, conservation, and forest harvesting, which could be helpful in obtaining a job.

Most construction laborers learn their skills informally, observing and learning from experienced workers. Individuals who learn the trade on the job usually start as helpers. Becoming a fully skilled construction laborer by training on the job normally takes longer than the two to four years required to complete an apprenticeship program.

Formal apprenticeship programs provide more thorough preparation than on-the-job training. Local apprenticeship programs are operated under guidelines established by the Laborers-Associated General Contractors of America Education and Training Fund. Most apprenticeship programs require workers to be at least 18 years old and physically able to perform the work. Many apprenticeship programs require a high school diploma or equivalent.

Relevant work experience that provides construction-related job skills can often reduce or eliminate a wide range of training and apprenticeship requirements. Most apprenticeship programs, local unions, and employers look very favorably on military service and/or service in the Job Corps, as veterans and Job Corps graduates have already demonstrated a high level of responsibility and reliability and may have gained many valuable job skills.

Experience, Special Skills, and Personality Traits

Combat Engineers must meet very demanding physical requirements. They need agility and balance and must be able to perform strenuous physical activities over long periods of time. Combat Engineers lift and move heavy objects. Some specialties require good swimming abilities. Also helpful is the ability to use hand and power tools and to think and remain calm under stress as well as a preference for working outdoors.

Forest, conservation, and logging workers must be in good health, able to work as part of a team, have physical strength, stamina, maturity, good judgment, mechanical aptitude, and coordination.

Construction laborers need good manual dexterity, hand-eye coordination, balance and the ability to read and comprehend warning signs and labels. They should be capable of working as a member of a team, have basic problem-solving and math skills. They should also be hardworking, reliable, and diligent.

Unions and Associations

For information about timber cutting and logging careers and secondary and postsecondary programs offering training for logging occupations, contact the Northeastern Loggers Association and the Forest Resources Association, Inc. Schools of forestry at states' land-grant colleges or universities also should be able to provide useful information. A list of state forestry associations and other forestry-related state associations is available at most public libraries.

For information about jobs as construction laborers, contact local building or construction contractors, local joint labor-management apprenticeship committees, apprenticeship agencies, or the local office of your State Employment Service. For general information about the work of construction laborers, contact the Laborers' International Union of North America.

INFANTRYMAN

Duties: Operate, clean, and store automatic weapons; parachute from troop transport airplanes; fire armor-piercing missiles from hand-held antitank missile launchers; carry out scouting missions to spot enemy troop movements and gun locations; operate two-way radios and signal equipment; drive vehicles mounted with machine guns or small missiles; perform hand-to-hand combat drills; set firing angles and fire mortar shells at targets; dig foxholes, trenches, and bunkers

Alternate Title(s): None

Availability: Army, Marine Corps

Military Salary: See How to Use This Book

Civilian Salary: Varies by industry

Civilian Employment Prospects: Fair

Civilian Advancement Prospects: Fair

Prerequisites:

Rank—Enlisted

Education and Training—None required

Experience—None required

Special Skills and Personality Traits—Readiness to accept a challenge and face danger, ability to stay in top physical condition, interest in working as a member of a team; able to follow orders and stay calm under pressure

> **Varies by industry**

Position Description

Since the beginnings of organized warfare, the infantry has always been the primary land combat force of any military. When not at war, the infantry's role is to stay ready to defend our country. It is maintained through regular infantry troops, and their twin back-up forces, the reserve units of each branch and the national guard. During times of combat, the essential role of the infantry is to capture or destroy enemy ground forces and repel enemy attacks. Infantrymen operate weapons and equipment to engage and destroy enemy ground forces.

At a moment's notice, Infantrymen can be called upon to perform some or all of the following duties in any corner of the world. They operate, clean, and store automatic weapons, such as rifles and machine guns, parachute from troop trans-

port airplanes while carrying weapons and supplies, and fire armor-piercing missiles from hand-held antitank missile launchers. Infantrymen carry out scouting missions to spot enemy troop movements and gun locations, operate two-way radios and signal equipment to relay battle orders, and drive vehicles mounted with machine guns or small missiles. They also perform hand-to-hand combat drills that involve martial arts tactics, set firing angles and fire mortar shells at targets, and dig foxholes, trenches, and bunkers for protection against attacks.

Because it is vital to both their own safety and safety of the nation, Infantrymen must be extremely well trained. Since they must be prepared to go anywhere in the world they are needed as quickly as possible, they work and train in all climates and weather conditions. During training exercises, as in real combat, Infantrymen work, eat, and sleep outdoors. When not training, or in actual combat situations, however, Infantrymen work and live on military bases.

The position of Infantryman has very demanding physical requirements, possibly the most demanding of all positions within the modern military. Infantrymen must perform strenuous physical activities, such as marching long distances while carrying heavy equipment, digging foxholes, and climbing over obstacles. Infantrymen need good hearing and clear speech to use two-way radios, and good night vision and depth perception to see targets and signals.

Currently this occupation is open only to men.

Civilian Salaries

Civilian salaries will vary widely by industry. Once an Infantryman has chosen a field to pursue, he may contact related organizations for salary information or consult general career resources for that field.

Civilian Employment Prospects

Employment prospects for Infantryman will vary widely by industry. Although the job of Infantryman has no equivalent in civilian life, the close teamwork, discipline, and leadership experiences it provides are helpful in many civilian jobs. Since the skills gained in the military may be applied to a wide number of fields, Infantrymen stand a fair chance of finding employment since they can choose to look in areas offering the most openings.

Civilian Advancement Prospects

Advancement for Infantrymen in civilian careers will vary by industry and the skills and personality of each worker.

Some workers may move into supervisory positions. In some fields workers may advance by starting their own business or becoming an independent contractor. While most Infantrymen should enjoy the benefit of their discipline, training, and physical condition when pursuing a career, this may not offer any special advantage in many industries.

Education and Training

Training for the infantry starts with basic training, which lasts roughly for two months. Advanced training in infantry skills lasts for another two months. While some of the training is in the classroom, most is in the field under simulated combat conditions. In reality, training for an infantry soldier never stops. Infantry soldiers keep their skills sharp through frequent squad maneuvers, target practice, and war games. War games conducted without live ammunition allow soldiers to practice scouting, troop movement, surprise attack, and capturing techniques.

Experience, Special Skills, and Personality Traits

Those looking to join the infantry should have a readiness to accept a challenge and face danger, the ability to stay in top physical condition as well as an interest in working as a member of a team. Infantrymen must be dedicated to their mission goals and ready to follow the orders of their superiors.

Unions and Associations

There are no unions or associations specifically for Infantrymen. Helpful organizations may exist for various civilian industries an Infantryman may choose to enter after service.

INFANTRY OFFICER

CAREER PROFILE

Duties: Gather and evaluate intelligence on enemy strength and positions; develop offensive and defensive battle plans; coordinate plans with armor, artillery, and air support units; direct construction of bunkers and fortifications; direct the use of infantry weapons and equipment; develop and supervise infantry unit training; direct administrative activities

Alternate Title(s): None

Availability: Army, Marine Corps

Military Salary: See How to Use This Book

Civilian Salary: Varies by industry

Civilian Employment Prospects: Fair

Civilian Advancement Prospects: Fair

Prerequisites:
   Rank—Officer
   Education and Training—Four-year college degree
   Experience—None required
   Special Skills and Personality Traits—Strong leadership and motivational skills; enjoy challenges; willingness to face danger; interest in land battle history and strategy; excellent physical condition; good eyesight; endurance; comfortable outdoors in all weather and climates

CAREER LADDER

```
┌─────────────────────────────────┐
│   Independent Business Owner     │
└─────────────────────────────────┘

┌─────────────────────────────────┐
│           Supervisor             │
└─────────────────────────────────┘

┌─────────────────────────────────┐
│             Worker               │
└─────────────────────────────────┘
```

Position Description

The role of the infantry in the modern military is twofold. During times of peace, infantry forces must stand ready to defend our country anywhere in the world, sometimes at a moment's notice. During times of combat, the infantry is deployed to capture or destroy enemy forces on the ground and to repel enemy invasions. In both times of peace and war, an Infantry Officer directs, trains, and leads infantry units.

Infantry Officers must gather and evaluate intelligence on enemy strength and positions, develop offensive and defensive battle plans, and coordinate plans with armor, artillery, and air support units. They must direct the construction of bunkers, fortifications, and obstacles to support and camouflage infantry positions, and direct the use of infantry weapons and equipment, such as machine guns, mortars, rocket launchers, and armored personnel carriers.

They also develop and supervise infantry unit training and direct various administrative activities.

Because Infantry Officers must be prepared to lead their troops anywhere in the world, these officers must work and train in all climates and weather conditions. They must be capable of enduring themselves any place they can expect to send the men under them. During training exercises, as in real combat situations, infantry officers work, eat, and sleep outdoors and in tents. When not in the field, infantry officers perform administrative and management duties in offices.

Infantry Officers must meet the same demanding physical requirements as the infantrymen under their command. They must be in excellent physical condition to perform strenuous activities over long periods of time, sometimes without sleep or rest.

The occupation of Infantry Officer is currently open only to men.

Civilian Salaries

Civilian salaries will vary widely by industry. Once an Infantry Officer has chosen a field to pursue, he may contact related organizations for salary information or consult general career resources for that field.

Civilian Employment Prospects

Employment prospects for Infantry Officers will vary widely by industry. Although the job of Infantry Officers has no equivalent in civilian life, the close teamwork, discipline, and leadership experiences it provides are helpful in many civilian jobs. Since the skills gained in the military may be applied to a wide number of fields, Infantry Officers stand a fair chance of finding employment since they can choose to look in areas offering the most openings.

Civilian Advancement Prospects

Advancement paths will be determined by industry, but Infantry Officers should find their chances fair if they can successfully apply the discipline and planning skills learned in the service. Leadership skills make it possible for Infantry Officers to move into supervisory positions in civilian industry or to open their own business or become independent contractors.

Education and Training

In the military, those interested in this career receive two to three-and-a-half months of classroom instruction, depending on specialty, and field training under simulated combat conditions. Classes usually contain such courses as infantry leadership roles, infantry squad and platoon tactics and modern offensive and defensive combat techniques. As with most officer slots, a four-year college degree is normally required to enter this occupation. Helpful fields of study would include engineering, history, physical education, and business or public administration.

Experience, Special Skills, and Personality Traits

Those interested in a military career as an Infantry Officer should have the ability to motivate and lead others and the willingness to accept a challenge and face danger. An interest in land battle history and strategy is helpful. Candidates should possess excellent communications skills and good interpersonal abilities. Decisiveness and remaining calm under pressure are useful. They must also be willing to follow orders as well as issue orders they know will endanger the lives of the men under their command.

Unions and Associations

There are no unions or associations specifically for Infantry Officers. Helpful organizations may exist for various civilian industries an Infantry Officer may choose to enter after service.

MISSILE SYSTEM OFFICER

CAREER PROFILE

Duties: Stand watch as members of missile launch crews; direct testing and inspection of missile systems; direct missile maintenance operations; direct early-warning launch training exercises; direct security operations at missile sites; direct the storage and handling of nuclear warheads; direct operation of fail-safe and code verification systems

Alternate Title(s): None

Availability: Army, Navy, Air Force, Marine Corps

Military Salary: See How to Use This Book

Civilian Salary: Varies by industry

Civilian Employment Prospects: Fair

Civilian Advancement Prospects: Fair

Prerequisites:
   Rank—Officer
   Education and Training—Four-year college degree
   Experience—None required
   Special Skills and Personality Traits—Good motivational and leadership skills; ability to remain calm in stressful situations; capable of mastering and following complex procedures; good judgment; able to follow orders

CAREER LADDER

Independent Business Owner

Supervisor

Worker

Position Description

Although the combat soldier is still the backbone of the modern military, no one can deny the importance ballistic weapons play in modern warfare. Ballistic missiles are extremely powerful weapons that travel thousands of miles to their targets. They are fired from underground silos, submarines, and land-based launchers.

Missile System Officers direct missile crews as they target, launch, test, and maintain ballistic missiles. Working in underground launch command centers, in submarines, and in ground-level missile sites, Missile System Officers perform a variety of duties, including standing watch as members of missile launch crews, directing the testing and inspection of missile systems and missile maintenance operations, and conducting early-warning launch training exercises. These Officers also direct security operations at missile sites, and oversee the storage and handling of

nuclear warheads and the operation of fail-safe and code verification systems.

Civilian Salaries

Civilian salaries will vary widely by industry. Once a Missile System Officer has chosen a field to pursue, he may contact related organizations for salary information or consult general career resources for that field.

Civilian Employment Prospects

Employment prospects for Missile System Officer will vary widely by industry. Although the job of Missile System Officer has no equivalent in civilian life, the close teamwork, discipline, and leadership experiences it provides are helpful in many civilian jobs. Since the skills gained in the military may be applied to a wide number of fields, Missile System

Officers stand a fair chance of finding employment since they can choose to look in areas offering the most openings. The experience of Missile System Officers could translate well to technology, manufacturing, or aerospace industries.

Civilian Advancement Prospects

Advancement prospects will be determined by industry. Some workers may move into supervisory positions or become consultants. In some fields workers may advance by starting their own business or becoming an independent contractor. Missile System Officers should find good opportunities for advancement based on their discipline and training.

Education and Training

In the military, those interested in this career receive four to five months of classroom instruction, as well as training on missile system simulations. Training length varies depending on specialty. Classroom study generally includes courses such as missile targeting, security and code authentication, launch operations, and the necessary maintenance programs. Further training occurs on the job and through advanced courses.

A four-year college degree is normally required to enter this occupation. For some specialties, a master's degree in management is preferred. Helpful preparatory fields of study include engineering, physics, computer science, and business or public administration.

Experience, Special Skills, and Personality Traits

Those interested in a military career as a Missile System Officer should have the ability to motivate and lead others, as well as the abilities to remain calm in stressful situations and to master complex procedures. They must also be quick thinkers and capable of making solid decisions in a short period of time. They should be detail-oriented and have good interpersonal and communication skills. Any knowledge of or experience with technology can be a plus.

Unions and Associations

There are no unions or associations specifically for Missile System Officers. Helpful organizations may exist for various civilian industries a Missile System Officer may choose to enter after service.

SPECIAL OPERATIONS FORCES TEAM MEMBER

CAREER PROFILE

Duties: Go behind enemy lines to recruit, train, and equip friendly forces; carry out demolition raids against enemy military targets; clear mine fields; conduct missions to gather intelligence information on enemy military forces; conduct offensive raids or invasions of enemy territories; destroy enemy ships in coastal areas

Alternate Title(s): None

Availability: Army, Navy, Air Force, Marine Corps

Military Salary: See How to Use This Book

Civilian Salary: Varies by industry

Civilian Employment Prospects: Good

Civilian Advancement Prospects: Good

Prerequisites:
  Rank—Enlisted
  Education and Training—None
  Experience—None
  Special Skills and Personality Traits—Ability to work as a team member; readiness to accept challenges and face danger; ability to stay in top physical condition; ability to remain calm in stressful situations

CAREER LADDER

Varies by industry

Position Description

Not every battle is won by throwing overwhelming force at the enemy. There are many instances when a more subtle approach is called for. When the military has these difficult and dangerous covert missions to perform, they call upon special operations teams. These elite forces stay in a constant state of readiness, always prepared to strike anywhere in the world on a moment's notice. Special Operations Forces Team Members conduct offensive raids, demolition, intelligence, search and rescue, and other missions from aboard aircraft, helicopters, ships, or submarines. Since they can be called upon to go into action in any corner of the globe under any conditions, these men must be trained swimmers, parachutists, and survival experts, in addition to also being combat ready.

Special operations forces are constantly being called upon to go behind enemy lines to recruit, train, and equip friendly forces for guerrilla raids. They also carry out demolition raids against enemy military targets, such as bridges, railroads, and fuel depots; clear mine fields, both underwater and on land; and conduct missions to gather intelligence information on enemy military forces. These forces also conduct offensive raids or invasions of enemy territories and destroy enemy ships in coastal areas, using underwater explosives.

Most of the time, Special Operations Forces Team Members work and train on military bases or ships and submarines. But, since they must be prepared to go anywhere in the world they are needed, they often train and work in all climates, weather conditions, and settings. They may dive from submarines or small underwater craft.

The special operations forces have very demanding physical requirements. Since these forces may be exposed to harsh temperatures, often without protection, during missions in enemy-controlled areas, all members must be in top physical condition. Also, good eyesight, night vision, and physical conditioning are required to reach mission objectives by parachute, overland, or underwater. Also required is excellent hand-eye coordination to detonate or deactivate explosives. Most Special Operations Forces Team Members are required to be qualified divers, parachutists, and endurance runners. This occupation is open only to men.

Although the job of Special Operations Forces Team Members has no actual equivalent in the civilian world, training in explosives, bomb disposal, scuba diving, and swimming may be helpful in such civilian jobs as blaster, police bomb disposal specialist, diver, or swimming instructor. The discipline and dependability of special operations forces are assets in many civilian occupations.

The careers this field can possibly prepare one for are many and varied. For instance, explosives workers, ordnance handling experts, and blasters place and detonate explosives to demolish structures or to loosen, remove, or displace earth, rock, or other materials. On the other hand, such training is also the perfect background for one who might want to become a sports instructor or coach.

Civilian Salaries

Civilian salaries will vary widely by industry. Once a Special Operations Forces Team Member has chosen a field to pursue, he may contact related organizations for salary information or consult general career resources for that field.

Civilian Employment Prospects

Employment prospects for Special Operations Forces Team Members will vary widely by industry. Although the job of Special Operations Forces Team Member has no equivalent in civilian life, the close teamwork, discipline, and leadership experiences it provides are helpful in many civilian jobs. Since the skills gained in the military may be applied to a wide number of fields, Special Operations Forces Team Members stand a fair chance of finding employment since they can choose to look in areas offering the most openings.

Civilian Advancement Prospects

Most civilian opportunities open to Special Operations Forces Team Members tend to be blue-collar jobs, offering little chance for direct advancement. Some workers may move into supervisory positions. In some fields workers may advance by starting their own business or becoming an independent contractor.

Education and Training

In the military, those interested in this career receive at least a year and a half of classroom instruction and practice exercises. Classes usually consist of such courses as physical conditioning, parachuting, swimming, and scuba diving, using land warfare weapons and communications devices, handling and using explosives and bomb and mine disposal.

It should be noted that additional training occurs on the job and that the basic skills of special operations forces team members are kept sharp through frequent practice exercises under simulated mission conditions.

Experience, Special Skills, and Personality Traits

Those hoping to become Special Operations Forces Team Members face a daunting challenge. This is one of the military's elite positions, suitable for only "the best of the best" as the saying goes. Those who wish to enter this field must have the ability to work as a team member, be constantly ready to accept challenges and face danger, and possess the ability to stay in top physical condition as well as the ability to remain calm in stressful situations.

Unions and Associations

There are no unions or associations specifically for Special Operations Forces Team Members. Helpful organizations may exist for various civilian industries a Special Operations Forces Team Member may choose to enter after service.

SPECIAL OPERATIONS OFFICER

CAREER PROFILE

Duties: Train personnel in parachute, scuba diving, and special combat techniques; plan missions; train personnel for special missions; lead special forces teams; direct and supervise administrative activities of special forces units

Alternate Title(s): None

Availability: Army, Navy, Air Force, Marine Corps

Military Salary: See How to Use This Book

Civilian Salary: Varies by industry

Civilian Employment Prospects: Fair

Civilian Advancement Prospects: Fair

Prerequisites:

Rank—Officer

Education and Training—Four-year college degree

Experience—Prior military experience often required; candidate must be a qualified swimmer, parachutist, and endurance runner.

Special Skills and Personality Traits—Good eyesight and night vision; physical strength; good eye-hand coordination; the ability to remain calm and decisive under stress; a willingness to accept a challenges and face danger; willingness to stay in top physical condition; determination to complete a very demanding training program

CAREER LADDER

Independent Business Owner

Supervisor

Worker

Position Description

The role of the military is not always one of national defense. Often times our nation requires small, precise operations of all types, from covert missions to humanitarian rescues, and thus each branch of the service has specially trained forces to perform rapid strike missions. These elite forces stay in a constant state of readiness to strike anywhere in the world on a moment's notice.

Special Operations Officers lead special operations forces on missions of all types: offensive raids, demolitions, intelligence gathering, and search and rescue missions. Due to the wide variety of missions, Special Operations Officers are trained swimmers, parachutists, and survival experts and possess expertise in a wide variety of other skills. These Officers must train personnel in parachute, scuba diving,

and special combat techniques; plan missions; coordinate plans with other forces as needed; and train personnel for special missions using simulated mission conditions. They also lead Special Forces teams in accomplishing mission objectives and direct and supervise administrative activities of Special Forces units.

Because Special Operations Officers must be prepared to go anywhere in the world they are needed, they continually train and work in all climates, weather conditions, and settings. They must work in cold water and dive from submarines or small underwater craft. They must also prepare to be exposed to harsh temperatures, often without protection, during missions into enemy-controlled areas.

Currently this occupation is open only to men.

Civilian Salaries

Civilian salaries will vary widely by industry. Once a Special Operations Officer has chosen a field to pursue, he may contact related organizations for salary information or consult general career resources for that field.

Civilian Employment Prospects

Employment prospects for special operations officers will vary widely by industry. Although the job of Special Operations Officer has no equivalent in civilian life, the close teamwork, discipline, and leadership experiences it provides are helpful in many civilian jobs, particularly in the field of law enforcement. Since the skills gained in the military may be applied to a wide number of fields, Special Operations Officers stand a fair chance of finding employment since they can choose to look in areas offering the most openings. Some may choose to start their own business in an area of expertise learned during their military service, such as a skydiving or scuba agency.

Civilian Advancement Prospects

Advancement prospects for Special Operations Officers will vary by industry, though their discipline and training will give them an edge in meeting their goals. Some workers may move into supervisory positions. In some fields workers may advance by starting their own business or becoming an independent contractor. Special Operations Officers' variety of skills should serve them well in finding ways to advance their careers.

Education and Training

In the military, those interested in this career receive up to five months of classroom instruction, depending on specialty. Classes usually contain such courses as physical conditioning, scuba diving, swimming, parachuting, mission planning techniques, handling and using explosives, and reconnaissance techniques. Additional training does occur on the job. Basic skills for this occupation must be kept sharp through planning and conducting exercises under simulated mission conditions.

A four-year college degree is normally required to enter this occupation. Selection as a Special Operations Officer is very competitive. Helpful fields of study for this position include physical education, engineering, physical sciences, history, and business or public administration.

Experience, Special Skills, and Personality Traits

Special Operations Officers must meet very demanding physical requirements. Good eyesight, night vision, and physical conditioning are required to reach mission objectives by parachute, over land, or under water. Good eye-hand coordination is required to detonate or deactivate explosives. In most instances, Special Operations Officers are required to be qualified swimmers, parachutists, and endurance runners.

Those interested in a military career as a Special Operations Officer should also have the ability to remain calm and decisive under stress, a willingness to accept a challenge and face danger as well as the willingness to stay in top physical condition and the determination to complete a very demanding training program. They must also be willing to follow orders as well as issue orders they know will endanger the lives of the men under their command.

Unions and Associations

There are no unions or associations specifically for Special Operations Officers. Helpful organizations may exist for various civilian industries a Special Operations Officer may choose to enter after service.

TANK CREW MEMBER

CAREER PROFILE

Duties: Drive tanks or amphibious assault vehicles in combat formations; operate target sighting equipment to aim guns; load and fire guns; operate two-way radios and signaling equipment to receive and relay battle orders; gather and report information about the terrain, enemy strength, and target locations; perform preventive maintenance on tanks, guns, and equipment; read maps, compasses, and battle plans

Alternate Title(s): None

Availability: Army, Marine Corps

Military Salary: See How to Use This Book

Civilian Salary: Varies by industry

Civilian Employment Prospects: Fair

Civilian Advancement Prospects: Fair

Prerequisites:
 Rank—Enlisted
 Education and Training—None required
 Experience—None required
 Special Skills and Personality Traits—Work well with a team; ready to accept a challenge and face danger; ability to follow directions and execute orders quickly and accurately; physical strength and stamina; good eyesight and normal color vision; perform well under pressure; mechanical aptitude helpful; comfortable working in a confined space for long periods of time

CAREER LADDER

```
Independent Business Owner
```

```
Supervisor
```

```
Worker
```

Position Description

The role of tank and armor units, the modern day equivalent of the horse cavalry, is twofold. In peacetime these units stay ready to defend our country anywhere in the world. In combat they operate tanks and amphibious assault vehicles to seek out, engage, and destroy the enemy. Tanks also conduct scouting missions and support infantry units during combat. Tank Crew Members work as a team to operate armored equipment and fire weapons to destroy enemy positions. Tank Crew Members normally specialize by type of armor, such as tanks or amphibious assault vehicles.

At a moment's notice, Tank Crew Members can be called upon to perform some or all of the following duties in any corner of the world. These warriors drive tanks or amphibious assault vehicles in combat formations over roadways, rough terrain, and in heavy surf. They operate target sighting equipment to aim guns, load and fire guns, and operate two-way radios and signaling equipment to receive and relay battle orders. They also gather and report information about the terrain, enemy strength, and target location, perform preventive maintenance on tanks, guns, and equipment, and read maps, compasses, and battle plans.

Because it is vital to both their own safety and safety of the nation, Tank Crew Members must be extremely well-trained. Since they must be prepared to go anywhere in the world, they work and train in all climates and weather conditions.

During training exercises, as in real combat, Tank Crew Members work, eat, and sleep outdoors and in tanks. When not training, or in actual combat situations, however, Tank Crew Members work and live on military bases.

Currently this occupation is open only to men.

Civilian Salaries

Civilian salaries will vary widely by industry. Once a Tank Crew Member has chosen a field to pursue, he may contact related organizations for salary information or consult general career resources for that field. Some likely fields for Tank Crew Members might be truck driving, operating heavy construction vehicles, or jobs involving mechanical work, though tank experience doesn't limit one's range of options.

Civilian Employment Prospects

Employment prospects for Tank Crew Members will vary widely by industry. Although the job of Tank Crew Member has no equivalent in civilian life, the close teamwork, discipline, and leadership experiences it provides are helpful in many civilian jobs. Since the skills gained in the military may be applied to a wide number of fields, Tank Crew Members stand a fair chance of finding employment since they can choose to look in areas offering the most openings.

Civilian Advancement Prospects

Most civilian opportunities open to Tank Crew Members without additional education or training tend to be blue-collar jobs, offering little chance for direct advancement. Some workers may move into supervisory positions. In some fields workers may advance by starting their own business or becoming an independent contractor. Others may choose to continue their education and go into unrelated fields. Opportunities for advancement will vary by industry.

Education and Training

In the military, those interested in this career receive one-and-a-half to three months of classroom instruction, depending on specialty. Classes usually contain courses such as tank operations, armor offensive and defensive tactics, tank gunnery, map-reading, and scouting techniques.

Further training occurs both on the job and through extensive training exercises. Tank crews often take part in war games, which simulate combat conditions. They divide into teams and practice battle tactics on military exercise ranges. Instead of firing live ammunition tanks "shoot" harmless light beams at one another to determine war game victors.

Experience, Special Skills, and Personality Traits

Those interested in a military career as a Tank Crew Member should have the ability to work as a member of a team, a sense of readiness to accept a challenge and face danger and the ability to follow directions and execute orders quickly and accurately. The position of Tank Crew Member also has very demanding physical requirements. Candidates must be in peak physical condition and have exceptional stamina. They must also be able to work inside the confined area of a tank for long periods of time. Good vision and normal color vision are required in order to read maps, drive vehicles around obstacles, and locate targets.

Unions and Associations

There are no unions or associations specifically for Tank Crew Members. Helpful organizations may exist for various civilian industries a Tank Crew Member may choose to enter after service.

TANK OFFICER

CAREER PROFILE

Duties: Gather and evaluate intelligence or enemy strength and positions; formulate battle plans; coordinate actions with infantry, artillery, and air support units; plan and direct communications; direct operations of assault vehicles and support equipment; plan and supervise tactical and technical training of a tank unit; direct unit administrative activities

Alternate Title(s): None

Availability: Army, Marine Corps

Military Salary: See How to Use This Book

Civilian Salary: Varies by industry

Civilian Employment Prospects: Fair

Civilian Advancement Prospects: Fair

Prerequisites:
   Rank—Officer
   Education and Training—A four-year college degree
   Experience—None required
   Special Skills and Personality Traits—Ability to motivate and lead others; willingness to accept a challenge and face danger; decisiveness; interest in both tanks and battlefield strategy; physical strength and stamina; good eyesight; excellent communication skills; able to follow orders

CAREER LADDER

Varies by industry

Position Description

Outside of small regional skirmishes, after the military's air forces have softened enemy forces, it is up to the modern ground cavalry to take over and win the day. In peacetime, tank and armor units stay ready to defend the nation's interests anywhere in the world. During wartime they operate tanks, armored vehicles, and amphibious assault vehicles to engage and destroy the enemy. Tank Officers lead tank and armor units. They normally specialize by type of tank unit, such as armor, cavalry, or amphibious assault.

No matter what their specialty, however, all Tank Officers must be ready to gather and evaluate intelligence on enemy strength and positions, formulate battle plans, and coordinate actions with infantry, artillery, and air support units. They must also plan and direct communications, direct operations of tanks, amphibious assault vehicles, and support equipment, plan and supervise tactical and technical training of a tank unit, and direct unit administrative activities.

Although it must be noted that the job of Tank Officer has no actual equivalent in the civilian world, the leadership and administrative skills it provides are similar to those used in many civilian managerial occupations.

Because of the requirements of their position, Tank Officers must work and train in all climates and conditions the year round. To remain ready for combat, tank units regularly train under simulated combat conditions on all manner of terrain in all manner of weather. During these exercises, Tank Officers are on the move, working, eating, and sleeping outdoors and in tents under the same conditions as the men under their command. Tank Officers must meet the same demanding physical requirements as their troops. They must be physically fit and able to hold up under the stress of combat conditions. When not in training, Tank Officers perform administrative duties in offices.

This occupation is open only to men.

Civilian Salaries

Civilian salaries will vary widely by industry. Once a Tank Officer has chosen a field to pursue, he may contact related organizations for salary information or consult general career resources for that field.

Civilian Employment Prospects

Employment prospects for Tank Officers will vary widely by industry. Although the job of Tank Officer has no exact equivalent in civilian life, the close teamwork, discipline, and leadership experiences it provides are helpful in many civilian jobs. Since the skills gained in the military may be applied to a wide number of fields, Tank Officers stand a fair chance of finding employment since they can choose to look in areas offering the most openings.

Civilian Advancement Prospects

Most civilian opportunities open to Tank Officers tend to be blue-collar jobs, offering little chance for direct advancement. Some workers may move into supervisory positions. In some fields workers may advance by starting their own business or becoming an independent contractor.

Education and Training

In the military, those interested in this career receive at least one to five months of classroom instruction and field training, depending on specialty. Classes usually consist of such courses as weapons and equipment maintenance, tank and armor operations, principles, and tactics, night maneuvers, and the role of the platoon leader. Further training occurs on the job and through specialized courses.

A four-year college degree is normally required to enter this occupation. Also, those interested in this field should first think of adding experience or training in such fields of study as engineering, geography, physical sciences, history, and business or public administration to their résumés.

Experience, Special Skills, and Personality Traits

Those looking to join the ranks of the military's Tank Officers should have the ability to motivate and lead others, a willingness to accept a challenge and face danger. They must be decisive and interested in both tanks and battlefield strategy. Tank Officers must be in excellent physical condition and be able to stay calm under pressure. They require excellent communication skills.

Unions and Associations

There are no unions or associations specifically for Tank Officers. Helpful organizations may exist for various civilian industries Tank Officers may choose to enter after service.

CONSTRUCTION AND MACHINE OPERATIONS

CONSTRUCTION EQUIPMENT OPERATOR

CAREER PROFILE

Duties: Drive heavy equipment to cut and level earth for runways and roadbeds; move heavy building materials using winches, cranes, and hoists; use power shovels, scrapers and snow blowers; operate mixing plants, paving machines and drilling rigs; place and detonate explosives

Alternate Title(s): Operating Engineer; Heavy Equipment Operator; Well Driller; Rigger

Availability: All branches

Military Salary: See How to Use This Book

Civilian Salary: $8.51 to $27.29/hour

Civilian Employment Prospects: Good

Civilian Advancement Prospects: Good

Prerequisites:
  Rank—Enlisted
  Education and Training—High school diploma with courses in science and mechanical drawing
  Experience—Any experience operating related mobile equipment, such as farm tractors or heavy machinery
  Special Skills and Personality Traits—Mechanical aptitude; interest in automobile mechanics; interest in operating heavy construction equipment; preference for working outdoors; good physical condition; good eyesight; stamina; able to follow instructions; good foot-hand-eye-coordination

CAREER LADDER

```
┌─────────────────────────────┐
│     Heavy Construction      │
│     Equipment Operator      │
└─────────────────────────────┘

┌─────────────────────────────┐
│     Light Construction      │
│     Equipment Operator      │
└─────────────────────────────┘

┌─────────────────────────────┐
│     Trainee or Apprentice   │
└─────────────────────────────┘
```

Position Description

The military is always building something. Millions of tons of steel, concrete, asphalt, and sweat must be moved, mixed, spread, and spent to build the airfields, roads, dams, and buildings necessary to make possible the military's various projects and duties. And it all must come together safely and on schedule. Construction Equipment Operators use bulldozers, cranes, graders, and numerous other pieces of heavy equipment in military construction.

Construction Equipment Operators drive bulldozers, roadgraders, and other heavy equipment. They use winches, cranes, and hoists. They dig holes and trenches with power shovels and remove ice and snow from runways and roads with scrapers and snow blowers. They mix concrete and asphalt and then they spread it with paving machines. They drill wells using drilling rigs, and they place and detonate explosives. In short, they work outdoors in all kinds of weather, and sit for long periods while being pounded by loud noise and vibrations. The only time they work indoors is while repairing equipment.

The list of duties Construction Equipment Operators can perform is long. There are paving, surfacing, and tamping equipment operators, as well as pile driver operators, who operate excavation and loading machines that dig into the earth, then load it into trucks or onto conveyors. They operate trench excavators, road graders. They can be called upon to maneuver industrial trucks or tractors equipped with fork-lifts or booms for lifting materials, or hitches for pulling trailers. They operate and maintain air compressors and pumps as well as machines that spread and level asphalt or concrete. They work with tamping machines that compact earth and other materials for roadbeds. They cut or break up old pavement and drive guardrail posts where needed. They operate pile drivers mounted on skids, barges, or cranes, and sometimes on the land, ships, or offshore oil rigs.

Construction Equipment Operators work outdoors in every type of climate and weather condition. The work is cold in the winter and hot in the summer, often leaving the operator filthy. Most of the machines involved are extremely loud. Most of them shake or jolt the operator. Heavy construction equipment can certainly be dangerous, but most accidents can be avoided by simply observing proper operating procedures and safety practices.

In the civilian world, Construction Equipment Operators work for building contractors, state highway agencies, rock quarries, well drillers, and construction firms. Since most construction projects by necessity must continue around the clock, construction work of this type calls for irregular hours. Such jobs are often located in remote locations (cutting highways through mountains, building dams, etc.), which can call for the operator to live on site for days, or even months, on end. This can increase one's pay greatly, but it does cut one off from the usual benefits of a 9-to-5 occupation.

Civilian Salaries

In 2000, the average hourly salary for Construction Equipment Operators was $15.99. The middle 50 percent made between $12.21 and $21.68. The lowest 10 percent earned less than $10.00, the highest 10 percent earned more than $27.29.

The average hourly salary for paving, surfacing, and tamping equipment operators was $12.88. The middle 50 percent made between $10.04 and $17.57. The lowest 10 percent made less than $8.51, the highest 10 percent made over $23.57.

The average hourly salary for pile driver operators was $19.85. The middle 50 percent earned between $13.36 and $26.03. The lowest 10 percent earned less than $10.99, the highest 10 percent earned more than $31.04.

Earnings were found to be higher in metropolitan areas. The overall annual earnings of some workers were lower than their hourly rates might suggest due to bad weather limiting their available work time.

Civilian Employment Prospects

Job opportunities are good for Construction Equipment Operators despite slower-than-average employment growth. The hourly pay is relatively high but, because construction equipment operators cannot work in adversely inclement weather, their total yearly earnings can be reduced. Openings will fluctuate with the rise and fall of the economy and the rate of new constructions being built.

In 2000, Construction Equipment Operators held slightly under 416,000 positions. These jobs were to be found in every section of the country. About three out of every five of these positions was to be found in the construction industry. Many equipment operators worked in heavy construction, building highways, bridges, or railroads. Slightly over 80,000 of all Construction Equipment Operators worked in state and local government. Some worked in mining, or for utility companies. Only one in 20 were self-employed.

Civilian Advancement Prospects

From now through 2010 job opportunities are expected to remain excellent, due in part to the shortage of adequate training programs. Also, many Construction Equipment Operators who could handle the work prefer careers that are less strenuous and more comfortable. Well-trained workers in this field will have especially favorable opportunities.

Employment of Construction Equipment Operators is expected to increase more slowly than the average for all occupations through the year 2010. Technological advances are expected to raise worker productivity and to moderate demand for new workers. Job opportunities are expected to increase as population (as well as business) growth creates a need for new homes, schools, hospitals, and other structures.

Education and Training

Job training consists of one to three months of classroom instruction. This includes practice in both operating different types of construction equipment as well as instruction in its maintenance and repair. Additional training occurs on the job and through advanced courses. The army and the navy both offer certified apprenticeship programs.

Although many Construction Equipment Operators acquire their skills on the job, it is generally accepted that formal training provides more comprehensive skills. Some Construction Equipment Operators train in formal apprenticeship programs. These are administered by both the International Union of Operating Engineers and the Associated General Contractors of America. Since apprentices learn to operate a wider variety of machines than other beginners, they usually have better job opportunities. Apprenticeship programs consist of at least 6,000 hours (within three years) of on-the-job training and 144 hours a year of related classroom instruction.

Construction Equipment Operators employers generally prefer to hire high school graduates, although some will train those having less education to operate some types of equipment. More technologically advanced construction equipment has computerized controls and improved hydraulics and electronics, requiring more skill to operate than was necessary for older machines. Operators of such equipment may need more training and some understanding of electronics. Experience operating related mobile equipment in the armed forces or elsewhere is a valuable asset.

Experience, Special Skills, and Personality Traits

High school courses in shop or auto mechanics can prove helpful in this field as well as courses in science and mechanical drawing. An interest in operating heavy construction equipment as well as a preference for working outdoors would also be a plus. Also one should be in good physical condition and have a good sense of balance, the ability to judge distance, and eye-hand-foot coordination.

Whereas some of the more refined specialties within the field can require normal hearing, color vision, heavy lifting or the ability to work at heights, there actually are no special requirements for this career on the whole.

Unions and Associations

Some Construction Equipment Operators train in formal three-year operating engineer apprenticeship programs administered by union-management committees of the International Union of Operating Engineers and the Associated General Contractors of America. For further information about apprenticeships or work opportunities for construction equipment operators, contact a local of the International Union of Operating Engineers, a local apprenticeship committee or the nearest office of the state apprenticeship agency or employment service. For general information about the work of Construction Equipment Operators contact the Associated General Contractors of America.

CONSTRUCTION SPECIALIST

CAREER PROFILE

Duties: Build foundations, floors, and walls; erect wood framing for buildings using hand and power tools; lay roofing materials; install plasterboard, plaster, and paneling to form interior walls and ceilings; lay wood and ceramic tile floors; build steps, staircases, and porches; erect temporary shelters for storage while on training maneuvers

Alternate Title(s): Bricklayer; Stonemason; Cement Mason; Cement Finisher; Carpenter; Cabinetmaker; Brickmason; Blockmason; Concrete Finisher; Terrazzo Worker

Availability: All branches

Military Salary: See How to Use This Book

Civilian Salary: $8.31 to $30.02/hour

Civilian Employment Prospects: Good

Civilian Advancement Prospects: Good

Prerequisites:

Rank—Enlisted

Education and Training—High school classes in math, woodworking, industrial arts, general science, shop, blueprint reading, mechanical drawing, and carpentry; apprenticeship

Experience—Any training and work experience obtained in the armed services or Job Corps; two to four years training

Special Skills and Personality Traits—A preference for physical work; ability to work with blueprints; an interest in using power tools; manual dexterity; eye-hand coordination; physical fitness; good sense of balance; the ability to solve arithmetic problems quickly

CAREER LADDER

Construction Specialist, Supervisor, or Independent Contractor

Construction Specialist

Apprentice

Position Description

The military needs hundreds of temporary as well as new permanent structures built each year. These must be built with accuracy and care, but also with speed. Lumber, plywood, plasterboard, concrete and bricks, stone and concrete blocks are the essential building blocks for most of these projects. Construction Specialists must be ready at all times to build and repair buildings, bridges, foundations, dams, and bunkers. As essential cogs in the vast military construction apparatus, they must be ready on a moment's notice to build foundations, floor slabs, and walls with brick, cement block, mortar, or stone. They must erect wood framing for buildings using hand and power tools, such as hammers, saws, levels, and drills; lay roofing materials, such as asphalt, tile, and wooden shingles; and install plasterboard, plaster, and paneling to form interior walls and ceilings. They will lay both wood and ceramic tile floors, and build steps, staircases, and porches. While on training maneuvers they will build temporary shelters for storing supplies and equipment.

In civilian life, Construction Specialists usually work for construction or remodeling contractors, government agencies, utility companies, or manufacturing firms. They will be called upon to work indoors and outdoors. They may have to lift and carry heavy building materials and climb and work from ladders and scaffolding.

The eight main types of construction specialists are carpenters, brickmasons, blockmasons, stonemasons, cement masons, concrete finishers, segmental pavers, and terrazzo workers.

Carpenters cut, fit, and assemble wood; build doors or brattices; set forms for concrete construction; erect scaffolding; install interior and exterior trim; frame walls and partitions; put in doors and windows; build stairs; lay hardwood floors; and hang kitchen cabinets. They must know the local building codes. They must understand layout-measuring, marking, and arranging materials; cut and shape wood, plastic, fiberglass, or drywall; and join materials. They must check the accuracy of their work and make any necessary adjustments. They must be able to work with prefabricated components, switch from residential building to commercial construction or remodeling work and be able to perform a variety of installation and maintenance work.

Brickmasons, blockmasons, and stonemasons mostly work outdoors, lifting heavy bricks and blocks and working on scaffolds. They build and repair walls, floors, partitions, fireplaces, chimneys, and other structures, install firebrick linings and work with all kinds of stone. They repair imperfections and cracks and replace broken or missing masonry units in walls and floors. Some brick and blockmasons install structural insulated wall panels and masonry accessories used in many high-rise buildings.

Cement masons, concrete finishers, segmental pavers and terrazzo workers all work with concrete. Cement masons and concrete finishers place and finish concrete, color concrete surfaces and expose aggregate and fabricate concrete beams, columns, and panels.

Segmental pavers lay out, cut, and install pavers, which are flat pieces of masonry usually made from compacted concrete or brick. Terrazzo workers create attractive walkways, floors, patios, and panels by exposing marble chips and other fine aggregates on the surface of finished concrete.

Construction Specialists usually work outdoors and are exposed to the elements. The work is fast-paced and strenuous, requiring continuous physical effort. These specialists generally do work that is filthy, standing, kneeling, and bending for long periods. They often have to lift heavy materials. Common hazards include injuries from tools and falls from scaffolds, but these can often be avoided when proper safety practices are followed.

Civilian Salaries

In 2000, the average hourly salary for carpenters was $15.69. The middle 50 percent earned between $11.99 and $20.86. The lowest 10 percent earned less than $9.48, and the highest 10 percent earned more than $26.73. The average hourly salary in the industries employing the largest numbers of carpenters in 2000 are shown below:

Masonry, stonework, and plastering	$19.27
Nonresidential building construction	$17.43
Heavy construction, except highway	$16.74
Carpentry and floor work	$15.51
Residential building construction	$15.26

In 2000, the average hourly salary for brickmasons and blockmasons was $19.37. The middle 50 percent earned between $15.00 and $24.48. The lowest 10 percent earned less than $11.20, and the highest 10 percent earned more than $30.02. The average hourly salary in the industries employing the largest number of brickmasons in 2000 are shown below:

Miscellaneous special trade contractors	$22.87
Masonry, stonework, and plastering	$19.55
Nonresidential building construction	$19.02
Residential building construction	$18.10

In 2000, the average hourly salary for stonemasons in 2000 was $14.98. The middle 50 percent earned between $10.78 and $19.24. The lowest 10 percent earned less than $9.09 and the highest 10 percent earned more than $23.03.

In 2000, the average hourly salary for cement masons and concrete finishers was $13.50. The middle 50 percent earned between $10.55 and $18.41. The top 10 percent earned over $24.22, and the bottom 10 percent earned less than $8.31.

In 2000, the average hourly salary for terrazzo workers and finishers was $15.06 and average hourly salary for segmental pavers was $12.46.

The earnings of all construction trades workers can be reduced on occasion because poor weather and downturns in construction activity limit the time they can work.

Civilian Employment Prospects

Job opportunities are excellent for all Construction Specialists. This is largely due to the numerous openings arising each year as experienced workers leave the occupation. Also, many prefer to work under less strenuous, more comfortable conditions. Well-trained workers will have especially favorable opportunities.

In 2000, 5 percent of all cement masons, concrete finishers, segmental pavers, and terrazzo workers, 25 percent of all carpenters, 33 percent of all brickmasons, blockmasons, and stonemasons were self-employed.

Construction activity parallels the movement of people and businesses and reflects differences in local economic conditions. Therefore, the number of job opportunities and apprenticeship opportunities in a given year may vary widely from area to area.

Many builders use specialty subcontractors who do one or two work activities, so versatile Construction Specialists able to switch specialties should have the best opportunities for steady work. Because there are no strict training requirements for entry, many people with limited skills take jobs as in these fields but eventually leave the occupation because they dislike the work or cannot find steady employment.

Employment of Construction Specialists is sensitive to changes in the economy. When the level of construction activity falls, workers in these trades can experience periods of unemployment.

Civilian Advancement Prospects

From now through 2010 job opportunities are expected to grow for all types of Construction Specialists. The expectations for new positions in these fields are excellent.

Carpenters held about 1.2 million jobs in 2000. Brickmasons, blockmasons, and stonemasons held about 158,000 jobs in 2000. Cement masons, concrete finishers, segmental pavers, and terrazzo workers held about 166,000 jobs in 2000.

Some Construction Specialists may advance their careers through becoming self-employed, growing their business, and taking on more and higher profile projects.

Education and Training

Job training consists of one to two months of instruction, including practice with carpentry and masonry tools. Courses are typically in building construction, masonry construction methods, types and uses of construction joints and braces, interpretation of blueprints and drawings, and how to mix and set concrete, mortar, and plaster.

Further training occurs on the job and through advanced courses. The army, navy and marine corps all offer certified apprenticeship programs in this occupation.

Helpful high school subjects include woodworking, industrial arts, general science, shop, blueprint reading, mechanical drawing, carpentry, and general mathematics.

All Construction Specialists generally learn their trade through on-the-job training, as well as formal training programs or apprenticeships. Apprenticeship programs are administered by local joint union-management committees of the United Brotherhood of Carpenters and Joiners of America, the Associated General Contractors, Inc., and the National Association of Home Builders. In addition, training programs are administered by local chapters of the Associated Builders and Contractors and by local chapters of the Associated General Contractors, Inc. These programs combine on-the-job training with related classroom instruction.

Apprenticeships for brickmasons, blockmasons, and stonemasons usually are sponsored by local contractors or by local union-management committees. The apprenticeship program requires three years of on-the-job training, in addition to a minimum 144 hours of classroom instruction each year in subjects such as blueprint reading, mathematics, layout work, and sketching. Applicants must be at least 17 years old and in good physical condition. The International Masonry Institute (IMI), a joint trust of the International Union of Bricklayers and Allied Craftsworkers and the contractors who employ its members, operates training centers in several large cities that help jobseekers develop the skills needed to successfully complete the formal apprenticeship program.

Most cement masons, concrete finishers, segmental pavers, and terrazzo workers learn their trades either through on-the-job training as helpers, or through three-year apprenticeship programs. Three-year apprenticeship programs, usually jointly sponsored by local unions and contractors, provide on-the-job training in addition to a recommended minimum of 144 hours of classroom instruction each year. A written test and a physical exam may be required.

Experience, Special Skills, and Personality Traits

Construction Specialists should have a preference for physical work, an ability to work with blueprints, an interest in using power tools, manual dexterity, good hand-eye coordination, physical fitness, a good sense of balance, and the ability to solve arithmetic problems quickly. Workers should enjoy doing demanding work and take pride in craftsmanship. They should be patient and methodical. Good communications skills are needed for dealing with clients and coworkers. They should be able to work without close supervision and get along with others.

Unions and Associations

Apprenticeship programs are administered by local joint union-management committees of the United Brotherhood of Carpenters and Joiners of America, the Associated General Contractors, Inc. and the National Association of Home Builders. Training programs are administered by local chapters of the Associated Builders and Contractors and by local chapters of the Associated General Contractors, Inc. For information about carpentry apprenticeships or other work opportunities in this trade, contact local carpentry contractors, locals of the union mentioned above, local joint union-contractor apprenticeship committees or the nearest office of the state employment service or apprenticeship agency.

For information on training opportunities and carpentry in general, contact the Associated Builders and Contractors, the Associated General Contractors of America, Inc., the National Association of Home Builders and the United Brotherhood of Carpenters and Joiners of America.

For details about apprenticeships or other work opportunities in these trades, contact local bricklaying, stonemasonry, or marble-setting contractors; a local of the union listed above; a local joint union-management apprenticeship committee or the nearest office of the state employment service or apprenticeship agency.

For general information about the work of brickmasons, blockmasons, or stonemasons contact the International Union of Bricklayers and Allied Craftsworkers and the International Masonry Institute, the Associated General Contractors of America, Inc., the Brick Industry Association, the National Association of Home Builders and the National Concrete Masonry Association.

For information about apprenticeships and work opportunities, contact local concrete or terrazzo contractors, locals of unions previously mentioned, a local joint union-management apprenticeship committee, or the nearest office of the state employment service or apprenticeship agency.

For general information about cement masons, concrete finishers, segmental pavers, and terrazzo workers contact the Associated General Contractors of America, Inc., the International Union of Bricklayers and Allied Craftworkers, the Operative Plasterers' and Cement Masons' International Association of the United States and Canada, the National Terrazzo and Mosaic Association, the Portland Cement Association and the United Brotherhood of Carpenters and Joiners of America.

MACHINIST AND CNC PROGRAMMER

CAREER PROFILE

Duties: Use machine tools (lathes, drill presses, milling machines) to produce precision metal parts; plan and carry out the operations needed to make machined products that meet precise specifications; review blueprints; plan the sequence of cutting and finishing operations; check computer programs to ensure that machinery will function properly and the output will meet specifications

Alternate Title(s): Numerical Control Machine Tool Programmer; Tool and Die Maker; Metalworking and Plastics-Working Machine Operator; Tool Planner; Instrument Maker

Availability: All branches

Military Salary: See How to Use This Book

Civilian Salary: $17,800 to $72,290

Civilian Employment Prospects: Good

Civilian Advancement Prospects: Good

Prerequisites:

Rank—Enlisted

Education and Training—Bachelor's degree in aeronautical, astronautical, or mechanical engineering required for civilian employment

Experience—Strong educational background; on-the-job training

Special Skills and Personality Traits—Mechanically inclined; able to work independently; highly accurate; stamina; able to concentrate under deadline pressure; manual dexterity; strong interpersonal skills

Licensure/Certification—Optional certification

CAREER LADDER

Supervisor or Manager

Machinist or CNC Programmer

Apprentice

Position Description

Machinists make extensive use of machines such as lathes, drill presses, and milling machines to produce precision metal parts. They produce both large quantities of a single part and small batches of specialty pieces or one-of-a-kind items. They also plan and carry out the making of machined products that meet precise specifications. Before Machinists can machine any part, they must carefully plan and prepare the operation. First they review blueprints or the written specifications for a job. Second they calculate the precise

cut or drill points for a work-piece, how fast to feed metal into the proper machine, and how much metal to remove. They are responsible for selecting both the proper tools and materials for the job, the planning of the cutting and finishing operations, and marking the metal stock to show where all cuts or bores must be made.

Once the preliminary work is finished, the machining operations must be attended to—metal stock must be positioned, controls must be set, and all cuts or bores made. They must constantly monitor the machinery feed and speed. Since the machining of metal products gives off a great deal of heat, Machinists also ensure that the work-piece is being properly lubricated and cooled. Production Machinists often generate large quantities of one part, especially those requiring complex operations and great precision. Large numbers of parts requiring more routine operations are produced by metalworking and plastics-working machine operators. Some Machinists repair or build new parts for existing machinery.

Often times the machine tools used to produce metal parts contain computer controllers that direct the machine's operations. These are known as CNC (computer numerically controlled). The controller reads a coded list of steps necessary to perform a specific machining job and runs the machine tool's mechanisms through the steps. CNC machine tools enable Machinists to be more productive and to produce parts with a level of precision not possible with traditional machining techniques. Precise movements are recorded in a program that can be saved and used again in the future, allowing high levels of precision to be consistently repeated. The quality of the products these machines produce depends largely on the programs, which may be produced by Machinists or by CNC Programmers.

CNC Programmers also analyze blueprints, compute the size and position of the cuts, determine the sequence of machine operations, select tools, and calculate machine speeds and feed rates. Then they write a program and store it. Machinists work alone or with CNC Programmers to check new programs, make certain that machinery will function properly, and that the output will meet exact specifications. Because any problem with the program could ruin expensive machines and tools, computer simulations may be used instead of a trial run to check the program. If errors are found, the program must be changed and retested until the problem is worked out.

Even though machine shops are usually properly illuminated and ventilated, working with machine tools presents certain dangers. Machinists wear safety glasses to shield against bits of flying metal and earplugs to dampen machinery noise. They must exercise caution when handling and feeding metal that is being worked. They must also stand throughout the day and often need to do moderately heavy lifting.

CNC Programmers work in offices. Although often close to the shop floor, they are removed from the workplace itself. These offices are generally clean, properly illuminated and relatively quiet. Both Machinists and CNC Programmers generally work a 40-hour week. Evening and weekend shifts are becoming more common, however, and overtime is often common.

Civilian Salaries

Machinists annual earnings averaged around $28,860 in 1998. The middle 50 percent earned between $22,670 and $36,100. The lowest 10 percent dropped to less than $17,800, while the top 10 percent jumped upward to over $42,480. In 1997, the median annual earnings in those industries employing the largest number of Machinists:

Aircraft and parts	$32,200
Metalworking machinery	$28,300
Industrial machinery	$26,500

For CNC Programmers, medial annual earnings were roughly $40,490 in 1998. The middle 50 percent earned between $33,230 and $49,620; the lowest 10 percent less than $27,170; and the top 10 percent, more than $72,290.

Civilian Employment Prospects

Machinists and CNC Programmers held approximately 434,000 jobs in 1998. Most of these jobs were Machinist positions. Most were in small machining shops or in manufacturing firms that produce durable goods, such as metalworking and industrial machinery or with transportation producers, such as the aircraft or automotive industries. Maintenance Machinists work in most industries that use production machinery. Although Machinists and CNC Programmers can find employment in almost any area of the country, the most jobs are concentrated in the Northeast, Midwest, and all along the West Coast.

Although employment growth has been slower than average lately, job opportunities should remain good. Those industries concerned constantly report difficulties in finding workers with the necessary skills and knowledge to fill machining and CNC programming openings. Job openings arise each year from the need to replace experienced Machinists and Programmers who retire or transfer to other occupations. It is expected that more Machinists will be needed than CNC Programmers mainly because there is always more regular machining work to be done.

Jobs for Machinists and CNC Programmers aren't expected to grow as quickly as the average for all occupations through 2008. Rising productivity, resulting from the expanding use of computer controls, among Machinists and CNC Programmers is limiting their employment growth. Fewer Machinists are accomplishing the same amount of work it took more workers to accomplish previously. Technology isn't expected to affect Machinists employment as significantly as most other production occupations, however. For the most part, the precision mental operations performed by Machinists cannot be efficiently automated. Also, companies usually try to retain their most skilled workers to have someone competent to put on new or improved machinery as it is added to the inventory.

Jobs for CNC Programmers are also not expected to grow as quickly as the average for all occupations through 2008. As advanced machine tool technology allows programming and minor adjustments to be performed on the shop floor by others in the field, there will be less call for CNC Programmers.

Also, demand for CNC Programmers is being cut due to the increasing use of software that automatically translates part and product designs into CNC machine tool instructions.

As demand for machined goods falls, Machinists and CNC Programmers involved in production may find their hours cut, or be laid off completely in times of economic cutback. Those working in plant maintenance, however, have less to fear as the proper maintenance and repair of costly equipment remain vital concerns, even when production levels are reduced.

Civilian Advancement Prospects

Both Machinists and CNC Programmers tend to receive additional training from their companies when new machines or technological controls are introduced into the workplace. A few companies offer tuition reimbursement for job-related courses. As far as advancement is concerned, experienced Machinists may become CNC Programmers. Some are promoted to supervisory or administrative positions in their firms. Some open their own companies.

Education and Training

Training for Machinist positions can vary from formal apprenticeships and post-secondary programs to far less structured on-the-job training situations. Apprentice programs consist of classroom work and shop training. Apprentices learn handtapping, filing, and dowel fitting, as well as the operation of machine tools. Classroom studies cover blueprint reading, mechanical drawing, math, and physics as well as basic shop practices. Machine shops also increasingly use computer-controlled equipment, making training in the operation and programming of this equipment a further requirement.

Special Requirements

A number of training facilities and colleges have recently begun offering curriculums based on the national skills standards developed by NIMS (National Institute of Metalworking Skills). NIMS credentials are granted to trainees who complete one of these courses and are generally accepted as formal recognition of competency in a metalworking field. Such credentials are often helpful, either to confirm one's skills at job interviews, or when trying for advancement once one is already within a company.

Experience, Skills, and Personality Traits

Previous experience with machine tools is extremely important. Those seeking to become Machinists or CNC Programmers should be mechanically inclined and be able to work independently, performing highly accurate work that requires concentration and physical effort.

CNC Programmers' qualifications vary from job to job. Basic requirements parallel those of Machinists. Companies, however, often prefer Machinists with either previous experience or with technical school training. Companies may even require an engineering degree for some specialized types of programming. CNC Programmers must have a basic knowledge of computers and electronics. Hands-on experience with machine tools is very helpful. In the classroom trainees will start by writing simple programs under the direction of an experienced programmer. Even though manufacturing companies are looking to standardize programming languages, there are still many in use. Due to this factor CNC Programmers should be able to master new programs and languages relatively quickly.

Unions and Associations

The Precision Machined Products Association and The National Tooling and Machining Association offer membership to Machinists and CNC Programmers. The National Institute of Metalworking Skills offers continuing education and training courses to earn certifications in specific fields.

POWER PLANT OPERATOR

CAREER PROFILE

Duties: Produce electric power; regulate power plants; monitor and control nuclear reactors that produce electricity and power ships and submarines; operate and maintain stationary engines, such as steam engines, air compressors, and generators; operate auxiliary equipment, such as pumps, fans, and condensers; maintain and operate steam turbines that generate power for ships and inspect equipment for malfunctions

Alternate Title(s): Boiler Operator; Stationary Engineer; Nuclear Reactor Operator; Diesel Plant Operator; Chemical Plant and System Operator; Petroleum Pump System Operator; Refinery Operator; Gauger; Water and Wastewater Treatment Plant and System Operator

Availability: Army, Navy, Marine Corps, Coast Guard

Military Salary: See How to Use This Book

Civilian Salary: $24,470 to $74,370

Civilian Employment Prospects: Fair

Civilian Advancement Prospects: Fair

Prerequisites:
  Rank—Enlisted
  Education and Training—High school math and shop mechanics
  Experience—Any training and work experience obtained in the armed services or Job Corps, especially the navy or the merchant marine
  Special Skills and Personality Traits—An interest in working with large machinery and in nuclear power as well as mechanical aptitude, manual dexterity, and good physical condition
  Licensure/Certification—State or federal license required for some positions

CAREER LADDER

Senior Power Plant Operator

Plant Operator

Power Plant Laborer

Position Description

The military uses many different types of power plants to generate electricity for ships, submarines, and both temporary and permanent bases. These are fueled by oil, coal, and nuclear power. Power Plant Operators control generating plants on land and aboard ships and submarines. They monitor and operate control boards to regulate boilers, turbines, nuclear reactors, and portable generators. They operate and maintain diesel generating units to produce electric power, stationary engines, such as steam engines, air compressors, and generators, and auxiliary equipment, including pumps, fans, condensers, and auxiliary boilers. They monitor and control nuclear reactors that produce electricity and power ships and submarines, operate the steam turbines that generate power for ships, and inspect all equipment for malfunctions.

After the service, Power Plant Operators can find work with power companies, factories, schools, and hospitals. They perform duties similar to military Power Plant Operators. They control and monitor boilers, turbines, generators, and auxiliary equipment in power generating plants. Operators distribute power demands among generators, combine the current from several generators, and monitor instruments to maintain voltage and regulate electricity flows from the plant. When power requirements change, these workers start or stop generators and connect or disconnect them from circuits. They often use computers to keep records of switching operations and loads on generators, lines, and transformers.

Since providing electricity is a twenty-four hour job, Operators usually work one of three daily eight-hour shifts or one of two 12-hour shifts on a rotating basis. Rotating shifts can be stressful and fatiguing. Operators generally sit or stand at a control station. This work is not physically strenuous but requires constant attention. Nuclear Power Plant Operators are subject to random drug and alcohol tests, as are most workers at nuclear power plants.

Although the work is usually indoors, they are still subject to high temperatures, dust and excessive noise. They also must lift heavy parts or tools and also have to stoop and kneel and work in awkward positions. Operators who work outside the control room may be exposed to danger from electric shock, falls, and burns.

Stationary engineers and boiler operators control and maintain heating, air-conditioning, and ventilation systems. They start up, regulate, and shut down equipment, while ensuring that it operates safely, economically, and within established limits. They manually control equipment, make adjustments, use hand and power tools to perform repairs and maintenance, and record relevant events and facts concerning operation and maintenance. They must perform routine maintenance, test boiler water, and add chemicals to prevent corrosion and harmful deposits and may also check the air quality of the ventilation system and make adjustments to keep quality within mandated guidelines.

Such engineers usually have steady, year-round employment. The average workweek is forty hours. They also usually work rotating shifts. Weekend and holiday work often is required. While their work areas are usually clean and well lit, stationary engineers and boiler operators are still often exposed to high temperatures, dust, dirt, and high noise levels. General maintenance duties are required and workers spend much of the time on their feet. They also have to crawl inside boilers and work in cramped positions to inspect, clean, and repair equipment.

Stationary engineers and boiler operators work around potentially hazardous machinery such as boilers and electrical equipment. They must follow procedures to guard against burns, electric shock, and exposure to hazardous materials such as asbestos or chemicals.

Civilian Salaries

In 2000, the average yearly earnings of Power Plant Operators were $46,090. The middle 50 percent earned between $37,320 and $54,200 a year. The lowest 10 percent earned less than $28,700, and the highest 10 percent earned more than $62,020 a year. Average yearly earnings of Power Plant Operators in 2000 were $48,350 in electric services and $40,160 in local government.

In 2000, the average yearly earnings of power reactor operators were $57,220. The middle 50 percent earned between $50,720 and $67,320 a year. The lowest 10 percent earned less than $46,890, and the highest 10 percent earned more than $74,370 a year.

In 2000, the average yearly earnings of power distributors and dispatchers were $48,570. The middle 50 percent earned between $39,880 and $58,290 a year. The lowest 10 percent earned less than $31,760, and the highest 10 percent earned more than $69,260 a year. Average yearly earnings in electric services, the industry employing the largest numbers of power distributors and dispatchers, were $49,070.

In 2000, the average yearly earnings of stationary engineers and boiler operators were $40,420 in 2000. The middle 50 percent earned between $31,490 and $51,090 a year. The lowest 10 percent earned less than $24,470, and the highest 10 percent earned more than $61,530 a year. Average yearly earnings of stationary engineers and boiler operators in 2000 were $46,600 in local government and $37,680 in hospitals.

Civilian Employment Prospects

Job opportunities look to be fair at best for Power Plant Operators, distributors, and dispatchers due to increasing industry competition. Though opportunities will be best for operators with training in automated systems, still declining employment and low turnover will result in few job opportunities.

In 2000, Power Plant Operators, distributors, and dispatchers held roughly 55,000 jobs. Jobs are located throughout the country. About one in five worked for utility companies and government agencies that produced electricity.

In 2000, stationary engineers and boiler operators held roughly 57,000 jobs. They worked in factories, hospitals, hotels, office and apartment buildings, schools, and shopping malls throughout the country, generally in the more heavily populated areas in which large industrial and commercial establishments are located.

Civilian Advancement Prospects

Employers prefer high school graduates with strong math and science skills for entry-level Power Plant Operator, distributor, and dispatcher positions. College-level courses or prior experience in a mechanical or technical job may be helpful as well as computer proficiency. Most entry-level positions are helper or laborer jobs. Depending on the results of aptitude tests, worker preferences, and availability of openings, workers may be assigned to train for one of many utility positions.

Workers selected for training undergo extensive on-the-job and classroom training. Several years of training and experience are required to become fully qualified. With further training and experience, workers may advance to shift supervisor. Since utilities usually promote from within opportunities to advance by moving to another employer are limited.

Extensive training and experience are also necessary to pass the Nuclear Regulatory Commission examinations for reactor operators. To maintain their license, operators must pass an annual practical plant operation exam and a biennial written exam. Training may include simulator and on-the-job training, classroom instruction, and individual study. Entrants to nuclear power plant operator trainee jobs must have strong math and science skills. Experience in other power plants or with navy nuclear propulsion plants also is helpful. With further training and experience, reactor operators may advance to senior reactor operator positions.

Through 2010 the job market for Power Plant Operators is expected to decline slightly as the industry continues to restructure in response to both deregulation and increasing competition. People should expect keen competition for these high-paying jobs. The slow pace of new plant construction also will limit opportunities as will the increasing use of automatic controls and more efficient equipment.

Education and Training

Job training consists of three to eight months of classroom instruction, including practice in operating power plants and courses in the operation and maintenance of pressure boilers, reactor control systems, and mechanical systems on nuclear powered ships and submarines. Nuclear specialties have training programs that last one year or more, covering all aspects of nuclear power plant operations.

Power Plant Operators usually acquire their skills through a formal apprenticeship program or informal on-the-job training supplemented by courses at a trade or technical school. In addition, valuable experience can be obtained in the navy or the merchant marine.

The International Union of Operating Engineers sponsors apprenticeship programs. In selecting apprentices, most local labor-management apprenticeship committees prefer applicants with education or training in mathematics,

computers, mechanical drawing, machine-shop practice, physics, and chemistry.

Those who acquire their skills on the job may supplement this practical experience with postsecondary vocational training in computerized controls and instrumentation. Operators advance by being placed in charge of larger, more powerful, or more varied equipment, usually as they obtain higher-class licenses. Some stationary engineers and boiler operators advance to boiler inspectors, chief plant engineers, building and plant superintendents, or building managers. A few obtain jobs as examining engineers or technical instructors.

Special Requirements

Most states and cities have licensing requirements for Power Plant Operators. Additional certification may be available depending on one's field. The Nuclear Regulatory Commission issues examinations for reactor operators and provides licenses to those who pass. A license to operate boilers, ventilation, air conditioning, and other equipment is required in most states and cities. There are several classes of stationary engineer licenses, and each class specifies the type and size of equipment the engineer can operate without supervision. For more information contact state licensing boards or one of the groups listed below.

Experience, Special Skills, and Personality Traits

Job opportunities will be best for workers with computer skills. Most employers prefer to hire persons with at least a high school diploma, or equivalent. Many stationary engineers and boiler operators have some college education. Nuclear specialties require successful completion of high school algebra.

Useful school subjects include math and shop mechanics. Also important: an interest in working with large machinery and in nuclear power, as well as mechanical aptitude, manual dexterity, and good physical condition.

Unions and Associations

Apprenticeship, vocational training, and work opportunity information is available from state employment service offices, local chapters of the International Union of Operating Engineers, vocational schools, and state and local licensing agencies. Questions about specific branches of power plant operation or state requirements should be addressed to the International Union of Operating Engineers, the National Association of Power Engineers, Inc., and the Building Owners and Managers Institute International.

PRINTING SPECIALIST

CAREER PROFILE

Duties: Reproduce printed matter; prepare photographic negatives and layouts of artwork, photographs, and text; produce brochures, newspapers, maps, and charts; bind printed material into hardback or paperback books; maintain printing presses

Alternate Title(s): Offset Printing Press; Lithograph Press and Offset Duplicating Machine Operators; Lithograph Photographers; Machine Setters; Tenders-Metal and Plastic; Bookbinders; Bindery Workers; Prepress Technicians

Availability: Army, Navy, Air Force, Marine Corps

Military Salary: See How to Use This Book

Civilian Salary: $6.06 to $21.92/hour

Civilian Employment Prospects: Fair

Civilian Advancement Prospects: Fair

Prerequisites:

Rank—Enlisted

Education and Training—High school classes in shop mechanics and photography; training in graphic arts

Experience—Any training and work experience obtained in the armed services or Job Corps

Special Skills and Personality Traits—Normal color vision; basic mathematics and language skills; detail-oriented; patient; neat and well-organized; good eyesight; manual dexterity; mechanical aptitude; artistic ability; imagination; basic computer skills; a preference for doing physical work; an interest in learning about printing

CAREER LADDER

Supervisor

Worker

Trainee

Position Description

Every branch of the military needs a variety of publications and other printed materials constantly. Each branch has its own newspapers, booklets, training manuals, maps, and charts. Printing Specialists in the military are trained to perform some or all of the following duties: they reproduce printed matter using offset lithographic printing processes; they prepare photographic negatives and transfer them to printing plates using copy cameras and enlargers; and they prepare layouts of artwork, photographs, and text for lithographic plates. They produce brochures, newspapers, maps, and charts, bind printed material into hardback or paperback books using binding machines and maintain their own printing presses at the same time.

In the civilian world, these duties easily translate into any of the following jobs: printing machine operator, photographic process worker, processing machine operators, bookbinders, and bindery workers.

The duties of printing machine operators can vary greatly according to the type of press they operate. Essentially, however, they must prepare presses for printing, ensure that paper and ink meet specifications, adjust margins and the flow of ink, feed paper through the press cylinders, adjust feed and tension controls, and then monitor the entire operation until completion. They will also perform preventive maintenance.

The job is physically and mentally demanding. It can become tedious, especially considering that operators are on their feet most of the time. There is pressure to meet deadlines and to avoid waste. Pressrooms are noisy, and the machinery can be hazardous, although most accidents can be avoided when safe work practices are observed. Press operators often work evening, night, and overtime shifts.

Amateur and professional photographers need photographic process workers and processing machine operators to develop film, make prints or slides, enlarge or retouch photographs, etc. Photographic processing machine operators often have specialized jobs. Film process technician, color printer operator, photographic process worker, airbrush artist, photographic retoucher, colorist, and photographic spotter are all careers that can start with work as a photographic processing machine operator.

Unlike printing machine operators, photographic process workers and processing machine operators generally spend their work hours in clean, well-lit offices or laboratories. Some photographic workers are exposed to the chemicals and fumes associated with developing and printing. They must wear rubber gloves and aprons and take precautions against these hazards. They also do repetitive work at a fast pace. Most photo process workers maintain a normal, 40-hour week.

Bookbinders and bindery workers take printed sheets and turn them into books, magazines, catalogs, folders, directories, etc. Job duties depend on the kind of material being bound. Some types of binding require only one step, but others take many. Bookbinding is hard work. The conditions are often noisy. There is also usually a good deal of lifting, standing, and carrying as well as stooping, kneeling, and crouching, plus the assembly line-like repetition of the work.

Civilian Salaries

In 2000, the average hourly wage for printing machine operators was $13.57. The middle 50 percent earned between $10.38 and $17.80 an hour. The lowest 10 percent earned less than $8.09 and the highest 10 percent earned more than $21.92 an hour. The average hourly wage in the industries employing the largest numbers of printing machine operators in 2000 were:

Commercial printing	$14.91
Newspapers	$14.71
Paperboard containers and boxes	$14.44
Miscellaneous converted paper products	$13.78
Mailing, reproduction, and stenographic services	$10.92

In 2000, the average hourly wage for photographic process workers was $9.44. The middle 50 percent earned between $7.56 and $12.54. The lowest 10 percent earned less than $6.44 and the highest 10 percent earned more than $16.61.

In 2000, the average hourly wage in miscellaneous business services, including photofinishing laboratories was $9.55.

In 2000, the average hourly wage for photographic processing machine operators was $8.39. The middle 50 percent earned between $7.06 and $10.56. The lowest 10 percent earned less than $6.06 and the highest 10 percent earned more than $14.48.

In 2000, the average hourly wage for bookbinders was $11.42. The middle 50 percent earned between $9.14 and $15.71 an hour. The lowest 10 percent earned less than $7.28 and the highest 10 percent earned more than $20.11.

In 2000, the average hourly wage for bindery workers was $10.05. The middle 50 percent earned between $7.88 and $13.27 an hour. The lowest 10 percent earned less than $6.57 and the highest 10 percent earned more than $17.22.

Employment Prospects After Military Service

In 2000, printing machine operators held roughly 222,000 positions, mostly in newspaper plants or in commercial or business printing firms. Such jobs can be found throughout the country, but are concentrated in New York, Los Angeles, Chicago, Philadelphia, Washington, D.C., and Dallas.

Photographic process workers and processing machine operators held just more than 76,000 positions during the same year. These were found mostly in photofinishing laboratories, department and drug stores, one-hour minilabs, portrait studios, and commercial laboratories.

Bookbinders and bindery workers held roughly 115,000 jobs in 2000. These were mostly to be found in commercial printing plants or bindery trade shops. Such positions are concentrated in New York, Chicago, Washington, D.C., Los Angeles, Philadelphia, and Dallas.

Civilian Advancement Prospects

Through experience and demonstrated ability, printing machine operators can advance to a more complex printing press, a move meaning more pay and responsibility. They may also advance to pressroom supervisor.

Those looking for work in this area will find stiff competition from experienced operators and prepress workers who have been displaced by new technology. Openings for press operators are expected to grow slower than the average for all occupations through 2010. More efficient, computerized printing presses are expected to replace many operators who retire or leave the occupation.

New jobs will result from American expansion into foreign markets, the growing use of direct mail by advertisers, the need for updated textbooks and magazines as school enrollments rise and old books grow outdated, and as growth in the portion of the population reaching retirement age spurs adult education and leisure reading.

Photographic process machine workers can sometimes advance from jobs as machine operators to supervisory positions in laboratories or to management positions within retail stores. It also seems that there will be little or no change through the year 2010 in their job opportunities. Even though the use of digital cameras has grown rapidly (reducing the need for traditional photographic processing), conventional cameras are expected to continue to be the camera of choice.

Opportunities for bookbinders are expected to grow more slowly than average, reflecting increasingly productive bindery operations through 2010. Binding is slowly becoming a job for computers, making it hard for the newcomer to find employment as the workforce shrinks. Experienced workers will continue to have the best opportunities.

Education and Training

Job training consists of two to five months of classroom instruction, including practice in operating printing presses. Courses will include such topics as photolithography techniques, the operation of offset presses, techniques for making printing plates, and binding techniques. The army, navy, and marine corps offer certified apprenticeship programs in this occupation.

Printing machine operators can complete a formal apprenticeship or a postsecondary program in printing equipment operation (one of the best ways to learn the trade), but most are still trained informally on the job while working as assistants or helpers. Apprenticeships in commercial shops take four years. Formal postsecondary programs in printing equipment operation offered by technical and trade schools and community colleges are growing in importance, however, because they provide the theoretical knowledge needed to operate advanced equipment.

Most photographic process workers and processing machine operators start as assistants and receive on-the-job training from experienced workers. New employees gradually learn to use the machines and chemicals that develop and print film. High school graduates and those with some experience in the field are preferred. Familiarity with computers is essential for photographic processing machine operators. The ability to perform simple mathematical calculations also is helpful. Photography courses that include instruction in film processing are valuable preparation. Some workers attend periodic training seminars to maintain a high level of skill.

Most bookbinders and bindery workers learn the craft through on-the-job training. Formal apprenticeships are not common, but are offered by some employers. Employers prefer to hire experienced individuals, but will train workers with some basic knowledge of binding operations.

Experience, Special Skills, and Personality Traits

High school courses in shop mechanics, chemistry, electronics, color theory, physics, and photography are helpful. So are a preference for doing physical work, and an interest in learning about printing. Good eyesight and normal color vision are required.

Printing machine operators need mechanical aptitude to make press adjustments and repairs. Writing and mathematical skills are necessary, as well as basic computer skills.

Bindery work requires careful attention to detail so accuracy, patience, neatness, good eyesight, manual dexterity, mechanical aptitude, artistic ability, and imagination are necessary. Training in graphic arts also can be an asset.

Unions and Associations

For information about employment opportunities in photographic laboratories and schools that offer degrees in photographic technology contact the Photo Marketing Association International.

For information about apprenticeships and other training opportunities contact local printing industry associations, local bookbinding shops, local offices of the Graphic Communications International Union or local offices of the state employment service.

For general information on bindery occupations contact the Bindery Industries Association, International and the Graphic Communications International Union.

For information on careers and training programs in printing and the graphic arts contact the Graphic Communications Council, the Printing Industries of America and the Graphic Arts Technical Foundation.

WATER AND SEWAGE TREATMENT PLANT OPERATOR

CAREER PROFILE

Duties: Operate pumps; transfer water from reservoirs and storage tanks to treatment plants; purify water for drinking or clean it for safe disposal; test water for chlorine content, acidity, oxygen demand, and impurities; regulate its flow to meet demand; clean and maintain treatment machinery; keep records of chemical treatments, water pressure, and maintenance

Alternate Title(s): Water Treatment Plant Operator; Waterworks Pump Station Operator; Wastewater Treatment Plant Operator; Chemical Plant and System Operator; Gas Plant Operator; Petroleum Pump System Operator; Refinery Operator and Gauger; Power Plant Operator, Distributor, or Dispatcher; and Stationary Engineer; Boiler Operator

Availability: All branches

Military Salary: See How to Use This Book

Civilian Salary: $19,120 to $47,370

Civilian Employment Prospects: Good

Civilian Advancement Prospects: Good

Prerequisites:
  Rank—Enlisted
  Education and Training—High school diploma
  Experience—Any training and work experience received in the armed forces or Job Corps
  Special Skills and Personality Traits—High school chemistry, math, and shop mechanics; enjoy working with mechanical equipment; an interest in chemistry and pollution control; normal color vision; good eyesight
  Licensure/Certification—State license required

CAREER LADDER

> **Plant Supervisor or Superintendent**

> **Operator**

> **Attendant or Operator-in-Training**

Position Description

The military maintains and operates their own water treatment plants when public facilities cannot be utilized safely. These plants provide drinking water and safely dispose of sewage. Water and Sewage Treatment Plant Operators maintain the systems that purify water and treat and dispose of sewage.

Military Water and Sewage Treatment Plant Operators are trained to perform a number of duties. They operate pumps to transfer water from reservoirs and storage tanks to treatment plants, and add the proper amounts of chemicals and operate the machinery that purifies water for drinking or cleans it for safe disposal. They test water for chlorine content, acidity, oxygen demand, and impurities; regulate the flow of drinking water to meet what can be an ever-changing demand; and clean and maintain water treatment machinery. They are also required to keep records of chemical treatments, water pressure, and maintenance.

In the civilian world, employment for Water and Sewage Treatment Plant Operators is concentrated in municipal public works and private water supply and sanitary services companies. There, operators either treat water so that it is safe to drink or remove pollutants from it so that it is safe to return to the environment.

Both types of operators control processes and equipment to remove or destroy harmful materials, chemical compounds, and microorganisms from the water. They also control pumps, valves, and other processing equipment to move the water or liquid waste through the various treatment processes, and dispose of the removed waste materials. They read, interpret, and adjust meters and gauges to make certain plant equipment and processes are working properly. They operate chemical-feeding devices, take samples of the water or liquid waste, perform chemical and biological laboratory analyses, and adjust the amount of chemicals, such as chlorine, in the water. They use a variety of instruments to sample and measure water quality, and common hand and power tools to make minor repairs to valves, pumps, and other equipment. They rely on computers to help in all these duties.

Sometimes operators must work under emergency conditions—rainstorms can cause large amounts of liquid waste to exceed a plant's treatment capacity, chlorine gas leaks or oxygen deficiencies can occur inside plants, etc. During such conditions, operators work under pressure to correct problems as quickly as possible. These periods may create dangerous working conditions, and operators must be extremely cautious.

Operators must also be completely familiar with the guidelines established by federal regulations and how they affect their plant. In addition to federal regulations, they must also be aware of any guidelines imposed by the state or locality in which the plant operates.

Operators work both indoors and outdoors, and may be exposed to noise from machinery and unpleasant odors. Their work is physically demanding and often performed in unclean locations. They must pay close attention to safety procedures. Plants operate every minute of every day which means operators must work one of three eight-hour shifts, including weekends and holidays, on a rotating basis.

Civilian Salaries

In 2000, the average yearly salary of plant and system operators was $31,380. The middle 50 percent earned between $24,390 and $39,530. The lowest 10 percent earned less than $19,120. The highest 10 percent earned more than $47,370.

In 2000, the average yearly salary of plant and systems operators was $31,120 in local government and $29,810 in water supply.

In addition to their annual salaries, water and liquid waste treatment plant and system operators usually receive benefits that may include health and life insurance, a retirement plan, and educational reimbursement for job-related courses.

Some may also receive overtime pay for working during emergencies or on holidays or for putting in extra hours.

Civilian Employment Prospects

In 2000, plant and system operators held just under 90,000 jobs, mostly in local governments. Operators are employed throughout the country, but most jobs are in larger towns and cities. Although nearly all work full time, those who work in small towns may only work part time at the treatment plant.

From now through 2010 job opportunities are expected to grow as fast as the average for all occupations. Since the number of applicants is normally low, job prospects will be good for qualified applicants.

Civilian Advancement Prospects

Economic growth and the increasing population expected to boost demand for Water and Sewage Treatment Plant Operators. As new plants are constructed to meet this demand, employment of water and liquid waste treatment plant and system operators will increase.

Note that federal certification requirements have increased reliance on private firms specializing in the operation and management of water and liquid waste treatment facilities. As a result, employment in privately owned facilities will grow faster than the average. Increased pretreatment activity by manufacturing firms also will create new job opportunities.

Some operators become responsible for more complex treatment processes through promotion to plant supervisor or superintendent. Others advance by transferring to a larger facility. Postsecondary training in water and liquid waste treatment, coupled with increasingly responsible experience as an operator, may be sufficient to qualify for superintendent of a small plant. With each promotion, the operator must have greater knowledge of federal, state, and local regulations. Superintendents of large plants generally need an engineering or science degree.

A few operators get jobs with state drinking water or water pollution control agencies as technicians, who monitor and provide technical assistance to plants throughout the state. Vocational-technical school or community college training generally is necessary for technician jobs. Experienced operators may transfer to related jobs with industrial liquid waste treatment plants, water or liquid waste treatment equipment, and chemical companies, engineering consulting firms, or vocational-technical schools.

Education and Training

Job training consists of two to two-and-a-half months of instruction, including practice operating water and sewage treatment equipment. Courses include operation of treatment systems, water testing and analysis, and maintenance and repair of pumps, compressors, and other equipment. Further training occurs on the job and through advanced courses.

The army and the navy offer certified apprenticeship programs for some specialties in this occupation. Postsecondary training is increasingly an asset as the number of regulated contaminants grows and treatment plants become more complex.

A high school diploma usually is required as well as some basic familiarity with computers. Applicants may be given a written examination testing mathematics skills, mechanical aptitude, and general intelligence.

Completion of an associate degree or one-year certificate program in water quality and liquid waste treatment technology increases an applicant's chances for employment and promotion because plants are becoming more complex.

Trainees usually start as attendants or operators-in-training and learn their skills on the job under the direction of an experienced operator. Larger treatment plants generally combine this on-the-job training with formal classroom or self-paced study programs.

Some operators take correspondence courses on subjects related to water and liquid waste treatment. Some employers pay part of the tuition for related college courses in science or engineering.

Special Requirements

Since passage of the Safe Drinking Water Act Amendments of 1996, operators must pass an examination to certify that they are capable of overseeing liquid waste treatment plant operations. The level of certification acquired depends on the operator's experience and training. Higher certification levels qualify the operator for a wider variety of treatment processes. Certification requirements vary by state and by size of treatment plants. Although relocation may mean having to become certified in a new location, many states accept other states' certifications. Most states offer training courses to improve operators' skills and knowledge.

Experience, Special Skills, and Personality Traits

Mechanical aptitude is necessary. A basic knowledge of math is required. Also needed are an understanding of basic mathematics, chemistry, and biology, and the ability to apply data to formulas of treatment requirements, flow levels, and concentration levels. An interest in working with mechanical equipment, chemistry, and pollution control is helpful. Good eyesight and normal color vision is needed to examine water for acidity and impurities.

Unions and Associations

For information on employment opportunities, contact state or local water pollution control agencies, state water and liquid waste operator associations, state environmental training centers or local offices of the state employment service. For information on certification, contact the Association of Boards of Certification. For educational information related to a career as a Water and Sewage Treatment Plant Operator, contact the American Water Works Association and the Water Environment Federation.

WELDER/METAL WORKER

CAREER PROFILE

Duties: Weld, braze, or solder metal parts together; repair automotive and ship parts; measure work with precision tools

Alternate Title(s): Machinists; Metal and Plastic Machine Setters, Operators, and Tenders; Computer-Control Programmers and Operators; Tool and Die Makers; Sheet Metal Workers; Boilermakers

Availability: All branches

Military Salary: See How to Use This Book

Civilian Salary: $8.86 to $20.74/hour

Civilian Employment Prospects: Excellent

Civilian Advancement Prospects: Good

Prerequisites:

Rank—Enlisted

Education and Training—High school classes in blueprint reading, shop mathematics, mechanical drawing, physics, chemistry, metallurgy, auto mechanics, and industrial arts are all useful

Experience—Any training and work experience obtained in the armed services or Job Corps

Special Skills and Personality Traits—A preference for physical work; an interest in repair tools; good eyesight and normal color vision; hand-eye coordination; manual dexterity; a solid understanding of computers

CAREER LADDER

Supervisor, Inspector, or Instructor

Welding Technician

Welder

Position Description

The military uses acres of sheet metal yearly as a building material in construction projects. Ships, tanks, and aircraft are made of heavy metal armor. Welders and Metal Workers in the services make and install sheet metal products such as roofs, air ducts, gutters, and vents, as well as custom parts to repair the structure of ships, submarines, landing craft, buildings, and equipment.

Military Welders and Metal Workers must weld, braze, or solder metal parts together, repair automotive and ship parts using welding equipment, and then measure their work with calipers, micrometers, and rulers.

In the civilian world Welders and Metal Workers work for metal repair shops, auto repair shops, construction companies, pipeline companies, aircraft manufacturing plants, shipyards, and marine servicing companies. They work indoors in metalworking shops and aircraft hangars. They also work outdoors at construction sites, on ships, and in the field. They often have to lift heavy metal parts and work in crouching or kneeling positions.

Welding is the most common way of permanently joining metal parts. It is used in shipbuilding, automobile manufacturing and repair, aerospace applications, etc. Welders use many types of welding equipment set up in a variety of positions. They may perform manual welding, in which they controlled the entire process or semiautomatic welding, in which the welder uses machinery to help in performing welding tasks.

Arc welding is the most common type of welding, followed by soldering and brazing. Skilled welding, soldering, and brazing workers generally plan work from drawings or specifications or use their knowledge of fluxes and base metals to analyze parts. These workers then select and set up welding equipment and examine welds to ensure that they meet standards or specifications. Some Welders only perform routine, preplanned jobs that don't require extensive knowledge of welding techniques.

During automated welding procedures, a machine or robot performs the welding tasks while monitored by a welding machine operator. Welding, soldering, and brazing machine setters, operators and tenders follow specified layouts, work orders, or blueprints. Operators must load parts correctly and constantly monitor the machine to ensure that it produces the desired bond.

Metal Workers are often exposed to potential hazards such as the intense light created by their arcs, hazardous fumes, and burns. For safety they wear safety shoes, goggles, hoods with protective lenses and other devices designed to prevent burns and eye injuries and to protect them from falling objects. They normally work in well-ventilated areas to limit their exposure to fumes.

Metal Workers may work outdoors, often in inclement weather, or indoors, sometimes in a confining area designed to contain sparks and glare. When outdoors, they may work on a scaffold or platform far above the ground. Also Metal Workers are often required to lift heavy objects and work in a variety of awkward positions, having to make welds while bending, stooping, or working overhead.

Although about half of Welders, solderers, and brazers work a 40-hour week, overtime is common, and some welders work up to 70 hours per week. Welders also may work in shifts as long as 12 hours. Some Welders, solderers, brazers, and machine operators work in factories that operate around-the-clock.

Civilian Salaries

In 2000, the average hourly salary of Welders and Metal Workers was $13.13. The middle 50 percent earned between $10.74 and $16.37. The lowest 10 percent had earnings of less than $8.86, while the top 10 percent earned over $20.74.

In 2000, the average hourly salary in the industries employing the largest numbers of Welders and Metal Workers were:

Construction and related machinery	$13.51
Motor vehicles and equipment	$13.43
Fabricated structural metal products	$12.91
Miscellaneous repair shops	$12.33
Personnel supply services	$10.55

Civilian Employment Prospects

In 2000, Welders and Metal Workers held nearly 525,000 jobs. Three out of four of these were found in manufacturing and services. Prospects should be excellent for skilled candidates, as many potential entrants who have the educational and personal qualifications to acquire the necessary skills may prefer to attend college or choose work that has more comfortable working conditions. Employment of welding, soldering, and brazing workers is expected to grow about as fast as the average for all occupations from now through 2010.

Because almost every manufacturing industry uses welding at some stage of manufacturing or in the repair and maintenance of equipment, a strong economy will keep demand for Welders high. A downturn affecting industries such as auto manufacturing or construction would have a negative impact on the employment of Welders.

Pressure to improve productivity and hold down labor costs is leading companies to invest heavily in computer- and robotically-controlled welding machinery. This will affect the demand for low-skilled manual Metal Workers because the jobs being automated are the simple, repetitive ones. The growing use of automation will increase the demand for highly skilled welding, soldering, and brazing machine setters, operators, and tenders. Welders working on construction projects or in equipment repair will not be affected by technology change to the same extent that other Welders are, because their jobs are not as easily automated.

Civilian Advancement Prospects

Welders can always advance to more skilled welding jobs with additional training and experience. They may become welding technicians, supervisors, inspectors, or instructors. Those who choose to learn computer skills may go on to use new technology as it becomes available. Some experienced Welders open their own repair shops.

Education and Training

Job training consists of one to four months of classroom instruction. Courses generally cover sheet metal layout and ductwork; procedures for cutting, brazing, and heat-treating; and the operation and care of welding, soldering, and brazing equipment.

Further training occurs on the job and through advanced courses. The army, navy and marine corps offer certified apprenticeship programs for some specialties in this occupation.

Formal training is available in high schools, vocational schools, and postsecondary institutions, such as vocational-technical institutes, community colleges, and private welding schools. Some employers provide training. Some Welders become certified at independent testing labs or technical schools where they are tested based on the standards and codes set by one of several industry associations.

Experience, Special Skills, and Personality Traits

High school classes in blueprint reading, shop mathematics, mechanical drawing, physics, chemistry, metallurgy, auto mechanics, and industrial arts are all useful.

Also helpful are a preference for physical work and an interest in working with repair tools as well as good hand-eye coordination, and manual dexterity. Good color vision is required for locating and marking reference points, setting and adjusting welding equipment, and matching paints. Welders should be able to concentrate on detailed work for long periods and be able to bend, stoop, and work in awkward positions.

A solid understanding of computers is important for welding, soldering, and brazing machine operators, who are becoming responsible for the programming of computer-controlled machines, including robots.

Unions and Associations

Many welders belong to the following unions: the International Association of Machinists and Aerospace Workers; the International Brotherhood of Boilermakers, Iron Ship Builders, Blacksmiths, Forgers and Helpers; the International Union of United Automobile, Aerospace and Agricultural Implement Workers of America; the United Association of Journeymen and Apprentices of the Plumbing and Pipe Fitting Industry of the United States and Canada; and the United Electrical, Radio, and Machine Workers of America. All provide opportunities for making contacts, learning about employment opportunities, and improving one's skills.

ELECTRICAL AND
ELECTRONIC REPAIRS

BUILDING ELECTRICIAN

CAREER PROFILE

Duties: Install and wire transformers, junction boxes, and circuit breakers; read blueprints, wiring plans, and repair orders; cut, bend, and string wires and conduits; inspect power distribution systems, shorts in wires, and faulty equipment; repair and replace faulty wiring and lighting fixtures and install lightning rods

Alternate Title(s): Heating, Air-Conditioning, and Refrigeration Mechanic/Installer; Line Installer/Repairer; Electrical and Electronics Installer/Repairer; Electronic Home Entertainment Equipment Installer/Repairers; Elevator Installer/Repairer; Electrician; Electrical Engineer; Electrical Contractor

Availability: All branches

Military Salary: See How to Use This Book

Civilian Salary: $11.31/hour to $31.71/hour

Civilian Employment Prospects: Good

Civilian Advancement Prospects: Good

Prerequisites:
　Rank—Enlisted
　Education and Training—Courses in mathematics, electricity, electronics, mechanical drawing, science, and shop
　Experience—Any training and work experience obtained in the armed services or Job Corps
　Special Skills and Personality Traits—The ability to use hand tools; a preference for doing physical work; an interest in electricity; good health; average physical strength; agility, dexterity, and good color vision

CAREER LADDER

Superintendent

Supervisor

Apprentice

Position Description

Like the rest of the world the military uses electricity to perform hundreds of tasks such as lighting hospitals, running power tools, and operating computers. Building Electricians install and repair electrical wiring systems in offices, repair shops, airplane hangars, and other buildings on military bases. They install and wire transformers, junction boxes, and circuit breakers, using wire cutters, insulation strippers, and other hand tools. They read blueprints, wiring plans, and repair orders to determine wiring layouts or repair needs and cut, bend, and string wires and conduits (pipe or tubing). They also inspect power distribution systems, shorts in wires, and faulty equipment using test meters, repair and replace faulty wiring and lighting fixtures and even install lightning rods to protect the electrical systems they create, use, and maintain.

In the civilian world Building Electricians generally work for building and electrical contracting firms. Some work as self-employed electrical contractors. They usually work indoors while installing wiring systems. They work outdoors while installing transformers and lightning rods.

Electricians install, connect, test, and maintain electrical systems for a variety of purposes including climate control, security, and communications. They also install and maintain the electronic controls for machines in business and industry.

Electricians work with blueprints when they install electrical systems. Blueprints indicate the locations of circuits, outlets, load centers, panel boards, and other equipment. Electricians must follow the National Electric Code and comply with state and local building codes when they install these systems. In addition to wiring a building's electrical system, electricians may install coaxial or fiber-optic cable for computers and other telecommunications equipment. Many install telephone systems, computer wiring and equipment, street lights, intercom systems, and fire alarm and security systems. They also connect motors to electrical power and install electronic controls for industrial equipment.

Maintenance work varies greatly, depending on where the electrician is employed. Maintenance electricians spend much of their time in preventive maintenance. They periodically inspect equipment, hopefully locating and correcting problems before breakdowns occur. Electricians advise management on whether continued operation of equipment could be hazardous. When breakdowns occur they must make all necessary repairs as quickly as possible in order to minimize inconvenience. When working with complex electronic devices they may work with engineers, engineering technicians, or industrial machinery installation, repair, and maintenance workers.

Electricians use hand tools such as screwdrivers, pliers, knives, and hacksaws. They also use power tools and testing equipment such as oscilloscopes, ammeters, and test lamps. Their work can be strenuous. They stand for long periods, frequently working on ladders and scaffolds. Their work can be dusty, dirty, hot, or wet, or in confined areas, ditches, or other uncomfortable places. Electricians risk injury from electrical shock, falls, and cuts.

Some electricians may have to travel great distances to job sites. Most work a standard 40-hour week, although overtime may be required. Those in maintenance work may work days and be on call nights, weekends, and holidays.

Civilian Salaries

In 2000, the average hourly wage of electricians was $19.29. The middle 50 percent earned between $14.49 and $25.41. The lowest 10 percent earned less than $11.31 and the highest 10 percent earned more than $31.71.

In 2000, the average hourly wage in the industries employing the largest numbers of electricians were as shown below:

Motor vehicles and equipment	$26.71
Local government	$19.88
Electrical work	$19.22
Heavy construction, except highway	$17.92
Plumbing, heating, and air-conditioning	$17.26

Civilian Employment Prospects

Qualified electricians held just under 700,000 jobs in 2000. About two-thirds were employed in the construction industry. About one-third worked as maintenance electricians and were employed outside the construction industry. Roughly 8 percent were self-employed.

Because of the widespread need for electrical services, jobs for electricians are found in all parts of the country. Job opportunities for skilled electricians are expected to be excellent, largely due to the numerous openings arising each year from experienced electricians who leave the occupation. In addition, many potential workers may prefer work that is less strenuous and has more comfortable working conditions. Well-trained workers will have especially favorable opportunities.

Population and economic growth will create an increased need for the installation and maintenance of electrical devices and wiring for homes, factories, offices, etc. New technologies are expected to continue to stimulate demand. Also, far more new buildings are now prewired during construction to accommodate use of computers and telecommunications equipment. Factories changing over to robotic and automated manufacturing systems will stimulate a further demand for electricians. Additional jobs will be created by rehabilitation and retrofitting of existing structures.

Because of their lengthy training and relatively high earnings, a smaller proportion of electricians than of other craftworkers leave their occupation each year. The number of retirements is expected to rise, however, as more electricians reach retirement age.

Job opportunities for electricians vary by area. Employment opportunities follow the movement of people and businesses among states and local areas, and reflect differences in local economic conditions. The number of job opportunities in a given year may fluctuate widely from area to area.

Civilian Advancement Prospects

From now through 2010 job opportunities are expected to increase for electricians about as fast as the average for all occupations through the year 2010.

Depending on experience, apprentices usually start at between 30 percent and 50 percent of the rate paid to experienced electricians. As they become more skilled, they receive periodic increases throughout the course of the apprenticeship program. Many employers also provide training opportunities for experienced electricians to improve their skills, which will lead to increases in pay and ranking upon completion.

Those who begin serve as either trainees or complete an apprenticeship can move on to become supervisors or superintendents. Those with sufficient capital and management skills may start their own contracting business, although this may require an electrical contractor's license.

Education and Training

Job training consists of two to three months of classroom instruction, including practice in the installation and repair of electrical wiring systems. Courses cover the fundamentals of electricity, electrical circuit troubleshooting, safety procedures, and techniques for wiring switches, outlets, and junction boxes.

Further training occurs on the job and through advanced courses. The army and marine corps offer certified apprenticeship programs for some specialties in this occupation.

Most electricians learn their trade by completing a four- to five-year apprenticeship program. Apprenticeship gives trainees a thorough knowledge of all aspects of the trade and generally improves their ability to find a job mainly because those who complete apprenticeship programs qualify to do both maintenance and construction work. Although more electricians are trained through apprenticeship than are workers in other construction trades, some still learn their skills informally, on the job.

The typical apprenticeship program provides some 144 hours of classroom instruction each year as well as 8,000 hours of on-the-job training over the course of the apprenticeship. In the classroom, apprentices learn blueprint reading, electrical theory, electronics, mathematics, electrical code requirements, and safety and first aid practices. They also may receive specialized training in welding, communications, fire alarm systems, and cranes and elevators. On the job, under the supervision of experienced electricians, apprentices must demonstrate mastery of the electrician's work. Those who do not enter a formal apprenticeship program can begin to learn the trade informally by working as helpers for experienced electricians.

Many trainees supplement this experience with trade school or correspondence courses. Special training offered in the armed forces and by postsecondary technical schools also is beneficial. Most localities require electricians to be licensed. Usually they must pass an examination that tests their knowledge of electrical theory, the National Electrical Code, and local electric and building codes. Electricians periodically take courses offered by their employer or union to keep abreast of changes in the National Electrical Code, materials, or methods of installation.

Experience, Special Skills, and Personality Traits

High school courses in mathematics, electricity, electronics, mechanical drawing, science, and shop as well as an ability to use hand tools, a preference for doing physical work and an interest in electricity.

Electricians need to be in good health and have at least average physical strength. Agility and dexterity also are important, as is good color vision since workers must frequently identify color-coded wiring and circuits.

Unions and Associations

Apprenticeship programs may be sponsored by joint training committees made up of local unions of the International Brotherhood of Electrical Workers and local chapters of the National Electrical Contractors Association or by local chapters of the Associated Builders and Contractors and the Independent Electrical Contractors Association. Training also may be provided by local chapters of the Associated Builders and Contractors and the Independent Electrical Contractors.

For details about apprenticeships or other work opportunities in this trade, contact the offices of the state employment service, the state apprenticeship agency, local electrical contractors, firms that employ maintenance electricians, or local union-management electrician apprenticeship committees. This information may also be available from local chapters of the Independent Electrical Contractors, Inc., the National Electrical Contractors Association, the Home Builders Institute, the Associated Builders and Contractors, and the International Brotherhood of Electrical Workers.

For general information about the work of electricians, contact: the Independent Electrical Contractors, Inc., the National Electrical Contractors Association, the International Brotherhood of Electrical Workers, the Associated Builders and Contractors, and the National Association of Home Builders.

COMMUNICATION EQUIPMENT REPAIRER

CAREER PROFILE

Duties: Maintain, test, and repair communications equipment; install and repair circuits and wiring; calibrate and align equipment components; string overhead communications and electric cables between utility poles

Alternate Title(s): Broadcast and Sound Engineering Technician and Radio Operator; Computer, Automated Teller, and Office Machine Repairer; Electronic Home Entertainment Equipment Installer and Repairer; Electrical or Electronics Installer and Repairer; Radio Repairer; Radio Mechanic; Teletype Repairer; Station Installer and Repairer

Availability: All branches

Military Salary: See How to Use This Book

Civilian Salary: $12.04 to $27.23/hour

Civilian Employment Prospects: Poor

Civilian Advancement Prospects: Poor

Prerequisites:

Rank—Enlisted

Education and Training—High school diploma; apprenticeship or postsecondary training in electronics; familiarity with computers

Experience—Any training and work experience obtained in the armed services or Job Corps

Special Skills and Personality Traits—High school courses in math, electricity, or electronics repair and shop mechanics; an interest in working with electrical, electronic, and electromechanical equipment; enjoy solving problems; normal color vision; good hearing; good physical condition

CAREER LADDER

Sales Worker, Maintenance Supervisor, or Service Manager

Communications Equipment Repairer

Trainee

Position Description

The military relies heavily on communication equipment to coordinate ground, sea, and air forces. This equipment allows commanders to track and direct troop, aircraft, and ship movements. Any modern combat force would be helpless without such equipment. Communications Equipment Repairers ensure this equipment operates properly.

Military Communications Equipment Repairers maintain, test, and repair communications equipment using frequency meters, circuit analyzers, and other electrical and electronic test equipment. They install and repair circuits and wiring using soldering iron and hand tools; calibrate and align equipment components using scales, gauges, and other measuring instruments, and string overhead communications and electric cables between utility poles.

In the civilian world, Communications Equipment Repairers work for firms that design and make communications and electronic equipment. They also work for the federal government as well as in repair shops and laboratories.

Central office installers set up switches, cables, and other equipment in central offices. PBX installers and repairers set up private branch exchange switchboards, by connecting the equipment to power lines and communications cables and installing frames and supports. They test the connections to ensure that adequate power is available and that the communication links function. They also install equipment such as power systems, alarms, and telephone sets. Then they perform tests to verify that the newly installed equipment functions properly.

When problems with telecommunications equipment arise, telecommunications equipment repairers diagnose the source of the problem by testing each of the different parts of the equipment. This requires an understanding of how the software and hardware interact. Repairers often use spectrum and/or network analyzers to locate the problem. To fix the equipment, repairers use hand tools to remove and replace defective components. Newer equipment is easier to repair, since whole boards and parts are designed to be quickly removed and replaced. Repairers also may install updated software or programs that maintain existing software.

Station installers and repairers install and repair telephone wiring and equipment on customers' premises. They install telephone service by connecting customers' telephone wires to outside service lines on telephone poles or in underground conduits. Once the telephone is connected, the line is tested to insure it is functioning.

Radio mechanics install and maintain radio transmitting and receiving equipment, including stationary equipment mounted on transmission towers and mobile equipment such as radio communications systems and emergency vehicles. Modern radio equipment is self-monitoring and may alert mechanics to potential malfunctions. When malfunctions occur, these mechanics examine equipment for damaged components and loose or broken wires. They use electrical measuring instruments to monitor signal strength, transmission capacity, interference, and signal delay, as well as hand tools to replace defective parts.

Communications Equipment Installers and Repairers generally work in clean, well-lighted, air-conditioned surroundings. Telephone installers and repairers work on rooftops, ladders, and telephone poles. Radio mechanics may maintain equipment located on the tops of transmissions towers. While working outdoors, these workers are exposed to a variety of weather conditions.

Nearly all radio and telecommunications equipment installers and repairers work full time. Many work regular business hours to meet the demand for repair services during the workday. Schedules are more irregular at companies that need repair services 24 hours a day or where installation and maintenance must take place after business hours. At these locations, weekend and holiday hours are common. Repairers may be on call around the clock in case of emergencies.

Also, the work of most repairers involves lifting, reaching, stooping, crouching, climbing, and crawling. Adherence to safety precautions is important to guard against work hazards such as falls, minor burns, electrical shock, and contact with hazardous materials.

Civilian Salaries

In 2000, the average hourly salary in the telephone communications industry was $22.88. The average hourly salary of telecommunications equipment installers and repairers, except line installers was $21.17. The middle 50 percent earned between $16.55 and $24.99. The bottom 10 percent earned less than $12.04, whereas the top 10 percent earned more than $27.23.

The average hourly salary for radio mechanics was $15.86. The middle 50 percent earned between $12.57 and $20.60. The bottom 10 percent earned less than $9.39, whereas the top 10 percent earned more than $25.62.

Civilian Employment Prospects

In 2000, radio and telecommunications equipment installers and repairers held over 195,000 jobs. Nearly 190,000 were telecommunications equipment installers and repairers, with the exception of line installers. The rest were radio mechanics. Most worked for telephone communications companies but many radio mechanics worked in electrical repair shops.

Through 2010 the employment of radio and telecommunications equipment installers and repairers is expected to decline. Even though the need for installation work will actually be increasing, the need for maintenance workers is not expected to grow due to the increasing reliability of self-monitoring and self-diagnosing equipment. Also the replacement of two-way radio systems by wireless systems has virtually eliminated the need for on-site radio mechanics. Applicants with electronics training and computer skills will have the best opportunities for radio and telecommunications equipment installer and repairer jobs.

Opportunities should be available for central office and PBX installers and repairers as the Internet, expanded multimedia offerings, and other telecommunications services continue to place additional demand on telecommunications networks. These new services require high data transfer rates that can only be achieved by installing new optical switching and routing equipment. Extending high-speed communications from central offices to customers also will require the installation of more advanced switching and routing equipment.

Prewired buildings and the increasing reliability of telephone equipment will reduce the opportunities for station installers and repairers. Pay phone usage is declining as cellular telephones increased in popularity. This is having an adverse affect on employment in this specialty as pay phone installation and maintenance is one of its major functions.

Civilian Advancement Prospects

From now through 2010 job opportunities are expected to decline. Those with the most specialized electronics training as well as excellent computer skills should have the best opportunities.

Experienced repairers with advanced training may become specialists or troubleshooters who help other repairers diagnose difficult problems. They may also work with engineers in designing equipment and developing maintenance procedures. Because of their familiarity with equipment, repairers are particularly well qualified to become manufacturers' sales workers. Workers with leadership ability also may become maintenance supervisors or service managers. Some experienced workers open their own repair services or shops or become wholesalers or retailers of electronic equipment.

Education and Training

Job training consists of two to 10 months of classroom instruction, including practice with equipment. Courses are usually in mechanical, electronic, and electrical principles; preventive maintenance procedures; line installation and wiring techniques; and communication security policies and procedures.

The army, navy, and marine corps offer certified apprenticeship training programs for some specialties in this occupation. Most employers seek applicants with apprenticeships or postsecondary training in electronics as well as a familiarity with computers. Training sources include two- and four-year college programs in electronics or communications, trade schools, and equipment and software manufacturers. Military experience with communications equipment is highly valued by many employers.

Newly hired repairers usually receive some training from their employers, either formal classroom training in electronics, communications systems, or software and informal, hands-on training with communications equipment.

Experience, Special Skills, and Personality Traits

High school courses in math, electricity, or electronics repair and shop mechanics. Also helpful: an interest in working with electrical, electronic, and electromechanical equipment and in solving problems.

For some specialties, normal color vision is required, because wires are color-coded. Repairers must be able to hear distinctions in various tones. Those repairers who must climb poles and towers must be in good physical shape. Repairers who handle on-site assignments must be able to work without close supervision. Repairs who meet with customers need a pleasant personality, neat appearance, and good communications skills.

Unions and Associations

For general information about the work of communications equipment repairers, contact the International Brotherhood of Electrical Workers, the Communications Workers of America, the Electronics Technicians Association International or the National Association of Radio and Telecommunications Engineers.

COMPUTER EQUIPMENT REPAIRER

CAREER PROFILE

Duties: Install and repair computers and other data processing equipment; test and repair data processing equipment; locate defective data processing parts and replace them

Alternate Title(s): Data Processing Equipment Repairer; Computer Service Technician; Broadcast and Sound Engineering Technician and Radio Operator; Electronic Home Entertainment Equipment Installers and Repairer; Electrical and Electronics Installer and Repairer; Industrial Machinery Installation, Repair, and Maintenance Worker; Radio and Telecommunications Equipment Installer and Repairer

Availability: Army, Navy, Air Force, Marine Corps

Military Salary: See How to Use This Book

Civilian Salary: $9.50 to $23.42/hour

Civilian Employment Prospects: Good

Civilian Advancement Prospects: Good

Prerequisites:
  Rank—Enlisted
  Education and Training—High school diploma; training in electronics from associate degree programs, the military, vocational schools, or equipment manufacturers
  Experience—Any training and work experience obtained in the armed services or Job Corps
  Special Skills and Personality Traits—An interest in working with electrical and electronic equipment; knowledge of electronics; good communications skills; normal color vision; a neat appearance
  Licensure/Certification—Optional certification

CAREER LADDER

```
┌─────────────────────────────────┐
│          Supervisor             │
└─────────────────────────────────┘

┌─────────────────────────────────┐
│  Bench-Technician or Specialist │
└─────────────────────────────────┘

┌─────────────────────────────────┐
│   Computer Equipment Repairer   │
└─────────────────────────────────┘
```

Position Description

Computers are as vital to the modern military as any weapon in their arsenal. They are crucial to the functioning of weapons systems, communications, and administration. Keeping these systems running at all times is of vital importance for all military operations. Computer Equipment Repairers install computers and other data processing equipment. They inspect it for defects in wiring, circuit boards, and other parts. They test and repair it using electri-cal voltage meters, circuit analyzers, and other special testing equipment, and they locate defective data processing parts using technical guides and diagrams. They usually work indoors in repair shops or data processing centers on land or aboard ships. Some specialties involve flying.

In the civilian world they work for computer manufacturers, repair services, and other businesses with large computer facilities. Also known as data processing equipment repairers, they service mainframe, server, and personal computers as well as printers and disc drives. They repair, maintain, and install computers and related equipment. Computer support specialists provide technical assistance, in person or by telephone, to computer system users. Automated teller machines (ATMs) are also installed, repaired, and serviced by Computer Equipment Repairers, as are photocopiers, cash registers, mail processing equipment, and fax machines.

They may also install operating software and peripheral equipment, checking that all components are configured to correctly function together.

Field technicians travel to customers' workplaces or other locations to make the necessary repairs when equipment breaks down. They often have assigned areas in which they perform preventive maintenance on a regular basis. Bench technicians work in repair shops located in stores, factories, or service centers.

Computer Equipment Repairers replace defective components instead of repairing them because components are inexpensive and businesses are reluctant to shut down their computers for time-consuming repairs. When ATMs malfunction, computer networks recognize the problem and alert field technicians.

Workers use a variety of tools including multimeters to measure voltage, current, resistance, and other electrical properties; signal generators to provide test signals and oscilloscopes to monitor equipment signals. They also use software programs to diagnose computerized equipment. To repair or adjust equipment, workers use hand tools, such as pliers, screwdrivers, soldering irons, and wrenches.

Repairers work in clean, well-lighted surroundings. Because computers and office machines are sensitive to extreme temperatures and humidity, shops must be air-conditioned and well ventilated. Field repairers must travel to various locations to install, maintain, or repair equipment and may have to perform their jobs in small, confined spaces.

Data processing equipment repairers and ATM field technicians often work around the clock, their schedules often including evening, weekend, and holiday shifts (which may be assigned on the basis of seniority). Office machine and cash register servicers usually work regular business hours.

Although their job is not strenuous, repairers must lift equipment and work in a variety of postures. Repairers of computer monitors need to discharge voltage from the equipment to avoid electrocution and sometimes wear protective goggles.

Civilian Salaries

In 2000, the average hourly salary of computer, automated teller, and office machine repairers was $15.08. The middle 50 percent earned between $11.80 and $19.20. The lowest 10 percent earned less than $9.50 and the highest 10 percent earned more than $23.42. The average hourly salary in the

industries employing the largest numbers of computer repairers in 2000 were:

Professional and commercial equipment	$15.28
Computer and data processing services	$15.05
Radio, television, and computer stores	$13.16

Civilian Employment Prospects

Job opportunities look to be good for computer, automated teller, and office machine repairers. In 2000 they held over 170,000 jobs. Wholesale trade establishments employed slightly less than one-half of them. Others were employed in computer and data processing services, as well as in appliance, radio, television, and music stores. More than one in seven computer, automated teller, and office machine repairers were self-employed.

Through 2010 employment of these workers is expected to grow about as fast as the average for all occupations. Job growth should blossom due to increasing dependence of business and residential customers on computers and other sophisticated office machines. The need to maintain this equipment in working order will create new jobs for repairers.

Job prospects will be best for applicants with knowledge of electronics as well as repair experience, especially considering the fact employers continue to report difficulty in finding qualified applicants. Business and the general public are becoming increasingly reliant on computers, ATMs, fax machines, etc. Since most businesses find it more cost-efficient to bring in repair people rather than keep them on staff, and most personal computer operators do not have the skills necessary to repair their own machines, opportunities for repairers are expected to multiply exponentially.

Office machines, such as digital copiers and other new office machines are costly and complex. This equipment is often computerized, designed to work on a network, and able to perform multiple functions. The growing need for repairers to service such sophisticated equipment and systems will result in more job opportunities.

Civilian Advancement Prospects

With experience, Computer Equipment Repairers can advance to positions maintaining more sophisticated systems, such as networking equipment and servers. Field repairers of ATMs may advance to bench-technician positions responsible for more complex repairs. Experienced workers may also become specialists, helping other repairers diagnose difficult problems or work with engineers both designing equipment and developing maintenance procedures. Experienced workers can also move into management positions, supervising other repairers.

Because of their familiarity with equipment, experienced repairers may also move into customer service or sales positions. Some experienced workers open their own repair shops or become wholesalers or retailers of electronic equipment.

Education and Training

Job training consists of six to nine months of classroom instruction, including hands-on computer equipment repair practice. Courses are usually in electronic principles and concepts, operation of various computer systems and equipment, use of test equipment, and repair of data processing equipment.

Workers receive training in electronics from associate degree programs, the military, vocational schools, equipment manufacturers, or employers. The army, navy, and marine corps offer certified apprenticeship programs for some specialties in this occupation. Those specialties that involve flying require passing a special physical exam.

Employers prefer those certified as repairers or who have training in electronics from associate degree programs, the military, vocational schools, or equipment manufacturers. Employers generally provide some training to new repairers on specific equipment but expect workers to arrive on the job with a basic understanding of equipment repair. Employers may send experienced workers to training sessions to keep up with changes in technology and service procedures.

Most office machine and ATM repairer positions require an associate degree in electronics. A basic understanding of mechanical equipment also is important, as many of the parts that fail in office machines and ATMs are mechanical, such as paper loaders. Entry-level employees at large companies normally receive on-the-job training lasting several months.

Special Requirements

Several organizations administer certification programs for electronic or computer equipment Repairers. Numerous certifications, including A+, Net+, and Server+, are available through the Computing Technology Industry Association (CompTIA). To receive the certifications, candidates must pass several tests that assess computer repair skills. The International Society of Certified Electronics Technicians (ISCET) and the Electronics Technicians Association (ETA) also administer certification programs. Repairers may specialize in computer repair or a variety of other skills. To receive certification, repairers must pass qualifying exams corresponding to their level of training and experience. Both programs offer associate certifications to entry-level repairers.

Experience, Special Skills, and Personality Traits

High school math and electronic equipment repair courses are helpful. Also useful is an interest in working with electrical and electronic equipment, knowledge of electronics, good communications skills, and a neat appearance.

Field technicians must have a driver's license. Normal color vision is required to work with color-coded wiring.

Unions and Associations

For information on certification programs, contact the Computing Technology Industry Association, the International Society of Certified Electronics Technicians, and the Electronics Technicians Association.

ELECTRICAL AND ELECTRONICS ENGINEER

CAREER PROFILE

Duties: Direct research to improve and develop computer, navigation, and other electronic systems; direct equipment installation and repair; develop test standards and operating instructions; design and develop test instruments; test new or modified equipment; review test data; report results, and recommend actions

Alternate Title(s): Electronics Design Engineer; Electronics Test Engineer

Availability: All branches

Military Salary: See How to Use This Book

Civilian Salary: $41,740 to $94,490 (electrical engineers)/$43,070 to $94,330 (electronics engineers)

Civilian Employment Prospects: Good

Civilian Advancement Prospects: Good

Prerequisites:
  Rank—Officer
  Education and Training—A four-year college degree in electrical, electronic, or communications engineering
  Experience—Any training and work experience obtained in the armed services or Job Corps
  Special Skills and Personality Traits—Creativity; inquisitiveness; analytical; detail-oriented; an interest in engineering concepts and principles; able to plan and direct research projects; good with mathematical formulas; good team-worker; strong communication skills
  Licensure/Certification—State license required

CAREER LADDER

Electrical and Electronics Supervisor

Electrical and Electronics Technical Specialist

Electrical and Electronics Engineer

Position Description

The modern military, although still highly dependent on ground troops and such traditional weapons as the tank and assault helicopter, has moved into a new age where its first line of defense often lies solely in the realm of projectiles guided by advanced electronics. These intricate systems are also at the heart of defensive weapons as well, such as radar, communications equipment, and even the aforementioned tanks and helicopters. This equipment, an integral part of all offensive and defensive weapons, must be maintained at all costs. Electrical and Electronics Engineers design, develop,

and test electrical and electronic equipment. They also direct equipment installation and repair.

Usually working from offices (although they sometimes move outdoors when overseeing the installation of new equipment) these Electrical and Electronics Engineers direct research to improve and develop computer, navigation, and other electronic systems, direct equipment installation, and repair and develop test standards and operating instructions for electrical and electronic systems. They also design and develop test instruments, test new or modified equipment to check its performance and reliability, and review test data, report results, and recommend actions.

In the civilian world, Electrical and Electronics Engineers work on everything from geographical information systems to giant electric power generators. These engineers design, develop, test, and supervise the manufacture of electrical and electronic equipment. They work on the power generating, controlling, and transmission devices used by electric utilities; as well as electric motors, machinery controls, lighting, and wiring in buildings, automobiles, aircraft, radar and navigation systems, and broadcast and communications systems.

Workers in this field design new products, write performance requirements, develop maintenance schedules, test equipment, solve operating problems, and estimate the time and cost of engineering projects. Some specialize in areas such as power generation, transmission, and distribution; communications; and electrical equipment manufacturing.

Most work in office buildings, laboratories, or industrial plants. Others may spend time outdoors at construction sites, mines, and oil and gas exploration and production sites, where they monitor or direct operations or solve on-site problems. Some engineers travel extensively to plants or worksites. Most work a standard 40-hour week.

Civilian Salaries

In 2000, the average yearly salary for Electrical Engineers was $64,910. The middle 50 percent earned between $51,700 and $80,600. The lowest 10 percent earned less than $41,740. The highest 10 percent earned more than $94,490.

In 2000, the average yearly salaries in the industries employing the largest numbers of Electrical Engineers were:

Computer and office equipment	$69,700
Measuring and controlling devices	$67,570
Search and navigation equipment	$67,330
Electronic components and accessories	$65,830
Engineering and architectural services	$65,040

In 2000, the average yearly salary for Electronics Engineers was $64,830. The middle 50 percent earned between $52,430 and $79,960. The lowest 10 percent earned less than $43,070. The highest 10 percent earned more than $94,330.

In 2000, the average yearly salaries in the industries employing the largest numbers of electronics engineers were:

Federal government	$70,890
Search and navigation equipment	$68,930
Electronic components and accessories	$63,890
Electrical goods	$62,860
Telephone communication	$57,710

Civilian Employment Prospects

In 2000, Electrical and Electronics Engineers held nearly 290,000 jobs, mostly in engineering and business consulting firms, government agencies, and manufacturers of electrical and electronic and computer and office equipment, industrial machinery, and professional and scientific instruments. Transportation, communications, and utilities firms as well as personnel supply services and computer and data processing services firms accounted for most of the remaining jobs. Practically one-third of these positions was located in only four states: California, Texas, New York, and New Jersey.

Through 2010, opportunities for Electrical and Electronics Engineers are expected to grow about as fast as the average for all occupations. This growth should come mainly from increased demand for electrical and electronic goods, as well as from the need for electronics manufacturers to invest heavily in research and development to remain competitive and gain a scientific edge. Opportunities for Electronics Engineers in defense-related firms should improve as aircraft and weapons systems are upgraded. Growth is expected to be fastest in services industries, particularly consulting firms that provide electronic engineering expertise.

Civilian Advancement Prospects

Newly hired engineers usually work under the watchful eye of experienced engineers until they have gained sufficient knowledge to be entrusted with more difficult projects. From there engineers can advance to become technical specialists or to supervisory positions in charge of a team of engineers and technicians. Some may eventually become engineering managers or enter other managerial or sales jobs.

Education and Training

In the military, those interested in this career usually are provided with on-the-job training. Classroom training is only provided for some specialties. These classroom sessions can contain such courses as combat and tactical communications systems, telecommunications center systems, and signal center site defense systems.

A four-year college degree in electrical, electronic, or communications engineering is required for almost all entry-level engineering jobs. Most engineering degrees are granted in electrical, electronics, mechanical, or civil engineering, but engineers trained in one branch may work in related branches. This flexibility allows engineers to shift to fields with better employment prospects or to those that more closely match their interests.

Most engineering programs involve a concentration of study in an engineering specialty, along with courses in both mathematics and science. Most programs include a design course, sometimes accompanied by a computer or laboratory class or both. In addition to the standard engineering degree, many colleges offer two- or four-year degree programs in engineering technology. Some employers regard technology program graduates as having skills between those of a technician and an engineer. Graduate training is essential for engineering faculty positions and many research and development programs, but is not required for the majority of entry-level engineering jobs.

Some 330 colleges and universities offer bachelor's degree programs in engineering that are accredited by the Accreditation Board for Engineering and Technology (ABET), and about 250 colleges offer accredited bachelor's degree programs in engineering technology. ABET accreditation is based on an examination of an engineering program's student achievement, program improvement, faculty, curricular content, facilities, and institutional commitment. Few of these institutions offer programs in the smaller specialties. Also, programs of the same title may vary in content among institutions.

Undergraduate admissions requirements include a solid background in math (algebra, geometry, trigonometry, calculus) and science (biology, chemistry, physics), and courses in English, social studies, humanities, and computers. In a typical four-year college curriculum, the first two years are spent studying mathematics, basic sciences, introductory engineering, humanities, and social sciences. In the last two years, most courses are in engineering, usually with a concentration in one branch.

Continuing education is important for electrical and electronics engineers. Engineers who fail to keep up with the rapid changes in technology risk becoming more susceptible to layoffs or, at a minimum, more likely to be passed over for advancement.

Special Requirements

All 50 states and the District of Columbia usually require licensure for engineers who offer their services directly to the public. Engineers who are licensed are called Professional Engineers. This licensure generally requires a degree from an ABET-accredited engineering program, four years of relevant work experience, and successful completion of a state examination. Recent graduates can start the licensing process by taking the examination in two stages. The initial Fundamentals of Engineering examination can be taken upon graduation. Engineers who pass this examination commonly are called Engineers in Training or Engineer Interns. The EIT certification usually is valid for 10 years. After acquiring suitable work experience, EITs can take the second examination, the Principles and Practice of Engineering Exam. Several states have imposed mandatory continuing education requirements for renewal of licensure. Most states recognize licensure from other states. Many civil, electrical, mechanical, and chemical engineers are licensed as PEs.

Experience, Special Skills, and Personality Traits

All engineers should be creative, inquisitive, analytical, and detail-oriented. They should have an interest in engineering concepts and principles, in planning and directing research projects and in working with mathematical formulas. They should also be able to work as part of a team and to communicate well, both verbally and in print.

Unions and Associations

For information on electrical and electronics engineers contact the Institute of Electrical and Electronics Engineers. Those interested in obtaining information on ABET-accredited engineering programs should contact the Accreditation Board for Engineering and Technology, Inc. Nonlicensed engineers and college students interested in obtaining information on Professional Engineer licensure should contact the National Society of Professional Engineers and the National Council of Examiners for Engineers and Surveying. For information on general engineering education and career resources contact the American Society for Engineering Education.

ELECTRICAL PRODUCTS REPAIRER

CAREER PROFILE

Duties: Maintain, test, and repair electric motors in various machines; inspect and repair electrical, medical, dental equipment, and other electric instruments; replace worn gaskets and seals; maintain and repair portable electric tools, such as saws and drills, and nonportables such as submarine periscopes

Alternate Title(s): Electric Tool Repairer; Electrical Instrument Repairer; Electromedical Equipment and Electric Motor Repairer; Broadcast and Sound Engineering Technician; Radio Operator; Computer, Automated Teller, and Office Machine Repairer; Electronic Home Entertainment Equipment Installer or Repairer; Radio and Telecommunications Equipment Installer or Repairer

Availability: Army, Navy, Marine Corps, Coast Guard

Military Salary: See How to Use This Book

Civilian Salary: $7.98 to $29.00/hour

Civilian Employment Prospects: Fair

Civilian Advancement Prospects: Good

Prerequisites:

Rank—Enlisted

Education and Training—High school diploma; advanced training from vocational schools, community colleges, or the military

Experience—Any training and work experience obtained in the armed services or Job Corps; on-the-job training

Special Skills and Personality Traits—Skilled with tools; an interest in electric motors and appliances; good problem-solving skills; good eyesight and normal color vision; strong communications skills; well-organized; detail-oriented; good interpersonal skills; neat appearance

CAREER LADDER

```
┌─────────────────────────────────┐
│  Electrical Products Repairer,   │
│  Supervisor                      │
└─────────────────────────────────┘

┌─────────────────────────────────┐
│  Electrical Products Repairer,   │
│  Specialist                      │
└─────────────────────────────────┘

┌─────────────────────────────────┐
│  Electrical Products Repairer,   │
│  Trainee                         │
└─────────────────────────────────┘
```

Position Description

Today the majority of the modern military's equipment is electrically powered. This equipment requires constant, careful maintenance and repair. Electrical Products Repairers perform these duties, specializing by type of equipment. In the military, Electrical Products Repairers maintain, test, and repair electric motors in various machines such as lathes, pumps, office machines, and kitchen appliances. They inspect and repair electrical, medical, and dental equipment as well as electric instruments, such as voltmeters. They replace worn gaskets and seals in watertight electrical equipment. They also maintain and repair portable electric tools such as saws and drills and even submarine periscopes.

In civilian life, Electrical Products Repairers work in many industries, including hospitals, manufacturing firms, and governmental agencies. They also work in independent repair shops. They perform duties similar to military Electrical Products Repairers working in repair shops on land or aboard ships.

All businesses these days depend on electronic equipment. Electrical equipment and electronics equipment are two distinct types of industrial equipment. Electrical portions of equipment provide the power for the equipment while electronic components control the device. Many installers and repairers, known as field technicians, travel to on-site locations to repair equipment. Usually, they have assigned areas where they perform preventive maintenance on a regular basis.

When equipment breaks down, field technicians go to a customer's site to repair the equipment. Bench technicians work in repair shops located in factories and service centers on those components that cannot be repaired on the factory floor. Repairers first check for common causes of trouble, such as loose connections or obviously defective components. If routine checks do not locate the trouble, they will refer to schematics and manufacturers' specifications that show connections and provide instructions on how to locate problems or use software programs and testing equipment to diagnose malfunctions.

In this work they use multimeters (to measure voltage, current, and resistance), advanced multimeters (to measure capacitance, inductance, and current gain of transistors), signal generators (which provide test signals), and oscilloscopes (which graphically display signals) as well as hand tools such as pliers, screwdrivers, soldering irons, and wrenches to adjust equipment and replace faulty parts.

Since factories cannot allow production equipment to stand idle, repairers on the factory floor simply remove and replace defective units, rather than fixing them. Defective units are thrown out, sent back to the manufacturer, or passed on to a specialized shop for repair. Bench technicians at these locations have the training, tools, and parts to thoroughly diagnose and repair circuit boards or other complex components. These workers also locate and repair circuit defects, such as poorly soldered joints, blown fuses, or malfunctioning transistors.

Electrical and electronics installers often refit outdated manufacturing equipment with new, automated control devices. Setting up and installing a new PLC involves connecting it to different sensors and electrically powered devices such as electric motors, switches, and pumps, and writing a computer program to operate the PLC. Electronics installers coordinate their efforts with other workers installing and maintaining equipment.

Motor vehicle electronic equipment installers and repairers install, diagnose, and repair communications, sound, security, and navigation equipment in motor vehicles. Most installation work involves either new alarm or sound systems. Such work can be as simple as removing a few screws and connecting a few wires or as complicated as having to build a fiberglass or wooden subwoofer box designed to fit in the unique dimensions of a particular vehicle. Installing sound-deadening material requires the removal and reinstallation of many parts of a car as well as the addition of sound-absorbing material in empty spaces. Motor vehicle electronic equipment installers and repairers also run new speaker and electrical cables, install additional fuses, run new electrical lines from batteries, and drill holes in fire walls.

Installers and repairers work on factory floors where they are subject to noise, dirt, vibrations, and heat. Bench technicians work primarily in repair shops that are relatively quiet, comfortable, and well-lighted. Field technicians spend much time on the road, traveling to different customer locations. They work at all hours since electronic equipment is critical to industries. Their schedules may include evening, weekend, and holiday shifts.

Installers and repairers may have some heavy lifting and often work in a variety of positions. They often wear protective goggles and hard hats and harnesses to prevent falls when working on elevated equipment. They also must take precautions against electric shock.

Civilian Salaries

In 2000, the average hourly wage for Electrical Products Repairers of commercial and industrial equipment was $17.75. The middle 50 percent earned between $13.92 and $21.32. The lowest 10 percent earned less than $10.90. The highest 10 percent earned more than $25.78.

In 2000, the average hourly wage for electric motor, power tool, and related repairers was $15.80. The middle 50 percent earned between $11.91 and $20.04. The lowest 10 percent earned less than $9.13. The highest 10 percent earned more than $25.17.

In the same year the average hourly wage for Electrical Products Repairers of powerhouses, substations, and relays was $23.34. The middle 50 percent earned between $19.07 and $26.21. The lowest 10 percent earned less than $14.79. The highest 10 percent earned more than $29.00. For those employed working on transportation equipment, it was $16.93 in 2000. The middle 50 percent earned between $12.25 and $21.54. The lowest 10 percent earned less than $9.60. The highest 10 percent earned more than $25.76.

In 2000, the average hourly wage for Electrical Products Repairers of motor vehicles was $12.06 in 2000. The middle 50 percent earned between $9.60 and $15.25. The lowest 10 percent earned less than $7.98. The highest 10 percent earned more than $18.69.

Civilian Employment Prospects

In 2000, Electrical Products Repairers held just over 170,000 jobs. Many worked for wholesale trade companies, general electrical work companies, the federal government, electrical repair shops, and manufacturers of electronic components and accessories and communications equipment.

Job opportunities look to be fair for installers and repairers. Employment growth is expected to be slower than average, but will vary by occupational specialty. Opportunities will be best for applicants with a thorough knowledge of electrical and electronic equipment, as well as repair experience.

Average employment growth is projected for electrical and electronics installers and repairers of transportation equipment as well as for electronics installers and repairers of motor vehicles. Employment opportunities for electric motor, power tool, and related repairers are expected to grow more slowly than the average, however. Worse yet, employment of electrical and electronics installers and repairers of powerhouses, substations, and relays is expected to decline slightly.

Civilian Advancement Prospects

Experienced Electrical Products Repairers with advanced training may become specialists or troubleshooters who help other repairers diagnose difficult problems. Workers with leadership ability may become supervisors and move on to other management positions. Some experienced workers open their own repair shops.

Education and Training

Job training consists of one to six months of classroom instruction, including practice in repairing electrical products. Instruction usually includes such courses as maintenance and repair procedures and the use of electrical test equipment.

Further training occurs on the job and through advanced courses. The army, navy, and marine corps offer certified apprenticeship programs for some specialties in this occupation.

Knowledge of electrical equipment and electronics is necessary for employment. Many applicants complete one to two years at vocational schools and community colleges, although some less skilled repairers may have only a high school diploma. These entry-level repairers may have to work closely with more experienced technicians who will provide the necessary technical guidance.

Special Requirements

The International Society of Certified Electronics Technicians and the Electronics Technicians Association administer certification programs for electronics installation and repair technicians. Both programs offer associate certifications to entry-level repairers.

Experience, Special Skills, and Personality Traits

High school math, electricity, and shop mechanics course are good. Helpful attributes include the ability to use tools as well as an interest in electric motors and appliances and in solving problems.

Electrical Products Repairers should have good eyesight in order to work with the intricate components used in electronic equipment. Normal color vision is required to work with color-coded wiring. Field technicians often need good communications skills, a neat appearance, and a driver's license.

Unions and Associations

The International Society of Certified Electronics Technicians and the Electronics Technicians Association offer membership to Electrical Products Repairers. They provide certification, networking opportunities, and other useful benefits.

ELECTRONIC INSTRUMENT REPAIRER

CAREER PROFILE

Duties: Test precision meteorological and medical instruments, navigational controls, and simulators; read technical diagrams and manuals; replace equipment

Alternate Title(s): Computer, Automated Teller, and Office Machine Repairer; Coin, Vending, and Amusement Machine Servicer and Repairer; Dental Laboratory and Ophthalmic Laboratory Equipment Repairer; Camera Repairer

Availability: All branches

Military Salary: See How to Use This Book

Civilian Salary: $6.48 to $31.47/hour

Civilian Employment Prospects: Fair

Civilian Advancement Prospects: Fair

Prerequisites:

　Rank—Enlisted

　Education and Training—High school diploma; postsecondary education; certified apprenticeship program or significant on-the-job training

　Experience—Any training and work experience obtained in the armed services or Job Corps; on-the-job training

　Special Skills and Personality Traits—Good math skills; general knowledge of science and electronic equipment repair; detail-oriented; good reading skills; manual dexterity; an interest in working with electronic equipment; enjoy solving problems; good fine motor skills; excellent vision; normal color vision

　Licensure/Certification—Optional

CAREER LADDER

```
┌─────────────────────────────────┐
│  Electronic Instrument Repairer, │
│            Supervisor            │
└─────────────────────────────────┘

┌─────────────────────────────────┐
│   Electronic Instrument Repairer │
└─────────────────────────────────┘

┌─────────────────────────────────┐
│  Electronic Instrument Repairer, │
│            Apprentice            │
└─────────────────────────────────┘
```

Position Description

Many areas of the military use electronic instruments, including health care, weather forecasting, flight control, combat, and so on. Electronic Instrument Repairers maintain and repair electronic instruments, such as precision measuring equipment, navigational controls, photographic equipment, and biomedical instruments. Electronic Instrument Repairers normally specialize by type of equipment or instrument. Their duties can include testing meteorological and medical instruments, navigational controls, and simulators; using electronic and electrical test equipment; reading technical diagrams and manuals in order to locate, isolate, and repair instrument parts; and replacing equipment parts such as resistors, switches, and circuit boards.

In the civilian world, most Electronic Instrument Repairers work for manufacturing, medical research, satellite communications firms, commercial airlines, and government agencies, such as the Federal Aviation Administration, the National Aeronautics and Space Administration, or the National Weather Service. They perform the same kind of duties as military Electronic Instrument Repairers, usually working in repair shops and laboratories.

Repairing and maintaining watches, cameras, musical instruments, medical equipment, and similar items requires a high level of skill and attention to detail. Some devices contain tiny gears that must be manufactured to within one one-hundredth of a millimeter of design specifications; others contain equally small, sophisticated electronic controls.

Camera and photographic equipment repairers must first determine whether a repair would be profitable, since inexpensive cameras often cost more to repair than to replace. If they decide to proceed, they diagnose the problem, often by disassembling numerous small parts in order to reach the source, then make needed adjustments or replace a defective part. Camera repairers also maintain cameras by removing and replacing broken or worn parts and cleaning and lubricating gears and springs. When camera parts are no longer available repairers must build replacement parts or strip junked cameras. Repairers also repair the increasingly popular digital cameras.

Watch and clock repairers work almost exclusively on expensive timepieces. Expensive timepieces still employ old-style mechanical movements and manual controls that require adjustment and maintenance. This means the disassembly of many fine gears and components. Each part is inspected for wear. All parts will be cleaned and oiled, but only some may need to be replaced or machined. Again, when parts are unavailable repairers must machine their own parts using small lathes and other machines.

Musical instrument repairers and tuners work in four specialties—band instruments, pianos and organs, violins, and guitars. Band, brass, wind, and percussion instrument repairers focus on woodwind, brass, reed, and percussion instruments. They move mechanical parts or play scales to find problems. They may unscrew and remove rod pins, keys, worn cork pads, and pistons and remove soldered parts using gas torches. They repair dents in metal and wood using filling techniques or a mallet. Drums often need new drumheads, which are cut from animal skin. These repairers use gas torches, grinding wheels, shears, mallets, and small hand tools. Piano repairers use similar techniques, skills, and tools. Violin and guitar repairers adjust and repair string instruments. They play and inspect instruments to find defects, then replace or repair cracked or broken sections and damaged parts. They also restring instruments and repair damage to their finish.

Although medical equipment repairers work on fine mechanical systems, the machines that they repair—electric wheelchairs, mechanical lifts, hospital beds, customized vehicles—often require less precision. Medical equipment repairers use various tools, including ammeters, voltmeters, and other measuring devices to diagnose problems. They use hand tools and machining equipment, such as small lathes and other metalworking equipment, to make repairs.

Camera, watch, and musical instrument repairers work under low-stress conditions in quiet, well-lighted work or repair shops. Some travel to the instrument being repaired (pianos, organs, or grandfather clocks).

Medical equipment and precision instrument and equipment repairers usually work daytime hours. They also work in a variety of conditions—hot, dirty, noisy factories; air-conditioned workshops; or outdoor fieldwork. Their work can involve dangerous machinery and toxic chemicals.

Civilian Salaries

In 2000, earnings ranged from less than $6.48 for the lowest 10 percent of watch repairers to more than $31.47 for the highest 10 percent of musical instrument repairers and tuners.

Medical equipment repairers	$16.99
Musical instrument repairers and tuners	$15.10
Camera and photographic equipment repairers	$13.94
Watch repairers	$12.08
All other Electronic Instrument Repairers	$19.87

Civilian Employment Prospects

In 2000, Electronic Instrument Repairers held slightly fewer than 65,000 jobs. Most medical equipment repairers and other Electronic Instrument Repairers were wage and salary workers. Conversely, approximately one out of four watch, camera, and photographic equipment and musical instrument repairers were self-employed. The following lists employment by occupation:

Medical equipment repairers	28,000
All other Electronic Instrument Repairers	15,000
Camera and photographic equipment repairers	7,200
Musical instrument repairers and tuners	7,100
Watch repairers	5,200

Good opportunities are expected for most types of jobs as overall employment is expected to grow about as fast as average from now through 2010. This projected growth varies by detailed occupation, however.

Job growth among medical equipment repairers should grow about as fast as the average for all occupations over the projected period. On the other hand, employment of musical instrument repairers is expected to increase more slowly than average. The employment of camera and photographic equipment repairers is expected to decline. The employment of watch repairers is also expected to grow more slowly than average.

The projected slower than average employment growth of other Electronic Instrument Repairers reflects the expected lack of employment growth in manufacturing and other industries in which they are employed. Nevertheless, good employment opportunities are expected for other Electronic Instrument Repairers due to the relatively small number of people entering the occupation and the need to replace repairers who retire.

Civilian Advancement Prospects

From now through 2010 job opportunities for Electronic Instrument Repairers are expected to be fair to good, depending on the individual repairer's specialty. There are some opportunities for advancement, but most supervisory positions in these fields require additional formal education. Some Electronic Instrument Repairers may go on to form their own independent business.

Education and Training

Job training consists of four to eight months of classroom instruction, including practice in repairing and replacing electronic instrument parts. Training length varies depending on specialty. Training includes courses in the principles of electronics, the use and maintenance of electrical and electronic test equipment, and equipment repair exercises.

Most employers require a high school diploma and, in some cases, postsecondary education, coupled with significant on-the-job training. The navy and the Marine Corps offer certified apprenticeship programs for some specialties in this occupation.

The educational background required for camera and photographic equipment repairers varies, but some background in electronics is necessary. The job requires the ability to read an electronic schematic diagram and comprehend other technical information. New employees first assist a senior repairer for half a year, then they refine their skills by performing repairs on their own for the next half-year. Afterward they continually improve their skills by attending manufacturer-sponsored seminars on the specifics of particular models.

Medical equipment repairers often specialize in a model or brand. Medical equipment repair requires less training than other precision equipment repair specialties. There are no schools to train these repairers; they learn through hands-on experience and observation. New repairers begin by observing and assisting an experienced worker over three to six months. Then they begin working independently while still under close supervision.

Training varies for watch and clock repairers as well. Some must earn certifications that can be completed in a few months; some require simply passing an examination. Some repairers opt to learn through assisting a master watch repairer. Nevertheless, developing proficiency in watch or clock repair requires several years of education and experience.

Musical instrument repairers and tuners need post–high school training in music repair technology. A few technical schools and colleges offer courses in instrument repair. Graduates of these programs normally receive additional training on the job, working with an experienced repairer.

Special Requirements

No certification is required, but some, like those offered by the American Watchmakers-Clockmakers Institute (AWI) and the National Association of Watch and Clock Collectors, can be helpful. Independent business owners may need the usual business licenses.

Experience, Special Skills, and Personality Traits

Repairers need to understand blueprints, electrical schematic diagrams, and electrical, hydraulic, and electromechanical systems. High school math, science, and electronic equipment repair are useful. The ability to read is important and some background in electronics is necessary. Also, Electronic Instrument Repairers must be able to pay close attention to details and have the desire to disassemble machines to see how they work, as well as the confidence to put them back together.

They must be able to work alone with minimal supervision, have good manual dexterity, an interest in working with electronic equipment and in solving problems. Good fine motor skills and excellent vision are also important, as is normal color vision.

Unions and Associations

Several associations, including the American Watchmakers-Clockmakers Institute (AWI) and the National Association of Watch and Clock Collectors, offer certifications.

For additional information about camera repair careers, contact the National Association of Photo Equipment Technicians. For additional information on medical equipment repair, contact your local medical equipment repair shop or hospital. For information on musical instrument repair, including schools offering training, contact the National Association of Professional Band Instrument Repair Technicians. For additional information on piano repair work, contact the Piano Technicians Guild. For information about training, mentoring programs, and schools with programs in precision instrument repair, contact the ISA—The Instrumentation, Systems, and Automation Society. And for information about watch and clock repair and a list of schools with related programs of study contact the American Watchmakers-Clockmakers Institute.

PRECISION INSTRUMENT REPAIRER

CAREER PROFILE

Duties: Calibrate weather instruments; repair gyrocompasses; adjust and repair weapon-aiming devices; calibrate engineering instruments; calibrate and repair instruments used in aircraft; repair watches, clocks, and timers; calibrate electrical test instruments

Alternate Title(s): Instrument Mechanic; Calibration Specialist; Computer, Automated Teller, and Office Machine Repairer; Coin, Vending, and Amusement Machine Servicer and Repairer; Dental Laboratory and Ophthalmic Laboratory Technician; Camera Repairer

Availability: Army, Navy, Air Force, Marine Corps

Military Salary: See How to Use This Book

Civilian Salary: $6.48 to $31.47/hour

Civilian Employment Prospects: Fair

Civilian Advancement Prospects: Fair

Prerequisites:
  Rank—Enlisted
  Education and Training—High school math, science, electronics, and shop mechanics; postsecondary education; certified apprenticeship program
  Experience—Any training and work experience obtained in the armed services or Job Corps
  Special Skills and Personality Traits—An interest in machines and how they work; the ability to solve mechanical problems; enjoy working with tools; good fine motor skills; good vision; excellent manual dexterity; normal color vision; detail-oriented; able to read and understand technical manuals, blueprints, and electrical schematic diagrams; understanding of electrical, hydraulic, and electromechanical systems
  Licensure/Certification—Optional

CAREER LADDER

```
┌─────────────────────────────────┐
│  Precision Instrument Repair     │
│  Supervisor                      │
└─────────────────────────────────┘

┌─────────────────────────────────┐
│  Precision Instrument Repairer   │
└─────────────────────────────────┘

┌─────────────────────────────────┐
│  Precision Instrument Repair     │
│  Trainee                         │
└─────────────────────────────────┘
```

Position Description

Precision instruments are measuring devices, as simple as a thermometer or as complex as a gyrocompass. In the military, precision instruments are used to measure distance, pressure, altitude, underwater depth, and many other things. Precision Instrument Repairers keep measuring devices in good working order.

In repair shops on land or aboard ships they calibrate gauges and meters, such as barometers and thermometers, to give correct readings. They repair gyrocompasses, adjust and repair weapon-aiming devices, such as range finders, telescopes, periscopes, and ballistic computers, calibrate engineering instruments, such as transits, levels, telemeters, and stereoscopes. They also calibrate and repair instruments used in aircraft and electrical test instruments as well as repair watches, clocks, and timers.

In the civilian world, Precision Instrument Repairers work for firms that manufacture or use precision instruments, such as manufacturing firms, airlines, machinery repair shops, maintenance shops, and instrument makers. Their work requires a high level of skill and attention to detail.

Camera and photographic equipment repairers first determine whether a repair would be cost-effective, since inexpensive cameras often cost more to repair than to replace. If the repairer decides to proceed, they diagnose the problem, disassemble numerous small parts in order to reach the source, then make needed adjustments or replace a defective part. Repairers also maintain cameras by removing and replacing broken or worn parts, cleaning and lubricating gears and springs, and building replacement parts. When machining new parts, they use a small lathe, a grinding wheel, and other metalworking tools. They also repair digital cameras.

Watch and clock repairers work almost exclusively on expensive timepieces, employing old-style mechanical movements and manual mechanisms. This type of timepiece requires regular adjustment and maintenance, which means the disassembly of many fine gears and components and inspection for wear. All parts are cleaned and oiled, some may need to be replaced or machined. When replacement parts are unavailable repairers must machine their own parts, employing small lathes and other machines.

Musical instrument repairers and tuners work in four specialties: band instruments, pianos and organs, violins, and guitars. Band, brass, wind, and percussion instrument repairers focus on woodwind, brass, reed, and percussion instruments. They move mechanical parts or play scales to find problems. They unscrew and remove rod pins, keys, worn cork pads, and pistons, and remove soldered parts using gas torches. They repair dents in metal and wood using filling techniques or a mallet. Drums often need new drumheads, which are cut from animal skin. These repairers use gas torches, grinding wheels, shears, mallets, and small hand tools. Piano repairers use similar techniques, skills, and tools. Violin and guitar repairers adjust and repair string instruments. They play and inspect instruments to find defects, then replace or repair cracked or broken sections and damaged parts. They also restring the instruments and repair damage to their finish.

Although medical equipment repairers work on fine mechanical systems, including electric wheelchairs, mechanical lifts, hospital beds, and customized vehicles, the larger scale of their tasks requires less precision. They use various tools including ammeters, voltmeters, and other measuring devices to diagnose problems. They also use hand tools and machining equipment such as small lathes and other metalworking equipment.

Civilian Salaries

In 2000, Precision Instrument Repairers' earnings ranged from less than $6.48 an hour for the lowest 10 percent of watch repairers to more than $31.47 an hour for the highest 10 percent of musical instrument repairers and tuners. The average hourly rates for various types of precision instrument and equipment repairers were as follows:

Medical equipment repairers	$16.99
Musical instrument repairers and tuners	$15.10
Camera and photographic equipment repairers	$13.94
Watch repairers	$12.08
All other precision instrument and equipment repairers	$19.87

Civilian Employment Prospects

In 2000, Precision Instrument Repairers held just under 65,000 jobs. Most medical equipment repairers and other precision instrument and equipment repairers were wage and salary workers. About one in four watch, camera, and photographic equipment and musical instrument repairers were self-employed. The following shows employment by occupation:

Medical equipment repairers	28,000
All other precision instrument and equipment repairers	15,000
Camera and photographic equipment repairers	7,200
Musical instrument repairers and tuners	7,100
Watch repairers	5,200

Through 2010 good opportunities are expected for most types of Precision Instrument Repairer jobs. Overall employment is projected to grow about as fast as the average for all occupations during this period, though projected growth varies by detailed occupation.

Medical equipment repairers' opportunities should grow about as fast as the average for all occupations. On the other hand, employment of musical instrument repairers is expected to increase more slowly than average. Employment of camera and photographic equipment repairers is expected to decline, and employment of watch repairers is expected to grow more slowly than average.

Civilian Advancement Prospects

From now through 2010 job opportunities are expected to be good for most types of Precision Instrument Repairer jobs. Overall employment is projected to grow about as fast as the average for all occupations during this period, though projected growth varies by detailed occupation. Some advancement opportunities exist, but many supervisory positions require additional formal education or higher-level business training.

Education and Training

Job training consists of three to nine months of classroom instruction, including practice in repairing precision instruments. Training courses include calibration and repair of precision measuring instruments and the use of blueprints and schematics.

Training requirements include a high school diploma and, often, postsecondary education coupled with significant on-the-job training. The army and navy offer certified apprenticeship programs for some specialties in this occupation.

Much training takes place on the job. The educational background required for camera and photographic equipment repairers varies, but some background in electronics is necessary. New repairers assist a senior repairer for half a year, then refine their skills by performing repairs on their own for another half year. Then they hone their skills by attending manufacturer-sponsored seminars on the specifics of particular models. Medical equipment and camera repairers often specialize in a model or brand. There are no schools to train these repairers; they learn through hands-on experience and observation. New repairers begin by observing and assisting an experienced worker.

Certifications are available in some areas of watch repair, but some repairers opt to learn through assisting a master watch repairer. Nevertheless, developing proficiency in watch or clock repair requires several years of education and experience.

Musical instrument repairers and tuners are generally trained in music repair technology. A few technical schools and colleges offer courses in instrument repair. Graduates of these programs normally receive additional training on the job from an experienced repairer. Some repairers and tuners begin learning their trade on the job as assistants, but employers strongly prefer those with technical school training.

Special Requirements

Several associations, including the American Watchmakers-Clockmakers Institute and the National Association of

Watch and Clock Collectors, offer certifications for watch and clock repairers.

Experience, Special Skills, and Personality Traits

High school studies should include math, science, electronics, and shop mechanics. Also helpful are interest in machines and how they work as well as the ability to solve mechanical problems and to work with tools. Good fine motor skills and vision, manual dexterity, and normal color vision are all necessary. Also, repairers must be able to pay close attention to details, enjoy problem solving, and be able to work alone with minimal supervision.

The ability to read and understand technical manuals, blueprints, electrical schematic diagrams is required. Also important is an understanding of electrical, hydraulic, and electromechanical systems.

Unions and Associations

For additional information about camera repair careers, contact the National Association of Photo Equipment Technicians. For additional information on medical equipment repair, contact your local medical equipment repair shop or hospital. For information on musical instrument repair, including schools offering training, contact the National Association of Professional Band Instrument Repair Technicians. For additional information on piano repair work, contact the Piano Technicians Guild. For information about training, mentoring programs, and schools with programs in precision instrument repair, contact the ISA—The Instrumentation, Systems, and Automation Society. For information about watch and clock repair and a list of schools with related programs of study, contact the American Watchmakers-Clockmakers Institute.

The American Watchmakers-Clockmakers Institute provides continuing education courses at its training center in Harrison, Ohio. They also provide the following technical services to its members: technical bulletins, parts lists, and movement bank/material search.

The Instrumentation, Systems, and Automation Society provides home-based and on-site training via the Web, videotape, or CD-Rom.

ENGINEERING, SCIENCE, AND TECHNICAL

AEROSPACE ENGINEER

CAREER PROFILE

Duties: Design and direct the development and construction of military airplanes, satellites, spacecraft, and missiles; see that all needs and specifications are met; choose civilian contractors; test prototypes

Alternate Title(s): Aeronautical Engineer; Astronautical Engineer

Availability: All branches

Military Salary: See How to Use This Book

Civilian Salary: $42,659 to $93,880

Civilian Employment Prospects: Fair

Civilian Advancement Prospects: Fair

Prerequisites:
  Rank—Officer
  Education and Training—Bachelor's degree in aeronautical, astronautical, or mechanical engineering required for civilian employment
  Experience—Strong educational background; on-the-job training
  Special Skills and Personality Traits—Inquisitiveness; love of tinkering; imagination and practicality

CAREER LADDER

```
┌─────────────────────────────────────┐
│        Consulting Engineer           │
└─────────────────────────────────────┘

┌─────────────────────────────────────┐
│  Project Engineer, Research Engineer,│
│            Management                │
└─────────────────────────────────────┘

┌─────────────────────────────────────┐
│           Staff Engineer             │
└─────────────────────────────────────┘
```

Position Description

Aerospace Engineers develop and create an amazing array of machines, including airplanes, satellites, and spacecraft, but they also contribute to such vehicular systems as high-speed trains, submarines, and hydrofoils. They play an important role in the conception, design, and construction of defense systems technology. Their research efforts have led to such innovative spin-off products derived from aerospace projects as Teflon and freeze-dried food. Their work is also applied to many other fields, such as studying the effects of wind on structural elements to aid in improving architectural design for skyscrapers.

Aerospace Engineers study a wide range of scientific disciplines including propulsion, acoustics, aerodynamics, celestial mechanics, flight and space mechanics, thermodynamics, and energy conservation. Those who work with aircraft are known as aeronautical engineers, while those involved in space travel are called astronautical engineers.

Aerospace Engineers often specialize further in areas like structural design, guidance systems, navigation and control systems, instrumentation, communication, or production methods. Another method of specialization might find them concentrating their efforts on a particular type of aerospace product. Thus engineers may focus on commercial transports, military fighter jets, missiles and rockets, spacecraft, or helicopters. Also, it should be noted that there are many civilian companies at present drawing up plans for space-related businesses (such as tourist flights and hotels) who may begin actual hiring and building within the next decade.

More recently, aerospace professionals have recognized the growing trend of aerospace vehicles becoming integral parts of information collection and dissemination systems (for example, the Hubble telescope). On board information systems now account for more than half of all defense procurements and are becoming the core business for many aerospace companies.

Military Aerospace Engineers work closely with private companies hired by the armed forces to conduct research, develop new aircraft or related technologies, and build it. They review all steps of the process, select plans, and decide which prototypes should be built and tested further. Once a new design is accepted, Aerospace Engineers oversee the production and deployment of the new equipment.

Aerospace Engineers can pursue opportunities in industry, business, government, or education. Whatever the focus of their efforts—research, development, design, testing, manufacturing, operation and maintenance, marketing and sales, administration, or teaching—Aerospace Engineers face great challenges and can reap tremendous satisfaction.

Civilian Salaries

Average annual earnings for Aerospace Engineers were $66,950 in 1998. The lowest 10 percent earned less than $42, 650 and the highest 10 percent earned in excess of $93,880. The median annual earnings for the industries employing the largest numbers of Aerospace Engineers in 1997 were:

Aircraft and parts	$72,200
Federal government	$70,000
Guided missiles, space vehicles, and parts	$58,200

According to the National Association of Colleges and Employers' 1999 salary survey, bachelor's degree candidates in aerospace engineering received starting offers of $40,700 per year on average. Candidates with master's degrees received offers that averaged $54,200 and Ph.D. candidates were getting offers that averaged $64,400 to start.

Civilian Employment Prospects

Aerospace Engineers held some 53,000 jobs in 1998. Nearly half worked in aircraft and parts, and guided missile and space vehicle manufacturing industries. One out of every seven jobs was provided by such federal government agencies as the Department of Defense and the National Aeronautics and Space Administration. Most of the remaining jobs were accounted for by business services, engineering and architectural services, electrical and electronics manufacturing, research and development services, and testing facilities. California, Washington, Texas, and Florida are home to the largest concentrations of aerospace firms and, consequently, employ the most Aerospace Engineers. The remainder worked as consultants or as educators.

In coming years, the number of graduates in the field of aerospace engineering is expected to exceed the number of available positions, creating serious competition for openings. Aerospace engineering opportunities are expected to grow more slowly than the average for other occupations through 2008, mostly due to the mergers and consolidations of defense companies necessary to cope with the decline in defense spending. The federal government is also spending less on research and development of new systems.

There is a projected increase in the civilian sector as airlines move to replace aging fleets with quieter, more fuel-efficient aircraft. However, the bulk of new openings are expected to be those necessary to fill positions vacated by engineers leaving the labor force or transferring to other industries.

Civilian Advancement Prospects

With the job market tightening for Aerospace Engineers, opportunities for advancement will be fewer and the competition will be strong. Engineers tend to rise up the same type of ladder, beginning with a position as a staff engineer and working on a team. After sufficient experience, the engineer is placed in charge of projects, with a staff of newer engineers to supervise. Finally, the engineer begins a consulting practice, hiring on to advise and assist on specific projects that require someone with his/her expertise.

Education and Training

Aerospace engineering is a profession that requires specific skills. Students can begin to prepare while still in high school by enrolling in certain courses to prepare them for acceptance into engineering programs at a college or university. At the high school level, the emphasis is on mathematics. Two years of algebra are generally required, as are courses in geometry and trigonometry. Calculus is strongly recommended.

High school students should also take one year each of chemistry and physics, including laboratory work in both courses, and four years of English.

Aerospace engineering is a math and science intensive profession requiring a minimum of four years college education in an accredited engineering college and a commitment to lifelong learning. However, the more education an engineer has undergone, the better chance that engineer has of securing a good position in this fast-moving field, where up-to-date knowledge and skills are the currency of advancement.

Experience, Special Skills, and Personality Traits

Aerospace Engineers can be most easily described as pragmatic dreamers, grounded in reality but always reaching for the sky and beyond. They cannot resist the challenge of learning how things work and, in many instances, trying to find ways to improve them. They are math- and science-oriented with good imaginations, an artistic bent, and a willingness to put in as much time as it takes to solve a problem. They are also committed to a lifetime of learning as the field is a dynamic, constantly evolving discipline that requires its practitioners to remain current. Computer skills are a must. Business management skills will be required for those seeking to advance to supervisory positions.

Unions and Associations

Aerospace Engineers have a number of professional organizations with which they can become associated. The American Institute of Aeronautics and Astronautics is a national professional society with over 34,000 members serving the aerospace engineering community. The American Astronautical Society is the premier independent scientific and technical group exclusively dedicated to the advancement of space science and exploration in the United States. The American Society of Mechanical Engineers, the National Academy of Engineering, the Society of Women Engineers, and the National Institute of Standards and Technology are some additional examples.

CHEMICAL LABORATORY TECHNICIAN

CAREER PROFILE

Duties: Obtain petroleum test samples; test fuels and oils for water, sediment, and other contaminants; analyze chemicals; perform chemical and physical tests on clothing, food, paints, and plastics; keep detailed laboratory records and files

Alternate Title(s): Science Technician; Biological Technician; Chemical Technician; Environmental Science and Protection Technician; Forensic Science Technician; Forest and Conservation Technician; Nuclear Technician

Availability: Army, Navy, Coast Guard

Military Salary: See How to Use This Book

Civilian Salary: $17,483 to $53,143

Civilian Employment Prospects: Good

Civilian Advancement Prospects: Good

Prerequisites:

Rank—Enlisted

Education and Training—Minimum associate's degree; bachelor's degree may be required.

Experience—Any training and work experience obtained in the armed services

Special Skills and Personality Traits—Strong computer skills; communication skills; the ability to work well with others; organizational ability; an eye for detail; skill in interpreting scientific results; normal color vision; an interest in performing technical work and in working with chemicals and lab equipment; the ability to follow detailed procedures

CAREER LADDER

```
┌─────────────────────────────┐
│         Supervisor          │
└─────────────────────────────┘

┌─────────────────────────────┐
│          Trainee            │
└─────────────────────────────┘
```

Position Description

To be safely used in any type of aircraft or vehicles, fuels and oils of any kind must be free of water and other contaminants. The same is true for all the other chemicals and materials used by the military. To this end, Chemical Laboratory Technicians test fuels, oils, chemicals, and other materials for quality, purity, and durability.

Working in laboratories on military bases and aboard ships, laboratory technicians obtain petroleum test samples from storage tanks, barges, and tankers, test fuels and oils for water, sediment, and other contaminants using laboratory equipment, and analyze chemicals for strength, purity,

and toxic qualities. They also perform chemical and physical tests on clothing, food, paints, and plastics and keep detailed laboratory records and files.

In the civilian world, Chemical Laboratory Technicians work for petroleum refineries, chemical companies, manufacturing firms, and government agencies. Some specialize in particular industries, such as petroleum, food processing, or medical drugs.

Science technicians use science and mathematics principles and theories to solve research and development problems as well as to invent and improve products and processes. They set up, operate, and maintain laboratory instruments, monitor experiments, make observations, calculate and record results, and develop conclusions. They must keep detailed logs of all their work-related activities. Those who work in production monitor manufacturing processes and may be involved in ensuring quality by testing products for proper proportions of ingredients, purity, or for strength and durability.

Biological technicians work with biologists studying living organisms. Many assist scientists who conduct medical research or who help develop and manufacture medicinal and pharmaceutical preparations. They also analyze organic substances, such as blood, food, and drugs, and even examine evidence in criminal investigations.

Chemical technicians work with chemists and chemical engineers, developing and using chemicals and related products and equipment. Most do research and development, testing, or other laboratory work. Some, however, collect and analyze samples of air and water to monitor pollution levels. Those within chemical plants (referred to as process technicians) operate equipment, monitor plant processes, and analyze plant materials.

Environmental science and protection technicians perform laboratory and field tests to monitor environmental resources and determine the contaminants and sources of pollution. Some are responsible for waste management operations, control and management of hazardous materials inventory, or general activities involving regulatory compliance. Forensic science technicians investigate crimes by collecting and analyzing physical evidence. They perform tests on weapons or substances to determine their significance to an investigation. They also prepare reports to document their findings and the laboratory techniques used.

Forest and conservation technicians compile data on the size, content, and condition of forest land tracts. They travel through sections of forest to gather basic information. Geological and petroleum technicians measure and record physical and geologic conditions in oil or gas wells, using instruments lowered into wells or by analysis of the mud from wells. Nuclear technicians operate nuclear test and research equipment, monitor radiation, and assist nuclear engineers and physicists in research. Other science technicians collect weather information or assist oceanographers.

Most science technicians work regular hours, indoors, usually in laboratories. Production technicians usually work in eight-hour shifts around the clock. Agricultural, forest and conservation, geological and petroleum, and environmental science and protection technicians, perform much of their work outdoors, sometimes in remote locations.

Some workers in these occupations may be exposed to hazards from equipment, chemicals, toxic materials or chemicals, radioactive isotopes or radiation, disease-causing organisms, or even human body fluids and firearms. These working conditions tend to pose little risk, however, if proper safety procedures are followed.

Civilian Salaries

In 2001, science technicians working for the federal government started at $17,483, $19,453, or $22,251, depending on education and experience. The average yearly salary for biological science technicians in nonsupervisory, supervisory, and managerial positions was $32,753; for physical science technicians, $42,657; for geodetic technicians, $53,143; for hydrologic technicians, $39,518; and for meteorologic technicians, $48,630.

In 2001, science technicians working outside the federal government started at the following hourly rates:

Nuclear technicians	$28.44
Forensic science technicians	$18.04
Geological and petroleum technicians	$17.55
Chemical technicians	$17.05
Environmental science and protection technicians (including health)	$16.26
Biological technicians	$15.16
Forest and conservation technicians	$14.22
Agricultural and food science technicians	$13.02

Civilian Employment Prospects

In 2000, science technicians held nearly 198,000 jobs. Chemical technicians, concentrated in chemical manufacturing, held over 30,000 jobs. Nearly 45 percent of biological technicians worked in research and testing firms. Most of the rest of biological technicians worked in drug manufacturing or for federal, state, or local governments as did many environmental science and protection technicians. Others worked for engineering and architectural services, management and public relations firms, food processing companies, nonveterinary animal services, oil and gas extraction companies, and for federal, state, and local government agencies.

Through 2010, opportunities for science technicians are expected to increase about as fast as the average for all occupations. There is a continuing growth in the fields of scientific and medical research, technical products' development and production, and quality assurance that will stimulate the demand for these workers, as well as the demand for more intense regulation of waste products, environmental protection, and responsible land management. Also foreseen at this time is a need for more biotechnology research as it becomes increasingly important to balance greater agricultural output with protection and preservation of soil, water, and the ecosystem.

Opportunities look best for qualified graduates of science technician training programs or applied science technology programs who are well-trained on equipment used in industrial and government laboratories and production facilities. As the instrumentation and techniques used in industrial research, development, and production become increasingly more complex, employers are seeking well-trained individuals with highly developed technical and communication skills.

Civilian Advancement Prospects

Science technicians usually begin work as trainees in routine positions. As they gain experience, technicians take on more responsibility and carry out assignments under only general supervision, and some eventually become supervisors.

Education and Training

In the military, those interested in this career receive two weeks to three months of classroom instruction, depending on specialty, including practice in testing different products. Classes usually contain such course as testing methods, the use of lab equipment, such as centrifuges and spectrometers and physical and chemical properties of fuel, oils, and other products. Further training occurs on the job and through advanced courses. The army and the navy offer certified apprenticeship programs for one specialty in this occupation.

Many employers prefer applicants with at least two years of specialized training or an associate degree in applied science or science-related technology. Many technical and community colleges offer associate degrees in specific technologies as well as general education in science and mathematics. About 20 colleges or universities offer bachelor's degree programs in forensic technology, often with an emphasis in a specialty area. In contrast to some other science technician positions that require only a two-year degree, a four-year degree in forensics science is usually necessary to work in the field.

Those interested in careers as science technicians should take as many high school science and math courses as possible. Science courses taken beyond high school should be laboratory-oriented, with an emphasis on bench skills.

Experience, Special Skills, and Personality Traits

Technicians should have strong computer skills because computer equipment is often used in research and development laboratories. Communication skills are also important, as are the ability to work well with others, organizational ability, an eye for detail, and skill in interpreting scientific results. Also required are normal color vision, an interest in performing technical work and in working with chemicals and lab equipment, and the ability to accurately follow detailed procedures.

Unions and Associations

For information about a career as a chemical technician, contact the American Chemical Society. For career information and a list of undergraduate, graduate, and doctoral programs in forensics sciences, contact the American Academy of Forensic Sciences. For information on forestry technicians and lists of schools offering education in forestry, contact the Society of American Foresters.

CHEMIST

CAREER PROFILE

Duties: Conduct experiments to establish strength and durability standards for materials; test materials to identify defects; conduct chemical research for military and medical uses; oversee research projects, prepare technical reports, and make research recommendations

Alternate Title(s): R&D Chemist; Materials Scientist; Analytical Chemist; Organic Chemist

Availability: Army, Navy, Air Force, and Marine Corps

Military Salary: See How to Use This Book

Civilian Salary: $29,620 to $88,030

Civilian Employment Prospects: Good

Civilian Advancement Prospects: Good

Prerequisites:
  Rank—Officer
  Education and Training—A four-year degree in chemistry, chemical engineering, or biology
  Experience—Any training and work experience obtained in the armed services or in academic laboratories through internships, fellowships, or coop programs in industry
  Special Skills and Personality Traits—An interest in building scientific apparatus and performing laboratory experiments and computer modeling; perseverance and curiosity; the ability to concentrate on details and work independently; an interest in working with mathematical formulas and in general scientific study and research

CAREER LADDER

```
┌─────────────────────────────┐
│       Senior Chemist        │
└─────────────────────────────┘

┌─────────────────────────────┐
│      Assistant Chemist      │
└─────────────────────────────┘
```

Position Description

The fields of chemistry and biochemistry are both used by the modern military to develop new materials for equipment, better medicines, and defenses against biological and chemical agents. Chemists conduct and manage research in chemical synthesis, structure, and interactions. They establish strength and durability standards for materials used to build aircraft, ships, and other equipment. They test materials to identify defects and determine if they meet minimum military standards; conduct chemical research for military and medical uses, such as protecting people from radiation, chemicals, and biological agents; oversee research projects under contract to universities and

industrial firms; and prepare technical reports and make research recommendations.

In the civilian world, Chemists work in research and development for private industry. They also work for government agencies, colleges and universities, specializing in areas such as organic chemistry, inorganic chemistry, physical chemistry, or biochemistry. Whatever their specialty, however, Chemists and materials scientists search for and use new knowledge about chemicals. Chemical research has discovered and developed new and improved synthetic fibers, paints, adhesives, drugs, cosmetics, electronic components, lubricants, and much more. Chemists and materials scientists have developed processes that save energy and reduce pollution and have spurred advances in medicine, agriculture, food processing, and other fields.

R&D (research and development) Chemists and materials scientists investigate the properties, composition, and structure of matter, as well as the laws that govern the combination of elements, and reactions of substances. They create new products and processes, or improve existing ones, often using knowledge gained from basic research. They use computers and a wide variety of sophisticated laboratory instrumentation for modeling and simulation in their work.

Chemists also work in production and quality control in chemical manufacturing plants. They prepare instructions for plant workers, monitor automated processes to ensure proper product yield, and test samples of raw materials or finished products to ensure that they meet industry and government standards. Chemists report and document test results and analyze those results in hopes of further improving existing theories or developing new test methods.

Analytical Chemists determine the structure, composition, and nature of substances by examining and identifying the various elements or compounds that make up a substance. They study the relations and interactions of the parts of compounds and develop analytical techniques. They also identify the presence and concentration of chemical pollutants in air, water, and soil.

Organic Chemists study the chemistry of the vast number of carbon compounds that make up all living things. Inorganic Chemists study compounds consisting mainly of elements other than carbon, such as those in electronic components. Physical and theoretical Chemists study the physical characteristics of atoms and molecules and the theoretical properties of matter, and investigate how chemical reactions work. Medicinal Chemists study the structural properties of compounds intended for applications to human medicine. Materials Chemists study and develop new materials to improve existing products or make new ones.

Chemists work in laboratories and offices. Although they observe strict safety precautions, they may be exposed to hazardous substances.

Salaries After Military Service

In 2000, the average yearly salary for Chemists was $50,080. The middle 50 percent earned between $37,480 and $68,240. The lowest 10 percent earned less than $29,620 and the highest 10 percent earned more than $88,030. In 2000, the average yearly salaries in the industries employing the largest numbers of Chemists were:

Federal government	$65,950
Drugs	$50,820
Research and testing services	$41,820

Civilian Employment Prospects

In 2000, Chemists and materials scientists held roughly 92,000 jobs. Over half of all Chemists are employed in manufacturing firms. Chemists also work for state and local governments and for federal agencies such as the U.S. Department of Health and Human Services, which is the major federal employer of Chemists. Other Chemists work for research, development, and testing services. Those with only a background in Chemistry can still hold teaching positions in high schools, colleges, and universities.

Job opportunities will be concentrated in pharmaceutical companies and in research and testing services firms in all parts of the country (but mainly concentrated in large industrial areas). Strong demand will exist for those with a master's or Ph.D.

Through 2010, employment of Chemists is expected to grow about as fast as the average for all occupations. Job growth will be strongest in drug manufacturing and in research, development, and testing services firms. With the demand for new and better pharmaceuticals and personal care products at an all time high, chemical firms are expected to continue to devote money to research and development, spurring employment growth.

Job opportunities are expected to be most plentiful in pharmaceutical and biotechnology firms. Strong competition among drug companies and an aging population are contributing to the need for innovative and improved drugs. Also, there is an increased demand for different and improved grooming products such as vegetable-based products, products with milder formulas, treatments for aging skin, and products that have been developed using more benign chemical processes. All this will increase the need for Chemists, as will growth in the field of environmental research.

Civilian Advancement Prospects

Innovators and those whose teams make the kinds of discoveries employers seek will find themselves rapidly elevated to senior positions within research and development areas. Chemists who hold a Ph.D. and have previous industrial experience may be particularly attractive to employers because such people are more likely to understand the complex regulations that apply to the pharmaceutical industry.

Education and Training

A four-year degree in chemistry, chemical engineering, biology, or a related discipline is the minimum educational requirement. Many research jobs, however, require a Ph.D. Many colleges and universities offer a bachelor's degree program in chemistry. In addition to required courses in analytical, inorganic, organic, and physical chemistry, undergraduate chemistry majors usually study biological sciences, mathematics, and physics. Those interested in the environmental field should also take courses in environmental studies and become familiar with current legislation and regulations. Computer courses have become essential as combinatorial chemistry techniques have grown to be more widely applied. Scientists with outdated skills or who are unfamiliar with combinatorial chemistry are often retrained by companies in-house.

Beginning Chemists generally perform analytical testing or assist senior Chemists in research and development laboratories. Many employers prefer Chemists with a Ph.D. or at least a master's to lead basic and applied research. Relevant work experience is an asset. Chemists who hold a Ph.D. and have previous industrial experience may be particularly attractive to employers because such people are more likely to understand the complex regulations that apply to the pharmaceutical industry. Within materials science, a broad background in various sciences is preferred. This broad base may be obtained through degrees in physics, engineering, or chemistry. While many companies prefer hiring Ph.D.'s, many materials scientists have bachelor's and master's degrees.

Experience, Special Skills, and Personality Traits

Courses in science and mathematics are a plus. Candidates should like working with their hands building scientific apparatus and performing laboratory experiments and computer modeling. Perseverance, curiosity, and the ability to concentrate on detail and to work independently are essential. As are an interest in working with mathematical formulas and in general scientific study and research.

Since Chemists and materials scientists are often expected to work on teams, understanding of other disciplines, leadership ability, and good oral and written communication skills have become highly desirable. Some employers prefer to hire individuals with several years of postdoctoral experience for this reason. Most employers provide new graduates additional training or education.

Unions and Associations

Information on career opportunities for Chemists is available from the American Chemical Society, Education Division. Information on obtaining a position as a Chemist with the Federal Government is available from the Office of Personnel Management on the OPM Internet site: http://www.usajobs.opm.gov.

For general information on materials science, contact the Materials Research Society.

CIVIL ENGINEER

CAREER PROFILE

Duties: Design and supervision of a wide variety of construction projects including buildings, transportation infrastructure, water and sewage systems, and other public works and facilities

Alternate Title(s): Structural Engineer; Environmental Engineer

Availability: All branches

Military Salary: See How to Use This Book

Civilian Salary: $30,000 to $100,000

Civilian Employment Prospects: Better than average

Civilian Advancement Prospects: Good

Prerequisites:
  Rank—Officer
  Education and Training—Four-year degree in civil engineering plus on-the-job training
  Experience—Field experience as a staffer; one year working with a senior engineer to meet licensing requirement
  Special Skills and Personality Traits—Focused, detail-oriented, and analytical; enjoys challenges; motivated to serve the community; good interpersonal skills
  Licensure/Certification—State license required

CAREER LADDER

```
┌─────────────────────────────┐
│   Civil Engineer, Supervisor │
│        or Consultant        │
└─────────────────────────────┘

┌─────────────────────────────┐
│  Civil Engineer, Project Designer │
└─────────────────────────────┘

┌─────────────────────────────┐
│            Staffer          │
└─────────────────────────────┘
```

Position Description

As members of the oldest engineering discipline, with roots stretching back to the ancient world, Civil Engineers have been responsible for such wonders as the Great Pyramid at Giza and the aqueducts of Rome. Today's Civil Engineers design and supervise the construction of roads, bridges and highways, water treatment and sewage systems, space satellites and launching facilities, irrigation projects, dams, airports, tunnels, offshore oil rigs, monuments, and buildings of all kinds.

Many Civil Engineers pursue a particular specialty such as structural, environmental, construction, transportation, water resources, or geotechnical engineering. Present focus on environmental issues has made environmental engineering an increasingly popular choice and some schools have elevated this discipline to a status equal to civil engineering. Environmental engineers are concerned with inspecting, analyzing and designing ways of minimizing the environmental impact of various engineering and construction projects, including noise impact and air quality issues.

Structural engineers are known as the "police" of the construction industry, as it is their job to ensure that a project is being built according to the relevant local and federal building and safety standards. Transportation engineers design and supervise the construction of roads, bridges, and tunnels or may further specialize in traffic engineering, designing and implementing signaling systems that facilitate traffic flow and safety. Water resources engineers specialize in water and sewage treatment systems and facilities. Geotechnical engineers work in the fields of earth, environmental, offshore site, and marine science, specifically dealing with the effect the physical environment will have on a construction project.

Civil Engineers must obtain professional engineer licenses. Although they generally work near major commercial and industrial centers, their work can take them to remote areas and foreign lands. Many Civil Engineers hold supervisory or administrative positions from supervisor of a construction site to city engineer. Others work in design, research, construction, or teaching.

Civil Engineers who concentrate their talents on the design side of the equation are leading users of leading edge technology. They generally work in offices, spending their days at computer terminals working with CAD (computer aided design) applications. Engineers who focus on the construction aspect spend the majority of their time in the field, supervising projects.

On average, Civil Engineers work an eight-hour day but extra hours are not uncommon. They are often called in when disasters strike; emergency flood relief projects keep Civil Engineers working seven days a week. At the beginning of their careers, Civil Engineers can earn up to $35,000 or $40,000 a year if they do not mind relocating frequently. (Engineers in the water or sewer treatment field who are adept at designing treatment systems command the highest salaries in the field.) There are more lucrative segments in engineering, but Civil Engineers choose the field because of the vast challenges it affords; following projects from start to finish provides a high level of satisfaction and a tangible result for their efforts. Service to the community is the core tenet of Civil Engineering and as such it tends to attract people who want to make a significant contribution to the betterment of their world and who enjoy the satisfaction of meeting tough challenges.

Civilian Salaries
Civil Engineers averaged approximately $53,000 in 1998. The full range ran from under $34,000 for the lowest 10 percent to more than $87,000 for the top 10 percent. Median annual salaries for industries that employ the largest numbers of Civil Engineers in 1997 were:

Federal government	$64,000
Heavy construction, except highway	$61,300
Local government, except education and hospitals	$52,100
Engineering and architectural services	$49,300
State government, except education and hospitals	$48,900

In 1999, the National Association of Colleges and Employers conducted a salary survey. Their results showed that bachelor's degree candidates in civil engineering received starting offers averaging about $36,100 a year; master's degree candidates in civil engineering, $42,300; and Ph.D. candidates in civil engineering, $58,600.

Civilian Employment Prospects
The prospects for the employment of Civil Engineers are positive. Through 2008, the increase in Civil Engineer employment is expected to outperform the average for all occupations. In response to general population growth and a robust economy, there will be an expanding need for Civil Engineers to design and construct large buildings and complexes, water supply and pollution control systems, and higher capacity transportation systems; and to repair or replace the existing roads, bridges, and other public structures.

In addition to the expected job growth, more engineers will be needed to replace those who transfer to other occupations or leave the labor force.

As of 1998, there were nearly 200,000 Civil Engineers in the United States. Between 30 percent and 40 percent are government employees, working as municipal employees for the federal, state, or local governments. The rest work in construction, public utilities, transportation, and manufacturing. Nearly half work for engineering consulting services, primarily developing designs for new construction products. Approximately 6 percent are self-employed, most often as consultants. Approximately 95 percent of Civil Engineers are male, but female engineers are making inroads and their numbers are expected to rise significantly in the coming decade.

Since many Civil Engineers are employed by firms that provide design and support services for construction projects, employment opportunities will vary by geographic area and will be affected by economic conditions such as slowdowns, which can often curtail new construction.

Civilian Advancement Prospects
In their first year on the job, Civil Engineers complete their licensing exams and work for senior engineers. For example, a field position as a staffer for a resident engineer at a highway company can provide valuable experience in civil engineering, especially for those who are interested in becoming designers. Work availability varies by region and fluctuates with the economy—good times see more projects. After about five years, many Civil Engineers design or direct projects of their own. After 10 to 15 years, many Civil Engineers go into private consulting.

Education and Training
A four-year degree in civil engineering is necessary. Additional education can enhance skills or facilitate specialization. Once on the job, Civil Engineers work toward fulfilling their licensing requirements and completing their exams. Many fine universities offer degree programs in civil engineering.

Special Requirements
State license required. Candidates must have appropriate experience in the field working with senior engineers and pass all exams.

Experience, Special Skills, and Personality Traits

Engineers should be, by nature, analytical, detail-oriented, and highly focused and motivated individuals. Problem-solving skills are indispensable. For supervisory positions, good people skills and a talent for motivation are helpful. The financial rewards are not large enough to make this a field that will ensure the accumulation of wealth. It is primarily for individuals who seek a high degree of personal satisfaction in meeting challenges, following difficult projects through to completion and receiving some tangible evidence of the importance of their efforts.

Unions and Associations

A number of professional organizations exist for Civil Engineers. The National Society of Professional Engineers, The American Society of Civil Engineers and the International Association for Bridge and Structural Engineers are some examples. All offer opportunities for networking, education, and professional advancement.

COMPUTER PROGRAMMER

CAREER PROFILE

Duties: Organize and arrange computer programs into logical steps; determine and analyze computer systems requirements; code programs into languages that computers can read; design, test, and debug computer programs; review and update old programs as new information is received or changes are needed

Alternate Title(s): Computer Systems Analysts

Availability: Air Force, Marine Corps, Navy, Coast Guard

Military Salary: See How to Use This Book

Civilian Salary: $57,590

Civilian Employment Prospects: Good

Civilian Advancement Prospects: Good

Prerequisites:
  Rank—Enlisted
  Education and Training—Math, business administration, and computer science courses
  Experience—Any training and work experience obtained in the armed services or Job Corps
  Special Skills and Personality Traits—The ability to understand math concepts; an interest in computers; an interest in solving problems using rules of logic; patience; persistence; the ability to focus on exacting analytical work, especially under pressure; ingenuity; imagination
  Licensure/Certification—Optional certification; may be required to work on some systems

CAREER LADDER

```
┌─────────────────────────────────┐
│            Manager              │
└─────────────────────────────────┘

┌─────────────────────────────────┐
│    Lead Computer Programmer     │
└─────────────────────────────────┘

┌─────────────────────────────────┐
│       Computer Programmer       │
└─────────────────────────────────┘
```

Position Description

The modern military uses as much, if not more, data processing equipment as any organization in the world. Communications, personnel, finance, and supply information is needed for planning and management. Computer Programmers plan and prepare programs that command computers to solve problems and organize data.

Working aboard ships, in missile facilities, or in space command centers, military programmers organize and arrange computer programs into logical steps, which direct computers to solve problems. They determine and analyze computer systems requirements, code programs into languages that computers can read, such as COBOL and FOR-

TRAN, design, test, and debug computer programs and also review and update old programs as new information is received or changes are needed.

In the civilian world, Computer Programmers work for manufacturing firms, banks, data processing organizations, government agencies, and private corporations. These employers handle large amounts of information that programmers organize for convenient use.

Programmers write, test, and maintain the programs their computers must follow to perform their functions. They also conceive, design, and test logical structures for solving problems by computer. Programs vary widely depending upon the type of information to be accessed or generated.

Although simple programs can be written in a few hours, there are many complex needs for which a year or more of work may be called for to complete a single program.

Programmers write programs according to the specifications determined primarily by computer software engineers and system analysts. After the design process is complete, it is the job of the Programmer to convert that design into a logical series of instructions the computer can follow. They then code these instructions in a conventional programming language, such as COBOL, Prolog, Java, C++, or Smalltalk. Different programming languages are used depending on the purpose of the program.

Many programmers update, repair, modify, and expand existing programs. Programmers test a program by running it to ensure the instructions are correct and it produces the desired information. If errors do occur, the programmer must make the appropriate change and recheck the program until it produces the correct results. Programmers often are grouped into two broad types—applications programmers and systems programmers. Applications programmers write programs to handle specific jobs. Systems programmers write programs to maintain and control computer systems software.

Programmers generally work in offices in comfortable surroundings. Many programmers may work long hours or weekends. Such conditions leave programmers susceptible to eyestrain, back discomfort, and hand and wrist problems such as carpal tunnel syndrome.

Civilian Salaries

In 2000, the average yearly salary for Computer Programmers was $57,590. The middle 50 percent earned between $44,850 and $74,500 a year. The lowest 10 percent earned less than $35,020, The highest 10 percent earned more than $93,210. In 2000, the average yearly salaries in the industries employing the largest numbers of Computer Programmers were:

Personnel supply services	$65,780
Professional and commercial equipment	$63,780
Computer and data processing services	$61,010
Commercial banks	$60,180
Management and public relations	$57,120

The National Association of Colleges and Employers reports that in 2001 starting salary offers for graduates with a bachelor's degree in computer programming averaged $48,602 a year.

Robert Half International reports that in 2001 starting salaries for applications development programmers/developers ranged from $58,500 to $90,000, for software development programmers/analysts from $54,000 to $77,750 and for Internet programmers/analysts ranged from $56,500 to $84,000.

Civilian Employment Prospects

In 2000, Computer Programmers held close to 600,000 jobs. Programmers are employed in nearly every industry, with the largest concentration in the computer and data processing services industry. Programmers also work for firms that provide engineering and management services, telecommunications companies, manufacturers of computer and office equipment, financial institutions, insurance carriers, educational institutions, and government agencies.

Employment growth will be considerably slower than that of other computer specialists, due to the spread of prepackaged software solutions. Three out of five Computer Programmers held at least a bachelor's degree in 2000.

Prospects are best for college graduates with knowledge of a variety of programming languages and tools.

Many programmers are employed on a temporary or contract basis or work as independent consultants. Rather than hiring programmers as permanent employees, employers contract with temporary help agencies, consulting firms, or directly with programmers themselves, hiring programmers only for the time it takes to complete a particular job. Such jobs may last anywhere from several weeks to a year or longer. In 2000 there were 22,000 self-employed Computer Programmers.

Through 2010 employment of programmers is expected to grow about as fast as the average for all occupations. Jobs for both systems and applications programmers should be most plentiful in data processing service firms, software houses, and computer consulting businesses. As organizations attempt to control costs and keep up with changing technology, they will need programmers to assist in conversions to new computer languages and systems.

Employment of programmers, however, is expected to grow much slower than that of other computer specialists. With the rapid gains in technology, sophisticated computer software now has the capability to write basic code, eliminating the need for more programmers to do this routine work. Employers will continue to need programmers who have strong technical skills, however, and who understand an employer's business and its programming needs. This means programmers will need to keep up with changing programming languages and techniques. Companies will be looking for programmers who can support data communications and help implement electronic commerce and intranet strategies. Demand for programmers with strong object-oriented programming capabilities and technical specialization in areas such as client/server programming, multimedia technology, and graphic user interface should arise from the expansion of intranets, extranets, and Internet applications. Programmers also will be needed to create and maintain expert systems and embed these technologies in more and more products.

As programming tasks become increasingly sophisticated employers will demand an additional level of skill and experience, and prospects will be best for college graduates with knowledge of, and experience working with, a variety of programming languages and tools, including C++ and other object-oriented languages like Java. Experience with newer, domain-specific languages that apply to computer networking, data base management, and Internet application development will be useful, as well. Obtaining vendor or language specific certification can also provide a competitive edge.

Civilian Advancement Prospects

For skilled workers who keep up to date with the latest technology, the prospects for advancement are good. In large organizations, programmers may be promoted to lead programmer and be given supervisory responsibilities. Some applications programmers may move into systems programming after they gain experience and take courses in systems software. With general business experience, programmers may become programmer analysts or systems analysts or be promoted to a managerial position. Other programmers, with specialized knowledge and experience with a language or operating system, may work in research and development areas, such as multimedia or Internet technology. As employers increasingly contract out programming jobs, more opportunities to work as consultants should arise for experienced programmers with expertise in a specific area.

Education and Training

Job training consists of two to three months of classroom instruction, including practice in program coding. Courses should include program structuring; coding and debugging; analysis and design of computer systems; preparation of block diagrams, flow charts, and program codes; and FORTRAN, COBOL, and other computer programming languages. Further training occurs on the job and through advanced courses in specific computer systems and languages.

Bachelor's degrees are commonly required, although some programmers may qualify for certain jobs with two-year degrees or certificates. Employers are primarily interested in programming knowledge. College graduates who are interested in changing careers or developing an area of expertise also may return to a two-year community college or technical school for additional training. In the absence of a degree, substantial specialized experience or expertise may be needed. Even with a degree, employers appear to be placing more emphasis on previous experience.

Required skills vary from job to job, but the demand for various skills generally is driven by changes in technology. Employers will sometimes prefer applicants who have general business skills and experience related to the operations of the firm. Students can improve their employment prospects by participating in a college work-study program or by undertaking an internship. Most systems programmers hold a four-year degree in computer science. Programmers must continuously update their training by taking courses sponsored by their employer or software vendors.

Special Requirements

Technical or professional certification is a way to demonstrate a level of competency or quality. In addition to language-specific certificates that a programmer can obtain, product vendors or software firms also offer certification and may require professionals who work with their products to be certified. Voluntary certification also is available through other organizations. Professional certification may provide a job seeker a competitive advantage.

Experience, Special Skills and Personality Traits

School subjects such as math, business administration and computer science are helpful. Employers also look for the ability to understand math concepts, an interest in solving problems using rules of logic, patience, persistence, and the ability to concentrate on exacting analytical work, especially under pressure. Ingenuity and imagination are important, as are the ability to work with abstract concepts and to do technical analysis.

Unions and Associations

For information about certification as a computing professional contact the Institute for Certification of Computing Professionals. Further information about computer careers is available from the Association for Computing Machinery, the IEEE Computer Society, Headquarters Office and the National Workforce Center for Emerging Technologies. These associations also provide valuable opportunities for networking and education.

COMPUTER SYSTEMS SPECIALIST

CAREER PROFILE

Duties: Identify computer user problems and coordinate to resolve them; install, configure, and monitor local and wide area networks, hardware, and software; compile, enter, and process information; provide customer and network administration services

Alternate Title(s): Network Support Technician; Computer Operator; Data Processing Technician

Availability: All branches

Military Salary: See How to Use This Book

Civilian Salary: $17,350 to $43,950

Civilian Employment Prospects: Fair

Civilian Advancement Prospects: Fair

Prerequisites:

Rank—Enlisted

Education and Training—Four-year college degree preferred; on-the-job training

Experience—Any training and work experience obtained in the armed services or Job Corps

Special Skills and Personality Traits—High adaptability; a willingness to learn; analytical thinker; technical expertise; good communication skills; the ability to work independently; an interest in work requiring accuracy and attention to detail; good interpersonal skills

CAREER LADDER

```
┌─────────────────────────────────────┐
│     Supervisor or Programmer         │
└─────────────────────────────────────┘

┌─────────────────────────────────────┐
│   Network or Systems Administrator   │
└─────────────────────────────────────┘

┌─────────────────────────────────────┐
│     Computer Support Specialist      │
└─────────────────────────────────────┘

┌─────────────────────────────────────┐
│        Computer Operator             │
└─────────────────────────────────────┘
```

Position Description

Computers are used to store and process data on personnel, weather, finances, and much more. Every large organization in the world is dependent on computers these days, and the modern military is no exception. Before any information can be processed, however, computer systems must be set up, data entered, and computers operated. Working in offices or at computer sites on military bases or aboard ships, Computer Systems Specialists ensure information is entered, stored, processed, and retrieved in a way that meets the military services' needs. These specialists identify computer user problems and coordinate to resolve them. They also install, configure, and monitor local and wide area networks, hardware, and software; compile, enter, and process information; and provide customer and network administration services, such as passwords, electronic mail accounts, security, and troubleshooting.

In the civilian world, these specialists work for everyone: banks, hospitals, retail firms, manufacturers, government agencies, firms that design and test computer systems, and any other organization with large amounts of data to input, process, and analyze. Wherever they are employed, Computer Systems Specialists ensure that the computer hardware systems under their care are used as efficiently as possible, be they mainframes, minicomputers, or networks of personal computers. Although they are responsible for solving any problems that occur during operations, their main duty is to anticipate problems before they can halt operations and take preventive action.

Computer Systems Specialists' exact duties vary with the size of the installation, the type of equipment under their control, and their employer's specific policies. On the whole operators control the console of either a mainframe digital computer or a group of minicomputers. Working from operating instructions they set controls on the computer and any other devices required to run a particular job. Computer operators load equipment with tapes, disks, and paper, as needed. They must monitor their control console and respond to operating and computer messages. They must make quick, intelligent decisions to locate and correct the problem indicated, or to stop the program in error before the mistake costs the company too greatly. Operators also must list each job that is run in a record book or log, as well as all occurrences on their shift, such as machine malfunctions. On occasion operators will help programmers and systems analysts test and debug new programs.

It should be noted that as technology advances, the responsibilities of many Computer Systems Specialists are shifting to areas such as network operations, user support, and database maintenance. Automation, in the form of sophisticated software coupled with robotics, is constantly allowing computers to take over more and more of the routine tasks once performed by computer operators. Those with limited skills will find themselves left behind in the future.

Computer operators generally work in well-lighted, air-conditioned areas. Since many large computer systems are operated 24 hours a day, evening, night, and weekend shifts are common. Computer operators must spend a great deal of time in front of computer monitors, as well as performing repetitive tasks such as loading and unloading printers. Because of these factors, their positions are highly susceptible to eyestrain, back discomfort, and hand and wrist problems.

Civilian Salaries

In 2000, the average yearly salary for Computer Systems Specialists was $27,670. The middle 50 percent earned between about $21,280 and $35,320 a year. The highest 10 percent earned more than $43,950. The lowest 10 percent earned less than $17,350.

In 2000, the average yearly salaries for Computer Systems Specialists in the industries employing them in the largest numbers were:

Computer and data processing services	$28,530
Hospitals	$26,550
Commercial banks	$22,840
Personnel supply services	$22,130
Miscellaneous business services	$21,980

In 2001, the average yearly salary for computer operators employed by the federal government was $37,574. According to Robert Half International, in 2001 the average starting salaries for operators ranged from $28,250 to $40,500.

Median annual earnings of computer support specialists were $36,460 in 2000. The middle 50 percent earned between $27,680 and $48,440.

Median annual earnings of network and computer systems administrators were $51,280 in 2000. The middle 50 percent earned between $40,450 and $65,140.

Employment Prospects After Military Service

In 2000, Computer Systems Specialists held just under 195,000 jobs. Most were in wholesale trade establishments, manufacturing companies, business services firms, financial institutions, and government agencies. A large number of Computer Systems Specialists were also employed by service firms in the computer and data-processing services industry, a growth field as more companies continue to contract out the operation of their data-processing centers.

Through 2010 opportunities for computer operators are expected to decline sharply. Advances in technology are reducing both the size and cost of computer equipment, while increasing the capacity for data storage and processing automation. Such sophisticated computer hardware and software are now used in practically every industry with the need for massive amounts of data processing. The expanding use of software that automates computer operations gives companies the option of making systems user-friendly, greatly reducing the need for operators. Such improvements require operators to monitor a greater number of operations at the same time and be capable of solving a broader range of problems that may arise. The result is that fewer operators will be needed to perform more highly skilled work. Thus those opportunities that will be available will go to those operators who have superior, formal computer-related education, are familiar with a variety of operating systems, and keep up-to-date with the latest technology.

Those Computer Systems Specialists initially displaced by automation may be reassigned to support staffs that maintain their company's personal computer networks or given the chance to assist other members of the organization. Operators who stay abreast with changing technology by updating their skills and enhancing their training, however, should be able to move into other areas within their organization, such as network administration or technical support. Still others may be retrained to perform different yet related functions. Computer operators coming into the field in the near future will need a far more thorough knowledge of programming, automation software, graphics interface, client/server environments, and open systems to be able to find employment.

Civilian Advancement Prospects

A Computer Systems Specialist's chance to advance to a supervisory job or higher within most of today's data-processing or computer-operations centers are slim if the operator does not have an advanced, formal education, such as a bachelor's or higher degree. With on-the-job experience and additional formal education, some operators will be able to advance to areas such as network operations or support. As they gain experience in programming, some may even advance to jobs as programmers or analysts. These type of moves are becoming much more difficult, however, as employers increasingly require candidates for these positions to possess at least a bachelor's degree.

Education and Training

In the military, those interested in this career receive two to three months of classroom instruction, depending on specialty. Classes usually include courses in the use of computer consoles and peripheral equipment; computer systems concepts; and the planning, designing, and testing computer systems.

In the civilian world, computer operators usually receive on-the-job training in order to become acquainted with their employer's equipment and routines. The length of training will, of course, vary with the job and the previous experience of the worker. Previous work experience, such as that gained in the military, is the key to obtaining an operator job in many large establishments. Employers generally look for specific, hands-on experience with the type of equipment and related operating systems that they use. Also, formal computer-related training (obtained possibly through a community college or technical school) is recommended for those who do not obtain it through the armed forces. Certification in specific fields and in the use of certain operating systems and their attendant software packages are available through technical schools that are affiliated with manufacturers and software firms.

Experience, Special Skills, and Personality Traits

Since levels of computer technology changes with an incredible speed, Computer Systems Specialists must be highly adaptable and particularly willing to learn. Analytical and technical expertise are needed, especially by operators working in automated data centers. Operators must also have good communication skills; work effectively with programmers, users, and other operators; be able to work independently; and have an interest in work requiring accuracy and attention to detail.

Unions and Associations

Computer Systems Specialists may join associations groups such as the Association of Computer Support Specialists, Association of Support Professionals, or the System Administrators Guild. Other applicable organizations may include the Association for Computing Machinery, the Data Processing Management Association, or the Association for System Management. Information about work opportunities in computer operations may also be obtained by contacting banks, manufacturing and insurance firms, colleges and universities, data processing service organizations, and other such establishments with large computer centers. The local office of the state employment service can also supply information about employment and training opportunities.

ENVIRONMENTAL HEALTH AND SAFETY OFFICER

CAREER PROFILE

Duties: Determine methods to collect environmental data; analyze data to identify pollution problem areas; inspect food samples; develop pollution control plans and policies; conduct health education programs; work with civilian public health officials

Alternate Title(s): Environmental Scientist; Air Pollution Analyst; Soil Analyst; Industrial Hygienist; Water Quality Analyst; Agricultural Inspector; Construction and Building Inspector; Correctional Officer; Financial Examiner; Fire Inspector; Transportation Inspector; Occupational Health and Safety Inspector; Industrial Hygienist

Availability: All branches

Military Salary: See How to Use This Book

Civilian Salary: $23,780 to $106,040

Civilian Employment Prospects: Good

Civilian Advancement Prospects: Good

Prerequisites:
Rank—Officer
Education and Training—A four-year college degree
Experience—Any training and work experience obtained in the armed services or Job Corps
Special Skills and Personality Traits—Good interpersonal skills; strong oral and written communication skills; a second language; physical stamina; an open mind; the ability to think logically; interest in protecting the environment; enjoy conducting research and analytical studies; accurate and detail-oriented

CAREER LADDER

```
┌─────────────────────────────────────┐
│  Project Leader or Program Manager   │
└─────────────────────────────────────┘

┌─────────────────────────────────────┐
│           Field Researcher           │
└─────────────────────────────────────┘

┌─────────────────────────────────────┐
│         Research Assistant           │
└─────────────────────────────────────┘
```

Position Description

Like all branches of the U.S. government, the modern military labors to ensure safe working conditions and a clean environment. In the military today, Environmental Health and Safety Officers study the air, ground, and water to identify and analyze sources of pollution and its effects. They also direct programs to control safety and health hazards in the workplace.

Working mainly in offices or research laboratories, but moving outdoors while conducting environmental studies and surveys or inspecting facilities, these officers determine methods to collect environmental data for research projects and surveys, analyze data to identify pollution problem areas, and inspect food samples to detect any spoilage or disease. They also develop pollution control plans and policies, conduct health education programs and work with civilian public health officials in performing studies and analyzing results.

In the civilian world, environmental scientists and geoscientists locate water, mineral, and energy resources; protect the environment; predict future geologic hazards; and offer advice on construction and land use projects.

Environmental scientists conduct research to identify and eliminate sources of pollutants that affect people, wildlife, and their environments. Geoscientists study the composition, structure, and other physical aspects of the Earth. Geoscientists are subsequently classified in one of several closely related fields of geoscience: geology, geophysics, and oceanography. Geophysicists use the principles of physics, mathematics, and chemistry to study not only the Earth's surface, but also its internal composition. Oceanographers use their knowledge of geology and geophysics, in addition to biology and chemistry, to study the world's oceans and coastal waters.

Many further subdisciplines fall under the two major disciplines of geology and geophysics that further differentiate the type of work geoscientists do. These include petroleum geologists, engineering geologists, mineralogists, paleontologists, stratigraphers, volcanologists, geodesists, seismologists, geochemists, geomagnetists, paleomagnetists, hydrologists, physical oceanographers, chemical oceanographers, geological and geophysical oceanographers, and biological oceanographers.

Occupational health and safety specialists and technicians help keep workplaces safe and workers unscathed. They analyze work environments and design programs to control, eliminate, and prevent disease or injury caused by chemical, physical, and biological agents or ergonomic factors. They identify hazardous conditions and practices, sometimes developing methods to predict hazards from experience, historical data, and other information sources. They also inspect and test machinery and equipment, check that personal protective equipment is being used in workplaces according to regulations, check that dangerous materials are stored correctly, test and identify work areas for potential accident and health hazards, such as toxic fumes and explosive gas-air mixtures, and may implement appropriate control measures, such as adjustments to ventilation systems.

Occupational health and safety specialists and technicians often do considerable fieldwork, traveling frequently. Many occupational health and safety specialists and technicians work long and often irregular hours.

Civilian Salaries

In 2000, the average yearly salary for environmental scientists was $44,180. The middle 50 percent earned between $34,570 and $58,490. The lowest 10 percent earned less than $28,520. The highest 10 percent earned more than $73,790.

In 2000, the average yearly salary for occupational health and safety specialists and technicians was $42,750. The middle 50 percent earned between $32,060 and $54,880. The lowest 10 percent earned less than $23,780. The highest 10 percent earned over $67,760.

In 2000, the average yearly salary for geoscientists was $56,230. The middle 50 percent earned between $43,320 and $77,180. The lowest 10 percent earned less than $33,910. The highest 10 percent earned more than $106,040.

In 2000, the average yearly salary for hydrologists was $55,410. The middle 50 percent earned between $43,740 and $68,500. The lowest 10 percent earned less than $35,910. The highest 10 percent earned more than $85,260.

Civilian Employment Prospects

In 2000, environmental scientists and geoscientists held roughly 97,000 positions. Environmental scientists accounted for 64,000; geoscientists, 25,000; hydrologists, 8,000. The remainder held faculty positions in colleges and universities.

Through 2010, opportunities for environmental scientists, geoscientists, and hydrologists is expected to grow faster than or as fast as the average for all occupations. Driving this growth will be the continuing need for companies and organizations to comply with environmental laws and regulations, particularly those regarding groundwater contamination and flood control. Issues of water conservation, deteriorating coastal environments, and rising sea levels also will stimulate employment growth of these workers. Hydrologists and environmental scientists also will be needed to conduct research on hazardous waste sites to determine the impact of hazardous pollutants on soil and groundwater so engineers can design remediation systems. The need for environmental scientists and geoscientists who understand both the science and engineering aspects of waste remediation is growing. An expected increase in highway building and other infrastructure projects will be an additional source of jobs for engineering geologists.

In 2000, occupational health and safety specialists and technicians held around 35,000 jobs. The federal government employed 8 percent; state governments: 17 percent; local governments: 19 percent. The remainder was employed in schools, hospitals, management consulting firms, public utilities, and manufacturing firms.

Through 2010, opportunities for occupational health and safety specialists and technicians is expected to grow about as fast as the average for all occupations. This growth will reflect not only industry growth, but also the continuing self-enforcement of government and company regulations and policies.

Civilian Advancement Prospects

Environmental scientists and geoscientists usually start in field positions or as research assistants or technicians. As they gain experience, they may be promoted to project leader, program manager, or another management and research position.

Federal occupational health and safety specialists whose job performance is satisfactory advance through their career ladder to a specified full-performance level. For positions above this level, usually supervisory positions, advancement is competitive and based on agency needs and individual merit.

Education and Training

In the military, no initial job training is provided to officers in this occupation. A four-year college degree is normally required to enter this occupation. While a degree in biomedical or biological science is required to enter some specialties in this occupation, a bachelor's degree in geology or geophysics is adequate for entry-level jobs; better jobs with good advancement potential usually require at least a master's degree (for instance, a Ph.D. degree is required for most research positions in colleges and universities and in government).

Many colleges and universities offer a bachelor's degree in geology; fewer schools offer programs in geophysics, hydrogeology, or other geosciences such as geophysical technology, geophysical engineering, geophysical prospecting, engineering geology, petroleum geology, geohydrology, and geochemistry. Also, several hundred universities award advanced degrees in geology or geophysics.

Those students interested in working in the environmental or regulatory fields should take courses in hydrology, hazardous waste management, environmental legislation, chemistry, fluid mechanics, and geologic logging. An understanding of environmental regulations and government permit issues is also valuable for those planning to work in mining and oil and gas extraction. Hydrologists and environmental scientists should have some knowledge of the potential liabilities associated with some environmental work. Students with some experience with computer modeling, data analysis and integration, digital mapping, remote sensing, and geographic information systems will be the most prepared for the job market. Knowledge of the Global Positioning System is also helpful.

Special Requirements

All occupational health and safety specialists and technicians are trained in the applicable laws or inspection procedures through a combination of classroom instruction and on-the-job training. Certification is available through the Board of Certified Safety Professionals and the American Board of Industrial Hygiene. The BCSP offers the Certified Safety Professional credentials, while the ABIH proffers the Certified Industrial Hygienist credential. Also, the Council on Certification of Health, Environmental, and Safety Technologists awards the Occupational Health and Safety Technologist credentials. Requirements for this credential are less stringent than those for the CSP or CIH. Once education and experience requirements have been met, certification may be obtained through an examination. Continuing education is required for recertification. Although voluntary, many employers encourage certification.

Experience, Special Skills, and Personality Traits

Those wishing to enter the environmental sciences should possess good interpersonal skills, strong oral and written communication skills, a second language, physical stamina, an open mind, and the ability to think logically, as well as an interest in protecting the environment, in conducting research or analytical studies and in work requiring accuracy and attention to detail.

Unions and Associations

For information on training and career opportunities for geologists contact the American Geological Institute, the Geological Society of America, and the American Association of Petroleum Geologists. For information on training and career opportunities for geophysicists contact the American Geophysical Union and the Society of Exploration Geophysicists.

For information on a career as an industrial hygienist and a list of colleges and universities offering programs in industrial hygiene, contact the American Industrial Hygiene Association. For a list of colleges and universities offering safety and related degrees, including correspondence courses, contact the American Society of Safety Engineers. For information on the Certified Safety Professional credential, contact the Board of Certified Safety Professionals. For information on the Certified Industrial Hygiene credential, contact the American Board of Industrial Hygiene. For information on the Occupational Health and Safety Technologist credential, contact the Council on Certification of Health, Environmental, and Safety Technologists.

GEOSCIENTIST

CAREER PROFILE

Duties: Manage personnel who collect geological and oceanographic data; conduct research; direct the preparation of charts, maps, and publications; oversee the preparation of geological surveys and oceanographic and weather forecasts; collect information on ice conditions and ocean currents; advise commanders about terrain and ocean and sea conditions

Alternate Title(s): Environmental Scientist; Oceanographer; Petroleum Geologist; Land and Engineering Geologist; Mineralogist; Paleontologist; Geochemist; Stratigrapher; Volcanologist; Geodesist; Seismologist; Geomagnetist; Paleomagnetist; Hydrologist; Physical Oceanographer; Chemical Oceanographer; Geological and Geophysical Oceanographer; Biological Oceanographer

Availability: Navy, Coast Guard

Military Salary: See How to Use This Book

Civilian Salary: $28,520 to $106,040

Civilian Employment Prospects: Good

Civilian Advancement Prospects: Good

Prerequisites:

Rank—Officer

Education and Training—A bachelor's degree in geology, geophysics, or related field for entry-level jobs; Ph.D. required for most college, university, and government research positions

Experience—Any training and work experience obtained in the armed services or Job Corps

Special Skills and Personality Traits—Excellent interpersonal skills; strong oral and written communication skills; a preference for doing scientific work; computer skills; an interest in being outdoors or in sailing and being at sea; an interest in conducting research or analytical studies; the ability to think logically; an open mind; physical stamina; an understanding of environmental regulations and government permit issues; experience with computer modeling, data analysis and integration, digital mapping, remote sensing, and geographic information systems; knowledge of the Global Positioning System

CAREER LADDER

```
┌─────────────────────────────────────────┐
│  Project Leader or Program Manager        │
└─────────────────────────────────────────┘


┌─────────────────────────────────────────┐
│             Geoscientist                  │
└─────────────────────────────────────────┘
```

Position Description

Geoscientists use sophisticated instruments and analyses of the earth and water to study the Earth's geologic past and present in order to make predictions about its future. Many are involved in the search for oil and gas. Others work closely with environmental scientists in preserving and cleaning up the environment. Geologists and geophysicists examine the chemical and physical properties of specimens. They study fossil remains of animal and plant life or experiment with the flow of water and oil through rocks. Geoscientists working in mining or the oil and gas industry sometimes process and interpret data produced by remote sensing satellites to help identify potential new mineral, oil, or gas deposits. There are numerous specialties within this field.

Oceanographers provide precise navigational charts and maps vital to the modern military's ability to safely travel the oceans and patrol our coastlines. Accurate oceanographic and weather forecasts are needed to plan military operations. Oceanographers study ocean tides, currents, weather, and the physical features of the ocean floor. They also direct personnel who collect oceanographic data, conduct research on the effects of water and atmosphere on military warning and weapon systems, direct the preparation of ocean, sea, and waterway charts, maps, and publications, and oversee the preparation of oceanographic and weather forecasts. They collect information on ice conditions in ocean shipping lanes and about ocean currents for support of military operational planning, and they make recommendations to commanders about ocean and sea conditions to assist in search and rescue missions.

In the civilian world oceanographers usually work as researchers for colleges and universities. Some work for federal government agencies and for state and local governments that border on the ocean. Many Geoscientists work in the petroleum and natural gas industry. Environmental scientists and Geoscientists locate water, mineral, and energy resources; protect the environment; predict future geologic hazards; and offer advice on construction and land use projects.

Environmental scientists analyze and report measurements and observations of air, water, soil, and other sources to make recommendations on how best to clean and preserve the environment. They design and monitor waste disposal sites, preserve water supplies, and reclaim contaminated land and water to comply with federal environmental regulations.

Petroleum geologists explore for oil and gas deposits by studying and mapping the subsurface of the ocean or land or engineering geologists who apply geologic principles to the fields of civil and environmental engineering. Mineralogists analyze and classify minerals and precious stones according to composition and structure and study their environment in order to find new mineral resources. Paleontologists study fossils found in geological formations to trace the evolution of plant and animal life and the geologic history of the Earth. Stratigraphers study the formation and layering of rocks to understand the environment in which they were formed. Volcanologists investigate volcanoes and volcanic phenomena to try to predict the potential for future eruptions and possible hazards to human health and welfare.

Geodesists study the size and shape of the Earth, its gravitational field, tides, polar motion, and rotation. Seismologists interpret data from seismographs and other geophysical instruments to detect earthquakes and locate earthquake-related faults. Geochemists study the nature and distribution of chemical elements in ground water and Earth materials. Geomagnetists measure the Earth's magnetic field and use measurements taken over the past few centuries to devise theoretical models to explain the Earth's origin. Paleomagnetists interpret fossil magnetization in rocks and sediments from the continents and oceans, to record the spreading of the sea floor, the wandering of the continents, and the many reversals of polarity that the Earth's magnetic field has undergone through time. Hydrologists study the quantity, distribution, circulation, and physical properties of underground and surface waters.

Oceanography also is split in subdisciplines. Physical oceanographers study the tides, waves, currents, temperatures, density, and salinity of the oceans. Chemical oceanographers study the distribution of chemical compounds and chemical interactions that occur in the ocean and sea floor. Geological and geophysical oceanographers study the topographic features and the physical makeup of the ocean floor. Biological oceanographers, or marine biologists, study the distribution and migration patterns of the many diverse forms of sea life in the ocean.

Most Geoscientists split their time between fieldwork and office or laboratory work. Geologists often travel to remote field sites and cover large areas on foot. They often work in foreign countries in remote areas under difficult conditions. Oceanographers spend long stretches at sea. Fieldwork often requires working long hours, but is generally compensated by longer than normal vacations.

Civilian Salaries

In 2000, the average yearly salary for Geoscientists was $56,230. The middle 50 percent earned between $43,320 and $77,180. The lowest 10 percent earned less than $33,910. The highest 10 percent earned more than $106,040.

In 2000, the average yearly salary for environmental scientists was $44,180. The middle 50 percent earned between $34,570 and $58,490. The lowest 10 percent earned less than $28,520. The highest 10 percent earned more than $73,790.

In 2000, the average yearly salary for hydrologists was $55,410. The middle 50 percent earned between $43,740 and $68,500. The lowest 10 percent earned less than $35,910. The highest 10 percent earned more than $85,260.

In 2000, the average yearly salary in the industries employing the largest number of Geoscientists and environmental scientists were:

Federal government	$59,590
Engineering and architectural services	$43,920
Management and public relations	$43,900
Local government	$42,880
State government	$39,330

Civilian Employment Prospects

In 2000, environmental scientists and Geoscientists held close to 100,000 jobs. Environmental scientists accounted for 64,000 of the total; Geoscientists, 25,000; Hydrologists, 8,000.

Geoscientists, environmental scientists, and hydrologists were employed in engineering and management services, oil and gas extraction companies, metal mining companies, management and public relations, engineering and architectural services, and for local, state, and the federal government.

Through 2010 employment of environmental scientists and hydrologists is expected to grow faster than the average for all occupations while employment of Geoscientists is expected to grow only as fast as the average. Driving the growth of environmental scientists and Geoscientists will be the continuing need for companies and organizations to comply with environmental laws and regulations. As for Geoscientists, those who speak a foreign language and who are willing to work abroad should enjoy the best opportunities.

The need for companies to comply with environmental laws and regulations is expected to contribute to the demand for environmental scientists and some Geoscientists, especially hydrologists and engineering geologists. Employment of environmental scientists and Geoscientists is more sensitive to changes in governmental energy or environmental policy than employment of other scientists. If environmental regulations are rescinded or loosened, job opportunities will shrink. On the other hand, increased exploration for energy sources will result in improved job opportunities for Geoscientists.

Civilian Advancement Prospects

Environmental scientists and Geoscientists often start as field explorers, research assistants, or technicians. As they gain experience they may be promoted to project leader, program manager, or some other management or research position.

Education and Training

A bachelor's degree in geology or geophysics is adequate for entry-level jobs; better jobs with good advancement potential usually require at least a master's degree. A Ph.D. is required for most research positions in colleges, universities, and in government.

Hundreds of colleges and universities offer a bachelor's degree in geology; some offer programs in geophysics, hydrogeology, or other geosciences. There are also several hundred universities that award advanced degrees in geology or geophysics.

Traditional geoscience courses emphasizing mineralogy, petrology, paleontology, stratigraphy, structural geology, etc., make up the core of the Geoscientist's college training. Those studying physics, chemistry, biology, mathematics, engineering, or computer science may also qualify for some environmental science and geoscience positions if their coursework includes study in geology. Those students interested in working in the environmental or regulatory fields should take courses in hydrology, hazardous waste management, environmental legislation, chemistry, fluid mechanics, and geologic logging.

Experience, Special Skills, and Personality Traits

Environmental scientists need excellent interpersonal skills, strong oral and written communication skills, a preference for doing scientific work, computer skills, an interest in sailing and being at sea and in conducting research or analytical studies, the ability to think logically, an open mind and physical stamina.

An understanding of environmental regulations and government permit issues is valuable as is knowledge of the potential liabilities associated with environmental work; experience with computer modeling, data analysis and integration, digital mapping, remote sensing, and geographic information systems, and knowledge of the Global Positioning System.

Unions and Associations

Information on training and career opportunities for geologists is available from the American Geological Institute, the Geological Society of America and the American Association of Petroleum Geologists.

Information on training and career opportunities for geophysicists is available from the American Geophysical Union and the Society of Exploration Geophysicists.

A packet of free career information, and a list of education and training programs in oceanography and related fields priced at $6.00, is available from the Marine Technology Society.

Information on acquiring a job as a geologist, geophysicist, hydrologist, or oceanographer with the federal government may be obtained from the Office of Personnel Management. Information is also available at: http://www.usajobs.opm.gov.

METEOROLOGIST

CAREER PROFILE

Duties: Direct personnel who collect weather data; observe weather conditions, interpret weather data, and prepare weather forecasts; relay forecast updates and violent weather warnings; train staff in data collection and interpretation

Alternate Title(s): Weather Forecaster; Atmospheric Scientist

Availability: Navy, Air Force, Marine Corps

Military Salary: See How to Use This Book

Civilian Salary: $24,245 to $89,060

Civilian Employment Prospects: Good

Civilian Advancement Prospects: Good

Prerequisites:
    Rank—Officer
    Education and Training—Bachelor's degree in meteorology or a closely related field with courses in meteorology or atmospheric science
    Experience—Any training and work experience obtained in the armed services
    Special Skills and Personality Traits—An interest in scientific work; enjoy collecting and analyzing data; like working with mathematical formulas; well-organized; capable of planning and directing the work of others; computer skills; strong background in mathematics and physics; good communication skills
    Licensure/Certification—Voluntary certification

CAREER LADDER

```
┌─────────────────────────────┐
│       Administrator          │
└─────────────────────────────┘

┌─────────────────────────────┐
│       Meteorologist          │
└─────────────────────────────┘

┌─────────────────────────────┐
│          Trainee             │
└─────────────────────────────┘
```

Position Description

Throughout history, battles have been upset by acts of nature like unexpected rain or snow. Today, military operations such as troop movements, airplane flights, missile launches, and ship movements still have a crucial need for accurate weather information. In the military, Meteorologists study weather conditions and prepare current and long-range weather forecasts. They are responsible for directing personnel who collect weather data, observing weather conditions from airplanes, and interpreting weather data received from satellites and weather balloons. They also prepare short-range and long-range weather forecasts, relay forecast updates and violent weather warnings to military and civilian authorities, and train staff in data collection and interpretation.

Civilian Meteorologists work for government agencies, radio and television stations, and airlines. Working in weather stations or operations centers, they collect, analyze, and plot weather information using computers. Atmospheric scientists do more than just predict the weather, however. They study the atmosphere's physical characteristics, motions, processes, and the way it affects our entire environment. Their research can also be applied in air-pollution control, agriculture, air and sea transportation, global warming, droughts, and ozone depletion.

Atmospheric scientists study information on air pressure, temperature, humidity, and wind velocity. They apply physical and mathematical relationships to make short-term and long-range weather forecasts. They use weather satellites, weather balloons, weather radar, sensors, satellites, and observers spread across the world to collect data. Their forecasts are used by the general public to plan their daily lives, but also by the shipping, air transportation, agriculture, fishing, and utilities industries for both economic and safety reasons.

Physical Meteorologists study the atmosphere's chemical and physical properties—the transmission of light, sound, and radio waves—and the transfer of energy in the atmosphere, as well as factors affecting the formation of clouds, rain, snow, and other weather phenomena, such as severe storms. Synoptic Meteorologists develop new tools for weather forecasting using computers and sophisticated mathematical models. Climatologists collect, analyze, and interpret past records of wind, rainfall, sunshine, and temperature in specific areas or regions. Their studies are used to design buildings, plan heating and cooling systems, and aid in effective land use and agricultural production. Other research Meteorologists examine the most effective ways to control or diminish air pollution.

Weather stations operate every minute of the day, meaning night, weekend, and holiday work, often with rotating shifts. Emergencies such as hurricanes can spark long overtime hours. Operational Meteorologists are also often under pressure to meet forecast deadlines. Though many weather stations are located at airports or near large cities, just as many are located in remote areas. Some Meteorologists collect data from aircraft. Television and radio weather forecasters report from station studios and may work evenings and weekends.

Civilian Salaries

In 2000, the average yearly salary for atmospheric scientists was $58,510. The middle 50 percent earned between $39,780 and $72,740. The lowest 10 percent earned less than $29,880. The highest 10 percent earned more than $89,060.

In 2000, the average salary for Meteorologists employed by the federal government was roughly $68,100. Meteorologists in the federal government with a bachelor's degree, but no experience, received a starting salary of $24,245 to $29,440 depending on their college grades; a master's degree: $29,440 to $36,606; with a Ph.D.: $47,039 or $59,661.

Civilian Employment Prospects

In 2000, atmospheric scientists held just under 7,000 jobs. Through 2010 opportunities for atmospheric scientists is projected to increase about as fast as the average for all occupations. On the one hand, the National Weather Service has no plans to increase the number of weather stations or the number of Meteorologists in existing stations for many years. Employment of Meteorologists in other federal agencies is expected to decline slightly as efforts to reduce the federal government workforce continue.

On the other hand, opportunities for atmospheric scientists in the private sector are expected to be better than in the federal government during the same period. Though the federal government employs close to half of all atmospheric scientists, they are by no means the only employers. Demand is expected to grow for private weather consulting firms to provide more detailed information than has formerly been available, especially to weather-sensitive industries. Farmers, commodity investors, radio and television stations, as well as utilities, transportation, and construction firms have all reported needing weather information more specifically targeted to their needs than the general information provided by the National Weather Service.

There will also continue to be a need for atmospheric scientists to analyze and monitor the dispersion of pollutants into the air to ensure compliance with federal environmental regulations. However, newcomers to the field seeking employment may face competition for jobs if the number of degrees awarded in atmospheric science and meteorology remain near current levels.

Civilian Advancement Prospects

Beginning Meteorologists collect routine data as well as some basic computation, analysis, and forecasting. Within the federal government they are usually placed in intern positions for training and experience. They learn about the Weather Service's forecasting equipment and procedures, rotating to different offices to learn about various weather systems. After training they are assigned a permanent duty station.

Experienced Meteorologists may advance to supervisory or administrative jobs or may handle more complex forecasting jobs. Later, some even establish their own weather consulting services.

Education and Training

Job training consists of a month-and-a-half to four months of classroom instruction. Courses generally covered are identification of common weather patterns; methods of analyzing weather conditions; use of radar and satellite systems for weather data collection; use of computers for compiling, analyzing, and plotting weather data; and techniques and procedures of forecasting. It should be noted that those atmospheric specialties involving air observation require passage of a demanding flight physical exam.

A bachelor's degree in meteorology, or in a closely related field with courses in meteorology or atmospheric science is the minimum educational requirement; a master's degree is necessary for some positions, and a Ph.D. is required for most research positions.

Although those with a bachelor's degree can sometimes obtain positions in operational meteorology, a master's degree enhances employment opportunities and advancement potential. A master's degree is almost always necessary for conducting applied research and development. A Ph.D. is required for most basic research positions. Students planning on a career in research and development need not necessarily major in atmospheric science or meteorology. A bachelor's degree in mathematics, physics, or engineering provides an excellent preparation for graduate study in atmospheric science.

Special Requirements

The American Meteorological Society offers professional certification of consulting Meteorologists, administered by a Board of Certified Consulting Meteorologists. Applicants must meet formal education requirements, pass an examination to demonstrate thorough meteorological knowledge, have a minimum of five years of experience or a combination of experience plus an advanced degree and provide character references from fellow professionals.

Experience, Special Skills, and Personality Traits

One should have an interest in scientific work, in collecting and analyzing data, in working with mathematical formulas, and in planning and directing the work of others.

Computer science courses, additional meteorology courses, a strong background in mathematics and physics, and good communication skills are important. Those interested in air quality work should take courses in chemistry and supplement their technical training with coursework in policy or government affairs.

Unions and Associations

For information about careers in meteorology contact the American Meteorological Society. The Society also provides opportunities for certification, continuing education, and networking. Information on obtaining a meteorologist position with the federal government is available from the Office of Personnel Management. Information is also available from the Internet site: http://www.usajobs.opm.gov.

NUCLEAR ENGINEER

CAREER PROFILE

Duties: Researching, designing, maintaining, and operating nuclear power facilities; researching fission applications

Alternate Title(s): Mechanical Engineer (Nuclear)

Availability: Army, Navy, Marine Corps

Military Salary: See How to Use This Book

Civilian Salary: $48,830 to $106,400

Civilian Employment Prospects: Fair

Civilian Advancement Prospects: Good

Prerequisites:

Rank—Officer

Education and Training—Four-year college degree in physics, chemistry, or nuclear engineering required; some specialties require a master's degree

Experience—Primarily on-the-job training; any engineering-related experience should be helpful.

Special Skills and Personality Traits—Inquisitive; analytical; problem-solver; enjoy meeting a challenge; detail-oriented; strong interpersonal skills

CAREER LADDER

```
┌─────────────────────────────┐
│     Manager or Teacher       │
└─────────────────────────────┘

┌─────────────────────────────┐
│      Project Manager         │
└─────────────────────────────┘

┌─────────────────────────────┐
│    Staff Nuclear Engineer    │
└─────────────────────────────┘
```

Position Description

Nuclear engineering is a specialty within the larger field of mechanical engineering. Nuclear Engineers research and develop the processes and technologies that utilize the power of nuclear energy and radiation. They design, develop, monitor, and operate nuclear power plants.

The military has been a pioneer in the use of nuclear energy, using it for power plants, strategic weapons, and defense systems. Nuclear Engineers direct research and development projects to improve military uses of nuclear energy. They also direct nuclear power plant operations.

Nuclear Engineers in the military perform some or all of the following duties:

• Direct projects to improve nuclear power plants in ships and submarines
• Direct research on the uses and effects of nuclear weapons
• Develop safety procedures for handling nuclear weapons
• Assist high-level officials in creating policies for developing and using nuclear technology
• Direct operations and maintenance of nuclear power plants

Nuclear energy is relatively new, but it has rapidly attained importance as a source of efficient and inexpensive power. With more than 100 nuclear power plants currently in operation, providing nearly a quarter of the United States' electrical power needs, the nuclear energy industry requires substantial manpower.

Nuclear Engineers held about 12,000 jobs in 1998. Approximately 60 percent were employed by utilities, the federal government, and engineering consulting firms. Over 50 percent of the federally employed Nuclear Engineers were civilian employees of the navy and the bulk of the rest worked for either the Department of Energy or the Tennessee Valley Authority. Most of the private sector Nuclear Engineers worked for public utility companies or engineering consulting firms. A small percentage taught at universities. Nuclear Engineers may work on the production, handling, and use of nuclear fuel and the safe, efficient disposal of nuclear-generated waste products (known as the nuclear fuel cycle), or they may concentrate on fusion energy.

The nuclear industry is an extremely high-tech industry with a wide field of technical disciplines. Nuclear Engineers may choose to specialize in utilization of radioactivity and radiation in fields as disparate as medicine and the military; developing nuclear power sources for use in spacecraft to aid in outer solar system exploration; and utilizing nuclear engineering principles in high-tech imaging and scanning applications. An ongoing program at one university has developed an application whereby radiation diagnostics can be used to locate buried land mines. And the United States Navy has an extremely comprehensive nuclear program.

Despite some concern on the part of the public about the potential dangers of nuclear power, there seems little likelihood of it becoming any less prevalent. Although no new power stations are presently being constructed in the United States, the new uses being developed offer a wide and challenging array of opportunities for the Nuclear Engineers of the future.

Civilian Salaries

In 1998, the average salary of a Nuclear Engineer was $71,000. The lowest 10 percent earned less then $48,830 and the highest 10 percent earned over $106,400. Those employed by the federal government earned a lower average salary of about $67,000.

Civilian Employment Prospects

Nuclear Engineers have good employment prospects currently because the number of graduates in the field is low enough to roughly equal the number of available openings. Most of these openings exist due to the need to replace Nuclear Engineers who change occupations or leave the labor force.

Employment of Nuclear Engineers is expected to grow more slowly than the average for all occupations through 2008, due to the absence of new construction of nuclear power plants. However, the need for Nuclear Engineers to operate existing plants remains. In addition, Nuclear Engineers will be needed to continue efforts in defense-related areas, biomedical applications, and to improve and enforce the safety standards and waste management efforts.

Civilian Advancement Prospects

Nuclear Engineers follow the same general advancement ladder as other engineers in other fields, beginning with a staff position. In time, they advance to become responsible for their own projects or research efforts or move into management positions. Most round out their career as consultants, while some choose to cultivate the next crop of engineers through teaching positions.

Education and Training

Nuclear engineering is a subset of mechanical engineering. Minimum requirements are a bachelor's degree with a four-year curriculum rich in math and science, with additional courses in computing. Master's degrees require a more intensive mathematics curriculum.

Experience, Special Skills, and Personality Traits

Engineers should be, by nature, analytical, detail-oriented, and highly focused and motivated individuals. Problem-solving skills are indispensable. For supervisory positions, good people skills and a talent for motivation are helpful. The financial rewards are not large enough to make this a field that will ensure the accumulation of wealth. It is primarily for individuals who seek a high degree of personal satisfaction in meeting challenges, following difficult projects through to completion and receiving some tangible evidence of the importance of their effort.

Unions and Associations

Nuclear Engineers may become members of a number of professional organizations. The American Nuclear Society, the American Society of Mechanical Engineers, the National Academy of Engineering, the Society of Women Engineers, and the American Society for Engineering Education are some examples. All provide opportunities for networking, continuing education, and keeping up with trends in the field.

PHYSICIST

CAREER PROFILE

Duties: Plan and conduct experiments in aerodynamics, optics, geophysics, biophysics, and astrophysics; conduct research to improve methods of radiation detection and protection; analyze the properties of metals, plastics, and other materials; conduct studies regarding the use of nuclear-powered engines; write technical reports; assist in research and development projects; oversee research projects and manage laboratories or field staff to conduct experiments

Alternate Title(s): Astronomer

Availability: Army, Navy, Air Force, Coast Guard

Military Salary: See How to Use This Book

Civilian Salary: $51,680 to $116,290

Civilian Employment Prospects: Good

Civilian Advancement Prospects: Good

Prerequisites:

    Rank—Officer

    Education and Training—A four-year college degree in physics, chemistry, or nuclear engineering required; master's degree or higher required for some specialties

    Experience—Any training and work experience obtained in the armed services

    Special Skills and Personality Traits—Mathematical ability; problem-solving; analytical skills; an inquisitive mind; imagination and initiative important; good oral and written communication skills; an interest in scientific and technical work; patient; logical thinker

CAREER LADDER

```
┌─────────────────────────────────────┐
│          Senior Scientist           │
└─────────────────────────────────────┘

┌─────────────────────────────────────┐
│   Physicist, Postdoctoral Research   │
└─────────────────────────────────────┘

┌─────────────────────────────────────┐
│              Physicist              │
└─────────────────────────────────────┘

┌─────────────────────────────────────┐
│             Technician              │
└─────────────────────────────────────┘
```

Position Description

As with research anywhere, the objective of military research is to enhance existing technologies. The military, concerned as it must be with national defense, uses tools like physics research to look for new materials for building ships, aircraft, and weapons as well as addressing a host of other vital concerns. Working in research and development laboratories physicists in the military plan and conduct experiments in aerodynamics, optics, geophysics, biophysics, and astrophysics. They conduct research to improve methods of radiation detection and protection. They analyze the

strength, flexibility, weight, and other properties of metals, plastics, and other materials and conduct studies regarding the use of nuclear-powered engines. They write technical reports on the experiments performed. Physicists assist in research and development projects to improve radio and other communications equipment and oversee research projects under contract to universities and industrial firms.

In the civilian world, Physicists work primarily in research and development for private industry, colleges, universities, and government agencies. Usually specializing in one area of physics (nuclear, astronomical, health, medical physics), Physicists explore and identify basic principles governing the structure and behavior of matter, the generation and transfer of energy, and the interaction of matter and energy within the scope of their discipline.

Some Physicists use these principles in theoretical areas; others apply their physics knowledge to practical areas. They design and perform experiments with lasers, cyclotrons, telescopes, mass spectrometers, etc. Based on observations and analysis, they attempt to discover and explain laws describing the forces of nature, such as gravity, electromagnetism, and nuclear interactions. Physicists also find ways to apply physical laws and theories to problems in nuclear energy, electronics, optics, materials, communications, aerospace technology, navigation equipment, and medical instrumentation.

Astronomers use the principles of physics and mathematics to learn about the fundamental nature of the universe, including the sun, moon, planets, stars, and galaxies. They also apply their knowledge to solve problems in navigation, space flight, and satellite communications and to develop the instrumentation and techniques used to observe and collect astronomical data.

Most Physicists work in research and development, doing either basic or applied research. Physicists who conduct basic research work to increase scientific knowledge. Those in applied research build upon basic research discoveries to develop new devices, products, and processes. They also design research equipment. A small number of Physicists work in inspection, testing, quality control, and other production-related jobs in industry.

There are no limits in physics. Though the majority of physics research is done in small to medium-size laboratories, experiments in plasma, nuclear, and some other areas require extremely large pieces of expensive equipment such as particle accelerators.

Nearly all astronomers spend their time in research. Some act as theoreticians, others analyze large quantities of data gathered by observatories and satellites, writing scientific papers or reports on their findings. Some astronomers actually operate space-stationed or ground-based telescopes, but most spend only a few weeks each year making observations with optical and radio telescopes and other instruments. For many years, satellites and other space-based instruments have provided tremendous amounts of astronomical data. Some few astronomers work in museum planetariums. These astronomers develop and revise programs presented to the public and sometimes direct planetarium operations.

Physicists specialize in one of the many subfields of physics, or even in one of the subdivisions of one of those subfields. Their choices range from such broad categories as condensed matter physics, elementary particle physics, nuclear physics, atomic and molecular physics, optics, acoustics, or the physics of fluids to one of the more rarefied subdivisions. Consider that within condensed matter physics alone, specialties include superconductivity, crystallography, and semiconductors. Since all physics involves the same fundamental principles, however, specialties often overlap and Physicists can switch from one subfield to another without a great deal of difficulty. This has led to the recent growth in Physicists working in combined fields, such as biophysics, chemical physics, and geophysics.

Physicists work in clean, quiet surroundings, but are often compelled to work long or irregular hours. Observatory work usually involves travel to remote locations, long hours, and routine night work, which can possibly create stressful conditions. Also, both Physicists and astronomers, whose work depends on grant money, are often under stress to write grant proposals to acquire funding.

Civilian Salaries

In 2000, the average yearly salary for Physicists and astronomers was $82,535. The average yearly salary of astronomers was $74,510 while Physicists earned $83,310. The middle 50 percent of Physicists earned between $65,820 and $102,270. The lowest 10 percent earned less than $51,680 and the highest 10 percent earned more than $116,290.

In 2001, National Association of Colleges and Employers research showed the average annual starting salary offer to physics doctoral degree candidates was $68,273.

In 2000, the American Institute of Physics claimed an average annual salary of $78,000 for its members with Ph.D.'s; with master's degrees, $63,800; with bachelor's degrees, $60,000 (those in temporary postdoctoral positions earned significantly less).

Civilian Employment Prospects

In 2000, Physicists and astronomers held about 10,000 jobs (astronomers accounted for only 10 percent of the total). Some 40 percent of all nonfaculty Physicists and astronomers worked for commercial or noncommercial research, development, and testing laboratories. The federal government employed some 35 percent. Others worked in colleges and universities in nonfaculty positions, for state governments, drug companies, or electronic equipment manufacturers.

Through 2010 opportunities for Physicists and astronomers are projected to grow about as fast as the average for all occupations. The need to replace Physicists and astronomers who retire and increased funding for both the Department of Energy and the Department of Defense will account for most of these opening positions. Research and development budgets in private industry will also continue to grow.

Due to a glut in doctorates granted in physics in recent years, new Ph.D. graduates will face competition for basic research jobs. Competitive conditions have begun to ease, however, following recent declines in enrollment in graduate physics programs. However, new doctoral graduates should still expect to face competition for research jobs, not only from fellow graduates, but also from an existing supply of postdoctoral workers seeking to leave low-paying, temporary positions and non-U.S. citizen applicants. Opportunities may be more numerous for those with a master's degree, particularly graduates from programs preparing students for applied research and development, product design, and manufacturing positions in industry.

Civilian Advancement Prospects

Although most Physics and astronomy Ph.D.'s. begin their careers in postdoctoral research positions, by learning about and gaining experience within their specialty they can reach the position of senior scientist. With sufficient experience, those Physicists who develop new products or processes sometimes form their own companies or join new firms to exploit their own ideas.

Education and Training

A four-year college degree in physics, chemistry, or nuclear engineering is required to enter this field. Specialties require a master's degree; a doctoral degree is required for jobs in basic research and development. Additional experience and training in a postdoctoral research appointment, although not required, is important for Physicists and astronomers looking for permanent appointments in universities and government laboratories.

Master's degree holders qualify for many jobs requiring a physics background, including positions in manufacturing and applied research and development, as well as teaching jobs in two-year colleges. Bachelor's degree holders qualify for work in engineering-related areas, in software

development and other scientific fields, as technicians or to assist in setting up computer networks and sophisticated laboratory equipment. They may also qualify for applied research jobs in private industry or nonresearch positions in the federal government or positions as science teachers in secondary schools.

In 2000, over 500 colleges and universities offer a bachelor's degree in physics. More than 180 colleges and universities had departments offering Ph.D. degrees in physics. More than 70 offered a master's as their highest degree. Roughly 70 universities grant degrees in astronomy, either through an astronomy, physics, or combined physics/astronomy department. Applicants to astronomy doctoral programs face competition for available slots.

Experience, Special Skills, and Personality Traits

Mathematical ability, problem-solving, analytical skills, an inquisitive mind, imagination, and initiative are important traits. Good oral and written communication skills and an interest in scientific and technical work are also necessary.

Those hoping to become astronomers still need a very strong physics background. In fact, an undergraduate degree in either physics or astronomy is excellent preparation, followed by a Ph.D. in astronomy.

Physicists hoping to work in industrial laboratories or start their own companies should broaden their educational background to include courses like economics, computer technology, and business management.

Unions and Associations

General information on career opportunities in physics is available from both the American Institute of Physics and The American Physical Society. Both also offer general information about the field and networking opportunities.

SURVEYING, MAPPING, OR DRAFTING TECHNICIAN

CAREER PROFILE

Duties: Draw maps and charts; make scale drawings; conduct land surveys and compute survey results; draw diagrams for wiring and plumbing; build scale models of land areas and piece together aerial photographs to form large photomaps

Alternate Title(s): Land Surveyor; Cartographer; Cartographic Technician; Photogrammetrist; Surveying Technician; Mapping Technician; Geodetic Surveyor; Marine or Hydrographic Surveyor; Geophysical Prospecting Surveyor

Availability: All branches

Military Salary: See How to Use This Book

Civilian Salary: $19,570 to $62,980

Civilian Employment Prospects: Good

Civilian Advancement Prospects: Good

Prerequisites:

  Rank—Enlisted

  Education and Training—High school diploma minimum; four-year college degree preferred

  Experience—Any training and work experience obtained in the armed services or Job Corps

  Special Skills and Personality Traits—Ability to visualize objects, distances, sizes, and abstract forms; able to work with precision and accuracy; good physical condition; normal color vision; good eyesight and depth perception; coordination and hearing; good interpersonal skills; the ability to work as part of a team; good office and computer skills; ability to convert ideas into drawings, and to print and draw neatly; an interest in maps and charts and in working with drafting equipment

  Licensure/Certification—State license required; voluntary certification optional

CAREER LADDER

```
┌─────────────────────────────┐
│     Licensed Surveyor       │
└─────────────────────────────┘

┌─────────────────────────────┐
│     Party Chief or Senior   │
│     Surveying Technician    │
└─────────────────────────────┘

┌─────────────────────────────┐
│         Surveyor            │
└─────────────────────────────┘

┌─────────────────────────────┐
│        Apprentice           │
└─────────────────────────────┘
```

Position Description

In the modern military, Surveying, Mapping, and Drafting Technicians build and repair airstrips, docks, barracks, roads, and numerous other parts of the armed forces infrastructure every day. These workers draw maps and charts using drafting tools such as easels, templates, and compasses, make scale drawings of roads, airfields, buildings, and other military projects, and conduct land surveys and compute survey results. They also draw diagrams for wiring and plumbing of structures, build scale models of land areas that show hills, lakes, roads, and buildings, and piece together aerial photographs to form large photomaps. Their surveys and maps are also used to locate military targets and plot troop movements. They may work indoors or outdoors, in all climates and weather conditions, on ships or on land.

In the civilian world, Surveying, Mapping, and Drafting Technicians work for construction, engineering, and architectural firms and government agencies. Their work is used in planning projects such as highways, airport runways, dams, and drainage systems.

Land surveyors establish official land, air space, and water boundaries; write descriptions of land for deeds, leases, and other legal documents; define air space for airports; and measure construction and mineral sites. On their own or in survey parties, they measure distances, directions, and angles between points and elevations of points, lines, and contours on, above, and below the earth's surface. They plan fieldwork, select known survey reference points, and determine the precise location of important features in the survey area. They also research legal records for evidence of previous boundaries, analyze the data to determine the location of boundary lines, record the results of the survey, verify the accuracy of data, and finally prepare all the necessary plots, maps, and reports.

The Global Positioning System satellite system is becoming more important to the work of surveying as the cost of receivers falls. Consequently surveyors now must be able to interpret and verify the results produced by the new technology.

Professional land surveyors establish boundaries. They must be licensed by the state and are sometimes called to provide expert testimony in court cases concerning surveying matters.

Cartographers compile geographical, political, and cultural information and prepare maps of large areas. They collect, analyze, and interpret both spatial data—such as latitude, longitude, elevation, and distance—and nonspatial data—such as population density, land use patterns, annual precipitation levels, and demographic characteristics. They prepare digital or graphic maps as needed, using information provided by geodetic surveys, aerial photographs, and satellite data.

Geodetic surveyors use high-accuracy techniques, including satellite observations to measure large areas of the Earth's surface. Geophysical prospecting surveyors survey harbors, rivers, and other bodies of water to determine shorelines, topography of the bottom, water depth, and other features. Marine or hydrographic surveyors mark sites for later subsurface exploration. Photogrammetrists measure and analyze aerial photographs to prepare detailed maps and drawings of areas difficult to survey by other methods. Map editors develop and verify map contents from aerial photographs and other reference sources.

Surveying technicians assist land surveyors by operating survey instruments and collecting information in the field,

and by performing computations and computer-aided drafting in offices. Mapping technicians calculate map-making information from field notes and draw topographical maps and verify their accuracy.

Although they often spend a great deal of time outdoors, surveyors tend to work a regular 40-hour week. Summer can bring longer hours when weather and light conditions are most suitable for fieldwork. A surveyor's work is active and often strenuous. They stand for long periods, walk considerable distances, and climb hills with heavy packs of instruments and other equipment in all types of weather. They sometimes have to travel to remote or inaccessible locations and stay overnight. Cartographers, on the other hand, spend nearly all of their time in offices.

Civilian Salaries

In 2000, the average yearly salary for surveyors was $36,700. The middle 50 percent earned between $26,480 and $49,030. The lowest 10 percent earned less than $19,570. The highest 10 percent earned more than $62,980.

In 2000, the average yearly salary for cartographers and photogrammetrists was $39,410. The middle 50 percent earned between $29,200 and $51,930. The lowest 10 percent earned less than $23,560. The highest 10 percent earned more than $64,780.

In 2001, the average yearly salary for land surveyors in nonsupervisory, supervisory, and managerial positions in the federal government was $57,416; for cartographers, $62,369; for geodetic technicians, $53,143; for surveying technicians, $34,623; and for cartographic technicians, $40,775.

Civilian Employment Prospects

In 2000, surveyors, cartographers, photogrammetrists, and Surveying Technicians held just over 120,000 jobs. Engineering and architectural services firms employed more than half, and federal, state, and local governments employed another sixteen percent. Some 5,000 were self-employed.

Through 2010 opportunities for these workers are expected to grow about as fast as the average for all occupations. Prospects will be best for those who have at least a bachelor's degree and strong technical skills. Increasing demand for geographic data will certainly mean better opportunities for cartographers and photogrammetrists involved in the development and use of geographic and land information systems. New technologies, such as GPS and GIS, also may enhance employment opportunities for surveyors and Surveying Technicians who have the educational background enabling them to use these systems.

Civilian Advancement Prospects

High school graduates with no formal surveying training start as apprentices. Those with postsecondary school surveying training start as technicians or assistants. On-the-job experience and formal training allow workers to advance to senior survey technician, then to party chief, and finally to licensed surveyor.

Education and Training

In the military, those interested in this career receive two to eight months of classroom instruction, depending on specialty. Classes usually include surveying and drafting techniques, aerial photo interpretation, and architectural and structural drawing. Further training occurs in the field and through advanced courses. The army and marine corps offer certified apprenticeship programs for some specialties in this occupation.

High-school students interested in surveying should take courses in algebra, geometry, trigonometry, drafting, mechanical drawing, and computer science. Although it is possible to enter this field straight out of high school, recent technological advances are making a four-year college degree more of a prerequisite. Some 25 universities now offer four-year programs leading to a B.S. degree in surveying.

Special Requirements

All land surveyors must be licensed. Most state licensing boards require that individuals pass a written examination given by the National Council of Examiners for Engineering and Surveying and one prepared by the state licensing board. They must also meet varying standards of formal education and work experience in the field. Currently most states require some formal post-high school course work and some 10 to 12 years of surveying experience to gain licensure. The National Society of Professional Surveyors has a voluntary certification program for surveying technicians. Although not required for state licensure, many employers require certification for promotion to positions with greater responsibilities.

Cartographers and photogrammetrists need only a bachelor's degree in a field such as engineering, forestry, geography, or a physical science to enter their field.

Experience, Special Skills, and Personality Traits

Surveyors need the ability to visualize objects, distances, sizes, and abstract forms as well as the ability to work with precision and accuracy. They must be in good physical condition, have normal color vision, good eyesight, depth perception, coordination, and hearing as well as good interpersonal skills and the ability to work as part of a team. Also helpful are good office and computer skills, the ability to convert ideas into drawings and to print and draw neatly, as well as an interest in maps and charts and in working with drafting equipment.

Unions and Associations

For information about career opportunities, licensure requirements, and the Surveying Technician certification program, contact the National Society of Professional Surveyors. Information on a career as a geodetic surveyor is available from the American Association of Geodetic Surveying. General information on careers in photogrammetry and remote sensing is available from ASPRS: The Imaging and Geospatial Information Society.

HEALTH CARE

CARDIOPULMONARY AND EEG TECHNICIAN

CAREER PROFILE

Duties: Take patients' blood pressure; attach equipment to patients' bodies; help physicians revive heart attack victims; adjust settings and operate test equipment; watch dials, graphs, and screens during tests; confer with physicians about what tests or treatments are needed; keep records of test results and discuss them with medical staff; operate electrocardiographs, electroencephalographs, and other test equipment

Alternate Title(s): Cardiovascular Technologist; Vascular Technologist; Cardiac Sonographer

Availability: Army, Navy, Air Force

Military Salary: See How to Use This Book

Civilian Salary: $19,540 to $52,930

Civilian Employment Prospects: Good

Civilian Advancement Prospects: Good

Prerequisites:
  Rank—Enlisted
  Education and Training—Two- or four-year program at a junior or community college
  Experience—Any training and work experience obtained in the armed services
  Special Skills and Personality Traits—An interest in electronic equipment; able to follow strict standards and procedures; an interest in learning how the heart, lungs, and blood work; detail-oriented; reliable; mechanical aptitude; a pleasant, relaxed manner; normal color vision
  Licensure/Certification—Optional but preferred

CAREER LADDER

```
┌─────────────────────────────┐
│         Supervisor          │
└─────────────────────────────┘

┌─────────────────────────────┐
│         Technician          │
└─────────────────────────────┘
```

Position Description

The modern military provides its members every aspect of medical care available, including treatment for heart, lung, and brain disorders. Physicians need sophisticated tests to help diagnose and treat these problems. Cardiopulmonary and Electroencephalograph Technicians administer a variety of diagnostic tests of the heart, lungs, blood, and brain. Most work in hospitals and clinics, but technicians should be ready to work in mobile field hospitals during combat sit-

uations. Military Cardiopulmonary and EEG Technicians take patients' blood pressure readings, attach electrodes or microphones to patients' bodies, help physicians revive heart attack victims and adjust settings and operate test equipment. They also watch dials, graphs, and screens during tests, talk to physicians to learn what tests or treatments are needed, keep records of test results and discuss them with medical staff and operate electrocardiographs, electroencephalographs, and other test equipment.

In the civilian world, Cardiopulmonary and EEG Technicians work in hospitals, clinics, and physicians' offices. Here, as in the military, they assist physicians in diagnosing and treating cardiac (heart) and peripheral vascular (blood vessel) ailments. Cardiovascular technologists may specialize in the areas of invasive cardiology, echocardiography, and vascular technology. Cardiovascular technicians who specialize in electrocardiograms, stress testing, and Holter monitors are known as cardiographic or EKG technicians.

Cardiology technologists specialize in invasive procedures. They assist physicians with cardiac catheterization procedures where a small tube is wound through a patient's blood vessel from a spot on the patient's leg into the heart (to determine if a blockage exists in the blood vessels that supply the heart muscle or to help diagnose other problems). They also must position patients on an examining table, shave, clean, and administer anesthesia to the top of the patient's leg near the groin. During the procedure they monitor patients' blood pressure and heart rate using EKG equipment and must notify the physician if something appears wrong. Technologists also may prepare and monitor patients during open-heart surgery and the implantation of pacemakers.

Cardiovascular technologists who specialize in echocardiography or vascular technology often run noninvasive tests using ultrasound instrumentation (which transmits high frequency sound waves into areas of a body and then processes reflected echoes of the sound waves to form an image). While performing the scan, technologists check the image on a screen for subtle differences between healthy and diseased areas, decide which images to include, and judge if the images are satisfactory for diagnostic purposes. They also explain the procedure to patients, record additional medical history, select appropriate equipment settings, and change the patient's position as necessary.

Vascular technologists or vascular sonographers perform a medical history on a patient, then evaluate their pulses by listening to the sounds of their arteries for abnormalities. Then they use ultrasound instrumentation to record vascular information, such as vascular blood flow, blood pressure, limb volume changes, oxygen saturation, cerebral circulation, peripheral circulation, and abdominal circulation.

Cardiac sonographers, or echocardiographers, use ultrasound instrumentation to create images of the heart and its chambers called echocardiograms. They may also assist physicians who perform transesophageal echocardiography, which involves placing a tube in the patient's esophagus to obtain ultrasound images.

Electrocardiograph technicians take basic EKGs (which trace electrical impulses transmitted by the heart) by attaching electrodes to the patient's chest, arms, and legs, and then manipulating switches on an EKG machine to obtain a reading. A printout is made for interpretation by the physician. This test is done before most kinds of surgery and as part of a routine physical examination, especially for persons who have reached middle age or have a history of cardiovascular problems.

EKG technicians with advanced training perform Holter monitor and stress testing, where electrodes are placed on the patient's chest and attached to a portable EKG monitor on the patient's belt. Following 24 or more hours of normal activity for the patient, the technician removes a tape from the monitor and places it in a scanner. After checking the quality of the recorded impulses on an electronic screen, the technician prints the information from the tape for a physician's later use.

Technologists and technicians tend to work regular 40-hour weeks. This can include weekends and evenings. Some also schedule appointments, type doctor interpretations, maintain patient files, and care for equipment. Those in these professions spend a great deal of time walking and standing, and some face stressful working conditions, because of the life and death nature of many of their patients' ailments.

Civilian Salaries

In 2000, the average yearly salary for cardiovascular technologists and technicians was $33,350. The middle 50 percent earned between $24,590 and $43,450. The lowest 10 percent earned less than $19,540. The highest 10 percent earned more than $52,930.

In 2000, the average yearly salary for cardiovascular technologists and technicians was $33,100 in offices and clinics of medical doctors and $32,860 in hospitals.

Civilian Employment Prospects

In 2000, cardiovascular technologists and technicians held just fewer than 40,000 jobs. Some seven out of 10 of these positions were in hospitals, in both inpatient and outpatient settings, in hospital cardiology departments. The remainder of these jobs were in offices of cardiologists or other physicians, cardiac rehabilitation centers, or ambulatory surgery centers.

Through 2010, opportunities for cardiovascular technologists and technicians are expected to grow faster than the average for all occupations. Growth will occur as the population ages, because older people have a higher incidence of heart problems. Opportunities for vascular technologists and echocardiographers will also grow as advances in vascular technology and sonography reduce the need for more costly and invasive procedures. Employment of EKG technicians is expected to decline, however, as hospitals train nursing aides and others to perform basic EKG procedures. Individuals trained in Holter monitoring and stress testing are expected to have more favorable job prospects than those who can only perform a basic EKG.

Civilian Advancement Prospects

Beginning EKG technicians are usually trained on the job. With experience they can advance to the position of EKG supervisor. Some EKG technicians take extra courses so they can advance to become technologists. Others might pursue further medical education in order to advance their careers in new directions.

Education and Training

In the military, those interested in this career receive eight to nine-and-a-half months of classroom instruction. Classes usually contain such courses as diagnostic procedures, operation and maintenance of diagnostic equipment, preparation of patients for testing, and methods of resuscitation. Further training occurs on the job and through advanced courses.

In the civilian world, although some cardiovascular technologists, vascular technologists, and cardiac sonographers receive on-the-job training, the majority receive their training through two- to four-year programs at junior or community colleges.

There are currently 23 programs accredited by the Joint Review Committee on Education in Cardiovascular Technology. Graduates of any of these programs are eligible to obtain professional certification through Cardiovascular Credentialing International in cardiac catheterization, echocardiography, vascular ultrasound, and cardiographic techniques. Cardiac sonographers and vascular technologists may also obtain certification with the American Registry of Diagnostic Medical Sonographers.

For basic EKGs, Holter monitoring, and stress testing, one-year certificate programs exist, but most EKG technicians are still trained on the job by an EKG supervisor or a cardiologist. On-the-job training usually lasts about eight to 16 weeks. Most employers prefer to train people already in the health-care field. Some EKG technicians are students enrolled in two-year programs to become technologists, working part time to gain experience and make contact with employers.

Experience, Special Skills, and Personality Traits

Those interested in careers as cardiovascular technologists and technicians must have an interest in electronic equipment, the ability to follow strict standards and procedures, an interest in learning how the heart, lungs, and blood work together and the ability to keep accurate records. They must also be reliable, have mechanical aptitude, and possess a pleasant, relaxed manner as well as normal color vision.

Unions and Associations

For general information about a career in cardiovascular technology, contact the Alliance of Cardiovascular Professionals. For a list of accredited programs in cardiovascular technology, contact the Joint Review Committee on Education in Cardiovascular Technology. For information on vascular technology, contact the Society of Vascular Technology. For information on echocardiography, contact the American Society of Echocardiography. And for information regarding registration and certification, contact both the Cardiovascular Credentialing International and the American Registry of Diagnostic Medical Sonographers.

DENTIST

CAREER PROFILE

Duties: Examine patients' teeth and gums, examine X rays, locate and fill tooth cavities, perform oral surgery on teeth, gums, or jaws, develop and fit dentures, construct and fit dental devices, plan dental health programs

Alternate Title(s): Oral Pathologist; Endodontist; Oral Surgeon; Orthodontist; Pedodontist; Prosthodontist; Periodontist; Public Health Dentist

Availability: Army, Navy, Air Force, Coast Guard

Military Salary: See How to Use This Book

Civilian Salary: $129,030

Civilian Employment Prospects: Fair

Civilian Advancement Prospects: Fair

Prerequisites:

    Rank—Officer

    Education and Training—Doctor of dentistry degree; additional training in a dental specialty

    Experience—Any training and work experience obtained in the armed services

    Special Skills and Personality Traits—Diagnostic ability; good visual memory; excellent judgment of space and shape; a high degree of manual dexterity; good business sense; self-discipline; communication skills; a desire to help others; good eye-hand coordination

    Licensure/Certification—State license required; additional specialty license may be required

CAREER LADDER

```
┌─────────────────────────────┐
│         Specialist          │
└─────────────────────────────┘

┌─────────────────────────────┐
│          Dentist            │
└─────────────────────────────┘

┌─────────────────────────────┐
│         Associate           │
└─────────────────────────────┘
```

Position Description

Soldiers, like anyone else, need access to dental care. In the military, modern military Dentists examine, diagnose, and treat diseases and disorders of the mouth. Working in hospitals and dental clinics on land and aboard ships, they may practice general dentistry or work in one of several specialties. Military Dentists have many duties. They examine patients' teeth and gums to detect signs of disease or tooth decay, examine X rays to determine the soundness of teeth and the alignment of teeth and jaws. They locate and fill tooth cavities and perform oral surgery to treat problems with teeth, gums, or jaws. They also develop and fit dentures to replace missing teeth; construct and fit dental devices, such as braces and retainers, for straightening teeth; and plan dental health programs for patients to help prevent dental problems.

In the civilian world, Dentists diagnose, prevent, and treat teeth and tissue problems. They remove decay, fill cavities, examine X rays, place protective plastic sealants on children's teeth, straighten teeth, and repair fractured teeth. They also perform corrective surgery on gums and supporting bones to treat gum diseases, extract teeth, and make models and measurements for dentures to replace missing teeth. They also provide instruction on diet, brushing, flossing, and fluoride use, as well as administer anesthetics, and write prescriptions for antibiotics and other medications.

Dentists must be prepared to handle more than just their patient's teeth, however. Those in private practice must busy themselves with all manner of administrative tasks, including bookkeeping, buying equipment and supplies, as well as hiring and supervising dental hygienists, dental assistants, dental laboratory technicians, and receptionists.

Those Dentists who aren't general practitioners tend to specialize in one of the following areas: orthodontists, who straighten teeth by applying pressure to the teeth with braces or retainers; oral and maxillofacial surgeons, who operate on the mouth and jaws; pediatric dentists, who focus on dentistry for children; periodontists who treat gums and bone supporting the teeth; prosthodontists, who replace missing teeth with permanent fixtures; endodontists, who perform root canal therapy; public health dentists, who promote good dental health and preventing dental diseases within the community; oral pathologists, who study oral diseases; and oral and maxillofacial radiologists, who diagnose diseases in the head and neck through the use of imaging technologies.

The majority of Dentists work five days a week, some only four (though most provide some evening and weekend hours to meet their patients' needs). Most work an average of 40 hours a week. Initially, Dentists may work more hours as they establish their practice.

Civilian Salaries

In 2000, the average yearly salary for Dentists was $129,030. Earnings vary according to number of years in practice, location, hours worked, and specialty. Self-employed Dentists in private practice tend to earn more than salaried Dentists. These self-employed Dentists, one must remember, must provide their own health insurance, life insurance, and retirement benefits.

Civilian Employment Prospects

In 2000, Dentists held more than 150,000 jobs, some 80 percent of them in a private practice. According to the American Dental Association, roughly 13 percent of Dentists belong to a partnership. A small number of salaried Dentists work in private or public hospitals and clinics. Through 2010, opportunities for Dentists are expected to grow more slowly than the average for all occupations. Employment growth will provide some job opportunities, as will the need to replace the large number of Dentists projected to retire. Also, dental care demand should grow substantially as the baby-boom generation advances into middle age. Large numbers will need complicated dental work, such as partial plates and full bridges, but more of the elderly are likely to retain their teeth than in past generations, calling for dental services far into the senior years. There will also be a greater need for prevention, with Dentists increasingly called upon to provide care aimed at preventing tooth loss rather than simply providing treatments.

The reason the projection for opportunities for Dentists is so small is that despite what appears to be a growing need, established dentists are likely to hire more dental hygienists and dental assistants to handle routine services, enabling them to serve a greater number of patients.

Civilian Advancement Prospects

Many dental school graduates begin their careers working as associates for established Dentists. This generally lasts a year or two while the new Dentist both gains experience and saves money to open their own office. The majority of dental school graduates, however, purchase an established practice or open a new one immediately after graduation. Each year, about one-fourth to one-third of new graduates enroll in postgraduate training programs to prepare for a dental specialty.

Education and Training

In the military, those interested in this career receive no additional instruction. Most Dentists already have at least eight years of education beyond high school. Those high school and college students wishing to become dentists should take courses in biology, chemistry, physics, health, and mathematics.

A doctor of dentistry degree and additional training in a dental specialty are required to enter this occupation. Dental schools require a minimum of two years of college-level predental education. However, most dental students have at least a bachelor's degree. Predental education emphasizes coursework in the sciences. All dental schools require applicants to take the Dental Admissions Test. Students are generally selected according to the scores earned on the DAT, their grade point average, and information gathered through recommendations and interviews. Most dental schools award the degree of Doctor of Dental Surgery. The rest award the equivalent degree, Doctor of Dental Medicine.

Special Requirements

All of the states as well as the District of Columbia require dentists to be licensed. In most states this means graduation from a dental school accredited by the American Dental Association's Commission on Dental Accreditation, as well as passage of both written and practical examinations. Candidates may fulfill the written part of the state licensing requirements by passing the National Board Dental Examinations. Individual states or regional testing agencies administer the written or practical examinations.

At present, nearly 20 states require Dentists to obtain a specialty license before practicing as a specialist. Requirements can include two to four years of postgraduate education as well as completion of a special state examination. Most state licenses permit Dentists to engage in both general and specialized practice.

Experience, Special Skills, and Personality Traits

Dentists need diagnostic ability, good visual memory, excellent judgment of space and shape, a high degree of manual dexterity, good business sense, self-discipline, and communication skills. Also helpful are a desire to help others and good eye-hand coordination.

Unions and Associations

For information on dentistry as a career and a list of accredited dental schools, contact the American Dental Association. For information on admission to dental schools, contact the American Dental Education Association.

DIETITIAN

CAREER PROFILE

Duties: Set policies for hospital food service operations and inspect hospital food service and preparation areas; plan and organize training programs; develop special diets for patients, plan menus, interview patients; develop hospital food service budgets and provide information on nutrition to the military community

Alternate Title(s): Food Service Manager; Nutritionist

Availability: Army, Navy, Air Force, and Coast Guard

Military Salary: See How to Use This Book

Civilian Salary: $23,680 to $54,940

Civilian Employment Prospects: Good

Civilian Advancement Prospects: Good

Prerequisites:

Rank—Officer

Education and Training—Four-year college degree in food and nutrition or institutional management required

Experience—Any training and work experience obtained in the armed services

Special Skills and Personality Traits—A desire to help others; an interest in nutrition and food preparation; enjoy interpreting scientific and medical data

Licensure/Certification—Many states require a license or certification

CAREER LADDER

```
┌─────────────────────────────────┐
│            Dietitian            │
└─────────────────────────────────┘

┌─────────────────────────────────┐
│  Director, Dietetic Department  │
└─────────────────────────────────┘

┌─────────────────────────────────┐
│  Assistant, Dietetic Department │
└─────────────────────────────────┘
```

Position Description

Dietitians are an important part of the military's health care staff. Military personnel cannot be allowed the self-indulgent eating habits of civilian life, and yet, their meals must be satisfying. Military Dietitians are experts in the nutritional needs of hospital patients and outpatients. They manage medical food service facilities and plan meals for hospital patients and outpatients who need special diets.

Working in hospitals, clinics, and aboard ships they set policies for hospital food service operations, inspect hospital food service and preparation areas to be sure they meet sanitation and safety standards, and plan and organize training programs for medical food service personnel. They also develop special diets for patients based on instructions from doctors, plan menus for hospital meals,

and interview patients to determine whether they are satisfied with their diet. They also develop hospital food service budgets and provide information on nutrition to the military community.

In the civilian world, Dietitians and nutritionists work in hospitals, clinics, and other health-care facilities, college food services, restaurants, industrial food services, and research institutions. Civilian Dietitians sometimes specialize in specific areas such as consultation, clinical dietetics, and community health.

Wherever they work, Dietitians plan nutrition programs and supervise the preparation and serving of meals. They help prevent and treat illnesses by promoting healthy eating habits and suggesting diet modifications. They run food service systems for institutions such as hospitals and schools, promote sound eating habits through education, and conduct research.

In institutions such as hospitals and nursing homes, clinical Dietitians assess patients' nutritional needs, develop and implement nutrition programs, then evaluate and report the results. They also confer with doctors and other health-care professionals in order to coordinate medical and nutritional needs. Some specialize in the management of overweight patients, care of the critically ill, or of renal and diabetic patients.

Working in public health clinics, home health agencies, and health maintenance organizations, community Dietitians counsel individuals and groups on nutritional practices designed to prevent disease and promote good health. They evaluate individual needs, develop nutritional care plans, and instruct individuals and their families. They may also provide instruction on grocery shopping and food preparation to the elderly, individuals with special needs, and children.

In industry, the public's increased interest in nutrition has led to new opportunities for Dietitians. In food manufacturing, advertising, and marketing concerns, Dietitians now analyze foods, prepare literature for distribution, and report on issues such as the nutritional content of recipes, dietary fiber, or vitamin supplements.

Management Dietitians oversee large-scale meal planning and preparation in health-care facilities, company cafeterias, prisons, and schools. They hire, train, and direct other Dietitians and food service workers; budget for and purchase food, equipment, and supplies; enforce sanitary and safety regulations; and prepare records and reports. Consultant Dietitians, working for health-care facilities or in private practice, perform nutrition screenings for their clients and offer advice on diet-related concerns such as weight loss or cholesterol reduction. Some work for wellness programs, sports teams, supermarkets, and other nutrition-related businesses. They may consult with food service managers, providing expertise in sanitation, safety procedures, menu development, budgeting, and planning.

Dietitians work a regular 40-hour week with few calls for night work or weekend hours. By law they work in clean, well-lighted, well-ventilated areas. However, many must be on their feet for much of the workday.

Civilian Salaries

In 2000, the average yearly salary for Dietitians and nutritionists was $38,450. The middle 50 percent earned between $31,070 and $45,950 a year. The lowest 10 percent earned less than $23,680, and the highest 10 percent earned more than $54,940 a year. In 2000, the average yearly salary for Dietitians and nutritionists working in hospitals (the industry employing the largest numbers of them) was $39,450.

In 1999, the American Dietetic Association reported that the average yearly salaries for registered Dietitians for the following areas were:

Consultation and Business	$48,810
Food and Nutrition Management	$48,370
Education and Research	$47,040
Community Nutrition	$37,990
Clinical Nutrition	$37,565

Civilian Employment Prospects

In 2000, Dietitians and nutritionists held nearly 50,000 jobs. More than half worked in hospitals, nursing homes, or offices and clinics of physicians. Roughly one-tenth were employed by state and local governments in health departments and other public health related areas. Other jobs were in restaurants, social service agencies, residential care facilities, diet workshops, physical fitness facilities, school systems, colleges and universities, and the federal government. Some were employed by firms that provide food services on contract to such facilities as colleges and universities, airlines, correctional facilities, and company cafeterias. Still others were self-employed, working as consultants to facilities such as hospitals and nursing homes or providing dietary counseling to individual clients.

Through 2010, opportunities for Dietitians are expected to grow about as fast as the average for all occupations due to the increasing emphasis on disease prevention through improved dietary habits, according to the Bureau of Labor Statistics. A growing and aging population is already increasing the demand for meals and nutritional counseling in nursing homes, schools, prisons, community health programs, and home health-care agencies. Public interest in nutrition and the emphasis on health education and prudent lifestyles is spurring demand in management.

Civilian Advancement Prospects

As Dietitians and nutritionists gain experience they may expect to advance to assistant, associate, or director of a dietetic department, or become self-employed. Some Dietitians specialize in areas such as renal or pediatric dietetics. Others may leave the occupation to become sales representatives for equipment, pharmaceutical, or food manufacturers.

Education and Training

A four-year college degree in food and nutrition or institutional management is usually required to enter this occupation. Some specialties require completion of a general dietetic internship. However, the air force and army offer internship programs in dietetics that are approved by the American Dietetic Association.

High school students interested in entering these fields should take courses in biology, chemistry, mathematics, health, and communications. Dietitians and nutritionists need the minimum of a bachelor's degree in dietetics, foods and nutrition, food service systems management, or a related area. College students in these majors take courses in foods, nutrition, institution management, chemistry, biochemistry, biology, microbiology, and physiology. Other suggested courses include business, mathematics, statistics, computer science, psychology, sociology, and economics.

Special Requirements

Twenty-seven states require Dietitians and nutritionists to be licensed; 13 require certification; one requires registration. The Commission on Dietetic Registration of the American Dietetic Association awards the Registered Dietitian credential to those who pass a certification exam after completing their academic course work and supervised experience.

In 2001 there were 234 bachelor's and master's degree programs approved by the American Dietetic Association's Commission on Accreditation for Dietetics Education. Supervised practice experience can be acquired in two ways:

1. Completion of an ADA-accredited coordinated program (There are 51 accredited programs, which combine academic and supervised practice experience, lasting four to five years.)
2. Completion of 900 hours of supervised practice experience in any of the 258 CADE-accredited/approved internships (Internships may be full-time programs lasting six to 12 months or part-time programs lasting two years.)

Those interested in research, advanced clinical positions, or public health may need an advanced degree.

Experience, Special Skills, and Personality Traits

Dietitians and nutritionists need a desire to help others, an interest in nutrition and food preparation, and an interest in interpreting scientific and medical data. They should be well organized and analytical. Because they must convey important information to the general population, they should possess strong people skills and good written and oral communication abilities.

Unions and Associations

For a list of academic programs, scholarships, and other information about dietetics contact the American Dietetic Association. The ADA offers members opportunities to network, share information, and seek continuing training.

HEALTH SERVICE ADMINISTRATOR

CAREER PROFILE

Duties: Develop and manage budgets for health-care facilities; keep facilities running smoothly; plan for delivering health services during emergencies and test these plans during exercises; direct personnel activities and the day-to-day operations of the nursing and support departments, such as maintenance, food services, or administration

Alternate Title(s): Hospital Administrator; Nursing Services Director; Emergency Medical Services Coordinators; Outpatient Services Director

Availability: Army, Navy, Air Force, Coast Guard

Military Salary: See How to Use This Book

Civilian Salary: $28,600 to $124,500

Civilian Employment Prospects: Excellent

Civilian Advancement Prospects: Excellent

Prerequisites:

Rank—Officer

Education and Training—Bachelor's degree required for entry; master's degree and further education may be required for advancement; additional education may also be necessary

Experience—Any training and work experience obtained in the armed services; volunteer work at hospitals or clinics; first aid training

Special Skills and Personality Traits—Leadership; negotiation skills; good judgment; responsible; good communication skills; well organized; able to supervise others; capable of following orders precisely; desire to help others; self-confidence; ability to remain calm under pressure; interest in planning and organization; enjoy working closely with others; interest in health care

Licensure/Certification—State license required for nursing home administrators

CAREER LADDER

Health Service Administrator

Health Service Administrator, Specialized

Assistant Health Service Administrator

Position Description

The various departments of any health-care provider such as administration, nursing, X ray, emergency, maintenance, food service, and so on, cannot be run as individual departments divorced from one another. They must work together to provide quality health care and it is the job of the Health Services Administrator to manage hospitals, clinics, or other health-care facilities (as well as individual departments or specific health-care programs within their facility) so that they run smoothly and without mishap. Although most military Health Service Administrators work on land, there is an obvious need for them aboard hospital ships and ships with large sick bays as well.

The Health Service Administrator plans, directs, coordinates, and supervises the delivery of health care. These individuals can be generalists or specialists. Simply put, generalists oversee an entire facility while specialists run a specific or specialized department.

Health care is never static. The Health Service Administrator must be ready to handle the ever-changing world of integrated health-care delivery systems, technological innovations, and field-wide shifts in attention such as the recent increased focus on both preventive care and outpatient follow-up care. Larger facilities usually maintain at least a few assistant administrators to work under the chief administrator. Their duties could be to head up any of their facility's clinical areas, such as nursing, surgery, or therapy, or its nonmedical departments, such as housekeeping, or human resources. Conversely, the administrator of smaller facilities like nursing homes, and specialized clinics will often find themselves in charge of all or most of the daily operations.

Those managers of clinical departments will have far more specific responsibilities than generalists, and thus will be expected to have training and experience in a specific clinical area. For example, the director of pharmacology will be an experienced pharmacologist. In group practices the office administrator often handles only the business affairs of the group and leaves policy decisions to the doctors. Practices with 15 or fewer physicians might employ only one administrator to oversee personnel matters, including billing and collection, budgeting, planning, equipment outlays, and patient flow. Larger practices will have need for a top administrator with a staff of assistants, each responsible for different areas.

Those Health Service Administrators working for health maintenance organizations (HMOs) and other managed care settings would perform the same functions as those listed above. They would simply be expected to manage larger staffs. They are also generally expected to work in the areas of community outreach and preventive care as well.

Civilian Salaries

The average annual earnings of Health Service Administrators were $48,870 in 1998. The middle 50 percent earned between $37,900 and $71,580 a year. The lowest 10 percent earned below $28,600 and the highest 10 percent in excess of $88,730 a year. Average annual earnings in the industries employing the largest number of Health Service Administrators in 1997 were:

Hospitals	$52,600
Home health care services	$45,800
Health and allied services, not elsewhere classified	$44,700
Nursing and personal care facilities	$43,600
Offices and clinics of medical doctors	$39,600

The Buck Survey (conducted by the American Health Care Association) found that in 1997 nursing home administrators' average annual earnings were $52,800. The middle 50 percent earned between $44,300 and $60,300 a year. Assistant administrators had average annual earnings of about $35,000, with the middle 50 percent earning between $28,700 and $41,200.

Salaries will, of course, vary according to the size of a particular facility, as well as its geographic location. As with any job, the salaries of Health Service Administrators will also vary according to a number of other factors—the amount of responsibility the administrator is expected to handle, the type of facility in which they work, or the type of department of which they are in charge. For instance, the Medical Group Management Association reported that in 1998 the average salary for administrators of group practice (by size) was:

Fewer than seven physicians	$60,000
Seven to 25 physicians	$76,700
Twenty-six or more physicians	$124,500

Modern Healthcare magazine reported that the average annual compensation in 1998 for managers of various clinical departments was:

Respiratory therapy	$57,700
Home health care	$62,400
Ambulatory and outpatient services	$66,200
Radiology	$66,800
Clinical laboratory	$66,900
Physical therapy	$68,100
Rehabilitation services	$73,400
Nursing services	$100,200

Civilian Employment Prospects

As the elderly population in America continues to increase due to lower population replacement coupled with the constant advancement in age-increasing drugs and procedures, employment is expected to grow rapidly in home health agencies, residential care facilities, and practitioners' offices, and clinics. Health Service Administrators held roughly 222,000 jobs in 1998. Nearly one-half of these positions were in hospitals. One-quarter of them were in nursing and personal care facilities or physicians' offices and clinics. The remaining 25 percent were spread out over home health agencies, government ambulatory facilities, offices of dentists and other health practitioners, medical and dental laboratories, residential care facilities, and other social service agencies.

Hospitals will continue to employ the most administrators, although as hospitals continue to consolidate, centralize, and diversify functions the number of available positions within hospitals will slow as competition increases.

Civilian Advancement Prospects

As health services continue to expand and diversify the need for Health Service Administrators is expected to grow faster than the average for all occupations at least through 2008 and quite possibly beyond. While the elderly population in America continues to increase opportunities will be especially good in home health care and long-term care facilities. Managed care operations and consulting firms should prove to be good for Health Service Administrators with work experience in the health care field. It should be especially good for those with strong business and management skills.

Many services previously provided in hospitals are expected to shift to home health agencies, residential care facilities, and practitioners' offices and clinics. Medical group practice management is expected to flourish as group practices continue to grow larger and more complex. Health Service Administrators will also find their services in demand from health care management companies who provide management services to hospitals and other organizations.

Education and Training

Training is provided for some specialties in this occupation. It lasts between two to three months and consists of courses such as planning and directing health services, patient unit management, and nursing service administration. Of course, health services administrators must be familiar with management principles and practices. A bachelor's degree will suffice for some entry-level positions in smaller facilities or at the departmental level within HMOs, but a master's degree in health service administration, long-term care administration, health sciences, public health, public administration, or business administration is generally an absolute minimum requirement for most positions in this field. It is true, however, that some facilities may substitute on-the-job experience for formal education.

Clinical department heads might be able to get by with a degree in their field along with appropriate work experience, but a master's degree will almost certainly be required for them to progress beyond the entry level. Many colleges, universities, and other educational venues (schools of public health, medicine, public and business administration, etc.) offer B.A.s, M.A.s and doctoral degree programs in health administration. According to the Accrediting Commission on Education for Health Services Administrations, as recently as 1999, nearly 70 schools had accredited programs leading to the master's degree in health services administration. Graduate programs in this field will accept students with undergraduate degrees in business or health administration as well as those with a liberal arts or health profession background. Previous work experience in health care often factors in heavily when candidates for these programs are reviewed.

Special Requirements

All states and the District of Columbia require nursing home administrators to have a bachelor's degree, pass a licensing examination, complete a state-approved training program, and pursue continuing education.

Experience, Special Skills, and Personality Traits

There are no specific physical requirements for this career. Health Service Administrators must be strong leaders with excellent diplomatic skills. Since such an array of talents takes time to amass, most health services administrators need to start in small facilities. After gaining experience they then can move into more responsible and higher paying positions.

Health Service Administrators are often responsible for millions of dollars of facilities and equipment and hundreds of employees. They need to be open to different opinions. They must have a capacity for analyzing contradictory information and finding the correct path. They must understand finance and information systems, and be able to interpret data. Health Service Administrators must be strong leaders with excellent diplomatic skills.

Unions and Associations

Several groups offer Health Service Administrators opportunities to network with colleagues, stay in touch with their field, continue their education, and seek out certifications and job opportunities. They include the Association of University Programs in Health Administration, the Medical Group Management Association, and the Professional Association of Health Care Office Managers.

MEDICAL CARE TECHNICIAN

CAREER PROFILE

Duties: Provide bedside care in hospitals; feed, bathe, and dress patients; prepare patients, operating rooms, equipment, and supplies for surgery; make casts and other devices according to physicians' instructions; give medication to patients under the direction of physicians and nurses

Alternate Title(s): Nurse's Aide; Orderly; Operating Room Technician; Orthopedic Assistant; Practical Nurse; Nursing Assistant; Geriatric Aide; Unlicensed Assistive Personnel; Hospital Attendant; Mental Health Assistant; Psychiatric Nursing Assistant

Availability: Army, Navy, Air Force, Coast Guard

Military Salary: See How to Use This Book

Civilian Salary: $6.14/hour to $41,800

Civilian Employment Prospects: Good

Civilian Advancement Prospects: Good

Prerequisites:
   Rank—Enlisted
   Education and Training—High school diploma
   Experience—Any training and work experience obtained in the armed services or Job Corps
   Special Skills and Personality Traits—Tact; patience; understanding; good health; emotional stability; good communication skills; a willingness to perform repetitive, routine tasks; honesty; discretion; manual dexterity; quick reflexes; an interest in helping others; the ability to work under stressful or emergency conditions; the ability to follow directions precisely
   Licensure/Certification—State license; certification varies

CAREER LADDER

Varies by position

Position Description

Military Medical Care Technicians work with teams of physicians, nurses, and other health-care professionals to provide treatment to military personnel. They work in hospitals and clinics on land, or aboard ships, and in mobile field hospitals during combat situations. These technicians provide bedside care in hospitals, including taking patients' body temperature, pulse, and respiration rate; feeding, bathing, and dressing patients; and preparing patients, operating rooms, equipment, and supplies for surgery. They also make casts, traction devices, and splints according to physicians' instructions and give medication to patients under the direction of physicians and nurses.

In the civilian world nursing and psychiatric aides help care for physically or mentally ill, injured, disabled, or infirm individuals confined to hospitals, nursing and personal care facilities, and mental health settings. Home health aides duties are similar, but they work in patients' homes or residential care facilities. Nursing aides employed in nursing homes often are the principal caregivers, having far more contact with residents than other members of the staff.

Psychiatric aides care for mentally impaired or emotionally disturbed individuals. They work under a team that may include psychiatrists, psychologists, psychiatric nurses, social workers, and therapists. Home health aides help elderly, convalescent, or disabled persons live in their own homes instead of in a health facility. Under the direction of nursing or medical staff, they provide health-related services, such as administering oral medications.

Most full-time aides work 40 hours a week, but because patients need care 24 hours a day, some work evenings, nights, weekends, and holidays. Aides have many unpleasant duties. They spend many hours standing and walking, they must move patients in and out of bed or help them stand or walk, and they regularly face the hazards from minor infections and major diseases, such as hepatitis. They also empty bedpans, and change soiled bed linens.

Surgical technologists assist in surgical operations under the supervision of surgeons, registered nurses, or other surgical personnel. Surgical technologists are members of operating room teams, which most commonly include surgeons, anesthesiologists, and circulating nurses. During surgery, technologists pass instruments and other sterile supplies to surgeons and surgeon assistants. Surgical technologists work in clean, well-lighted, cool environments. They must stand and remain alert for long periods.

Licensed practical nurses care for the sick, injured, convalescent, and disabled under the direction of physicians and registered nurses. Most provide basic bedside care. Experienced LPNs may supervise nursing assistants and aides. Those in nursing homes provide routine bedside care, help evaluate residents' needs, develop care plans, and supervise the care provided by nursing aides. In doctors' offices and clinics, they also may make appointments, keep records, and perform other clerical duties.

Licensed practical nurses in hospitals and nursing homes work a 40-hour week. Because patients need around-the-clock care, some work nights, weekends, and holidays. They often stand for long periods and help patients move in bed, stand, or walk. LPNs face hazards from caustic chemicals, radiation, and infectious diseases.

Civilian Salaries

In 2000, the average hourly salary for nursing aides, orderlies, and attendants was $8.89 an hour. The middle 50 percent earned between $7.51 and $10.59 an hour. The lowest 10 percent earned less than $6.48. The highest 10 percent earned more than $12.69 an hour.

In 2000, the average hourly salary for psychiatric aides was $10.45 an hour. The middle 50 percent earned between $8.38 and $13.02 an hour. The lowest 10 percent earned less than $7.10. The highest 10 percent earned more than $15.50 an hour.

In 2000, the average hourly salary for home health aides was $8.23 an hour. The middle 50 percent earned between $7.13 and $9.88 an hour. The lowest 10 percent earned less than $6.14. The highest 10 percent earned more than $11.93 an hour.

In 2000, the average yearly income for surgical technologists was $29,020. The middle 50 percent earned between $24,490 and $34,160. The lowest 10 percent earned less than $20,490. The highest 10 percent earned more than $40,310.

In 2000, the average yearly income for licensed practical nurses was $29,440. The middle 50 percent earned between $24,920 and $34,800. The lowest 10 percent earned less than $21,520. The highest 10 percent earned more than $41,800.

Civilian Employment Prospects

In 2000, nursing, psychiatric, and home health aides held more than two million jobs. Most were employed by home health agencies, visiting nurse associations, social services agencies, residential care facilities, and temporary-help firms. Others worked for home health departments of hospitals and nursing facilities, public health agencies, and community volunteer agencies. Most psychiatric aides worked in psychiatric units of general hospitals, psychiatric hospitals, state and county mental institutions, homes for mentally retarded and psychiatric patients, and community mental health centers.

Through 2010, opportunities for nursing, psychiatric, and home health aides are projected to grow faster than the average. Home health aides are expected to grow the fastest, as a result of growing demand for home health care from an aging population and efforts to contain health-care costs by moving patients out of hospitals and nursing facilities as quickly as possible. Nursing aide employment will not grow as fast as home health aide employment, largely because nursing aides are concentrated in the relatively slower-growing nursing home sector. Opportunities for psychiatric aides are expected to grow as fast as the average.

In 2000, surgical technologists held more than 70,000 jobs. Nearly three-quarters are employed by hospitals, mainly in operating and delivery rooms. Others are employed in clinics and surgical centers, and in the offices of physicians and dentists who perform outpatient surgery. A few, known as private scrubs, are employed directly by surgeons who have special surgical teams, like those for liver transplants. Through 2010, opportunities for surgical technologists are expected to grow faster than the average for all occupations as the volume of surgery increases.

In 2000, licensed practical nurses held nearly 700,000 jobs. Twenty-nine percent of LPNs worked in nursing homes, 28 percent worked in hospitals, and 14 percent in physicians' offices and clinics. Others worked for home health-care services, residential care facilities, schools, temporary help agencies, or government agencies. Through 2010, opportunities for LPNs are expected to grow about as fast as the average for all occupations in response to the long-term care needs of a rapidly growing elderly population and the general growth of health care. Nursing homes will offer the most new jobs for LPNs as the number of aged and disabled persons in need of long-term care rises. In addition to caring for the aged and disabled, nursing homes will be called on to care for the increasing number of patients who have been discharged from the hospital but who have not recovered enough to return home.

Civilian Advancement Prospects

Opportunities for advancement within these occupations are limited unless one acquires additional formal training. Some employers and unions provide opportunities by simplifying the educational paths to advancement. Experience as an aide can also help individuals decide whether to pursue a career in the health-care field. Some medical care technicians might improve their job status by finding employment at larger facilities or taking on supervisory duties.

Education and Training

In the military, those interested in this career receive two months to one year of classroom instruction, depending on specialty, including patient care. Classes usually contain such courses as patient care techniques, emergency medical techniques, methods of sterilizing surgical equipment, and plaster casting techniques. Further training occurs on the job and through advanced courses.

Often, neither a high school diploma nor previous work experience is necessary for a job as a nursing, psychiatric, or home health aide. Hospitals may require experience, but nursing homes often hire inexperienced workers who must complete a minimum of 75 hours of mandatory training and pass a competency evaluation program within four months of employment. Aides who complete the program are certified and placed on the state registry of nursing aides. Some states require psychiatric aides to complete a formal training program.

Home health aides may take training before taking the competency test. Federal law suggests at least 75 hours of classroom and practical training supervised by a registered nurse. Training and testing programs must meet the standards of the Health Care Financing Administration. Training programs vary depending upon state regulations.

Nursing aide training is offered in high schools, vocational-technical centers, and some nursing homes and community colleges. Some facilities provide classroom instruction for newly hired aides, while others rely exclusively on informal on-the-job instruction from a licensed nurse or an experienced aide. Such training may last several days to a few months. From time to time, aides may also attend lectures, workshops, and in-service training.

Surgical technologists are trained in formal programs offered by community and junior colleges, vocational schools, universities, hospitals, and the military. In 2001, the Commission on Accreditation of Allied Health Education Programs recognized 350 accredited programs.

A high school diploma, or equivalent, usually is required for entry to nursing programs for licensed practical nurses, although some programs accept candidates without a diploma or are designed as part of a high school curriculum. In 2000, approximately 1,100 state-approved programs provided practical nursing training. Most practical nursing programs last about one year and include both classroom study and supervised clinical practice.

Special Requirements

Requirements vary, but most jobs in this area require some form of certification or state license.

Federal law requires home health aides to pass a competency test covering 12 areas: communication skills; documentation of patient status and care provided; reading and recording vital signs; basic infection control procedures; basic body functions; maintenance of a healthy environment; emergency procedures; physical, emotional, and developmental characteristics of patients; personal hygiene and grooming; safe transfer techniques; normal range of motion and positioning; and basic nutrition.

The National Association for Home Care offers national certification for home health aides. The certification is a voluntary demonstration that the individual has met industry standards.

Technologists may obtain voluntary professional certification from the Liaison Council on Certification for the Surgical Technologist by graduating from a CAAHEP-accredited program and passing a national certification examination. They may then use the designation Certified Surgical Technologist. Continuing education or reexamination is required to maintain certification, which must be renewed every six years. Certification may also be obtained from the National Center for Competency Testing.

All states and the District of Columbia require licensed practical nurses to pass a licensing examination after completing a state-approved practical nursing program.

Experience, Special Skills, and Personality Traits

Those desiring to be surgical technologists need to be tactful, patient, understanding, dependable, and have a desire to help people. They should be able to work as part of a team, have good communication skills, and be willing to perform repetitive, routine tasks. They need to be honest, discreet, and in good health. They must also have manual dexterity and be conscientious, orderly, and emotionally stable, have quick reflexes, an interest in helping others, the ability to work under stressful or emergency conditions and the ability to follow directions precisely.

Unions and Associations

For information about training and referrals to state and local agencies about opportunities for home health aides, a list of relevant publications, and information on certification, contact the National Association for Home Care.

For information on a career as a surgical technologist contact the Association of Surgical Technologists. For information on becoming a Certified Surgical Technologist, contact the Liaison Council on Certification for the Surgical Technologist.

For information on becoming a National Certified Technician O.R., contact the National Center for Competency Testing.

For information about practical nursing, contact the National League for Nursing, the National Association for Practical Nurse Education and Service, Inc., and the National Federation of Licensed Practical Nurses, Inc.

MEDICAL LABORATORY TECHNICIAN/TECHNOLOGIST

CAREER PROFILE

Duties: Use lab equipment to analyze specimens; examine blood and bone marrow; test specimens; draw blood; assist in collecting specimens at autopsies; record and file results of laboratory tests

Alternate Title(s): Clinical Laboratory Scientist; Medical Technologist; Clinical Laboratory Technician; Medical Technician; Phlebotomist; Histologist

Availability: Army, Navy, Air Force, Coast Guard

Military Salary: See How to Use This Book

Civilian Salary: $18,550 to $42,370 (technician)/$29,240 to $55,560 (technologist)

Civilian Employment Prospects: Good

Civilian Advancement Prospects: Good

Prerequisites:

Rank—Enlisted

Education and Training—Associate's degree minimum for clinical laboratory technicians; bachelor's degree in medical technology or a life science required for clinical laboratory technologists

Experience—Any training and work experience obtained in the armed services

Special Skills and Personality Traits—Normal color vision; good analytical judgment; the ability to work under pressure; detail-oriented; an interest in scientific and technical work; manual dexterity; computer skills; problem-solving abilities

Licensure/Certification—State license; certification

CAREER LADDER

```
┌─────────────────────────────────────┐
│    Medical Laboratory Supervisor     │
└─────────────────────────────────────┘

┌─────────────────────────────────────┐
│   Medical Laboratory Technologist    │
└─────────────────────────────────────┘

┌─────────────────────────────────────┐
│    Medical Laboratory Technician     │
└─────────────────────────────────────┘
```

Position Description

The staffs of military medical laboratories perform clinical tests required to detect and identify diseases among patients. Working in medical centers, clinics, and hospitals on land or aboard ships, military Medical Laboratory Technicians use lab equipment to analyze specimens of tissue, blood, and body fluids, examine blood and bone marrow under microscopes and test specimens for bacteria or viruses. They also draw blood from patients, assist in collecting specimens at autopsies, and record and file results of laboratory tests.

In the civilian world, clinical laboratory testing plays a crucial role in the detection, diagnosis, and treatment of disease. Clinical laboratory technologists examine and analyze body fluids, tissues, and cells. They look for bacteria, parasites, and other microorganisms; analyze the chemical content of fluids; match blood for transfusions; and test for drug levels in the blood to show how a patient is responding to treatment.

Medical and clinical laboratory technologists perform complex chemical, biological, hematological, immunologic, microscopic, and bacteriological tests. Technologists microscopically examine blood, tissue, and other body substances. They make cultures of body fluid and tissue samples, to determine the presence of bacteria, fungi, parasites, or other microorganisms. They analyze samples for chemical content or reaction and determine blood glucose and cholesterol levels. They also type and cross match blood samples for transfusions, evaluate test results, develop and modify procedures, and establish and monitor programs to ensure the accuracy of tests.

In large hospitals or in independent laboratories that operate continuously, personnel usually work the day, evening, or night shift and may work weekends and holidays. Laboratory personnel in small facilities may work on rotating shifts, rather than on a regular shift.

Laboratories usually are well-lighted and clean; however, specimens, solutions, and reagents used in the laboratory sometimes produce fumes. Laboratory workers may spend a great deal of time on their feet.

Civilian Salaries

In 2000, the average yearly salary for medical and clinical laboratory technicians was $27,540. The middle 50 percent earned between $22,260 and $34,320. The lowest 10 percent earned less than $18,550. The highest 10 percent earned more than $42,370.

In 2000, the average yearly salary for medical and clinical laboratory technologists was $40,510. The middle 50 percent earned between $34,220 and $47,460. The lowest 10 percent earned less than $29,240. The highest 10 percent earned more than $55,560.

Civilian Employment Prospects

In 2000, clinical laboratory technologists and technicians held nearly 295,000 jobs. Half worked in hospitals. Most of the remaining positions were found in medical laboratories or the offices and clinics of physicians. A small number were in blood banks, research and testing laboratories, and with the federal government, at U.S. Department of Veterans Affairs hospitals and U.S. Public Health Service facilities.

Through 2010, opportunities for clinical laboratory workers are expected to grow about as fast as the average for all occupations, as the volume of laboratory tests increases with population growth and the development of new types of tests. During this time, new, more powerful diagnostic tests will encourage additional testing and spur employment. At the same time, however, research and development efforts targeted at simplifying routine testing procedures may enhance the ability of non-laboratory personnel, physicians, and patients to perform tests now done in laboratories.

Civilian Advancement Prospects

Technologists may advance to supervisory positions in laboratory work or become chief medical or clinical laboratory technologists or laboratory managers in hospitals. Technicians can become technologists through additional education and experience. Some people in this field may choose to advance their career by going to other health careers such as becoming doctors or nurses.

Education and Training

In the military, those interested in this career receive three to nine months of classroom instruction, depending on specialty, including practice in testing specimens. Classes usually contain such courses as medical laboratory procedures, study of human parasites and diseases, laboratory administration, and record keeping.

Entry-level positions as medical or clinical laboratory technologists require a bachelor's degree with a major in medical technology or in one of the life sciences. Universities and hospitals offer medical technology programs. It also is possible to qualify through a combination of education, on-the-job, and specialized training. Medical and clinical laboratory technicians generally have either an associate's degree from a community or junior college or a certificate from a hospital, vocational, or technical school, or from one of the U.S. Armed Forces. A few technicians learn their skills on the job.

The National Accrediting Agency for Clinical Laboratory Sciences fully accredits 503 programs for medical and clinical laboratory technologists, medical and clinical laboratory technicians, histologic technologists and technicians, and pathologists' assistants. NAACLS also approves 70 programs in phlebotomy, cytogenetic technology, molecular biology, and clinical assisting. Other nationally recognized accrediting agencies include the Commission on Accreditation of Allied Health Education Programs and the Accrediting Bureau of Health Education Schools.

Special Requirements

Some states require laboratory personnel to be licensed or registered (information on licensure is available from individual state departments of health or boards of occupational licensing). Certification is a voluntary process by which a nongovernmental organization, such as a professional society or certifying agency, grants recognition to an individual whose professional competence meets prescribed standards. Agencies certifying medical and clinical laboratory technologists and technicians include the Board of Registry of the American Society for Clinical Pathology, the American Medical Technologists, the National Credentialing Agency for Laboratory Personnel, and the Board of Registry of the American Association of Bioanalysts.

Experience, Special Skills, and Personality Traits

Those working in clinical laboratories need normal color vision, good analytical judgment, and the ability to work under pressure. They must have the ability to pay close attention to details and an interest in scientific and technical work, as well as manual dexterity, computer skills, and problem-solving abilities. They must also be comfortable working with patients and handling patient samples.

Unions and Associations

For a list of accredited and approved educational programs for clinical laboratory personnel, contact the National Accrediting Agency for Clinical Laboratory Sciences. For information on certification contact the American Association of Bioanalysts, the American Medical Technologists, the American Society for Clinical Pathology, Board of Registry, and the National Credentialing Agency for Laboratory Personnel.

For further career information contact the American Association of Blood Banks, the American Society for Clinical Laboratory Science, and the American Society for Clinical Pathology.

MEDICAL RECORD TECHNICIAN

CAREER PROFILE

Duties: Fill out admission and discharge records for patients; assign patients to hospital rooms; prepare daily reports; organize, file, and maintain medical records; type reports; prepare tables of medical statistics; maintain libraries of medical publications

Alternate Title(s): Admitting Clerk; Discharge Clerk

Availability: Army, Navy, Air Force, Coast Guard

Military Salary: See How to Use This Book

Civilian Salary: $15,710 to $35,170

Civilian Employment Prospects: Good

Civilian Advancement Prospects: Good

Prerequisites:

Rank—Enlisted

Education and Training—Associate degree minimum

Experience—Any training and work experience obtained in the armed services or Job Corps

Special Skills and Personality Traits—Accurate; detail-oriented; good communications skills; excellent computer skills; knowledge of office equipment and filing systems; good interpersonal skills

Licensure/Certification—Optional certification

CAREER LADDER

```
┌─────────────────────────────────┐
│           Supervisor            │
└─────────────────────────────────┘

┌─────────────────────────────────┐
│ Senior Medical Record Technician │
└─────────────────────────────────┘

┌─────────────────────────────────┐
│    Medical Record Technician    │
└─────────────────────────────────┘
```

Position Description

Many positions within the modern military are support positions. In the field of health care, medical records are not only important, they are indispensable. Physicians need complete and accurate information about patient symptoms, test results, illnesses, and previous treatments to be able to provide proper treatment. Medical Record Technicians work in admissions or medical records sections of hospitals and clinics in land-based facilities and aboard ships. They fill out admission and discharge records for patients entering and leaving military hospitals, assign patients to hospital rooms, prepare daily reports about patients admitted and discharged, and organize, file, and maintain medical records. They also type reports of physical examinations, illnesses, and treatments, prepare tables of medical statistics and maintain libraries of medical publications.

Civilian Medical Record Technicians work in hospitals, clinics, and government health agencies. Every time they

treat a patient, they record what they observed, and how the patient was treated medically as well as information the patient provides concerning their symptoms and medical history, the results of examinations, reports of X rays and laboratory tests, diagnoses, and treatment plans.

Medical records and health information technicians start the process of building a patient's health information by ascertaining that their initial medical charts are complete, properly identified, and signed, and that all necessary information is in the computer. Sometimes, they communicate with physicians or others to clarify diagnoses or get additional information. Technicians use computer programs to tabulate and analyze data to help improve patient care, control costs, for use in legal actions, in response to surveys, or for use in research studies.

The duties of these technicians varies with the size of their facility. In large to medium facilities, technicians may specialize in one aspect of health information, or supervise health information clerks and transcriptionists while a medical records and health information administrator manages the department. In small facilities, a credentialed medical records and health information technician sometimes manages the department.

Medical records and health information technicians usually work a 40-hour week. Since many hospital health information departments are open 24 hours a day, seven days a week, technicians may work day, evening, and night shifts. Medical records and health information technicians work in pleasant and comfortable offices. Technicians who work at computer monitors for prolonged periods must guard against eyestrain and muscle pain.

Civilian Salaries

In 2000, the average yearly salary for medical records and health information technicians was $22,750. The middle 50 percent earned between $18,700 and $28,590. The lowest 10 percent earned less than $15,710. The highest 10 percent earned more than $35,170.

In 2000, the average yearly salaries in the industries employing the largest numbers of medical records and health information technicians were as follows:

Nursing and personal care facilities	$23,760
Hospitals	$23,540
Offices and clinics of medical doctors	$21,090

Civilian Employment Prospects

In 2000, medical records and health information technicians held slightly more than 135,000 jobs. Roughly 20 percent of these jobs were in hospitals. The rest were mostly in nursing homes, medical group practices, clinics, and home health agencies. Insurance firms that deal in health matters employ a small number of health information technicians to tabulate and analyze health information. Public health departments also hire technicians to supervise data collection from health-care institutions and to assist in research.

Through 2010, opportunities for formally trained technicians should be very good. Employment of medical records and health information technicians is expected to grow much faster than the average during this time due to rapid growth in the number of medical tests, treatments, and procedures which will be increasingly scrutinized by third-party payers, regulators, courts, and consumers.

Hospitals will continue to employ a large percentage of health information technicians, but growth will not be as fast as in other areas. Increasing demand for detailed records in offices and clinics of physicians should result in fast employment growth, especially in large group practices.

Civilian Advancement Prospects

Experienced medical records and health information technicians usually advance in one of two ways—by specializing or managing. Many senior technicians specialize in coding, particularly Medicare coding, or in tumor registry.

In large medical records and health information departments, experienced technicians may advance to section supervisor, overseeing the work of the coding, correspondence, or discharge sections, for example. Senior technicians with RHIT credentials may become director or assistant director of a medical records and health information department in a small facility. However, in larger institutions, the director is usually an administrator, with a bachelor's degree in medical records and health information administration.

Education and Training

In the military, those interested in this career receive one-and-a-half to four-and-a-half months of classroom instruction, depending on specialty. Classes usually contain such courses as medical terminology, medical records preparation and maintenance, maintenance of medical libraries, and basic typing skills.

Those still in high school can improve chances of acceptance into medical record and health information education programs by taking anatomy, biology, chemistry, health, general science, business administration, physiology, medical terminology, and computer courses. To actually enter the field, however, one must usually have an associate degree from a community or junior college. In addition to general education, coursework includes medical terminology, anatomy and physiology, legal aspects of health information, coding and abstraction of data, statistics, database management, quality improvement methods, and computer training. Hospitals sometimes advance promising health information clerks to jobs as medical records and health information technicians, although this practice may be less common in the future. Advancement usually requires two to four years of job experience and completion of a hospital's in-house training program.

Most employers prefer to hire Registered Health Information Technicians, who must pass a written examination offered by AHIMA. To take the examination, a person must graduate from a two-year associate degree program accredited by the Commission on Accreditation of Allied Health Education Programs of the American Medical Association. Technicians trained in non-CAAHEP accredited programs, or on the job, are not eligible to take the examination.

Special Requirements

In 2001, CAAHEP accredited 177 programs for health information technicians. Technicians who specialize in coding may also obtain voluntary certification.

Experience, Special Skills, and Personality Traits

Those who wish to enter this field should have an interest in work requiring accuracy and attention to detail, the ability to communicate well, and an interest in using computers and other office machines. Also required are strong interpersonal skills.

Unions and Associations

For information on careers in medical records and health information technology, including a list of CAAHEP-accredited programs, contact the American Health Information Management Association.

OPTOMETRIST

CAREER PROFILE

Duties: Check patient vision; examine eyes; measure vision problems using optical instruments; prescribe corrective lenses and training exercises; instruct patients on how to wear and care for contact lenses

Alternate Title(s): Doctor of Optometry; OD

Availability: Army, Navy, Air Force

Military Salary: See How to Use This Book

Civilian Salary: $60,130 to $120,000

Civilian Employment Prospects: Good

Civilian Advancement Prospects: Good

Prerequisites:
    Rank—Officer
    Education and Training—Doctor of Optometry degree
    Experience—Any training and work experience obtained in the armed services
    Special Skills and Personality Traits—Manual dexterity; a preference for working closely with people; desire to help others; detail-oriented; strong interpersonal skills; good communication skills; business ability; self-discipline; tact and sensitivity
    Licensure/Certification—State license

CAREER LADDER

```
┌─────────────────────────────┐
│         Specialist          │
└─────────────────────────────┘

┌─────────────────────────────┐
│        Optometrist          │
└─────────────────────────────┘
```

Position Description

Military Optometrists examine eyes and treat vision problems by prescribing glasses or contact lenses. They check patient vision using eye charts, examine eyes for glaucoma and other diseases, and measure patient nearsightedness, farsightedness, depth perception, and other vision problems using optical instruments. They prescribe corrective lenses and training exercises to strengthen weak eye muscles. They also instruct patients on how to wear and care for contact lenses and refer those with eye diseases to ophthalmologists.

In the civilian world, most Optometrists work in private practice. Some work for hospitals, clinics, public health agencies, or optical laboratories. Whether in private or public practice, however, these health care workers are essential as they provide primary vision care for the more than half of the people in the United States who wear glasses or contact lenses. Optometrists examine people's eyes to diagnose vision problems and eye diseases. They use instruments and observation to examine eye health and to test patients' visual acuity, depth and color perception and ability to focus and coordinate the eyes. Optometrists analyze test results and develop a treatment plan. Optometrists prescribe eyeglasses and contact lenses and provide vision therapy and low-vision rehabilitation. They administer drugs to patients to aid in the diagnosis of eye vision problems and prescribe drugs to treat some eye diseases and provide preoperative and postoperative care to cataract, laser vision correction, and other eye surgery patients. Some Optometrists specialize in work with the elderly, children, or partially sighted persons who need specialized visual devices. Others develop and implement ways to protect workers' eyes from on-the-job strain or injury. Some specialize in contact lenses, sports vision, or vision therapy. A few teach optometry, perform research, or consult.

Optometrists in private practice must also handle the business aspects of running an office, such as developing a patient base, hiring employees, keeping records, and ordering equipment and supplies. Whether in private or public practice, however, optometrists work in clean, well-lighted, comfortable surroundings. Most work only about 40 hours a week, although the hours may include weekends and evenings to suit the needs of patients.

Civilian Salaries

In 2000, the average yearly salary for salaried Optometrists was $82,860. The middle 50 percent earned between $60,310 and $111,520. In 2000, the average yearly salary for salaried Optometrists in offices and clinics of medical doctors was $89,460 and $85,470 in offices of other health practitioners. Salaried Optometrists tend to earn more initially than do optometrists who set up their own independent practice. In the long run, those in private practice usually earn more. In 2000 the American Optometric Association reported that the median net income for all Optometrists in private practice ranged from about $115,000 to $120,000.

Civilian Employment Prospects

In 2000, Optometrists held just over 30,000 jobs. The number of jobs is greater than the number of practicing Optometrists because some Optometrists hold two or more jobs. For example, an Optometrist just starting his private practice may work in another practice or a vision care center either to gain experience or simply to help balance the books while he gets his own practice off the ground.

Through 2010 opportunities for Optometrists are expected to grow about as fast as the average for all occupations due to the vision care needs of a growing and aging population. As baby boomers age, they will be more likely to visit Optometrists and ophthalmologists because of the onset of vision problems in middle age, including those resulting from the extensive use of computers. The demand for optometric services also will increase because of growth in the oldest age group, with their increased likelihood of cataracts, glaucoma, diabetes, and hypertension.

Because Optometrists usually remain in practice until they retire, replacement needs arise almost entirely from retirements.

Civilian Advancement Prospects

Optometrists wishing to teach or do research may study for a master's or Ph.D. in visual science, physiological optics, neurophysiology, public health, health administration, health information and communication, or health education. One-year postgraduate clinical residency programs are available for Optometrists who wish to specialize in family practice optometry, pediatric optometry, geriatric optometry, vision therapy, contact lenses, hospital-based optometry, primary care optometry, or ocular disease.

Education and Training

Competition for admission to optometry school is always keen, but it must be noted that the army has a program to provide financial support to optometry students in return for a period of obligated service.

Optometry programs include classroom and laboratory study of health and visual sciences, as well as clinical training in the diagnosis and treatment of eye disorders. Courses in pharmacology, optics, vision science, biochemistry, and systemic disease are included.

The Doctor of Optometry degree requires completion of a four-year program at an accredited optometry school preceded by at least three years of preoptometric study at an accredited college or university.

In 2000, 17 U.S. schools and colleges of optometry held an accredited status with the Accreditation Council on Optometric Education of the American Optometric Association. Requirements for admission to schools of optometry include courses in English, mathematics, physics, chemistry, and biology. A few schools require (or strongly recommend) courses in psychology, history, sociology, speech, or business. Applicants must take the Optometry Admissions Test, a measure of academic ability and scientific comprehension. Most applicants take the test after their sophomore or junior year.

Special Requirements

All areas of the country require optometrists to be licensed. They must have a Doctor of Optometry degree from an accredited optometry school and pass both a written and a clinical state board examination. In many states, applicants can substitute the examinations of the National Board of Examiners in Optometry, usually taken during the student's academic career, for part or all of the written examination. State licenses must be renewed (every one to three years depending on location). Continuing education credits are needed for renewal.

Experience, Special Skills, and Personality Traits

A Doctor of Optometry needs good manual dexterity, a preference for working closely with people, a desire to help others and an interest in work requiring accuracy and attention to detail. They must also have business ability, self-discipline, and the ability to deal tactfully with their patients.

Unions and Associations

For information on optometry as a career and a list of accredited optometric educational institutions, contact the Association of Schools and Colleges of Optometry and the American Optometric Association. The Board of Optometry in each state can supply information on licensing requirements.

PHARMACIST

CAREER PROFILE

Duties: Manage pharmacy technicians; advise doctors and patients about drugs and medicines; train medical, nursing, and pharmacy staff; consult on drug and medicine research programs; check drug and medicine supplies and reorder when necessary; direct pharmacy record keeping

Alternate Title(s): Radiopharmacist

Availability: Army, Navy, Air Force, Coast Guard

Military Salary: See How to Use This Book

Civilian Salary: $51,570 to $89,010

Civilian Employment Prospects: Good

Civilian Advancement Prospects: Good

Prerequisites:

    Rank—Officer

    Education and Training—Four-year college degree required

    Experience—Internship under a licensed pharmacist; any training and work experience obtained in the armed services

    Special Skills and Personality Traits—Scientific aptitude; good communication skills; a desire to help others; conscientiousness; an interest in chemical formulas and in understanding the effects of drugs and medicines; good interpersonal skills; sensitivity; honest; responsible

    Licensure/Certification—State license required

CAREER LADDER

```
┌─────────────────────────────────┐
│     Supervisor or Manager       │
└─────────────────────────────────┘

┌─────────────────────────────────┐
│          Pharmacist             │
└─────────────────────────────────┘

┌─────────────────────────────────┐
│   Pharmacy Technician or Aide   │
└─────────────────────────────────┘
```

Position Description

Military hospitals, clinics, and field care units have the same need for drugs and medicines as any other health-care venue. As in the civilian world, military Pharmacists manage the purchase, storage, and dispensation of drugs and medicines. Working in hospitals and clinics on land and aboard ships they manage pharmacy technicians who prepare, label, and dispense orders for drugs and medicines and advise doctors and patients on the proper use and side effects of drugs and medicines. They also train medical, nursing, and pharmacy staffs on the use of drugs, consult on drug and medicine research programs, check drug and medicine supplies, reorder when necessary, and perform clerical chores like directing pharmacy record keeping.

In the civilian world pharmacy technicians and pharmacy aides work for pharmacies, drug stores, and the drug departments of stores and supermarkets. They also work in hospitals, nursing homes, and clinics. Pharmacists who specialize in radioactive drugs are known as radiopharmacists. Those in other professions who may work with pharmaceutical compounds include biological and medical scientists and chemists and materials scientists.

Pharmacists dispense drugs to prescription holders. They also provide information to patients about medications and advise physicians and other health practitioners on the selection, dosages, interactions, and side effects of medications. Pharmacists do not just count out pills and pour prescribed dosages of medications into bottles. Compounding, the actual mixing of ingredients to form powders, tablets, capsules, ointments, and solutions, is only a small part of a pharmacist's practice. They must thoroughly understand the use; clinical effects; and composition of drugs, including their chemical, biological, and physical properties. Pharmacists are also becoming more involved in drug therapy decision making and patient counseling.

Pharmacists must counsel patients and answer questions about prescription drugs, provide information about over-the-counter drugs, and give advice about durable medical equipment and home health-care supplies. Those who own or manage community pharmacies may sell nonhealth-related merchandise, hire and supervise personnel, and oversee the general operation of the pharmacy. Some community pharmacists provide specialized services to help patients manage conditions such as diabetes, asthma, smoking cessation, or high blood pressure.

Hospitals and clinical Pharmacists dispense medications and advise the medical staff on the selection and effects of drugs. They make sterile solutions; buy medical supplies; assess, plan, and monitor drug programs or regimens; and counsel patients on the use of drugs while in the hospital and at home after a patient is discharged. Pharmacists also may evaluate drug use patterns and outcomes for patients in hospitals or managed care organizations. Home health-care Pharmacists monitor drug therapy and prepare infusions and other medications for use in the home.

Pharmacists keep confidential records of patients' drug therapies to ensure that harmful drug interactions do not occur. They frequently teach pharmacy students serving as interns in preparation for graduation and licensure. Some Pharmacists specialize in specific drug therapy areas, such as intravenous nutrition support, oncology, nuclear pharmacy, and pharmacotherapy.

Pharmacists usually work in clean, well-lighted, well-ventilated areas. Many spend most of the workday on their feet. Community and hospital pharmacies are open for extended hours, often around the clock, so Pharmacists may work evenings, nights, weekends, and holidays. Consultant Pharmacists may travel to nursing homes or other facilities to monitor patients' drug therapy.

Civilian Salaries
In 2000, the average yearly salary for Pharmacists was $70,950. The highest 10 percent earned more than $89,010 a year. The middle 50 percent earned between $61,860 and $81,690 a year. The lowest 10 percent earned less than $51,570. Many Pharmacists also receive compensation in the form of bonuses, overtime, and profit sharing.

In 2000, the average yearly salary in the industries employing the largest numbers of Pharmacists were as follows:

Department stores	$73,730
Grocery stores	$72,440
Drug stores and proprietary stores	$72,110
Hospitals	$68,760

Civilian Employment Prospects
In 2000, Pharmacists held nearly 220,000 jobs. Roughly three in five worked in community pharmacies, either independently owned or part of a drug store chain, grocery store, department store, or mass merchandiser. Most were salaried employees, but some were self-employed owners. Some 21 percent of salaried Pharmacists worked in hospitals, and others worked in clinics, mail-order pharmacies, pharmaceutical wholesalers, home health-care agencies, or for the federal government.

Through 2010, very good employment opportunities are expected for Pharmacists because the number of degrees granted in pharmacy are not expected to be as numerous as the number of job openings created by employment growth and the need to replace Pharmacists who retire or otherwise leave the occupation.

Through 2010, opportunities for Pharmacists are expected to grow faster than the average for all occupations due to the increased pharmaceutical needs of a larger and older population as well as an increase in the use of medication. The growing numbers of middle-aged and elderly people will continue to spur demand for Pharmacists in all practice settings.

Retail pharmacies are taking steps to increase their prescription volume. Automation of drug dispensing and greater use of pharmacy technicians and pharmacy aides will help them to dispense more prescriptions. The number of community Pharmacists needed in the future will depend on the rate of expansion of chain drug stores and the willingness of insurers to reimburse Pharmacists for providing clinical services to patients taking prescription medications.

Cost-conscious insurers and health systems should continue to emphasize the role of Pharmacists since they realize that the expense of using medication to treat diseases and conditions is often considerably less than the potential costs for patients whose conditions go untreated and eventually need costly operations or therapies. Pharmacists also can reduce the expenses resulting from unexpected complications due to allergic reactions or medication interactions.

With its emphasis on cost control, managed care encourages the growth of lower cost prescription drug distributors, such as mail-order firms, for certain medications. Faster than average employment growth is expected in retail pharmacies.

Employment in hospitals is expected to grow about as fast as average, as hospitals reduce inpatient stays, downsize, and consolidate departments. Pharmacy services are shifting to long-term, ambulatory, and home care settings, where opportunities for Pharmacists will be best. New opportunities are emerging for Pharmacists in managed-care organizations, where they analyze trends and patterns in medication use for their populations of patients (especially for those trained in research, disease management, and pharmacoeconomics—determining the costs and benefits of different drug therapies).

Civilian Advancement Prospects

Pharmacists in community pharmacies usually begin at the staff level. After they gain experience and secure the necessary capital, some become owners or part owners of pharmacies. Pharmacists in chain drug stores may be promoted to pharmacy supervisor or manager at the store level, then to manager at the district or regional level, and later to an executive position within the chain's headquarters.

Hospital Pharmacists may advance to supervisory or administrative positions. Pharmacists in the pharmaceutical industry may advance in marketing, sales, research, quality control, production, packaging, or other areas.

Education and Training

A four-year college degree in pharmacy, a state license to practice pharmacy, and an internship under a licensed Pharmacist are required to enter this occupation.

In 2000, more than 80 pharmacy colleges were accredited to confer degrees by the American Council on Pharmaceutical Education. Pharmacy programs grant the degree of Doctor of Pharmacy. This degree requires at least six years of postsecondary study and the passing of the licensure examination of a state board of pharmacy. These colleges require at least two years of college-level prepharmacy education. Entry requirements usually include mathematics and natural sciences, as well as courses in the humanities and social sciences. Some colleges require the applicant to take the Pharmacy College Admissions Test. All colleges of pharmacy offer courses in pharmacy practice, designed to teach students to dispense prescriptions and to communicate with patients and other health professionals.

Master's degrees and Ph.D.'s are awarded after completion of a Pharm. D. degree. These degrees are designed for those who want more laboratory and research experience. Some Pharmacists who run their own pharmacy obtain a master's degree in business administration. Areas of graduate study include pharmaceutics and pharmaceutical chemistry, pharmacology, and pharmacy administration.

Special Requirements

All Pharmacists must pass state examinations in order to be licensed to practice. State licensure requirements are available from each state's Board of Pharmacy.

Experience, Special Skills, and Personality Traits

Those seeking to be Pharmacists should have scientific aptitude, good communication skills, and a desire to help others. They must be conscientious and pay close attention to detail, and have an interest in chemical formulas and in understanding the effects of drugs and medicines.

Unions and Associations

For information on pharmacy as a career contact the American Association of Colleges of Pharmacy, the National Association of Boards of Pharmacy, and the National Association of Chain Drug Stores. These groups can provide guidance as well as networking opportunities. Information on specific college entrance requirements, curriculums, and financial aid is available from any college of pharmacy.

PHYSICAL AND OCCUPATIONAL THERAPIST

CAREER PROFILE

Duties: Test and interview patients; plan and manage individual physical or occupational therapy programs; consult with doctors and other therapists to discuss appropriate therapies; administer exercise, heat, and massage treatments; counsel patients and their families

Alternate Title(s): Industrial Therapist

Availability: Army, Navy, Air Force, Coast Guard

Military Salary: See How to Use This Book

Civilian Salary: $32,040 to $83,370

Civilian Employment Prospects: Good

Civilian Advancement Prospects: Good

Prerequisites:

Rank—Officer

Education and Training—Two-year associate's degree minimum; four-year college degree in physical or occupational therapy preferred; completion of a clinical program in physical or occupational therapy

Experience—Any training and work experience obtained in the armed services or Job Corps

Special Skills and Personality Traits—Patience; positive attitude; good physical condition; excellent communication skills; sensitive; desire to help others

Licensure/Certification—State license or eligibility for registration with the American Occupational Therapy Association may be required.

CAREER LADDER

```
┌─────────────────────────────────────┐
│   Private Practitioner, Physical     │
│   or Occupational Therapist          │
└─────────────────────────────────────┘

┌─────────────────────────────────────┐
│        Specialist, Physical          │
│     or Occupational Therapist        │
└─────────────────────────────────────┘

┌─────────────────────────────────────┐
│  Physical or Occupational Therapist  │
└─────────────────────────────────────┘
```

Position Description

Due to the nature of the military, there is little doubt of its need for Physical and Occupational Therapists. Working in hospitals, clinics, rehabilitation centers, and other medical facilities, these health workers create and administer programs of treatment and exercise for patients disabled from illness or injury. Moreover, they test and interview patients to determine the extent of their disabilities, plan and manage individual physical or occupational therapy programs, and consult with doctors and other therapists to discuss appropriate therapy and evaluate patients' progress. They handle

everything from administering exercise programs and heat and massage treatments to counseling patients and their families to create a positive attitude for recovery.

In the civilian world, Physical and Occupational Therapists work in hospitals, rehabilitation centers, nursing homes, schools, and community mental health centers, often specializing in treating a particular type of patient, such as children, the elderly, the severely disabled, amputees, or others.

Physical Therapists help restore function, improve mobility, and relieve the pain of patients suffering from injuries or disease. They restore, maintain, and promote overall fitness and health in accident victims and individuals with disabling conditions. After a thorough examination of patients' medical histories, Therapists test and measure the strength, range of motion, balance and coordination, posture, muscle performance, respiration, and motor function of the patient. They also determine their ability to be reintegrated into normal society while developing a treatment strategy. Treatment often includes exercise, electrical stimulation, hot packs or cold compresses, ultrasound to relieve pain and reduce swelling, and traction or deep-tissue massage to relieve pain. During treatment Physical Therapists document a patient's progress which they will then modify when progress, or a relapse, makes it necessary.

Physical Therapists can practice in hospitals, clinics, and private offices or treat patients at homes or in schools. Most work a regular 40-hour week. Therapists often have to stoop, kneel, crouch, lift, and stand for long periods.

Occupational Therapists use specialized knowledge to help patients with conditions that are mentally, physically, developmentally, or emotionally disabling to develop, recover, or maintain daily living and work skills. These Therapists help patients improve basic motor functions and reasoning abilities, and to compensate for permanent loss of function. They also assist clients in performing activities of all types, ranging from using a computer, to caring for daily needs such as dressing, cooking, and eating. In addition they use computer programs to help clients improve decision making, abstract reasoning, problem solving, and perceptual skills, as well as memory, sequencing, and coordination.

Therapists instruct those with permanent functional disabilities in the use of adaptive equipment such as wheelchairs, splints, and aids for eating and dressing. They also create special equipment needed at home or at work and develop computer-aided adaptive equipment that enables clients to communicate better and control their environment. They also treat individuals whose ability to function in a work environment has been impaired by arranging employment, planning work activities, and evaluating the patient's progress.

Occupational Therapists may work with individuals, certain age groups, or with particular disabilities. They also work with the mentally ill, mentally retarded, or emotionally disturbed. Recording a client's activities and progress is an important part of an occupational therapist's job. Accurate records are essential for evaluating clients, billing, and reporting to physicians and others.

Occupational Therapists generally work a 40-hour week. Their work keeps them on their feet much of the time.

Civilian Salaries

In 2000, the average yearly salary for Physical Therapists was $54,810. The middle 50 percent earned between $46,660 and $67,390. The lowest 10 percent earned less than $38,510. The highest 10 percent earned more than $83,370.

In 2000, the average yearly salaries in the industries employing the largest numbers of Physical Therapists were:

Offices and clinics of medical doctors	$58,390
Home health-care services	$57,830
Offices of other health practitioners	$55,830
Nursing and personal care facilities	$54,740
Hospitals	$54,430

In 2000, the average yearly salary for Occupational Therapists was $49,450. The middle 50 percent earned between $40,460 and $57,890. The lowest 10 percent earned less than $32,040. The highest 10 percent earned more than $70,810. In 2000, the average yearly salaries in the industries employing the largest numbers of occupational therapists were:

Nursing and personal care facilities	$51,220
Hospitals	$50,430
Offices of other health practitioners	$49,520
Elementary and secondary schools	$45,340

Civilian Employment Prospects

In 2000, Physical Therapists held more than 130,000 jobs in the United States. Occupational Therapists held more than 75,000. One in four Physical Therapists worked part time; one in six Occupational Therapists held more than one job.

Some two-thirds of Physical Therapists worked either in hospitals or physical therapy offices. Other jobs were in home health agencies, outpatient rehabilitation centers, offices and clinics of physicians, and nursing homes. Still others were self-employed in private practices, taught in academic institutions, or conducted research.

Occupational Therapists held jobs mostly in hospitals, including many in rehabilitation and psychiatric hospitals. Others worked in offices and clinics of Occupational Therapists and other health practitioners, school systems, home health agencies, nursing homes, community mental health centers, adult daycare programs, job training services, and residential care facilities. Some were self-employed in private practice.

Through 2010 opportunities for Physical Therapists are expected to grow faster than the average for all occupations as a result of growth in the number of individuals with disabilities or limited function. The rapidly growing elderly population is particularly vulnerable to chronic and debilitating conditions as well as heart attacks and strokes. Future medical developments and technological advances should save the lives of a larger proportion of newborns with severe birth defects while also allowing a higher percentage of trauma victims to survive, creating additional demands for Therapists.

Through 2010 opportunities for Occupational Therapists are also expected to increase faster than the average for all occupations as a result of growth in the number of individuals with disabilities or limited function requiring therapy services. The same aging of the population which should spur employment for Physical Therapists should benefit Occupational Therapists for the same reasons. Also, hospitals will continue to employ a large number of Occupational Therapists to provide therapy services to acutely ill inpatients and to staff their outpatient rehabilitation programs.

Civilian Advancement Prospects

Physical and Occupational Therapists who wish to advance can move into private practice, maintaining a position with a hospital or clinic while also treating their own clients. They may also specialize in areas such as pediatrics, geriatrics, orthopedics, sports medicine, neurology, and cardiopulmonary physical therapy. Others may move into supervisory positions within their organization. Those in private practice can advance their position by growing their practice and taking on more clients.

Education and Training

A four-year college degree in physical or occupational therapy and completion of a clinical program in physical or occupational therapy are required to enter this occupation. In the military, those interested in this career receive two to eight months of classroom instruction, depending on specialty. High school courses in biology, chemistry, physics, health, and the social sciences can give prospective Physical and Occupational Therapists a boost. College admissions offices also look favorably at paid or volunteer experience in the health-care field.

In 2001, the American Physical Therapy Association reported there were 199 accredited physical therapist programs—165 offering master's degrees and 33 offering doctoral degrees. Physical therapist programs start with biology, chemistry, and physics, and then move to specialized courses like biomechanics, neuroanatomy, human growth and development, manifestations of disease, examination techniques, and therapeutic procedures. Students also receive supervised clinical experience. A number of states require continuing education to maintain licensure.

In 1999, entry-level education was offered in 88 bachelor's degree programs; 11 postbachelor's certificate programs for students with a degree other than occupational therapy; and 53 entry-level master's degree programs. Occupational therapy programs include physical, biological, and behavioral sciences, and the application of occupational therapy theory and skills as well as six months of supervised fieldwork.

Special Requirements

A state physical therapy license or eligibility for registration with the American Occupational Therapy Association may also be required. Physical and occupational therapists must also pass a state licensure exam before they can practice.

Experience, Special Skills, and Personality Traits

Physical and Occupational Therapists need strong interpersonal skills, compassion, a desire to help others, interest in developing detailed plans and treatments, patience, and the ability to communicate effectively. They should also have excellent stamina and be in good physical condition. A positive attitude and the ability to motivate others are also important. Occupational Therapists also need ingenuity and imagination.

Unions and Associations

For information on a career as a Physical Therapist and a list of accredited educational programs in physical therapy contact the American Physical Therapy Association. For more information on occupational therapy as a career contact the American Occupational Therapy Association. Both can also provide information about certification programs, state licensing, and continuing education.

PHYSICIAN/SURGEON

Duties: Examine patients; determine presence and extent of illness or injury; develop treatment plans; perform surgery; advise patients on their health problems and personal habits; coordinate the activities of medical personnel; conduct medical research

Alternate Title(s): Doctor of Medicine; Doctor of Osteopathic Medicine; Allopathic Physician; General Practitioner; General Pediatrician

Availability: Army, Navy, Air Force, Coast Guard

Military Salary: See How to Use This Book

Civilian Salary: $120,000 to $240,000

Civilian Employment Prospects: Good

Civilian Advancement Prospects: Good

Prerequisites:

    Rank—Officer

    Education and Training—Four-year college degree; four-year medical school Doctor of Medicine or Osteopathy degree; advanced training in a medical specialty

    Experience—Three to eight years internship and residency; any training and work experience obtained in the armed services or Job Corps

    Special Skills and Personality Traits—A desire to serve others; self-motivation; good bedside manner; emotional stability; good communication skills; strong interpersonal skills; decisiveness; work well under pressure; stamina

    Licensure/Certification—State license; board certification

```
┌─────────────────────────────┐
│         Specialist          │
└─────────────────────────────┘

┌─────────────────────────────┐
│    Physician or Surgeon     │
└─────────────────────────────┘

┌─────────────────────────────┐
│     Intern or Resident      │
└─────────────────────────────┘
```

Position Description

Working in hospitals and clinics on land and aboard ships, military Physicians and Surgeons have an enormous responsibility to keep troops healthy and combat-ready. They must examine patients to detect any abnormalities and determine the presence and extent of illness or injury by reviewing medical histories, X rays, laboratory reports, and examination reports. They develop treatment plans that may include medication, therapy, or surgery, perform surgery to treat injuries or illnesses, and advise patients on their health problems and personal habits. They also coordinate the activities of nurses, physician assistants, medical specialists, therapists, and other medical personnel and conduct medical research.

In the civilian world, Physicians work for hospitals or clinics or in private practice to prevent, diagnose, and treat diseases, disorders, and injuries. They diagnose illnesses and prescribe and administer treatment for people suffering from injury or disease. Physicians examine patients, obtain medical histories, and order, perform, and interpret diagnostic tests. They counsel patients on diet, hygiene, and preventive health care.

The two types of Physicians are the Doctor of Medicine (M.D.) and the Doctor of Osteopathic Medicine (D.O.). Both use all accepted methods of treatment, but D.O.s place special emphasis on the body's musculoskeletal system, preventive medicine, and holistic patient care.

Common specialties for D.O.s include emergency medicine, anesthesiology, obstetrics and gynecology, psychiatry, and surgery. Common specialties for M.D.s include pulmonary diseases, surgical specialties, colon and rectal surgery, primary care, internal medicine, general and family practice, pediatrics, allergy, cardiovascular diseases, dermatology, general or neurological surgery, ophthalmology, orthopedic surgery, otolaryngology, plastic surgery, thoracic surgery, urological surgery, gastroenterology, obstetrics and gynecology, pediatric cardiology, aerospace medicine, anesthesiology, child psychiatry, diagnostic radiology, forensic pathology, neurology, pathology, radiology, and radiation oncology.

Primary care Physicians practice general and family medicine, general internal medicine, or general pediatrics. These are the first health professionals usually consulted by the average patient. These Physicians tend to see the same patients on a regular basis for preventive care as well as to treat them for injuries and ailments. Physicians in general internal medicine provide care mainly for adults with problems associated with the body's organs. General pediatricians focus on children. When appropriate, primary care physicians refer patients to specialists.

Physicians specializing in treatment through surgical procedure are called Surgeons. With patients under general or local anesthesia, they operate to correct physical deformities, repair bone, and tissue after injuries. They also perform preventive surgeries on patients with debilitating diseases or disorders. Common specialties for Surgeons include orthopedic surgery, ophthalmology, neurological surgery, and plastic or reconstructive surgery.

Most Physicians work in small private offices or clinics. Often they practice in groups or organizations that provide back-up coverage, allowing for more time off. Surgeons work in well-lighted, sterile environments while performing surgery and often stand for long periods. Most work long, irregular hours in hospitals or in surgical outpatient centers, often as much as 60 hours or more a week. Physicians and Surgeons must also travel frequently between office and hospital to care for their patients.

Civilian Salaries

In 1998, the average yearly salary, after expenses, for allopathic Physicians was about $160,000 in 1998. The middle 50 percent earned between $120,000 and $240,000 a year. Earnings vary according to number of years in practice, geographic region, hours worked, skill, personality, and professional reputation.

In 1998, according to the American Medical Association, the average yearly salaries of allopathic Physicians, after expenses, by specialty, were as follows:

Surgery	$240,000
Radiology	$230,000
Anesthesiology	$210,000
Obstetrics/gynecology	$200,000
Emergency medicine	$184,000
Pathology	$184,000
General internal medicine	$140,000
General/Family practice	$130,000
Psychiatry	$130,000
Pediatrics	$126,000

Civilian Employment Prospects

In 2000, Physicians and Surgeons held just under 600,000 jobs. About 20 percent were employed by hospitals. The majority of the others were in office-based practice although some did practice in the federal government. A growing number of Physicians are partners or salaried employees of group practices. These medical groups can afford expensive medical equipment and realize other business advantages.

Through 2010 opportunities for Physicians and Surgeons will grow about as fast as the average for all occupations. This is due to the current growing and aging population, which will continue to drive overall growth in the demand for physician services. In addition, new technologies will permit more intensive care: Physicians will be able to do more tests, perform more procedures, and treat conditions previously regarded as untreatable.

Although job prospects may be better for primary care Physicians such as general and family practitioners, general pediatricians, and general internists, a substantial number of jobs for specialists will also be created in response to patient demand for access to specialty care. Openings should remain numerous in rural and low-income areas, since many Physicians find these areas unattractive due to their lower earning potential and their isolation from medical colleagues.

Civilian Advancement Prospects

Through 2010 job opportunities for Physicians and Surgeons are expected to be excellent. Advancement in these professions comes mainly from lateral moves into a specialized field. Some opportunities exist in hospitals to advance to Chief of Staff, or as administrators or the heads of medical colleges.

Education and Training

A doctor of medicine or osteopathy degree and advanced training in a medical specialty are required to enter this occupation, the formal education and training requirements of which are among the most demanding of any field.

In the military, no initial job training is provided to officers; however, advanced courses and programs in medical specialties are available. In addition, scholarships for advanced medical training are available in return for an obligated period of military service.

To become a Physician takes four years of undergraduate school, four of medical school, and three to eight years of internship and residency, depending on the specialty selected. A few medical schools offer a combined undergraduate and medical school program that lasts only six years instead of eight.

Premedical students must complete undergraduate work in physics, biology, mathematics, English, and inorganic and organic chemistry. Students also take courses in the humanities and the social sciences.

There are 144 medical schools in the United States. Acceptance to medical school is very competitive. Applicants must submit transcripts, scores from the Medical College Admission Test, and letters of recommendation.

The first two years of medical school are spent taking courses such as anatomy, biochemistry, physiology, pharmacology, psychology, microbiology, pathology, medical ethics, and laws governing medicine. Students also learn to take medical histories, examine patients, and diagnose illness.

The last two years students work with patients under the supervision to learn acute, chronic, preventive, and rehabilitative care. Medical school is followed by a residency-graduate medical education in a specialty that takes the form of paid on-the-job training, usually in a hospital.

Special Requirements

All Physicians must be licensed which entails graduation from an accredited medical school, passing a licensing examination, and completion of one to seven years of graduate medical education. Those licensed in one state can usually get a license to practice in another without additional examination. Those seeking board certification in a specialty may spend up to seven years in residency training. For board certification by the American Board of Medical Specialists or the American Osteopathic Association, a final examination immediately after residency, or after one or two years of practice is also necessary. Certification in a subspecialty usually calls for another one to two years of residency.

Experience, Special Skills, and Personality Traits

Physicians must have a desire to serve, be self-motivated, and be able to survive the pressures and long hours of medical education and practice. They must also have a good bedside manner, emotional stability, and the abilities to express ideas clearly and concisely and to make decisions in emergencies. They should be meticulous, compassionate, and well organized.

Unions and Associations

For a list of medical schools and residency programs, as well as general information on premedical education, financial aid, and medicine as a career, contact the Association of American Medical Colleges, Section for Student Services and the American Association of Colleges of Osteopathic Medicine.

For general information on physicians, contact the American Medical Association, Department of Communications and Public Relations and the American Osteopathic Association, Department of Public Relations. These organizations also provide opportunities for networking with colleagues.

PSYCHOLOGIST

CAREER PROFILE

Duties: Conduct research on human and animal behavior as well as on aptitude and job performance; give psychological tests; treat patients; conduct experiments to determine the best equipment design, work procedures and training course content; write research reports and direct research projects performed by outside contractors

Alternate Title(s): Clinical Psychologist; Counseling Psychologist; Educational Psychologist; Experimental Psychologist; Social Psychologist; Psychometrician

Availability: Army, Navy, Air Force, Coast Guard

Military Salary: See How to Use This Book

Civilian Salary: $35,720 to $66,880

Civilian Employment Prospects: Good

Civilian Advancement Prospects: Good

Prerequisites:

Rank—Officer

Education and Training—A four-year college degree required for entry-level and trainee/assistant positions; doctorate required

Experience—Any training and work experience obtained in the armed services

Special Skills and Personality Traits—Emotional stability; maturity; outstanding interpersonal skills; sensitivity; compassion; the ability to lead and inspire others; excellent communication skills; patience; perseverance; an interest in scientific research, mathematics, and statistics

Licensure/Certification—State license; board certification

CAREER LADDER

```
┌─────────────────────────────┐
│        Psychologist         │
└─────────────────────────────┘

┌─────────────────────────────┐
│      Staff Psychologist     │
└─────────────────────────────┘

┌─────────────────────────────┐
│          Assistant          │
└─────────────────────────────┘
```

Position Description

It might surprise some, but psychological research and treatment are important to the modern military and national defense. Research can show how to improve military training, job assignment, and even equipment design. Treatment can help personnel cope with stress. Working in offices, hospitals, clinics, and other medical facilities on land and aboard ships, military Psychologists conduct research on human and animal behavior, emotions, and thinking processes. They conduct research on aptitude and job performance, administer psychological tests and interpret results to diagnose patients' problems and treat patients individually and in groups. They conduct experiments to determine the best equipment design, work procedures, and training course content, and write research reports and direct research projects performed by outside contractors.

In the civilian world, Psychologists treat patients in private practice, hospitals, school systems, and mental health centers. Like other social scientists, they formulate hypotheses and collect data to test their validity. Research methods vary depending on the topic under study. Psychologists sometimes gather information through controlled laboratory experiments or by administering personality, performance, aptitude, and intelligence tests or through observation, interviews, questionnaires, clinical studies, and surveys.

Clinical Psychologists help mentally and emotionally disturbed clients adjust to life. Some work in physical rehabilitation settings. Others help people deal with times of personal crisis. Some collaborate with physicians and other specialists to develop and implement treatment and intervention programs. Others work in universities and medical schools, where they train graduate students. Some administer community mental health programs.

Areas of specialization within clinical psychology include health psychology, neuropsychology, and geropsychology. Health Psychologists promote good health through health maintenance counseling programs designed to help people achieve goals such as to stop smoking or lose weight. Neuropsychologists study the relation between the brain and behavior, often working in stroke and head injury programs. Geropsychologists deal with the special problems faced by the elderly.

Counseling Psychologists advise people on how to deal with problems of everyday living. They work in settings such as university counseling centers, hospitals, and individual or group practices. School Psychologists work in elementary and secondary schools to resolve students' learning and behavior problems. Industrial-organizational Psychologists apply psychological principles and research methods to the workplace in the interest of improving productivity and the quality of work life. They also are involved in research on management and marketing problems.

Developmental Psychologists study the physiological, cognitive, and social development that takes place throughout life. They also study developmental disabilities and their effects. Social Psychologists examine people's interactions with others and with the social environment. They work in organizational consultation, marketing research, systems design, or other applied psychology fields. Experimental or research Psychologists work in university and private research centers and in business, nonprofit, and governmental organizations.

Clinical, school, and counseling Psychologists have their own offices and set their own hours. Those employed in hospitals, nursing homes and other health facilities may work shifts including evenings and weekends, while those who work in schools and clinics generally work regular hours. Many Psychologists experience pressures due to deadlines, tight schedules, and overtime work.

Civilian Salaries

In 2000, the average yearly salary for salaried psychologists was $48,596; for clinical, counseling, and school psychologists: $48,320; for industrial-organizational psychologists: $66,880.

In 2000, the average yearly salaries in the industries employing the largest numbers of psychologists were:

Hospitals	$52,460
Elementary and secondary schools	$51,310
Offices of other health practitioners	$50,990
Offices and clinics of medical doctors	$47,890
Individual and family services	$35,720

Civilian Employment Prospects

In 2000, Psychologists held just over 180,000 jobs. Educational institutions employed the largest number of salaried or staff Psychologists in positions other than teaching (counseling, testing, research, administration). Many were employed in hospitals, mental health clinics, rehabilitation centers, nursing homes, and other health facilities. Government agencies employed one in 10. More than two-fifths of all psychologists were self-employed.

Through 2010 opportunities for Psychologists are expected to grow about as fast as the average for all occupations. Employment in health care will grow fastest in outpatient mental health and substance abuse treatment clinics. Numerous job opportunities will also arise in schools, public and private social service agencies, management consulting services, and companies needing expertise in survey design, analysis, and research to provide marketing evaluation and statistical analysis.

Opportunities for people holding doctorates from leading universities in areas such as counseling, health, and educational psychology, as well as those with extensive training in quantitative research methods and computer science will be better than average. Few opportunities will exist for bachelor's degree holders. Some may find jobs as assistants in rehabilitation centers or in other jobs involving data collection and analysis. Those who meet state certification requirements may become high school psychology teachers.

Civilian Advancement Prospects

Psychologists do not so much advance, as graduate unto the position for which they have prepared. With experience, salaried Psychologists can gain the experience and credentials to open their own practice. They might also take on teaching positions or build their reputation by publishing significant research.

Education and Training

A four-year college degree in psychology is required to enter this occupation. A doctoral degree is required for employment as a licensed clinical or counseling Psychologist. Psychologists with a Ph.D. qualify for a wide range of teaching, research, clinical, and counseling positions in universities, health-care services, elementary and secondary schools, private industry, and government.

Psychologists with a Doctor of Psychology degree usually work in clinical positions or in private practices. An Educational Specialist degree will qualify an individual to work as a school psychologist. Persons with a master's degree in psychology may work as industrial-organizational Psychologists or psychological assistants. A bachelor's degree in psychology qualifies a person to assist Psychologists in community mental health centers, vocational rehabilitation offices, and correctional programs.

Clinical Psychologists usually must have completed the Ph.D. or Psy.D. requirements and served an internship. Vocational and guidance counselors usually need two years of graduate study in counseling and one of counseling experience. School psychology requires a master's degree followed by a one-year internship. A doctoral degree usually requires five to seven years of graduate study. The Ph.D. culminates in a dissertation based on original research. A master's degree in psychology requires at least two years of full-time graduate study.

The American Psychological Association accredits doctoral training programs in clinical, counseling, and school psychology. They also accredit institutions that provide internships for doctoral students in school, clinical, and counseling psychology. The National Council for Accreditation of Teacher Education, with the assistance of the National Association of School Psychologists, is involved in the accreditation of advanced degree programs in school psychology.

Special Requirements

Psychologists in independent practice or those who offer any type of patient care must meet certification or licensing requirements throughout the country. Clinical and counseling Psychologists usually require a doctorate in psychology, completion of an approved internship, and one to two years of professional experience. Also, all states require applicants pass an examination. Most administer a standardized test; many supplement that with additional oral or essay questions. Most states certify those with a master's degree as school Psychologists after completion of an internship; some require continuing education for license renewal.

The American Board of Professional Psychology recognizes professional achievement by awarding certification primarily in clinical psychology, clinical neuropsychology, counseling, forensic, industrial-organizational, and school psychology. Candidates for ABPP certification need a doctorate in psychology, five years of experience, professional endorsements, and a passing grade on an examination.

Experience, Special Skills, and Personality Traits

Psychologists interested in direct patient care must be emotionally stable, mature and able to deal effectively with people. Sensitivity, compassion, and the ability to lead and inspire others are particularly important qualities. Research Psychologists should be able to do detailed work independently, have excellent communication skills, patience, perseverance, and an interest in scientific research and in mathematics and statistics.

Unions and Associations

For information on careers, educational requirements, financial assistance, and licensing in all fields of psychology, contact the American Psychological Association. The National Association of School Psychologists provides information on the licensing of school psychologists, and information about state licensing requirements is available from the Association of State and Provincial Psychology Boards. Information on obtaining a position as a psychologist with the federal government may be obtained from the Office of Personnel Management. Information, online at: http://www.usajobs.opm.gov.

RADIOLOGIC (X-RAY) TECHNICIAN

CAREER PROFILE

Duties: Read requests or instructions from physicians; position patients under radiologic equipment; operate and adjust X-ray equipment; process X-ray pictures; prepare and administer radioactive solutions; keep records of patient treatment

Alternate Title(s): X-Ray Technologist; Nuclear Medical Technologist; Radiographer; CT Technologist; Magnetic Resonance Imaging Technologist; Radiologic Technologist

Availability: Army, Navy, Air Force, Coast Guard

Military Salary: See How to Use This Book

Civilian Salary: $25,310 to $52,050

Civilian Employment Prospects: Good

Civilian Advancement Prospects: Good

Prerequisites:

    Rank—Enlisted

    Education and Training—Certification; associate's degree or bachelor's degree in radiology

    Experience—Any training and work experience obtained in the armed services; on-the-job training

    Special Skills and Personality Traits—Sensitivity; detail-oriented; able to follow instructions; good team worker; mechanical ability; manual dexterity

    Licensure/Certification—License required in most states

CAREER LADDER

```
┌─────────────────────────────────┐
│    Administrator or Director     │
└─────────────────────────────────┘

┌─────────────────────────────────┐
│  Supervisor, Chief Radiologic    │
│          Technologist            │
└─────────────────────────────────┘

┌─────────────────────────────────┐
│           Specialist             │
└─────────────────────────────────┘

┌─────────────────────────────────┐
│        Staff Technologist        │
└─────────────────────────────────┘
```

Position Description

The modern military offers radiology (the use of X rays) to its members as a health-care service. X-ray photographs enable medical personnel to pinpoint injuries and detect illnesses. Radiology is also used to treat certain diseases, like cancer. Radiologic Technicians, working in hospitals, clinics, and even in mobile field hospitals, operate X-ray and related equipment used in diagnosing and treating injuries and diseases. They read requests or instructions from physicians to determine each patient's X-ray needs, position patients under radiologic equipment, operate X-ray equipment, and adjust X-ray equipment to the correct time and power of exposure. They also process X-ray pictures, prepare and administer radioactive solutions to patients, and keep records of patient treatment.

In the civilian world, Radiologic Technicians work in hospitals, diagnostic clinics, and medical laboratories where they operate sophisticated equipment to help physicians, dentists and other health practitioners diagnose and treat patients. Civilian Radiologic Technologists and technicians take X rays and administer nonradioactive materials into patients' bloodstreams for diagnostic purposes. Some specialize in diagnostic imaging technologies such as computed tomography and magnetic resonance imaging.

Radiologic Technicians produce X-ray films, or radiographs, of parts of the human body for use in diagnosing medical problems. They prepare patients for such examinations by explaining the procedure, removing articles such as jewelry, positioning patients so they may be appropriately radiographed, and surround the exposed area with protective lead shields to prevent unnecessary radiation exposure. They also are responsible for correctly positioning their equipment, setting its controls to produce radiographs of the appropriate density, detail, and contrast needed and then exposing and developing the film.

More experienced radiographers perform more advanced imaging procedures. When working with radiologists, the radiographer prepares a solution of contrast medium for the patient to drink. Placed behind a fluoroscope, the medium allows the radiologist to see soft tissues in the body. Some radiographers operate computerized tomography scanners to produce cross sectional images of patients. Others operate machines using strong magnets and radio waves rather than radiation to create an image.

Radiologic Technicians must follow physicians' orders precisely and conform to regulations concerning use of radiation to protect themselves, their patients, and coworkers from unnecessary exposure. Besides their other duties, they often prepare work schedules, evaluate equipment purchases, or manage a radiology department. Most work a regular 40-hour week.

Radiologic Technicians must be on their feet for long periods. They also sometimes need to lift or turn disabled patients. Physical stamina is important. Although most work in clean, well-lighted areas, some travel to patients in large vans equipped with sophisticated diagnostic equipment.

To guard against potential radiation hazards, Radiologic Technicians use lead aprons, gloves, and other shielding devices, as well as instruments monitoring radiation exposure. They also wear radiation-measuring badges and keep detailed records on their cumulative lifetime exposure.

Civilian Salaries

In 2000, the average yearly salary for Radiologic Technicians was $36,000. The middle 50 percent earned between $30,220 and $43,380. The lowest 10 percent earned less than $25,310. The highest 10 percent earned more than $52,050.

In 2000, the average yearly salaries in the industries employing the largest numbers of Radiologic Technicians were:

Medical and dental laboratories	$39,400
Hospitals	$36,280
Offices and clinics of medical doctors	$34,870

Civilian Employment Prospects

In 2000, Radiologic Technicians held nearly 170,000 jobs. Some 20 percent worked part time. Through 2010 opportunities for radiologic workers are expected to grow faster than the average for all occupations, as the population grows and ages, increasing the demand for diagnostic imaging. There are already reports of shortages of radiologic technologists and technicians.

Radiologic workers educated and credentialed in multiple forms of diagnostic imaging technology (radiography, sonography, nuclear medicine) will have better employment opportunities as hospitals continue to merge departments and look for other ways to control costs. Outside of hospitals, many new jobs will be found in physician's offices and clinics and diagnostic imaging centers. Through 2010 such facilities are expected to show rapid growth due to the strong shift toward outpatient care.

Civilian Advancement Prospects

Radiologic Technicians can become specialists with experience and additional training, performing CT scanning, angiography, and magnetic resonance imaging. With further experience they may also be promoted to supervisor, chief Radiologic Technician, on up to department administrator or director. Courses or a master's degree in business or health administration may be necessary for the director's position. Some advance by becoming instructors or directors in radiologic technology programs. Still others take jobs as sales representatives or instructors with equipment manufacturers.

Education and Training

Job training consists of three to five months of instruction, including practice with radiologic equipment. Extensive on-the-job training is also provided. Course work generally includes operation of X-ray equipment, radioactive isotope therapy, X-ray film processing, and anatomy and physiology.

Radiologic Technicians can prepare for their career in various hospitals, colleges, universities, vocational-technical institutes, and, of course, the U.S. Armed Forces. Formal training programs in radiography range in length from one to four years and lead to a certificate, associate's degree, or bachelor's degree. Two-year associate's degree programs are most prevalent. Some one-year certificate programs are available for experienced radiographers who want to change fields or specialize in computerized tomography or magnetic resonance imaging. A bachelor's or master's degree in one of the radiologic technologies is desirable and sometimes required for supervisory, administrative, or teaching positions.

In 2000, the Joint Review Committee on Education in Radiologic Technology, which accredits most formal training programs for this field, accredited 584 radiography programs. Radiography programs require, at a minimum, a high school diploma or the equivalent. High school courses in mathematics, physics, chemistry, and biology are helpful. The programs provide both classroom and clinical instruction in anatomy and physiology, patient care procedures, radiation physics, radiation protection, principles of imaging, medical terminology, positioning of patients, medical ethics, radiobiology, and pathology.

Special Requirements

As of 1999 35 States and Puerto Rico required licensing of Radiologic Technicians. The American Registry of Radiologic Technologists offers registration in radiography. To be eligible for registration, technologists generally must graduate from an accredited program and pass an examination.

Experience, Special Skills, and Personality Traits

Radiologic Technicians should be sensitive to patients' physical and psychological needs, able to focus on details, follow instructions, and work as part of a team. They also need mechanical ability and manual dexterity.

Unions and Associations

For information on a career in Radiology, send a stamped, self-addressed business-size envelope with your request to the American Society of Radiologic Technologists. For the current list of accredited education programs in radiography, write to the Joint Review Committee on Education in Radiologic Technology. And for information on certification, contact the American Registry of Radiologic Technologists.

REGISTERED NURSE

CAREER PROFILE

Duties: Assist physicians; give injections; change bandages and dressings; provide life support treatment; provide care for mental health patients; keep records of patients' condition; supervise support personnel

Alternate Title(s): Public Health Nurse; Nurse Practitioner; General Duty Nurse; Clinical Nurse Specialist; Certified Registered Nurse Anesthetist; Certified Nurse-Midwife

Availability: Army, Navy, Air Force, Coast Guard

Military Salary: See How to Use This Book

Civilian Salary: $31,890 to $64,360

Civilian Employment Prospects: Excellent

Civilian Advancement Prospects: Excellent

Prerequisites:

Rank—Enlisted

Education and Training—Associate degree, bachelor's degree or nursing diploma required; bachelor's degree may be required for advancement; additional education may also be necessary.

Experience—Any training and work experience obtained in the armed services; volunteer work at hospitals or clinics; first aid training

Special Skills and Personality Traits—Leadership; negotiation skills; good judgment; responsible; good communication skills; well-organized; able to supervise others; capable of following orders precisely; willing to seek consultation when required; desire to help others; self-confidence; ability to remain calm under pressure

Licensure/Certification—National license; additional certification required for specialization

CAREER LADDER

```
┌─────────────────────────────┐
│  Assistant Director, Director, │
│        Vice President         │
└─────────────────────────────┘

┌─────────────────────────────┐
│ Assistant Head Nurse or Head Nurse │
└─────────────────────────────┘

┌─────────────────────────────┐
│       Registered Nurse       │
└─────────────────────────────┘
```

Position Description

Registered Nurses are an instrumental part of the staff at hospitals and clinics. Some work in sick bays aboard ships or in mobile field hospitals. Others work in airplanes that transfer patients to medical centers. Wherever they are stationed, military nurses help physicians treat patients. They give injections of pain killers, antibiotics, and other medicines as prescribed by physicians; change bandages and dressings; assist physicians during surgery; and provide life support treatment for patients needing emergency care. They also provide care

for mental health patients; keep records of patients' condition; and supervise practical nurses, nurse aides, and other support personnel. Nurses also administer first aid.

In the civilian world, Registered Nurses work in hospitals, clinics, private medical facilities, public health agencies, schools, nursing homes, and rehabilitation centers. Civilian Registered Nurses work to promote health, prevent disease and help patients cope with illness. When providing direct patient care they observe, assess, and record symptoms, reactions, and progress; develop and manage nursing care plans; instruct patients and their families in proper care; and help individuals and groups take steps to improve or maintain their health.

The majority of all nurses work in hospitals, providing bedside nursing and carrying out medical regimens. They are usually assigned to one area such as surgery, maternity, pediatrics, emergency room, intensive care, etc.

Office Nurses work in physicians' offices, clinics, surgi-centers, and emergency rooms where they prepare patients for and assist with examinations, administer injections and medications, dress wounds and incisions, assist with minor surgery, and maintain records. Nursing home nurses man-age nursing care for residents with conditions ranging from a fracture to Alzheimer's disease. They also work in spe-cialty-care departments, such as long-term rehabilitation units for patients.

Home health nurses provide periodic services to patients at home, caring for a broad range of patients, such as those recovering from illnesses and accidents, cancer and child-birth. They must be able to work independently, and may supervise home health aides. Public health nurses work in government, private agencies, clinics, schools, retirement communities, etc. They work with individuals, groups and families to improve the overall health of communities. They give instruction on health issues and also arrange for immu-nizations, blood pressure testing, and other health screening.

Occupational health or industrial nurses provide nursing care at worksites to employees, customers, and others with minor injuries and illnesses. Head nurses or nurse supervi-sors direct nursing activities. They plan work schedules and assign duties to Nurses and aides, provide or arrange for training, and visit patients to observe Nurses and to ensure the proper delivery of care.

Most Nurses work in well-lighted, comfortable health-care facilities. They spend considerable time walking and standing. They need emotional stability to cope with human suffering, emergencies, and other stresses. Hospitals are 24 hour operations, meaning Nurses work nights, weekends, and holidays. Their work has its hazards, and Nurses must guard against disease and other dangers, such as those posed by radiation, chemicals used for sterilization of instruments, and anesthetics. In addition, they are vulnerable to back injury when moving patients, shocks from electrical equip-ment, hazards posed by compressed gases, etc.

Civilian Salaries

In 2000, the average yearly salary for Registered Nurses was $44,840. The middle 50 percent earned between $37,870 and $54,000. The lowest 10 percent earned less than $31,890. The highest 10 percent earned more than $64,360.

In 2000, the average yearly salaries in the industries employing the largest numbers of registered nurses were as follows:

Personnel supply services	$46,860
Hospitals	$45,780
Home health care services	$43,640
Offices and clinics of medical doctors	$43,480
Nursing and personal care facilities	$41,330

Civilian Employment Prospects

In 2000, registered nurses held in excess of two million jobs. Three out of five jobs were in hospitals, in inpatient and outpatient departments. The rest were divided between physicians' offices and clinics, home health-care agencies, nursing homes, temporary help agencies, schools, govern-ment agencies, residential care facilities, social service agencies, religious organizations, research facilities, man-agement and public relations firms, insurance agencies, and private households.

Opportunities seem excellent since nursing is one of the 10 occupations projected to have the largest numbers of new jobs. Through 2010, employment of Registered Nurses is expected to grow faster than the average for all occupa-tions. Some states are already reporting shortages of Regis-tered Nurses.

Employment in home health care and in nursing homes is expected to grow faster than average due to increases in the number of elderly, many of whom require long-term care. In addition, the financial pressure on hospitals to discharge patients as soon as possible should produce more home health-care needs and nursing home admissions. Also, because jobs in traditional hospital nursing positions are no longer the only option, Registered Nurses can create work to suit their own needs much more easily than in the past. Opportunities should be excellent, particularly for Nurses with advanced education and training.

Civilian Advancement Prospects

With experience and good performance reviews, Nurses can advance to assistant head nurse or head nurse. From there, they can advance to assistant director, director, and vice president. Increasingly, management-level nursing positions require a graduate degree in nursing or health ser-vices administration.

Within patient care, Nurses can advance to clinical Nurse specialist, Nurse practitioner, certified Nurse-midwife, or certified registered Nurse anesthetist. These positions require one or two years of graduate education, leading to a master's degree or, in some instances, to a certificate.

On the business side of health care, Nurses find their expertise and experience on a health-care team equip them to manage ambulatory, acute, home health, and chronic care services far better than those with no practical nursing experience. Health-care corporations employ Nurses for health planning and development, marketing, and quality assurance.

Education and Training

Graduation from an accredited school of nursing is required to enter this occupation. The three educational paths to registered nursing are the associate degree in nursing, the bachelor of science degree in nursing, and the diploma. A.D.N. programs take about two to three years. B.S.N. programs take four to five years. Diploma programs, administered in hospitals, last two to three years. Those who obtain a B.S.N. will find that their advancement opportunities are usually broader. Indeed, some career paths are open only to Nurses with bachelor's or advanced degrees, such as administrative positions or for admission to graduate nursing programs in research, consulting, teaching, or a clinical specialization.

Nursing education includes classroom instruction and supervised clinical experience in hospitals and other health facilities. Students take courses in anatomy, physiology, microbiology, chemistry, nutrition, psychology, and nursing. Coursework also includes the liberal arts.

Special Requirements

Throughout the country students must graduate from an approved nursing program and pass a national licensing examination to obtain a nursing license. Additional certifications can be required for specialized positions such as Nurse-practitioner and Nurse-midwife.

Experience, Special Skills, and Personality Traits

Nurses should be caring and sympathetic. Their work requires leadership, negotiation skills, good judgment, the ability to accept responsibility, to express ideas clearly and concisely, direct or supervise others, follow orders precisely, and determine when consultation is required. They should also have the desire to help others, self-confidence, and the ability to remain calm under pressure.

Unions and Associations

For information on a career as a Registered Nurse and nursing education, contact the National League for Nursing and the American Nurses Association. A list of B.S.N. and graduate nursing programs can be obtained by writing to the American Association of Colleges of Nursing.

SPEECH THERAPIST AND AUDIOLOGIST

CAREER PROFILE

Duties: Discuss hearing and speaking problems with patients; identify speaking and language problems; examine the ears and evaluate examination and test data

Alternate Title(s): Speech-Language Pathologist

Availability: Army, Navy, Air Force, Coast Guard

Military Salary: See How to Use This Book

Civilian Salary: $30,720 to $69,980

Civilian Employment Prospects: Good

Civilian Advancement Prospects: Good

Prerequisites:

   Rank—Officer

   Education and Training—A master's degree in either audiology or speech therapy

   Experience—Any training and work experience obtained in the armed services

   Special Skills and Personality Traits—Good communication skills essential; objectivity; patience and compassion; good listening skills; a desire to help others; an interest in scientific work

   Licensure/Certification—State license required; voluntary certification

CAREER LADDER

```
┌─────────────────────────────────┐
│   Doctor of Speech Therapy      │
│        or Audiology             │
└─────────────────────────────────┘


┌─────────────────────────────────┐
│   Certified Speech Therapist    │
│        or Audiologist           │
└─────────────────────────────────┘
```

Position Description

Military Speech Therapists work as part of medical teams to evaluate and treat patients with hearing and speech problems. In the military Speech Therapists work in therapy labs, clinics, and medical centers where they identify speaking and language problems and discuss with patients hearing and speaking problems and possible causes and treatment. They examine the ears, including the entire auditory system, and evaluate examination and test data to determine the type and amount of hearing loss. They also treat hearing problems using hearing aids and other treatments, assist patients in selecting and using hearing aids, conduct programs to help patients improve their speaking skills, and research new techniques for treating hearing and speaking problems.

In the civilian world Speech Therapists work in hospitals, clinics, schools, and research centers. There they assess, diagnose, treat, and help to prevent speech, language, cognitive, communication, voice, swallowing, fluency, and other related disorders. Audiologists identify, assess, and manage auditory, balance, and other neural systems. Speech-language pathologists work with people who cannot make speech sounds clearly or at all, those with speech rhythm and fluency problems, or with voice quality problems. They also work with people with problems understanding and producing language, who wish to modify an accent, those with cognitive communication impairments, and with people who have oral motor problems causing eating and swallowing difficulties.

Speech-language pathologists use written and oral tests, as well as special instruments, to diagnose the nature and extent of impairment and to record and analyze speech, language, and swallowing irregularities, then develop an individualized plan of care tailored to each patient's needs. For individuals with little or no speech capability, speech-language pathologists may select augmentative or alternative communication methods. They teach these individuals how to make sounds, improve their voices or increase their language skills to communicate more effectively. They also help patients develop or recover reliable communication skills.

Speech-language pathologists keep records on the initial evaluation, progress, and discharge of clients to help pinpoint problems, track client progress, and justify the cost of treatment when applying for reimbursement. They counsel individuals and their families concerning communication disorders and how to cope with the misunderstandings that accompany them. They also work with family members to recognize and change behavior patterns that impede communication and treatment and show them communication-enhancing techniques to use at home. Some speech-language pathologists conduct research on human communication. Others design and develop equipment or techniques for diagnosing and treating speech problems.

Audiologists provide direct clinical services to individuals with hearing or balance disorders. They use audiometers, computers, and other testing devices to measure the loudness at which a person begins to hear sounds, the ability to distinguish between sounds, and the nature and extent of hearing loss. Treatment for such losses may include examining and cleaning the ear canal, fitting and dispensing hearing aids or other assistive devices, and audiologic rehabilitation. Audiologists may recommend, fit, and dispense personal or large area amplification systems, such as hearing aids and alerting devices. Audiologists provide fitting and tuning of cochlear implants and the necessary rehabilitation for adjustment to listening with implant amplification systems.

Audiologists may conduct research on types of, and treatment for, hearing, balance, and related disorders. Others design and develop equipment or techniques for diagnosing and treating these disorders. They also measure noise levels in workplaces and conduct hearing protection programs in industry, as well as in schools and communities.

Speech Therapists and Audiologists usually work in clean, comfortable surroundings. The job requires attention to detail and intense concentration. Most Speech Therapists work about 40 hours per week. Those who work on a contract basis may spend a substantial amount of time traveling between facilities.

Civilian Salaries

In 2000, the average yearly salary for Speech Therapists was $46,640. The middle 50 percent earned between $37,670 and $56,980. The lowest 10 percent earned less than $30,720. The highest 10 percent earned more than $69,980.

In 2000, the average yearly salaries in the industries employing the largest numbers of speech-language pathologists were as follows:

Hospitals	$49,960
Offices of other health practitioners	$47,170
Elementary and secondary schools	$43,710

In 2000, the average yearly salary for Audiologists was $44,830. The middle 50 percent earned between $37,000 and $55,290. The lowest 10 percent earned less than $30,850. The highest 10 percent earned more than $68,570.

Civilian Employment Prospects

In 2000, Speech Therapists and Audiologists held over 100,000 jobs. Speech Therapists held nearly 90,000 jobs; Audiologists about 13,000. Roughly one-half of jobs for speech-language pathologists and Audiologists were in preschools, elementary and secondary schools, or colleges and universities. The remaining jobs were in offices of speech-language pathologists, Audiologists or physicians; hospitals; speech, language, and hearing centers; home health agencies, or other facilities. Audiologists are more likely to be employed in independent health-care offices, while speech-language pathologists are more likely to work in school settings.

Through 2010, employment is expected to grow much faster than the average for all occupations. Hearing loss is strongly associated with aging, and the coming rapid growth in the population age 55 and over will cause the number of persons with hearing, speech, and language impairments to increase markedly. Medical advances are improving the survival rate of premature infants and trauma and stroke victims, who then need assessment and possible treatment.

Also, federal law guarantees special education and related services to all eligible children with disabilities. This will increase employment along with the spreading awareness of the importance of early identification and diagnosis of speech, language, and hearing disorders.

Civilian Advancement Prospects

Speech Therapists advance their careers by moving to positions at larger or more prestigious hospitals, schools, or institutions. Those in private practice advance by increasing their number of clients or taking on more challenging cases. Some continue their education and conduct important research. Others may choose to teach at universities in addition to maintaining their own practice.

Education and Training

A master's degree in either audiology or speech therapy is required to enter this occupation. Over 240 colleges and universities offer graduate programs in speech-language pathology. Courses cover anatomy and physiology of the areas of the body involved in speech, language, and hearing; the development of normal speech, language, and hearing; the nature of disorders; acoustics; and psychological aspects of communication. Graduate students also learn to evaluate and treat speech, language, and hearing disorders and receive supervised clinical training in communication disorders. More than 110 institutions offer graduate programs in audiology. Course work includes anatomy; physiology; basic science; math; physics; genetics; normal and abnormal communication development; auditory, balance, and neural systems assessment and treatment; audiologic rehabilitation; and ethics.

Special Requirements

Of the states that regulate licensing, almost all require a master's degree or equivalent. Other requirements are 300 to 375 hours of supervised clinical experience, a passing score on a national examination, and nine months of postgraduate professional clinical experience. Forty-one states have continuing education requirements for licensure renewal. Medicaid, medicare, and private health insurers generally require a practitioner to be licensed to qualify for reimbursement.

Speech Therapists can acquire the Certificate of Clinical Competence in Speech-Language Pathology offered by the American Speech-Language-Hearing Association. Audiologists can earn the Certificate of Clinical Competence in Audiology. To earn one of these degrees a person must have a graduate degree and 375 hours of supervised clinical experience, complete a 36 week postgraduate clinical fellowship, and pass a written examination.

According to the American Speech-Language-Hearing Association, beginning in 2007 Audiologists will need to have a bachelor's degree and complete 75 hours of credit toward a doctoral degree in order to seek certification. Beginning in 2012, Audiologists will have to earn a doctoral degree in order to be certified.

Experience, Special Skills, and Personality Traits

Speech Therapists and Audiologists should be able to communicate effectively and maintain objectivity as well as show patience and compassion. Also important are good listening skills, a desire to help others and an interest in scientific work. They must be patient and committed to working long-term with their clients.

Unions and Associations

State licensing boards can provide information on licensure requirements. State departments of education can supply information on certification requirements for those who wish to work in public schools. For general information on careers in speech-language pathology and audiology contact the American Speech-Language-Hearing Association and the American Academy of Audiology. Both offer information about the field and opportunities for networking.

HUMAN RESOURCES
AND SERVICES

CHAPLAIN

CAREER PROFILE

Duties: Conduct worship services; perform religious rites and ceremonies; visit and provide spiritual guidance to personnel; counsel individuals who seek guidance; promote attendance at religious services; oversee religious education programs; train lay leaders who conduct religious education programs; prepare religious speeches and publications

Alternate Title(s): Priest; Minister; Rabbi; Clergy; Preacher; Reverend

Availability: Army, Navy, Air Force

Military Salary: See How to Use This Book

Civilian Salary: Varies

Civilian Employment Prospects: Good

Civilian Advancement Prospects: Good

Prerequisites:

Rank—Enlisted

Education and Training—Master's degree in theology, plus ordination and ecclesiastical endorsement from a recognized religious denomination

Experience—Any training and work experience obtained in the armed services or Job Corps

Special Skills and Personality Traits—Faith, confidence; motivation; tolerance; moral character; attentiveness; the ability to make difficult decisions; able to work under pressure; excellent communication skills; an interest in planning and directing the work of others; sensitivity and listening skills; willingness to make personal sacrifices

CAREER LADDER

Varies

Position Description

Soldiers are not machines. They are people with all the needs and weaknesses of any other human being, and, because human beings have needs beyond the merely physical or temporal, the military provides for the spiritual requirements of its personnel by offering religious services, moral guidance, and counseling through chaplains. Chaplains work in offices, hospitals, and places of worship on land and aboard ships, in and out of combat areas. They conduct worship services in a variety of religious faiths; perform religious rites and ceremonies, such as weddings and funeral services; visit and provide spiritual guidance to personnel in hospitals and

to their families; and counsel individuals who seek guidance. They also promote attendance at religious services, retreats, and conferences; oversee religious education programs, such as Sunday school and youth groups; train lay leaders who conduct religious education programs; and prepare religious speeches and publications.

In the civilian world, Chaplains work in places of worship, hospitals, universities, and correctional institutions, but they are, in almost all cases, affiliated with a particular religious faith. Within their sponsor faith, these clergy organize and lead regular religious services and officiate at ceremonies such as confirmations, weddings, and funerals. They lead worshipers in prayer, administer sacraments, deliver sermons, and read from sacred texts. They oversee religious education programs, visit the sick, provide comfort, counsel those seeking religious or moral guidance, and advise those who are troubled by family or personal problems.

Clergy work irregular hours and are frequently called on short notice to duties outside of their offices. They are on call 24 hours a day, seven days a week.

Civilian Salaries

Salaries of clergy vary substantially, depending on experience, denomination, geographic location, and the size and wealth of their congregation. For example, some Protestant denominations tie a minister's pay to the average pay of the congregation or the community. Catholic priests, on the other hand, take a vow of poverty and are supported by their religious order (this vow is recognized by the IRS, which exempts priests from paying federal income tax). Rabbis may earn additional income from gifts or fees for officiating at ceremonies such as bar or bat mitzvahs and weddings. Most clergy are provided some kind of annual salary, as well as benefits such as housing, a car allowance, health insurance, and a retirement plan.

Civilian Employment Prospects

Now through 2010, opportunities as Protestant ministers should be best for graduates of theological schools. The degree of competition for positions will vary among denominations and geographic regions. Newly ordained ministers unable to find parish positions may find work in youth counseling, family relations, and social welfare organizations; teaching in religious educational institutions.

Now through 2010, opportunities for rabbis are expected to decline in all four major branches of Judaism. Those willing to work in small, underserved communities should have the best prospects. Now through 2010, opportunities for Roman Catholic priests look very good as the current shortage of Roman Catholic priests is expected to continue.

Civilian Advancement Prospects

The clergy is far more a lifetime commitment than it is a job. Most clergy do not collect a salary. Those who enter this field, do so because they feel they have a calling, and not solely in the interest of building a career. Paths of advancement differ from faith to faith, but most promote outstanding members of their order to positions of higher authority by advancing them in rank in much the same manner as the military. For instance, in the Roman Catholic faith, priests may become monsignors, then bishops, cardinals, and then possibly pope.

Education and Training

In the military, those interested in this career receive one to two months of classroom instruction, depending on spe-

cialty. Classes usually consist of such courses as the role and responsibility of military chaplains, administration and leadership techniques, training and education methods, procedures for planning programs, and pastoral counseling methods. Further training occurs on the job and through advanced courses.

Educational requirements for entry into the clergy vary greatly. Some faiths require little more than a bachelor's degree, and not all require that, but often a master's degree in theology is required to enter this occupation. Almost always, ordination and ecclesiastical endorsement from a recognized religious denomination are also required.

Some faiths do not allow women to become clergy; however, those that do are experiencing increases in the numbers of women seeking ordination. Men and women considering careers in the clergy should consult their religious leaders to verify specific entrance requirements. Also, it must be noted that a career in the clergy is not just a career, but a way of life. Most members of the clergy remain in their chosen vocation throughout their lives.

In 1999–2000, the Association of Theological Schools in the United States and Canada accredited 206 Protestant denominational theological schools. These schools only admit students who have received a bachelor's degree or its equivalent from an accredited college. After college graduation, many denominations require a three-year course of professional study in one of these accredited schools, or seminaries, for the degree of Master of Divinity. Persons who have denominational qualifications for the ministry usually are ordained after graduation from a seminary or after serving a probationary pastoral period.

To become eligible for ordination as a rabbi, a student must complete a course of study in a seminary. Entrance requirements and the curriculum depend upon the branch of Judaism with which the seminary is associated. Most seminaries require applicants to be college graduates. Jewish seminaries typically take five years for completion of studies, with an additional preparatory year required for students without sufficient grounding in Hebrew and Jewish studies. In addition to the core academic program, training generally includes fieldwork and internships providing hands-on experience and, in some cases, study in Jerusalem. Seminary graduates are awarded the title Rabbi and earn the Master of Arts in Hebrew Letters degree. After more advanced study, some earn the Doctor of Hebrew Letters degree.

Preparation for the priesthood may begin in the first year of high school, at the college level, or in theological seminaries after college graduation. Nine high-school seminary programs—five free-standing high school seminaries and four programs within Catholic high schools—provided a college preparatory program in 2000. Those who begin training for the priesthood in college do so in one of 42 priesthood formation programs offered either through Catholic colleges or universities or in freestanding college seminaries. Preparatory studies usually include training in philosophy, religious studies, and prayer.

Today, most candidates for the priesthood have a four-year degree from an accredited college or university, then attend one of 46 theological seminaries and earn either the Master of Divinity or the Master of Arts degree. Young men are never denied entry into seminaries because of lack of funds. In seminaries for diocesan priests, scholarships or loans are available, and contributions of benefactors and the Catholic Church finance those in religious seminaries who have taken a vow of poverty and are not expected to have personal resources. Graduate work in theology beyond that required for ordination also is offered at a number of American Catholic universities or at ecclesiastical universities around the world, particularly in Rome. Also, many priests do graduate work in fields unrelated to theology. Priests are encouraged by the Catholic Church to continue their studies, at least informally, after ordination. In recent years, the Church has stressed continuing education for ordained priests in the social sciences, such as sociology and psychology.

Experience, Special Skills, and Personality Traits

Entering the clergy is a calling much more than a career; and those who choose this field are dedicating their life to the service of others and teaching the message of their faith. Religious leaders must exude confidence and motivation, while remaining tolerant and able to listen to the needs of others. They should be capable of making difficult decisions, working under pressure, and living up to the moral standards set by their faith and community. They should also have the ability to express ideas clearly and concisely, an interest in planning and directing the work of others and sensitivity to the needs of others. They must possess in the beliefs they profess and teach, and be able to abide the rules and dogma of their religion. Many clergy are required to take vows foregoing certain activities, so candidates must possess willingness for self-sacrifice.

Unions and Associations

Young men interested in careers in the Catholic Ministry should contact their local diocese or the Center for Applied Research in the Apostolate. Those interested in becoming rabbis should contact the Rabbinical Council of America, the Jewish Theological Seminary of America, the Hebrew Union College-Jewish Institute of Religion, and the Reconstructionist Rabbinical College. Those interested in entering the Protestant ministry should seek the counsel of a minister or church guidance worker.

COUNSELOR

CAREER PROFILE

Duties: Interview personnel, identify personal problems, and determine the need for professional help; counsel personnel and their families; administer and score psychological tests; teach classes; keep records of counseling sessions; give reports to supervisors

Alternate Title(s): Group Worker; Human Relations Counselor; Drug and Alcohol Counselor

Availability: All branches

Military Salary: See How to Use This Book

Civilian Salary: $15,790 to $67,170

Civilian Employment Prospects: Good

Civilian Advancement Prospects: Good

Prerequisites:

  Rank—Officer

  Education and Training—Bachelor's degree minimum; master's degree often required

  Experience—Any training and work experience obtained in the armed services or Job Corps.

  Special Skills and Personality Traits—A strong interest in helping others; the ability to inspire respect, trust, and confidence; the ability to speak clearly and distinctly; patience; sensitivity

  Licensure/Certification—State license required; additional certification may also be required.

CAREER LADDER

```
┌─────────────────────────────┐
│        Administrator        │
└─────────────────────────────┘

┌─────────────────────────────┐
│         Supervisor          │
└─────────────────────────────┘

┌─────────────────────────────┐
│         Counselor           │
└─────────────────────────────┘
```

Position Description

Soldiers are regular people, and, because all human beings can develop problems (drug or alcohol abuse, depression, etc.), the military provides caseworkers and Counselors to help military personnel and their families to overcome social problems. Working in offices or clinics, caseworkers and Counselors interview personnel who request help or are referred by their commanders, identify personal problems and determine the need for professional help, and counsel personnel and their families. They also administer and score psychological tests, teach classes on human relations, keep records of counseling sessions, and give reports to supervisors.

In the civilian world, caseworkers and Counselors work in rehabilitation centers, hospitals, schools, and public agen-

cies. There they assist people with personal, family, educational, mental health, and career decisions and problems. Their duties depend on the individuals they serve and on the settings in which they work.

Educational, vocational, and school counselors—in elementary, secondary, and postsecondary schools—help students evaluate their abilities, interests, talents, and personality characteristics in order to develop realistic academic and career goals.

School counselors help students understand and deal with social, behavioral, and personal problems. They provide students with life skills needed to deal with problems before they occur, and to enhance personal, social, and academic growth.

Vocational counselors help individuals make career decisions. They explore and evaluate the client's education, training, work history, interests, skills, and personal traits, and arrange for aptitude and achievement tests. They also work with individuals to develop job search skills and assist clients in locating and applying for jobs.

Rehabilitation counselors help people deal with the personal, social, and vocational effects of disabilities. They counsel people with disabilities, evaluate the strengths and limitations of individuals, provide personal and vocational counseling, and arrange for medical care, vocational training, and job placement.

Mental health counselors emphasize prevention, and work to promote optimum mental health. Substance abuse and behavioral disorder counselors help people who have problems with alcohol, drugs, gambling, and eating disorders. Marriage and family therapists apply principles, methods, and therapeutic techniques to individuals, family groups, couples, or organizations for the purpose of resolving emotional conflicts. A gerontological counselor provides services to elderly persons who face changing lifestyles because of health problems, and helps families cope with these changes. A multicultural counselor helps employers adjust to an increasingly diverse workforce.

Most Counselors work a standard 40-hour week (those connected to educational institutions follow the school year calendar of their school system). Self-employed counselors and those working in mental health and community agencies, such as substance abuse and behavioral disorder counselors, often work evenings to counsel clients who work during the day. Marriage and family counselors also often work flexible hours as well.

Civilian Salaries

In 2000, the average yearly salary for educational, vocational, and school counselors was $42,110. The middle 50 percent earned between $31,640 and $53,930. The lowest 10 percent earned less than $23,560. The highest 10 percent earned more than $67,170.

In 2000, the average yearly salary for substance abuse and behavioral disorder counselors was $28,510. The middle 50 percent earned between $23,280 and $35,250. The lowest 10 percent earned less than $18,850. The highest 10 percent earned more than $43,420.

In 2000, the average yearly salary for mental health counselors was $27,570. The middle 50 percent earned between $22,220 and $36,150. The lowest 10 percent earned less than $18,500. The highest 10 percent earned more than $46,270.

In 2000, the average yearly salary for rehabilitation counselors was $24,450. The middle 50 percent earned between $19,080 and $33,000. The lowest 10 percent earned less than $15,790. The highest 10 percent earned more than $42,790.

In 2000, the average yearly salary for marriage and family therapists was $34,660. The middle 50 percent earned

between $27,970 and $44,320. The lowest 10 percent earned less than $22,770. The highest 10 percent earned more than $44,320.

Civilian Employment Prospects

In 2000, Counselors held roughly 465,000 jobs. Educational, vocational, and school counselors held 205,000 positions; rehabilitation counselors held 110,000; mental health counselors held 67,000, substance abuse and behavioral disorder counselors held 61,000 and marriage and family therapists held some 21,000 positions.

Through 2010, opportunities for Counselors are expected to grow faster than the average for all occupations. Employment of educational, vocational, and school counselors is expected to grow as a result of increasing student enrollments; state legislation requiring counselors in elementary schools; and expansion of the responsibilities of counselors. The demand for vocational, or employment, counselors, who work primarily for state and local government, is expected to continue to grow as current welfare laws require welfare recipients to find jobs.

Demand is expected to be strong for substance abuse and behavioral, mental health, and marriage and family therapists and for rehabilitation counselors due to the increasing availability of funds to build statewide networks to improve services for children and adolescents with serious emotional disturbances and their family members. Also, insurance companies are increasingly providing for reimbursement of Counselors, enabling many Counselors to move to private practice.

Civilian Advancement Prospects

School counselors can move to a larger school; become directors or supervisors of counseling, guidance, pupil personnel services, counselor educators, counseling psychologists, or school administrators. Some Counselors choose to work for a state's department of education. For marriage and family therapists, doctoral education in family therapy emphasizes the training of supervisors, teachers, researchers, and clinicians in the discipline. Counselors can become supervisors or administrators in their agencies. Some Counselors move into research, consulting, or college teaching, or go into private or group practice.

Education and Training

In the military, those interested in this career receive two to two-and-a-half months of classroom instruction, including practice in counseling. Classes usually included courses in orientation to counseling and social service programs, interviewing and counseling methods, treatments for drug and alcohol abuse and psychological testing techniques. Further training occurs on the job and through advanced courses.

Half of all Counselors have a master's degree. Graduate-level counselor education programs in colleges and universities usually are in departments of education or psychology.

Courses are grouped into eight core areas: human growth and development, social and cultural diversity, relationships, groupwork, career development, assessment, research and program evaluation, and professional identity. In 2000, 149 institutions offered programs in counselor education that were accredited by the Council for Accreditation of Counseling and Related Educational Programs.

Vocational and related rehabilitation agencies usually require a master's degree in rehabilitation counseling, counseling and guidance, or counseling psychology for rehabilitation counselor jobs. Some, however, accept applicants with a bachelor's degree in rehabilitation services, counseling, psychology, sociology, or related fields. A bachelor's degree often qualifies a person to work as a counseling aide, rehabilitation aide, or social service worker. Experience in employment counseling, job development, psychology, education, or social work is helpful.

Special Requirements

In 2001, 46 States and the District of Columbia had some form of counselor credentialing, licensure, certification, or registry legislation governing practice outside schools. Requirements vary from state to state. In some states, credentialing is mandatory; in others, it is voluntary. All states require school counselors to hold state school counseling certification; however, certification requirements vary. Some states require public school counselors to have both counseling and teaching certificates.

A counselor may elect to be nationally certified by the National Board for Certified Counselors, Inc., which grants the general practice credential, "National Certified Counselor." To be certified, a Counselor must hold a master's or higher degree with a concentration in counseling from a regionally accredited college or university; have at least two years of supervised field experience in a counseling setting; provide two professional endorsements, one of which must be from a recent supervisor; and have a passing score on the NBCC's National Counselor Examination for Licensure and Certification.

The Commission on Rehabilitation Counselor Certification offers voluntary national certification for rehabilitation counselors. To become certified, rehabilitation counselors usually must graduate from an accredited educational program, complete an internship, and pass a written examination. After meeting these requirements, candidates are then designated as "Certified Rehabilitation Counselors."

Experience, Special Skills, and Personality Traits

Counselors need a strong interest in helping others as well as the ability to inspire respect, trust, and confidence. They need to be able to speak clearly and distinctly in order to teach classes and work with personnel who have problems. They also need patience for dealing with problems that take time and effort to overcome and sensitivity to the needs of others.

Unions and Associations

For general information about counseling, as well as information on specialties such as school, college, mental health, rehabilitation, multicultural, career, marriage and family, and gerontological counseling, contact the American Counseling Association.

For information on accredited counseling and related training programs, contact the Council for Accreditation of Counseling and Related Educational Programs. For information on national certification requirements for counselors, contact the National Board for Certified Counselors, Inc. And for information on certification requirements for rehabilitation counselors and a list of accredited rehabilitation education programs, contact the Commission on Rehabilitation Counselor Certification.

PERSONNEL SPECIALIST

CAREER PROFILE

Duties: Organize, maintain, and review personnel records; assign personnel to jobs; prepare organizational charts and reports; write official correspondence; provide career guidance and information about personnel programs and procedures to service men and women; assist personnel and their families who have special needs

Alternate Title(s): Human Resource Specialist; Training or Labor Relations Specialist; Public Relations Specialist; Recruiter

Availability: All branches

Military Salary: See How to Use This Book

Civilian Salary: $25,750 to $183,900

Civilian Employment Prospects: Good

Civilian Advancement Prospects: Good

Prerequisites:

Rank—Enlisted

Education and Training—Bachelor's degree in human resources or business management; graduate study in labor relations for some jobs; background in sociology or psychology may help

Experience—Internship; on-the-job training; any experience gained in the armed forces

Special Skills and Personality Traits—Excellent communication skills; public speaking skills; knowledge of business administration; typing; ability to follow detailed procedures and instructions; an interest in working closely with others

CAREER LADDER

> **Recruiting Manager**

> **Personnel Specialist**

> **Assistant Personnel Specialist**

Position Description

It is the duty of the Personnel Specialist to sift through the talent provided them and to match individuals to the jobs for which they are best suited. In the civilian world, the job of human resources, training, and labor relations specialists is to attract top talent to their workplace and then find suitable positions for where these individuals will be best suited. They will recruit and interview employees and then make recommendations following the policies of their employer.

Maintaining morale is often a part of this job. The personnel office must help reduce job turnover as well as seeing to it that their companies exploit employee skills effec-

tively. They must provide training opportunities to enhance those skills, and boost employee satisfaction with their jobs and working conditions. The responsibilities of human resources generalists can vary widely, depending on their employer's needs. Often they will specialize in one personnel field such as employment, compensation, benefits, training, and employee development, and so on.

Personnel Specialists search for talent. They must maintain contacts within the community and may travel extensively to search for promising applicants. They screen, interview, and test applicants as well as check references. They must be completely familiar with their firm's policies to discuss wages, working conditions, and promotional opportunities with applicants. Recruiters also must stay informed about federal regulations such as equal employment opportunity (EEO), affirmative action guidelines and laws, etc.

They may also be called upon to prepare job descriptions, explaining the duties, training, and skills each job requires. Whenever a large organization introduces a new job or reviews existing jobs, descriptions will have to either be revised or created anew. The human resources department will usually also be in charge of payroll. This means not only cutting and dispensing checks, but also making certain that their firm is paying fair and equitable rates. They may conduct surveys to see how their rates compare with others and to see that the firm's pay scale complies with changing laws and regulations.

They will handle a firm's employee benefits program, mainly health insurance and pension plans. They will often be call upon to implement various company-wide programs such as those covering occupational safety, health standards and practices, security, publications, company outings, car pooling, counseling services, etc.

Personnel Specialists will also find themselves in charge of creating labor policy, overseeing industrial labor relations, negotiating collective bargaining agreements, coordinating grievance procedures, and generally working on anything within the company that calls for the drawing up of new contracts or revising standing ones. There are also those specialists who handle human resources issues related to a company's foreign operations, as well as those who develop and apply computer programs to process personnel information, match job seekers with job openings and handle other personnel matters.

Civilian Salaries

The average yearly salary for personnel workers in this field was $49,010 in 1998. The middle 50 percent earned between $35,400 and $73,830. The lowest 10 percent earned less than $25,750 and the highest 10 percent earned more than $91,040. The average yearly earnings in the industries employing the largest numbers of human resources managers in 1997 were:

Local government, except education and hospitals	$50,800
Hospitals	$48,200
Management and public relations	$44,800
Labor organizations	$36,700
Personnel supply services	$35,900

A 1999 survey of the National Association of Colleges and Employers showed that bachelor's degree candidates majoring in human resources received starting offers averaging just under $30,000 a year. In November 1998 Abbott, Langer, and Associates of Crete, Illinois, conducted a survey of compensation in the human resources field which showed salaries ranging from $32,400 at the low end for human resources records specialists to a high of $183,900 for industrial and labor relations directors.

Candidates with a bachelor's degree or three years experience in the personnel field started at or around $23,300 a year in 1999 within the federal government. Those with a superior academic record or an additional year of specialized experience started at $28,000 a year. With a master's degree: $33,400; with a doctorate: $44,500.

Civilian Employment Prospects

The job market looks to remain highly competitive because of the abundant supply of qualified college graduates and experienced workers. Human resources, training, and labor relations specialists and managers held close to 600,000 jobs in 1998, working in practically all companies and every type of industry. Some federal, state, and local governments employed about 14 percent of human resources specialists and managers. They handled the recruitment, interviewing, job classification, training, salary administration, benefits, employee relations, and related matters of the nation's public employees.

Many job openings are expected to open in this field from the need to replace workers who transfer to other occupations or leave the labor force. Employment in this field is expected to grow about as fast as the average for all occupations through 2008. There will be an increased need for experienced Personnel Specialists for a number of reasons. First, firms are expected to devote greater resources to job-specific training programs in response to the increasing complexity of many jobs. Also, as the general workforce ages, the following generations are not replacing it in like numbers. And, rapid technological advances are leaving many employees with obsolete skills.

There is also the additional fact that excessive legislation and court rulings are causing an increased need for specialists in areas such as occupational safety and health, equal employment opportunity, wages, pension, family leave, etc. This is already increasing the demand for human resources, training, and labor relations experts. Rising health-care costs, in particular, should spur demand for specialists to develop creative compensation and benefits packages that firms can offer prospective employees.

Civilian Advancement Prospects

It is possible that job growth could be restricted by the growing use of computerized human resources information systems. Also, positions within human resources departments are no more shielded from corporate downsizing and restructuring than any other jobs, especially in larger firms.

However, employment demand is expected to be quite strong among those firms involved in management, consulting, and personnel supply as businesses increasingly contract out personnel functions or hire Personnel Specialists on a temporary basis. Demand should also increase in firms that develop and administer complex employee benefits and compensation packages for other organizations.

Exceptional human resources workers will often be promoted up the ladder until they reach top managerial or executive positions. Others may join consulting firms or open their own business.

Education and Training

Military training for this position consists of two to two-and-a-half months of classroom instruction. These courses usually include such things as basic typing skills, preparation of military correspondence and forms, personnel records management, and computer update and retrieval procedures.

In the private sector, the educational requirements for human resources personnel may vary considerably due to the wide range of duties and levels of responsibility to be found within such departments. In entry-level positions, employers prefer college graduates who have majored in human resources, personnel administration, or industrial and labor relations. They also search for those with a technical or business background or a well-rounded liberal arts education.

Depending on the school, courses leading to a career in human resources management may be found in departments of business administration, education, instructional technology, organizational development, human services, communication, or public administration.

An advanced degree is increasingly important for some jobs. A strong background in industrial relations and law is highly desirable for contract negotiators, mediators, and arbitrators; a background in law is desirable for those who must interpret the growing number of laws and regulations. A master's degree will be required for those seeking top (and even general) managerial positions. A Ph.D. is an asset for teaching, writing, or consulting work.

Entry-level employees usually learn their jobs by performing monitored duties—inputting data into computer systems, compiling employee handbooks, researching information, answering the phone, etc. They are often placed in on-the-job training programs after which they will be assigned to specific areas in the personnel department to gain experience.

Special Requirements

There are a number of organizations specializing in human resources which offer classes intended to enhance the marketable skills of their members. Some organizations offer certification programs, which are signs of competence and can enhance one's advancement opportunities. The International Foundation of Employee Benefit Plans confers the Certified Employee Benefit Specialist designation to persons who complete a series of college-level courses and pass exams covering employee benefit plans. The Society for Human Resources Management has two levels of certification—Professional in Human Resources, and Senior Professional in Human Resources; both require experience and a comprehensive exam.

Experience, Special Skills, and Personality Traits

A varied combination of courses in the social sciences, business, and behavioral sciences is useful when preparing for a personnel job. Some positions require a more technical or specialized background in engineering, science, finance, or law, while others demand experience or training in compensation, recruitment, training and development, or performance appraisal, as well as courses in everything from industrial psychology and business administration to sociology statistics and labor history. Of course, as in most fields these days, knowledge of computers and information systems is always useful.

Previous experience is an asset. For most advanced positions it is essential. This field demands of those within it the ability to work with individuals as well as a commitment to organizational goals. Other skills needed are the ability to use computers, to sell, teach, and supervise.

Personnel Specialists must speak and write effectively. They must be able to work with or supervise people from various cultures and backgrounds. They must be able to cope with conflicting points of view, function under pressure, and demonstrate discretion, integrity, fair-mindedness without ever losing their perspective. A cool head is not only valuable, it is a prerequisite.

Unions and Associations

There are numerous organizations for Personnel Specialists and human resources specialists. They include the American Society for Training and Development, the American Compensation Association, the International Foundation of Employee Benefit Plans, the Industrial Relations Research Association, and the American Society for Healthcare Human Resources Administration. Groups such as these offer opportunities for networking, training, continuing education, certification, and access to trends in the field.

RECRUITING MANAGER

CAREER PROFILE

Duties: Create programs to inform young people about military careers; direct the staff in local recruiting offices; speak with local civic groups, schools, parents, and young people about military careers; prepare reports and brief commanders on recruiting goals and results

Alternate Title(s): Human Resources Manager; Training and Labor Relations Specialists; Training Director; Recruitment and Interviewing Managers; Employee Assistance and Employee Counseling Specialists; Training Material Development Specialist; Employment Interviewing Specialist; Job Evaluation Specialist

Availability: All branches

Military Salary: See How to Use This Book

Civilian Salary: $25,750 to $183,900

Civilian Employment Prospects: Good

Civilian Advancement Prospects: Good

Prerequisites

Rank—Officer

Education and Training—Bachelor's degree in human resources or business management; graduate study in labor relations for some jobs; background in sociology or psychology may help

Experience—Internship; on-the-job training; any experience gained in the armed forces

Special Requirements—Well-organized; excellent communication skills; strong public relations skills; enjoy working with people; effective public speaking; detail-oriented; sensitive; good listener; good computer skills

Licensure/Certification—Optional; may be required by some employers

CAREER LADDER

```
┌─────────────────────────────┐
│    Director of Personnel     │
└─────────────────────────────┘

┌─────────────────────────────┐
│   Recruiting Manager or      │
│ Human Resources Specialist   │
└─────────────────────────────┘

┌─────────────────────────────┐
│ Assistant Recruiting Manager │
└─────────────────────────────┘
```

Position Description

More than 300,000 young people enlist in the military every year. The different service branches recruit individuals with the specific talents needed to succeed in today's military. Recruiting Managers plan and direct the activities of recruiting specialists who provide information to young people about military careers.

Military Recruiting Managers are uniquely qualified for moving into human resource-type positions after their term of service ends. Finding suitable employees and matching them to the jobs where they will best perform is important for the success of any organization. Human resources workers recruit and interview employees, and advise on hiring decisions. They also help their firms effectively use employee skills, provide training opportunities to enhance those skills, and boost employee satisfaction with their jobs and working conditions in an effort to improve morale and productivity and limit job turnover. Dealing with people is an essential part of the job.

Recruiting Managers maintain contacts within the community. They may travel extensively to search for promising job applicants. They screen, interview, and test applicants as well as check references, and extend job offers. Recruiters must be thoroughly familiar with both their organization and its personnel policies in order to discuss wages, working conditions, and promotional opportunities. They also investigate and resolve grievances and examine corporate practices for possible violations.

Human resources personnel collect and examine detailed information about job duties to prepare job descriptions that explain the duties, training, and skills each job requires. Whenever a new job is created, or existing jobs are reviewed, a firm will call upon the human resources department to handle the descriptive details.

Recruiting Managers handle their firm's employee benefits program, including its health insurance and pension plans. They can also find themselves responsible for a wide array of other programs covering occupational safety and health standards and practices; health promotion and physical fitness; medical examinations; plant security; publications; food service and recreation activities; car pooling, and many others.

They also supervise training. Human resources training specialists plan, organize, and direct a wide range of training activities. Planning and program development is an important part of their job. Trainers will confer with managers and supervisors, conduct surveys, and periodically evaluate training effectiveness. Training methods include on-the-job training; apprenticeship training; classroom training; programmed instruction, and so on.

Recruiting Managers also handle human resources issues related to a company's foreign operations, develop and apply computer programs to process personnel information, match job seekers with job openings, and handle other personnel matters.

Civilian Salaries

Average yearly earnings of human resources managers were $49,010 in 1998. The middle 50 percent earned between $35,400 and $73,830. The lowest 10 percent earned less than $25,750 and the highest 10 percent earned more than $91,040. Average yearly earnings in the industries employing the largest numbers of human resources managers in 1997 were:

Local government, except education and hospitals	$50,800
Hospitals	$48,200
Management and public relations	$44,800
Labor organizations	$36,700
Personnel supply services	$35,900

A 1999 salary survey conducted by the National Association of Colleges and Employers reported that bachelor's degree candidates majoring in human resources, including labor relations, received starting offers averaging $29,800 a year.

The November 1998 survey of compensation in the human resources field, conducted by Abbott, Langer, and Associates of Crete, Illinois, reported that the median total cash compensation for selected personnel and labor relations occupations were:

Industrial and labor relations directors	$183,900
Compensation and benefits directors	$88,000
Divisional human resources directors	$84,100
Training directors	$79,400
Recruitment and interviewing managers	$75,100
Employee and community relations directors	$73,500
Plant/location human resources managers	$62,000
Compensation supervisors	$53,300
Human resources information systems specialists	$49,300
Employee assistance and employee counseling specialists	$47,500
EEO and affirmative action specialists	$44,800
Training material development specialists	$43,500
Training generalists (computer)	$39,600
Classroom instructors	$35,300
Employment interviewing specialists	$35,100
Job evaluation specialists	$34,100
Human resources records specialists	$32,400

Civilian Employment Prospects

Human resources, training, and labor relations specialists and managers held roughly 600,000 jobs in 1998. These jobs could be found in virtually every industry. Specialists accounted for three-fifths of these positions, and managers for two-fifths. About 14,000 specialists were self-employed, working as consultants to public and private employers.

The private sector accounted for nearly 80 percent of salaried jobs. Services industries—including business, health, social, management, and educational services—accounted for about 40 percent of these salaried jobs; labor organizations, accounted for an additional 20 percent. Manufacturing industries accounted for another 17 percent, while finance, insurance, and real estate firms made up the remainder.

Federal, state, and local governments employed roughly 15 percent of human resources specialists and managers. They handled the recruitment, interviewing, job classification, training, salary administration, benefits, employee relations, and related matters of the nation's public employees.

All jobs in this market will likely remain competitive because of the abundant supply of qualified college graduates and experienced workers. In addition to openings due to growth, many job openings will result from the need to replace workers who transfer to other occupations or leave the labor force.

Civilian Advancement Prospects

Employment in these areas is expected to grow about as fast as the average for all occupations through 2008. New jobs will open due to both the aging of the workforce and technological advances that can leave employees with obsolete skills. Also, legislation and court rulings setting standards in various areas—occupational safety and health, equal employment opportunity, wages, health, pension, and family leave—are expected to increase demand for qualified individuals in these areas. Additional job growth may stem from increasing demand for specialists in international human resources management and human resources information systems.

Employment demand will rise among firms involved in management, consulting, and personnel supply as they increasingly contract out personnel functions or hire personnel specialists on a temporary basis. Demand will also increase in firms that develop and administer employee benefits and compensation packages for other organizations.

Exceptional human resources workers may be promoted to director of personnel or industrial relations. These positions can eventually lead to a top managerial or executive position. Others may join a consulting firm or open their own business. A Ph.D. is an asset for teaching, writing, or consulting work.

Education and Training

Because of the varied duties and levels of responsibility to be found in this career, the educational backgrounds of human resources personnel can vary considerably. In filling entry-level jobs, employers usually seek college graduates with an eye toward applicants who majored in human resources, personnel administration, or industrial and labor relations. Also highly regarded are graduates with technical or business backgrounds.

A large number of colleges and universities offer programs leading to such degrees. Some offer programs in personnel administration or human resources management, training and development, or compensation and benefits. Courses leading to a career in human resources management may be found in departments of business administration, education, instructional technology, organizational development, human services, communication, or public administration.

A combination of courses in the social sciences, business, and behavioral sciences is useful. Prospective human resources specialists should be trained in compensation, recruitment, training and development, and performance appraisal, as well as courses in principles of management, organizational structure, and industrial psychology. Other relevant courses include business administration, public administration, psychology, sociology, political science, economics, and statistics. Courses in labor law, collective bargaining, labor economics, labor history, and industrial psychology, also provide valuable background for the prospective labor relations specialist. A knowledge of computers and information systems is also useful.

Many labor relations jobs require graduate study in industrial or labor relations. A master's degree in human resources, labor relations, or in business administration with a concentration in human resources management is highly recommended for those seeking general and top management positions.

Previous experience is an extremely important asset for more advanced positions, including managers as well as arbitrators and mediators. Many employers prefer entry-level workers who have gained some experience through an internship or work-study program while in school while many other positions are filled by experienced individuals from other fields, including business, government, education, social services administration, and the military.

Special Requirements

Some organizations offer certification programs, which are signs of competence. These can enhance one's advancement opportunities. The International Foundation of Employee Benefit Plans confers the Certified Employee Benefit Specialist designation to persons who complete a series of college-level courses and pass exams covering employee benefit plans. The Society for Human Resources Management has two levels of certification—Professional in Human Resources, and Senior Professional in Human Resources. Both levels require experience and a comprehensive exam.

Experience, Skills, and Personality Traits

Human resources managers must speak and write effectively. They must work with or supervise people with various cultural backgrounds, levels of education, and experience. They must be able to cope with conflicting points of view, function under pressure, and demonstrate discretion, integrity, fair-mindedness, and a persuasive, congenial personality.

Good fields of study are personnel management, communications, and public relations. Helpful attributes include an interest in working closely with people as well as the ability to speak effectively to large and small groups.

A four-year college degree is normally required to enter this occupation. Depending on the job duties, a strong background in human resources, business, technical, or liberal arts subjects may be preferred.

Unions and Associations

There are numerous organizations for Recruiting Managers and human resources specialists. They include the

American Society for Training and Development, the American Compensation Association, the International Foundation of Employee Benefit Plans, the Industrial Relations Research Association, and the American Soci- ety for Healthcare Human Resources Administration. Groups such as these offer opportunities for networking, training, continuing education, certification, and access to trends in the field.

SOCIAL WORKER

CAREER PROFILE

Duties: Counsel military personnel; supervise counselors and caseworkers; survey military personnel; plan social action programs; plan and monitor equal opportunity programs; conduct research; organize community activities

Alternate Title(s): Social Group Worker; Medical Social Worker; Psychiatric Social Worker; Social Welfare Administrator

Availability: Army, Navy, Air Force

Military Salary: See How to Use This Book

Civilian Salary: $19,300 to $53,160

Civilian Employment Prospects: Good

Civilian Advancement Prospects: Good

Prerequisites:

  Rank—Officer

  Education and Training—Four-year college degree in social work or related social sciences; some specialties require a master's degree

  Experience—Any training and work experience obtained in the armed services or Job Corps

  Special Skills and Personality Traits—Emotional maturity; objectivity; sensitivity; a desire to help others; the ability to express ideas clearly and concisely; able to handle responsibility, work independently, and maintain good working relationships with clients and coworkers

  Licensure/Certification—State licensing and certification required; voluntary certifications optional

CAREER LADDER

```
┌─────────────────────────────────┐
│       Executive Director        │
└─────────────────────────────────┘

┌─────────────────────────────────┐
│  Supervisor, Program Manager,   │
│     or Assistant Director       │
└─────────────────────────────────┘

┌─────────────────────────────────┐
│          Social Worker          │
└─────────────────────────────────┘
```

Position Description

No military organization can function without cooperation and a spirit of teamwork motivating its members. Social Workers in the various branches of the service focus on improving conditions that cause social problems, such as drug and alcohol abuse, racism, and sexism. Working in offices or clinics throughout the armed services, they counsel military personnel and their family members, supervise counselors and caseworkers, survey military personnel to identify problems and plan solutions, and plan social action programs to rehabilitate personnel with problems. They also plan and monitor equal opportunity programs, conduct research on social problems and programs, and organize community activities on military bases.

In the civilian world, Social Workers work for hospitals, human service agencies, and federal, state, county, and city governments. They usually specialize in a particular field, however, such as family services, child welfare, or medical services.

Wherever they work, or whatever their specialty, Social Workers help people function as best they can within their environments, deal with their relationships, and solve personal and family problems. These workers often see clients who face life-threatening diseases, unmanageable social problems, or serious domestic conflicts.

Social Workers help people correctly identify their problems, consider effective solutions, and then arrange for specific services that can help them. They follow through to assure that services are helpful and that proper use is made of the services offered. Social Workers may review eligibility requirements, help fill out forms and applications, visit clients on a regular basis, and provide support during crises.

Social Workers' responsibilities vary depending on where they are employed. Some provide or arrange for support services. Others provide counseling services on marriage, family, and adoption matters, help people through personal or community emergencies, or help children, parents, and teachers cope with problems. They help people locate basic benefits, offer counseling to those receiving therapy for addictive or physical disorders in rehabilitation facilities, and counsel those with personal, family, professional, or financial problems. Some evaluate and counsel individuals in the criminal justice system to cope better in society.

Although some Social Workers conduct research or are involved in planning or policy development, most Social Workers prefer to specialize in an area of practice in which they may interact with a particular cross-section of clients. Some of the fields of specialty offered by this profession are: clinical social work, child welfare, child or adult protective services, mental health social work, health-care social work, school social work, substance abuse social work, criminal justice social work, occupational social work, and gerontology.

Social Workers generally work a standard 40-hour week in clean, well-lighted conditions. Some weekend and evening duties can occur. Their work can be immensely satisfying, but it can be emotionally draining as well as stressful.

Civilian Salaries

In 2000, the average yearly salary for child, family and school Social Workers was $31,470. The middle 50 percent earned between $24,910 and $40,170. The lowest 10 percent earned less than $20,120. The top 10 percent earned more than $50,280.

In 2000, the average yearly salary for medical and public health Social Workers was $34,790. The middle 50 percent earned between $27,800 and $43,450. The lowest 10 percent earned less than $22,490. The top 10 percent earned more than $53,160.

In 2000, the average yearly salary for mental health and substance abuse Social Workers was $30,170. The middle 50 percent earned between $23,840 and $39,190. The lowest 10 percent earned less than $19,300. The top 10 percent earned more than $48,750.

Civilian Employment Prospects

In 2000, Social Workers held nearly 470,000 jobs. Roughly one-third of the positions were in state, county, or municipal government agencies. Most nongovernment jobs were in social service agencies, hospitals, nursing homes, home health agencies, and other health centers or clinics.

Through 2010, opportunities for Social Workers are expected to increase faster than the average for all occupations, particularly among gerontology Social Workers. The number of Social Workers in hospitals and long-term care facilities will increase in response to the need to provide medical and social services for clients who leave the facility. Strong competition for jobs is expected in cities, but opportunities should be good in rural areas where it is often difficult to attract and retain qualified staff.

Employment is also expected to grow more rapidly for Social Workers employed in home health-care services and private social service agencies, as well as for substance abuse Social Workers and school Social Workers. Also, the growing popularity of employee assistance programs also is expected to spur some demand for an increase in private practitioners, some of whom provide social work services to corporations on a contractual basis.

Civilian Advancement Prospects

In social services advancement to positions such as supervisor, program manager, assistant director, or executive director of a social service agency or department is possible. Such upward movement, however, usually requires an advanced degree and related work experience. Other career options for Social Workers include teaching, research, and consulting. Those Social Workers in private practice are usually clinical Social Workers who provide psychotherapy. Private practitioners usually have at least a master's degree and a period of supervised work experience.

Education and Training

In the military those interested in this career receive four to six months of instruction with courses in such subjects as ways of controlling drug and alcohol abuse among military personnel and management of equal opportunity programs.

In the civilian world, a bachelor's degree is the minimum requirement, but a master's degree in social work or a related field has become the standard for many positions. However, majors in psychology, sociology, and related fields may be sufficient to qualify for some entry-level jobs, especially in small community agencies. A master's degree in social work is often necessary for positions in health and mental health settings, for certification for clinical work, jobs in public agencies and most supervisory, administrative, and staff training positions. College and university teaching positions and most research appointments normally require a doctorate in social work.

In 2000, the Council on Social Work Education accredited 421 bachelor's and 139 master's degree programs. The Group for the Advancement of Doctoral Education listed 71 doctoral programs for Ph.D.s in social work. Accredited bachelor's programs require at least 400 hours of supervised field experience. Master's degree programs last two years and include 900 hours of supervised field instruction, or internship.

Special Requirements

All segments of the country have licensing, certification, or registration requirements regarding social work practice and the use of professional titles. The National Association of Social Workers offers voluntary credentials. The Academy of Certified Social Workers grants certification to all Social Workers who have met established eligibility criteria. Clinical Social Workers may earn either the Qualified Clinical Social Worker credential or the advanced credential-Diplomate in Clinical Social Work. Social Workers holding clinical credentials also may list themselves in the biannual publication of the NASW Register of Clinical Social Workers.

Experience, Special Skills, and Personality Traits

Social Workers should be emotionally mature and objective. They must be sensitive to people and their problems, and possess a desire to help others. The ability to express ideas clearly and concisely is required, and candidates should be able to handle responsibility, work independently, and maintain good working relationships with clients and coworkers. An interest in research and teaching is important since the field requires ongoing education.

Unions and Associations

For information about career opportunities in social work and voluntary credentials for Social Workers, contact the National Association of Social Workers. For either accredited social work programs or to order a Directory of Colleges and Universities with Accredited Social Work Degree Programs contact the Council on Social Work Education. And, for information on licensing requirements and testing procedures for each state contact that state's licensing authorities, or the Association of Social Work Boards.

LAW AND PROTECTIVE SERVICES

FIREFIGHTER

CAREER PROFILE

Duties: Operate pumps, hoses, and extinguishers; force entry in order to fight fires and rescue personnel; drive firefighting emergency vehicles; give first aid; inspect aircraft, buildings, and equipment; teach fire protection procedures; repair firefighting equipment; fill fire extinguishers

Alternate Title(s): Fireman; Fire Inspector; Fire Chief

Availability: All branches

Military Salary: See How to Use This Book

Civilian Salary: $8.03/hour to $77,700/year

Civilian Employment Prospects: Fair

Civilian Advancement Prospects: Fair

Prerequisites:

Rank—Enlisted

Education and Training—High school diploma; undergraduate and graduate degrees may be necessary for advancement

Experience—Any training and work experience obtained in the armed services

Special Skills and Personality Traits—Mental alertness; self-discipline and courage; mechanical aptitude; endurance and strength; a sense of public service; initiative; good judgment; dependability; leadership; efficiency; the ability to remain calm under stress; a willingness to risk injury to help others; good vision; a clear speaking voice

Licensure/Certification—Certification from the National Fire Academy required for executive positions; various state certifications required, especially for fire chiefs

CAREER LADDER

```
┌─────────────────────────────────────────┐
│                  Chief                    │
└─────────────────────────────────────────┘

┌─────────────────────────────────────────┐
│   Battalion, Assistant or Deputy Chief    │
└─────────────────────────────────────────┘

┌─────────────────────────────────────────┐
│     Engineer, Lieutenant, Captain         │
└─────────────────────────────────────────┘

┌─────────────────────────────────────────┐
│              Firefighter                  │
└─────────────────────────────────────────┘
```

Position Description

Just as the modern military needs its own police services, it must also have its own fire departments. Working indoors and ·outdoors while fighting fires, they are exposed to smoke, heat, and flames. These firefighting units protect lives and property by putting out, controlling, and working to prevent fires in buildings, aircraft, and aboard ships. They also operate pumps, hoses, and extinguishers; force entry into aircraft, vehicles, and buildings in order to fight fires and rescue personnel; drive firefighting trucks and emer-gency rescue vehicles; and give first aid to injured personnel. Military Firefighters also inspect aircraft, buildings, and equipment for fire hazards; teach fire protection procedures; repair firefighting equipment; and fill fire extinguishers.

In the civilian world, Firefighters work for city and county fire departments, other government agencies, and industrial firms. They are also frequently the first emergency personnel at the scene of a traffic accident or medical emergency and may be called upon to put out a fire, treat injuries, or perform other vital functions.

Firefighting is dangerous and complex and requires organization and teamwork. At every emergency scene, Firefighters perform specific duties assigned by a superior officer. At fires, they connect hose lines to hydrants, operate pumps, position and climb ladders, rescue victims, provide emergency medical attention as needed, ventilate smoke-filled areas, and attempt to salvage the contents of buildings. Sometimes they remain at the site of a disaster for days at a time, rescuing trapped survivors and assisting with medical treatment. Firefighters may also be enlisted to investigate and determine the cause of a fire.

Firefighters receive training in emergency medical procedures, and many fire departments require them to be certified as emergency medical technicians. They also work in a variety of settings, including urban and suburban areas, airports, chemical plants, other industrial sites, and rural areas like grasslands and forests. In addition, some Firefighters work with hazardous materials units that are trained for the control, prevention, and cleanup of oil spills and other toxic materials incidents. In national forests and parks, Firefighters known as smoke jumpers, parachute from airplanes to reach otherwise inaccessible areas.

Between alarms, Firefighters clean and maintain equipment, conduct practice drills and fire inspections, and participate in physical fitness activities. They also prepare written reports on fire incidents and review fire science literature to keep abreast of technological developments and changing administrative practices and policies.

Most Firefighters work in excess of 50 hours a week. Some are on duty for 24 hours, then off for 48 hours. Still others rotate between a day shift and night shift. Also, Firefighters often work extra hours at various emergencies and are regularly assigned to work on holidays. Duty hours include time when Firefighters study, train, and perform fire prevention duties.

Firefighters must work whenever an emergency arises, no matter what the weather or hour. Firefighting involves risk of death or injury from many sources as well as the possibility of contact with poisonous, flammable, or explosive gases and chemicals, as well as radioactive or other hazardous materials. For these reasons, they must wear protective gear that can be very heavy and hot.

Civilian Salaries

In 2000, the average hourly pay for Firefighters was $16.43. The middle 50 percent earned between $11.82 and $21.75. The lowest 10 percent earned less than $8.03. The highest 10 percent earned more than $26.58.

In 2000, the average yearly salaries for first-line supervisors/managers of firefighting and prevention workers were $51,990. The middle 50 percent earned between $40,920 and $64,760. The lowest 10 percent earned less than $31,820. The highest 10 percent earned more than $77,700.

In 2000, the average yearly salaries for fire inspectors and investigators were $41,630. The middle 50 percent

earned between $31,630 and $53,130 a year. The lowest 10 percent earned less than $24,790. The highest 10 percent earned more than $65,030.

In 2000, the average yearly salaries for forest fire inspectors and prevention specialists were $32,140. The middle 50 percent earned between $22,930 and $41,150 a year. The lowest 10 percent earned less than $17,060. The highest 10 percent earned more than $50,680.

Firefighters who average more than a certain number of hours a week are required to be paid overtime. Firefighters' benefits usually include medical and liability insurance, vacation and sick leave, and some paid holidays. Most fire departments provide protective clothing, breathing apparatus, and dress uniforms. Firefighters are generally covered by pension plans, often providing retirement at half pay after 25 years of service or if disabled in the line of duty.

Civilian Employment Prospects

In 2000, paid career Firefighters held nearly 260,000 jobs. Some 90 percent worked in municipal or county fire departments. The last 10 percent worked in fire departments on federal and state installations, including airports.

Many people are attracted to firefighting because it is challenging and provides the opportunity to perform an essential public service, and because one can retire with a pension after only 20 years. Thus the number of qualified applicants usually exceeds the number of job openings, in most areas. Consequently, through 2010, opportunities for Firefighters are expected to increase more slowly than the average for all occupations.

Civilian Advancement Prospects

Opportunities for promotion depend upon written examination results, job performance, interviews, and seniority. The line of promotion usually is to engineer, lieutenant, captain, battalion chief, assistant chief, deputy chief, and chief.

Many fire departments now require a bachelor's degree (in fire science, public administration, or a related field) for promotion to positions higher than battalion chief. A master's degree is required for executive fire officer certification from the National Fire Academy and for State chief officer certification.

Education and Training

In the military, those interested in this career receive two to three months of classroom instruction, depending on specialty. Classes usually cover types of fires, firefighting equipment operations, firefighting procedures, first aid procedures, and rescue procedures. Further training occurs on the job. The army and the navy offer certified apprenticeship programs for some specialties in this occupation.

Applicants for municipal firefighting jobs generally must pass a written exam as well as tests of strength, physical stamina, coordination, and agility and a medical examination that includes drug screening. Examinations are generally open to persons who are at least 18 years of age and have a high school education or the equivalent. Those who receive the highest scores in all phases of testing have the best chances for appointment. The completion of community college courses in fire science may improve an applicant's chances for appointment. In recent years, an increasing proportion of entrants to this occupation has had some postsecondary education.

Entry-level Firefighters are trained at the department's training center or academy where they study firefighting techniques, fire prevention, hazardous materials control, local building codes, and emergency medical procedures, including first aid and cardiopulmonary resuscitation. They also learn how to use axes, chain saws, fire extinguishers, ladders, and other firefighting and rescue equipment.

Some fire departments have accredited apprenticeship programs that combine formal, technical instruction with on-the-job training under the supervision of experienced firefighters. Fire departments frequently conduct training programs, and some Firefighters attend training sessions sponsored by the U.S. National Fire Academy. Some states have extensive Firefighter training and certification programs. A number of colleges and universities offer courses leading to degrees in fire engineering or fire science. Many fire departments offer Firefighters incentives such as tuition reimbursement or higher pay for completing advanced training.

Most experienced Firefighters continue studying to improve their job performance and prepare for promotion examinations. To progress to higher level positions, they acquire expertise in advanced firefighting equipment and techniques, building construction, emergency medical technology, writing, public speaking, management and budgeting procedures, and public relations.

Experience, Special Skills, and Personality Traits

Firefighters need mental alertness, self-discipline, courage, mechanical aptitude, endurance, strength, and a sense of public service. Initiative and good judgment are also important, as well as dependability, leadership, discipline, efficiency, the ability to remain calm under stress, a willingness to risk injury to help others, good vision, and a clear speaking voice.

Unions and Associations

Information about a career as a Firefighter may be obtained from local fire departments and from both the International Association of Firefighters and the U.S. Fire Administration.

Information about Firefighter professional qualifications and a list of colleges and universities offering programs in fire science or fire prevention may be obtained from the National Fire Academy.

In addition there are many local and state firefighters associations. Check the Web for one in your area.

LAW ENFORCEMENT AND SECURITY OFFICER

CAREER PROFILE

Duties: Investigate criminal activities; interview witnesses and question suspects; guard correctional facilities; conduct searches; perform fire and riot control duties

Alternate Title(s): Detective; Private Investigator; Undercover Agent; Correction Officer; Guard; Bailiff

Availability: All branches

Military Salary: See How to Use This Book

Civilian Salary: $16,210 to $86,060

Civilian Employment Prospects: Good

Civilian Advancement Prospects: Good

Prerequisites:

Rank—Enlisted

Education and Training—High school diploma; college degree may be required for some positions; police academy training; pass written examinations

Experience—Any training and work experience obtained in the armed services

Special Skills and Personality Traits—Ingenuity; persistence; assertiveness; good communication skills; quick mental reflexes; good interviewing and interrogation skills; honesty; sound judgment; integrity; a sense of responsibility; good health; at least 20 years old; normal color vision; interest in law enforcement and crime prevention; willing to perform potentially dangerous work; ability to remain calm under pressure

Licensure/Certification—May be required in some cases, such as for private investigators

CAREER LADDER

```
┌─────────────────────────────────────────┐
│              Captain                      │
└─────────────────────────────────────────┘

┌─────────────────────────────────────────┐
│   Corporal, Sergeant, or Lieutenant       │
└─────────────────────────────────────────┘

┌─────────────────────────────────────────┐
│        Probationary Officer               │
└─────────────────────────────────────────┘
```

Position Description

The modern military maintains its own police force and Law Enforcement and Security Officers much like the civilian world. These law enforcement specialists investigate criminal activities and activities related to espionage, treason, and terrorism. They work mainly indoors, except when conducting investigations in the field or guarding prisoners in the exercise yards of military correctional facilities. They also interview witnesses and question suspects, sometimes using polygraph machines, and they conduct searches of inmates, cells, and vehicles and perform fire and riot control duties.

In the civilian world Law Enforcement and Security Officers work in federal, state, and local prisons; intelligence and law enforcement agencies; and private security companies. They may work as police and detectives, correctional officers, private detectives and investigators, and security guards and gaming surveillance officers, probation officers and correctional treatment specialists, bill and account collectors, claims adjusters, appraisers, examiners, and investigators.

Uniformed police officers work in municipal police departments. They maintain regular patrols, respond to calls for service, direct traffic, etc. Some work in special units, such as those on horseback, bicycle, or motorcycle or in the harbor patrol, canine corps, special weapons and tactics, and emergency response teams. Some work in special police agencies: public college, university, and public school district police, and agencies serving transportation systems. Police may specialize in fields such as chemical and microscopic analysis, training and firearms instruction, or handwriting and fingerprint identification.

Sheriffs and deputy sheriffs enforce the law on the county level. A deputy sheriff has law enforcement duties similar to those of officers in urban police departments. Police and sheriffs' deputies who provide security in city and county courts are sometimes called bailiffs. State police officers arrest criminals statewide and patrol highways to enforce motor vehicle laws and regulations. Detectives are plainclothes investigators who gather facts and collect evidence for criminal cases. They conduct interviews, examine records, observe the activities of suspects, and participate in raids or arrests.

Federal Bureau of Investigation agents are the government's principal investigators. U.S. Drug Enforcement Administration agents enforce laws and regulations relating to illegal drugs. U.S. marshals and deputy marshals protect the Federal courts and ensure the effective operation of the judicial system. U.S. Immigration and Naturalization Service agents and inspectors facilitate the entry of legal visitors and immigrants to the United States and detain and deport those arriving illegally. Bureau of Alcohol, Tobacco, and Firearms agents regulate and investigate violations of federal firearms and explosives laws, as well as federal alcohol and tobacco tax regulations.

Customs agents investigate violations of narcotics smuggling, money laundering, child pornography, customs fraud, and enforcement of the Arms Export Control Act. Customs inspectors inspect cargo, baggage, and articles worn or carried by people and carriers including vessels, vehicles, trains, and aircraft entering or leaving the United States to enforce laws governing imports and exports. U.S. Secret Service special agents protect the President and other dignitaries. They also investigate counterfeiting, forgery of government checks or bonds, and fraudulent use of credit cards.

The U.S. Department of State Bureau of Diplomatic Security special agents battle against terrorism. Other Federal agencies which employ police and special agents with sworn arrest powers and the authority to carry firearms are the U.S. Postal Service, the Bureau of Indian Affairs Office of Law Enforcement, the U.S. Forest Service, the National Park Service, and Federal Air Marshals.

Corrections officers are responsible for overseeing individuals who have been arrested and are awaiting trial or who have been convicted of a crime and sentenced to serve time in a jail, reformatory, or penitentiary. They maintain security and inmate accountability to prevent disturbances, assaults, or escapes.

Private detectives and investigators carry out investigations using various types of surveillance or searches. They offer many services, including executive, corporate, and celebrity protection; preemployment verification; and individual background profiles, assistance in civil liability and personal injury cases, insurance claims and fraud, child custody and protection cases, and premarital screening. They sometimes specialize as corporate or financial investigators and as retail store or hotel detectives.

Such work can be very dangerous and stressful. Officers need to be constantly alert and ready to deal appropriately with a number of threatening situations. Uniformed officers, detectives, agents, and inspectors are usually scheduled to work 40-hour weeks, but paid overtime is common. Some jobs, however, require extensive travel, often on very short notice. Most of the above jobs call for the law enforcement specialist to be armed. Work for all of them can be indoors or outdoors.

Private detectives and investigators often work irregular hours because of the need to conduct surveillance and contact people who are not available during normal working hours. Early morning, evening, weekend, and holiday work is common.

Civilian Salaries

In 2000, the average yearly salary for police and sheriff's patrol officers was $39,790. The middle 50 percent earned between $30,460 and $50,230. The lowest 10 percent earned less than $23,790. The highest 10 percent earned more than $58,900.

In 2000, the average yearly salary for police and detective supervisors was $57,210. The middle 50 percent earned between $43,630 and $70,680. The lowest 10 percent earned less than $34,660. The highest 10 percent earned more than $86,060.

In 2000, the average yearly salary for detectives and criminal investigators was $48,870. The middle 50 percent earned between $37,240 and $61,750. The lowest 10 percent earned less than $29,600. The highest 10 percent earned more than $72,160.

In 2000, the average yearly salary for corrections officers was $31,170. The middle 50 percent earned between $24,650 and $40,100. The lowest 10 percent earned less than $20,010. The highest 10 percent earned more than $49,310.

In 2000, the average yearly salary for first-line supervisors/managers of corrections officers was $41,880. The middle 50 percent earned between $32,460 and $55,540. The lowest 10 percent earned less than $28,280. The highest 10 percent earned more than $67,280.

In 2000, the average yearly salary for salaried private detectives and investigators was $26,750. The middle 50 percent earned between $20,040 and $38,240. The lowest 10 percent earned less than $16,210. The highest 10 percent earned more than $52,200.

Civilian Employment Prospects

In 2000, police and detectives held just under 835,000 jobs. About 80 percent were employed by local governments. Corrections officers held close to 460,000 jobs. Nearly 60 percent were in state correctional institutions such as prisons, prison camps, and youth correctional facilities. Private detectives and investigators held almost 40,000 jobs. Nearly two-fifths were self-employed.

The opportunity for public service through law enforcement work is attractive to many because the job is challenging and involves much personal responsibility. Also, most agencies allow retirement with a pension after only 20 to 25 years of service.

Through 2010, opportunities for police and detectives as well as for private detectives and investigators are expected to increase faster than the average for all occupations. Opportunities for corrections officers are expected to be excellent during the same period.

A more security-conscious society with concerns about drug-related crimes, street violence, terrorism, increased litigation, and the need to protect confidential information and property of all kinds will contribute to an increasing demand for police services. At the local and state levels, growth is likely to continue as long as crime remains a serious concern.

The number of qualified candidates exceeds the number of job openings in federal and state law enforcement agencies but is inadequate to meet growth and replacement needs in many local and special police departments. The largest number of employment opportunities will arise in urban communities with relatively low salaries and high crime rates.

Civilian Advancement Prospects

Police officers usually become eligible for promotion after a probationary period. Promotions to corporal, sergeant, lieutenant, and captain usually are made according to a candidate's position on a promotion list, as determined by scores on a written examination and on-the-job performance.

Corrections officers may advance to correctional sergeant. Correctional sergeants supervise correctional officers and usually are responsible for maintaining security and directing the activities of other officers during an assigned shift or in an assigned area.

Education and Training

In the military, those interested in this career receive one to three months of classroom instruction, depending on specialty. Classes usually include courses in civil and military laws, investigation procedures and techniques, and prisoner control and discipline.

In the civilian world, candidates for law enforcement positions must be U.S. citizens, usually at least 20 years of age, and must meet rigorous physical and personal qualifications. Physical examinations of vision, hearing, strength, and agility are often included, as well as performance in competitive written examinations, previous education, and experience.

In state and large local departments, recruits get training in their agency's police academy. In small agencies, recruits often attend a regional or state academy. To be considered as an FBI agent, an applicant either must be a graduate of an accredited law school or a college graduate with a major in accounting, fluency in a foreign language, or three years of related full-time work experience. All new agents undergo training at the FBI academy. Indeed, similar educational or work experience backgrounds are required of applicants seeking appointments to special agent jobs with any federal agency.

Many law enforcement agencies encourage applicants to take postsecondary school training in law enforcement-related subjects. Many junior colleges, colleges, and universities offer programs in law enforcement or administration of justice. Continuing training helps police officers, detectives, and special agents improve their job performance. Many agencies pay all or part of the tuition for officers to work toward degrees in criminal justice, police science, administration of justice, or public administration, and pay higher salaries to those who earn such a degree.

There are no formal education requirements for most private detective and investigator jobs, although many private detectives have college degrees and previous experience in other, related occupations. Private investigators must be licensed throughout most of the country.

Experience, Special Skills, and Personality Traits

Although many varied careers are profiled here, most of them require individuals with ingenuity, persistence, and assertiveness. Law enforcement agents must not be afraid of confrontation, should communicate well, and should be able to think on their feet. Good interviewing and interrogation skills are important as are honesty, sound judgment, integrity, and a sense of responsibility, good health, normal color vision, an interest in law enforcement and crime prevention, a willingness to perform potentially dangerous work and the ability to remain calm under pressure.

Unions and Associations

Information about entrance requirements may be obtained from federal, state, and local law enforcement agencies. Information about qualifications for employment as an FBI Special Agent is available from the nearest State FBI office. Information about career opportunities, qualifications, and training to become a deputy marshal is available from the

United States Marshals Service. Information on career opportunities, qualifications, and training for U.S. Secret Service Special Agents is available from the U.S. Secret Service.

For information on career opportunities in the U.S. Bureau of Alcohol, Tobacco, and Firearms or the United States Border Patrol, contact those specific agencies. Information about correctional jobs is available from the American Jail Association, the Federal Bureau of Prisons and the Office of Personnel Management. For information on local licensing requirements, contact your State Department of Public Safety, State Division of Licensing, or your local or state police headquarters. For information on a career as a legal investigator, contact the National Association of Legal Investigators.

LAWYER

CAREER PROFILE

Duties: Give legal advice; prepare pretrial advice in court-martial cases; act as prosecuting attorney, defense attorney, or judge; prepare legal documents; interpret laws, directives, regulations and court decisions; preside over court cases; help train new lawyers

Alternate Title(s): Attorney

Availability: All branches

Military Salary: See How to Use This Book

Civilian Salary: $44,590 to $145,600

Civilian Employment Prospects: Good

Civilian Advancement Prospects: Good

Prerequisites:

    Rank—Officer

    Education and Training—Four-year college degree; three-year law school and Juris Doctorate

    Experience—Any training and work experience obtained in the armed services

    Special Skills and Personality Traits—Good interpersonal skills; perseverance; creativity; reasoning ability; an interest in working with and researching legal concepts; good written and oral communication skills, including public speaking; sensitivity; well-organized

    Licensure/Certification—Pass a written bar examination; state license

CAREER LADDER

```
┌─────────────────────────────┐
│      Teacher or Judge        │
└─────────────────────────────┘

┌─────────────────────────────┐
│          Partner             │
└─────────────────────────────┘

┌─────────────────────────────┐
│         Associate            │
└─────────────────────────────┘
```

Position Description

The modern military has its own system of laws and courts as well as Lawyers who work within it. Working in legal offices and courtrooms on land and aboard ships, they perform legal research, prosecute and defend court cases, and preside over military courts. They provide legal services for military personnel and represent the services in civil and international legal matters. They also give legal advice about government real estate, commercial contracts, patents, and trademarks; provide pretrial advice for clients in court-martial cases; and prepare legal documents, such as wills and powers of attorney. They also interpret laws, directives, regulations, and court decisions; preside over court cases; make judgments based on the Uniform Code of Military Justice; and help train new Lawyers.

In the civilian world, Lawyers work in private practice and for law firms, government, corporations, and nonprofit groups, usually specializing in a particular field. It must also be noted that military Lawyers do not practice in several fields open to civilian Lawyers, such as divorce, trade, and antitrust.

All Lawyers act both as advocates and advisers. As advocates, they represent one of the parties in criminal and civil trials by presenting evidence and arguing in support of their client. As advisers, Lawyers counsel their clients concerning their rights and duties, and suggest appropriate courses of action. The majority of Lawyers are found in private practice where they concentrate on criminal or civil law. Some, though, are employed full time by a single client.

Lawyers who work for state attorneys general, prosecutors, public defenders, and courts play a key role in the criminal justice system. Others work for legal-aid societies. A small number of trained attorneys work in law schools as faculty members who specialize in one or more subjects. Others work full time in nonacademic settings and teach part time.

Lawyers do most of their work in offices, law libraries, and courtrooms, though they may meet in clients' homes or places of business, or in hospitals or prisons. They may travel to attend meetings, gather evidence, and appear before courts, legislative bodies, and other authorities.

Salaried Lawyers have structured work schedules. Those in private practice may work irregular hours. All Lawyers may face particularly heavy pressure and stress during trials.

Civilian Salaries

In 2000, the average yearly salary for all Lawyers was $88,280. Those in the middle half of the occupation earned between $60,700 and $130,170. The lowest paid 10 percent earned less than $44,590, and the highest paid 10 percent earned more than $145,600.

In 2000, the average yearly salaries in the industries employing the largest numbers of Lawyers were:

Legal services	$96,610
Federal government	$87,080
Fire, marine, and casualty insurance	$82,170
Local government	$66,280
State government	$64,190

Civilian Employment Prospects

In 2000, Lawyers held just over 680,000 jobs. Roughly 75 percent practiced privately in either law firms or solo practices. The rest held positions in government, mostly at the local level, or were employed as house counsel by public utilities, banks, insurance companies, real estate agencies, manufacturing firms, welfare and religious organizations, and other business firms and nonprofit organizations.

Through 2010, opportunities for Lawyers are expected to grow about as fast as the average. Demand will result from the growth of legal action in such areas as health care, intellectual property, international law, elder law, environmental law, and sexual harassment. The wider availability and affordability of legal clinics and prepaid legal service programs should result in increased use of legal services by middle-income people.

The large number of students graduating from law school each year will keep competition keen. Those with superior academic records from well-regarded law schools will have the best opportunities. Lawyers are also increasingly finding work in nontraditional areas for which legal training is an asset such as administrative, managerial, and business positions in banks, insurance firms, real estate companies, government agencies, and other organizations.

Opportunities in these areas are expected to continue to grow. Geographic mobility and work experience are an advantage in getting a job but, to be licensed in another state, a Lawyer may have to take an additional state bar examination.

Those wishing to work independently will find it easier to establish a practice in a small town or expanding suburban area, where competition from larger firms is likely to be less keen and new Lawyers may find it easier to become known to potential clients. Some Lawyers are adversely affected by cyclical swings in the economy.

Civilian Advancement Prospects

New Lawyers mainly start in salaried positions as associates, working with more experienced Lawyers or judges. After years of gaining more responsibilities, some are admitted to partnership in their firm or go into practice for themselves. Others become full-time law school faculty or administrators. Some use their legal training in administrative or managerial positions in various departments of large corporations. A transfer from a corporation's legal department to another department often is viewed as a way to gain administrative experience and rise in the ranks of management.

Education and Training

In the military, those interested in this career receive two to three months of classroom instruction, depending on specialty. Classes usually contain courses such as military trial procedures, application of the Uniform Code of Military Justice, methods of obtaining evidence, and court-martial advocacy techniques. Further training occurs on the job and through advanced courses.

In most states an applicant usually must obtain a college degree and graduate from a law school accredited by the American Bar Association or the proper state authorities. The ABA currently accredits 185 law schools; others are approved by state authorities only. With certain exceptions, graduates of schools not approved by the ABA are restricted to taking the bar examination and practicing in the state in which the school is located.

The required college and law school education usually takes four years of undergraduate study followed by three years of law school. Law school applicants must have a bachelor's degree to qualify for admission. Prospective Lawyers should develop proficiency in writing and speaking, reading, researching, analyzing, and thinking logically. Courses in English, foreign languages, public speaking, government, philosophy, history, economics, mathematics, and computer science are recommended among others.

Many law schools have clinical programs where students gain legal experience through practice trials and projects supervised by practicing Lawyers and law school faculty. Law school clinical programs might include work in legal aid clinics, or on the staff of legislative committees.

Part-time or summer clerkships in law firms, government agencies, and corporate legal departments also provide valuable experience that can lead directly to a job after graduation. Clerkships can also help students decide what kind of practice best suits them, as well as being an important source of financial aid.

Law school graduates receive the degree of juris doctor (J.D.) as the first professional degree. Advanced law degrees may be desirable for those planning to specialize, research, or teach. Some law students pursue joint degree programs, which usually require an additional semester or year. Joint degree programs are offered in a number of areas, including law and business administration or public administration.

After graduation Lawyers must keep informed about legal and nonlegal developments that affect their practice. Currently 39 states and jurisdictions mandate Continuing Legal Education. Many law schools and state and local bar associations provide continuing education courses that help lawyers stay abreast of recent developments.

Special Requirements

In the civilian world, to practice law a person must be licensed, or admitted to a state bar, under rules established by the jurisdiction's highest court. All states require applicants for admission to the bar pass a written bar examination; most also require applicants to pass a separate written ethics examination. Lawyers who have been admitted to the bar in one jurisdiction occasionally may be admitted to the bar in another without taking an examination, if they meet certain criteria. Federal courts and agencies set their own qualifications for those practicing before them.

All states (save Louisiana and Washington), the District of Columbia, Guam, the Northern Mariana Islands, Puerto Rico, and the Virgin Islands require the six-hour Multistate Bar Examination as part of the bar examination which covers issues of broad interest and is sometimes given in addition to a locally prepared state bar examination. The three-hour Multistate Essay Examination is used as part of the state bar examination in several states. Many states have begun to require Multistate Performance Testing to test the practical skills of beginning Lawyers. This program has been well received, and many more states are expected to require performance testing in the future. In 1999, 52 jurisdictions required law students to pass the Multistate Professional Responsibility Examination, which tests their knowledge of the ABA codes on professional responsibility and judicial conduct.

Experience, Special Skills, and Personality Traits

Those wishing to be Lawyers should like to work with people and be able to win the respect and confidence of others. Perseverance, creativity, and reasoning ability are also essential as are an interest in working with and researching legal concepts, the ability to write clearly and concisely and to speak effectively in public, plus sensitivity to the needs of others.

Unions and Associations

For information on law schools and a career in law contact the American Bar Association, which also offers members a forum for networking with colleagues and monitoring developments in the law. For information on the LSAT, the Law School Data Assembly Service, the law school application process, and the financial aid available for law students contact the Law School Admission Council. Information on obtaining a job as a lawyer with the Federal Government is available from the Office of Personnel Management.

MILITARY POLICE

CAREER PROFILE

Duties: Patrol designated areas; interview witnesses, victims, and suspects; collect evidence; arrest and charge criminal suspects; train and walk with police dogs; testify in court; guard entrances and direct traffic; enforce laws and prevent crime

Alternate Title(s): Detective; Private Investigator; Undercover Agent; Correction Officer; Guard; Bailiff

Availability: All branches

Military Salary: See How to Use This Book

Civilian Salary: $23,790 to $86,060

Civilian Employment Prospects: Good

Civilian Advancement Prospects: Good

Prerequisites:

Rank—Enlisted

Education and Training—High school diploma or higher, depending on position

Experience—Any training and work experience obtained in the armed services

Special Skills and Personality Traits—Ingenuity, persistence, and assertiveness; good communication skills; quick mental reflexes; good interviewing and interrogation skills; honesty; sound judgment; integrity; a sense of responsibility; good health; normal color vision; an interest in law enforcement and crime prevention; a willingness to perform potentially dangerous work; the ability to remain calm under pressure

CAREER LADDER

```
┌─────────────────────────────────────┐
│             Captain                 │
└─────────────────────────────────────┘

┌─────────────────────────────────────┐
│  Corporal, Sergeant, or Lieutenant  │
└─────────────────────────────────────┘

┌─────────────────────────────────────┐
│        Probationary Officer         │
└─────────────────────────────────────┘
```

Position Description

The military needs police for the same reasons all areas of civilization do. Working both indoors and outdoors, on foot, in cars, or in boats, Military Police control traffic, prevent crime, and respond to emergencies to protect lives and property on military bases by enforcing military laws and regulations. They also interview witnesses, victims, and suspects in the course of investigating crimes, collect fingerprints and other evidence, arrest and charge criminal suspects, train and walk with police dogs, and testify in court.

In the civilian world, police officers generally work for state, county, or city law enforcement agencies. Some work as security guards for industrial firms, airports, and other businesses and institutions. They maintain law and order, collect evidence and information, and conduct investigations and surveillance.

Law enforcement officers are expected to exercise authority when necessary, whether on or off duty. Uniformed Police officers who work in municipal police departments of various sizes, small communities, and rural areas have general law enforcement duties including maintaining regular patrols and responding to calls for service. In large police departments, officers usually are assigned to a specific type of duty.

Police agencies are usually organized into geographic districts, with uniformed officers assigned to patrol a specific area, such as part of the business district or outlying residential neighborhoods. Officers may work alone, or with a partner. While on patrol, officers attempt to become thoroughly familiar with their patrol area and remain alert for anything unusual. Some officers specialize in such diverse fields as chemical and microscopic analysis, training and firearms instruction, or handwriting and fingerprint identification. Others work with special units such as horseback, bicycle, motorcycle or harbor patrol, canine corps, special weapons and tactics, or emergency response teams.

Sheriffs and deputy sheriffs enforce the law on the county level. State police officers arrest criminals statewide and patrol highways to enforce motor vehicle laws and regulations. Detectives are plainclothes investigators who gather facts and collect evidence for criminal cases.

Federal Bureau of Investigation agents are the federal government's principal investigators, responsible for investigating violations of more than 260 statutes and conducting sensitive national security investigations. U.S. Drug Enforcement Administration agents enforce laws and regulations relating to illegal drugs. U.S. marshals and deputy marshals protect the Federal courts and ensure the effective operation of the judicial system. U.S. Immigration and Naturalization Service agents and inspectors facilitate the entry of legal visitors and immigrants to the United States and detain and deport those arriving illegally. Bureau of Alcohol, Tobacco, and Firearms agents regulate and investigate violations of federal firearms and explosives laws, as well as federal alcohol and tobacco tax regulations.

Customs agents investigate violations of narcotics smuggling, money laundering, child pornography, customs fraud, and enforcement of the Arms Export Control Act. Domestic and foreign investigations involve the development and use of informants, physical and electronic surveillance, and examination of records from importers/exporters, banks, couriers, and manufacturers. Customs inspectors inspect cargo, baggage, and articles worn or carried by people and carriers including vessels, vehicles, trains, and aircraft entering or leaving the United States to enforce laws governing imports and exports. U.S. Secret Service special agents protect the president and other dignitaries. They also investigate counterfeiting, forgery of government checks or bonds, and fraudulent use of credit cards.

The U.S. Department of State Bureau of Diplomatic Security special agents are engaged in the battle against terrorism. Other federal agencies employing police and special agents with sworn arrest powers and the authority to carry firearms include the U.S. Postal Service, the Bureau of Indian Affairs Office of Law Enforcement, the U.S. Forest Service, the National Park Service, the Federal Air Marshals and the General Services Administration's Federal Protective Service.

Police work can be very dangerous and stressful. In addition to the obvious dangers of confrontations with criminals, officers witness death and suffering resulting from accidents and criminal behavior. A career in law enforcement may take a toll on officers' private lives. In most jurisdictions, whether on or off duty, officers are expected to be armed and to exercise their arrest authority whenever necessary. Most law enforcement professionals work 40 hour weeks, but paid overtime is common.

Civilian Salaries

In 2000, average yearly salaries for police and sheriff's patrol officers were $39,790. The middle 50 percent earned between $30,460 and $50,230. The lowest 10 percent earned less than $23,790. The highest 10 percent earned more than $58,900.

In 2000, average yearly salaries for police and detective supervisors were $57,210. The middle 50 percent earned between $43,630 and $70,680. The lowest 10 percent earned less than $34,660. The highest 10 percent earned more than $86,060.

In 2000, average yearly salaries for detectives and criminal investigators were $48,870. The middle 50 percent earned between $37,240 and $61,750. The lowest 10 percent earned less than $29,600. The highest 10 percent earned more than $72,160.

Civilian Employment Prospects

In 2000, police and detectives held nearly 835,000 jobs. About 80 percent were employed by local governments. Through 2010, opportunities for police and detectives are expected to increase faster than the average for all occupations. A more security-conscious society and concern about drug-related crimes should contribute to the increasing demand for police services. At the local and state levels, growth is likely to continue as long as crime remains a serious concern.

Such positions are attractive to many because they are challenging and involve much personal responsibility. Also law enforcement officers may usually retire with a pension after only 20 to 25 years of service.

Opportunities will be best in local and special police departments, especially those offering relatively low salaries or urban communities where the crime rate is relatively high. Applicants with college training in police science, Military Police experience, or both should have the best opportunities.

Civilian Advancement Prospects

Police officers usually become eligible for promotion after a probationary period at which time they may be able to advance to detective or specialize in one type of police work, such as working with juveniles. Promotions to corporal, sergeant, lieutenant, and captain usually are made according to a candidate's position on a promotion list, as determined by scores on a written examination and on-the-job performance.

Education and Training

In the military, those interested in this career receive two to three months of classroom instruction, depending on specialty. Classes usually include military and civil laws and jurisdiction, crime and accident investigation procedures, evidence collection procedures, including fingerprinting and suspect questioning, the use of firearms, traffic and crowd control procedures, arrest and restraint of suspects and hand-to-hand defense techniques. Further training occurs on the job and through advanced courses. The navy offers a certified apprenticeship program for one specialty in this occupation.

Civil service regulations govern the appointment of police and detectives throughout the country. Candidates must be U.S. citizens, at least 20 years of age, and must meet rigorous physical and personal qualifications. Physical examinations include tests of vision, hearing, strength, and agility. Eligibility for appointment usually depends on performance in competitive written examinations and previous education and experience.

In state and large local departments, recruits get training in their agency's police academy. In small agencies, recruits often attend a regional or state academy. To be considered as an FBI agent, an applicant either must be a graduate of an accredited law school or a college graduate with a major in accounting, fluency in a foreign language, or three years of related full-time work experience. All new agents undergo training at the FBI academy. Indeed, similar educational or work experience backgrounds are required of applicants seeking appointments to special agent jobs with any federal agency.

Many law enforcement agencies encourage applicants to take postsecondary school training in law enforcement-related subjects. Many junior colleges, colleges, and universities offer programs in law enforcement or administration of justice. Continuing training helps police officers, detectives, and special agents improve their job performance. Many agencies pay all or part of the tuition for officers to work toward degrees in criminal justice, police science, administration of justice, or public administration, and pay higher salaries to those who earn such a degree.

Experience, Special Skills, and Personality Traits

Although many varied careers are profiled here, most of them require individuals with ingenuity, persistence, and assertiveness. Law enforcement agents must not be afraid of confrontation, should communicate well, and should be able to think on their feet. Good interviewing and interrogation skills are important as are honesty, sound judgment, integrity, and a sense of responsibility, good health, normal color vision, an interest in law enforcement and crime prevention, a willingness to perform potentially dangerous work, and the ability to remain calm under pressure.

Unions and Associations

Information about entrance requirements may be obtained from federal, state, and local law enforcement agencies. Further information about qualifications for employment as a FBI Special Agent is available from the nearest state FBI office. Information about career opportunities, qualifications, and training to become a deputy marshal is available from the United States Marshals Service.

Information on career opportunities, qualifications, and training for U.S. Secret Service Special Agents is available from the U.S. Secret Service. For information on career opportunities and U.S. Bureau of Alcohol, Tobacco, and Firearms operations, contact the U.S. Bureau of Alcohol, Tobacco, and Firearms. Information about careers in the United States Border Patrol is available from the U.S. Border Patrol.

In addition, there are numerous organizations for police officers including the National Association of Police Organizations, the International Police Association, and many local and state police officers associations. Check the Web for one in your area.

MEDIA AND PUBLIC AFFAIRS

AUDIOVISUAL AND BROADCAST DIRECTOR

CAREER PROFILE

Duties: Plan and organize audiovisual projects; determine the staff and equipment needed for productions; set production controls and performance standards; direct the preparation of scripts and determine camera-shooting schedules; direct actors and technical staff

Alternate Title(s): Production Coordinator; Assistant Director

Availability: Army, Navy, Air Force, Marine Corps

Military Salary: See How to Use This Book

Civilian Salary: $21,050 to $87,770

Civilian Employment Prospects: Good

Civilian Advancement Prospects: Good

Prerequisites:
   Rank—Officer
   Education and Training—A high school diploma
   Experience—Any training and work experience obtained in the armed services or Job Corps
   Special Skills and Personality Traits—Talent and creative ability; the ability to work with people; leadership qualities; capable of transforming ideas into visual images; business acumen; an interest in organizing and planning activities; an interest in planning and directing the work of others

CAREER LADDER

```
Producer
```

```
Director
```

```
Actor
```

Position Description

Audiovisual and Broadcast Directors working in the military produce motion pictures, videotapes, and TV and radio broadcasts used for training, news, and entertainment. Working in studios or offices, they manage audiovisual projects, direct day-to-day filming or broadcasting, manage other directors, and sometimes even direct film crews on location in military camps and combat zones. They also plan and organize audiovisual projects, including films, videotapes, TV and radio broadcasts, and artwork displays; determine the staff and equipment needed for productions; set production controls and performance standards for audiovisual projects; direct the preparation of scripts; determine camera-shooting schedules; and direct actors and technical staff during performances.

In the civilian world, Audiovisual and Broadcast Directors work for television networks and stations, motion picture companies, public relations and advertising firms, and government agencies. Although the perception is often that the vast majority of actors, producers, and directors work in either New York or Los Angeles, the truth is that far more work in local or regional television studios, theaters, or film production companies engaged in advertising, public relations, or independent, small-scale movie productions.

Producers oversee the business and financial decisions of a production. They select scripts, approve development of script ideas, arrange financing and determine the size and cost of stage, radio, television, video, or motion picture productions. Producers do most of the hiring and negotiating of contracts. They also coordinate the activities of writers, directors, managers, and agents to ensure that projects stay on schedule and within budget.

Directors are responsible for a production's creative decisions. They interpret scripts, express concepts to set and costume designers, audition and select cast members, conduct rehearsals, and direct the work of cast and crew. Directors also approve the design elements of a production.

Producers and directors work under constant pressure. They also experience vast amounts of stress due to the fact that their jobs are incredibly varied, with multiple, simultaneous responsibilities. Directors working on location shoots may work in the early morning or late evening hours to do nighttime filming or to tape scenes inside public facilities outside of normal business hours.

Civilian Salaries

In 2000, the average yearly salary for producers and directors was $41,030. The middle 50 percent earned between $29,000 and $60,330. The lowest 10 percent earned less than $21,050. The highest 10 percent earned more than $87,770.

In 2000, the average yearly salaries in the industries employing the largest numbers of producers and directors were:

Motion picture production and services	$50,280
Producers, orchestras, and entertainers	$38,820
Radio and television broadcasting	$34,630

Civilian Employment Prospects

In 2000, actors, producers, and directors held just under 160,000 jobs. These were primarily in motion pictures, theater, television, and radio. Since such jobs are generally work-for-hire, the total number of actors, producers, and directors available for work was higher. Others work in summer stock companies, on cruise lines, and in theme parks as well as with repertory companies, dinner theaters, and theaters affiliated with drama schools, acting conservatories, and universities.

Through 2010, opportunities for producers and directors are expected to grow faster than the average for all occupations. Competition for these jobs will always be great, however, in part because of the large number of qualified people seeking them. Only those individuals with the most stamina and talent will regularly find employment.

Expanding cable and satellite television operations, increasing production and distribution of major studio and independent films, and continued growth and development of interactive media, such as direct-for-Web movies and videos, should increase demand for producers and directors. A strong Broadway and Off-Broadway community and vibrant regional theater network are expected to offer many job opportunities.

Civilian Advancement Prospects

Producers often start in a theatrical management office, working for a press agent, managing director, or business manager. Some start in a performing arts union or service organization. As the reputations and box-office draw of producers and directors grow, they may work on bigger budget productions, on network or syndicated broadcasts, or in more prestigious theaters.

Education and Training

In the military, those interested in this career receive four month to two years of classroom instruction, depending on specialty. Classes usually include courses in public information management principles, management of military broadcasting facilities and motion picture and television production management.

There are no specific training requirements for producers or directors. Both come from many different backgrounds. Talent, experience, and business acumen are very important determinants of success for producers. Many people who start out as actors move into directing, while some directors try their hand at acting. Though no formal training exists for producers, a growing number of colleges and universities now offer degree programs in arts management and managing nonprofits.

Experience, Special Skills, and Personality Traits

Directors need talent, creative ability, and the ability to work with people as well as leadership qualities and the ability to transform ideas into visual images.

Producers need business acumen, an interest in organizing and planning activities and an interest in planning and directing the work of others.

Unions and Associations

For general information about theater arts and a list of accredited college-level programs, contact the National Association of Schools of Theater. For general information on actors, producers, and directors, contact the Actors Equity Association, the Screen Actors Guild and the American Federation of Television and Radio Artists-Screen Actors Guild.

AUDIOVISUAL AND BROADCAST TECHNICIAN

CAREER PROFILE

Duties: Work with writers, producers, and directors to plan and design production scenery, graphics, and special effects; operate media equipment and special effect devices; follow script and instructions of film or TV directors

Alternate Title(s): Motion Picture Camera Operator; Audiovisual Production Specialist; Sound Mixer; Recording Engineer; Broadcasting and Recording Technician

Availability: All branches

Military Salary: See How to Use This Book

Civilian Salary: $13,860 to $119,400

Civilian Employment Prospects: Good

Civilian Advancement Prospects: Good

Prerequisites:
  Rank—Enlisted
  Education and Training—A high school diploma
  Experience—Any training and work experience obtained in the armed services or Job Corps
  Special Skills and Personality Traits—Manual dexterity; an aptitude for working with electrical, electronic, and mechanical systems and equipment; an interest in creative and artistic work; a preference for working as part of a team; normal color vision; the ability to speak clearly
  Licensure/Certification—Optional certification from The Society of Broadcast Engineers

CAREER LADDER

```
┌─────────────────────────────┐
│       Chief Engineer        │
└─────────────────────────────┘

┌─────────────────────────────┐
│    Supervisory Technician   │
└─────────────────────────────┘

┌─────────────────────────────┐
│         Technician          │
└─────────────────────────────┘
```

Position Description

The modern military makes great use of both television and film productions. Working in studios or outdoors on location, sometimes from aircraft or ships, around the world in all climates and conditions, military Audiovisual and Broadcast Technicians make films used for training in many military occupations. They also record military operations, ceremonies, and news events. These Audiovisual and Broadcast Technicians work with writers, producers, and directors in preparing and interpreting scripts; plan and design production scenery, graphics, and special effects; operate media equipment and special effect devices including cameras, sound recorders, and lighting, and follow scripts and instructions from film or TV directors to move cameras, zoom, pan, or adjust focus.

In the civilian world, Audiovisual and Broadcast Technicians work for film production companies, government audiovisual studios, radio and television stations, and advertising agencies. There they install, test, repair, set up, and operate the electronic equipment used to record and transmit radio and television programs, cable programs, and motion pictures. They work with television cameras, microphones, tape recorders, lighting, sound effects, transmitters, antennas, and other equipment. Some broadcast and sound engineering technicians produce movie soundtracks in motion picture production studios, control the sound of live events, such as concerts, or record music in a recording studio.

They also operate equipment that regulates the signal strength, clarity, and range of sounds and colors of recordings or broadcasts and control panels to select the source of the material. Technicians switch from one camera or studio to another, from film to live programming, or from network to local programming. They also give technical directions to other studio personnel through both hand signals and telephone headsets, depending on the studio in which they are working.

Audio and video equipment operators operate specialized electronic equipment to record stage productions, live programs or events, and studio recordings. Radio operators mainly receive and transmit communications using a variety of tools. Broadcast and sound engineering technicians and radio operators perform a variety of duties in small stations. Transmitter operators monitor and log outgoing signals and operate transmitters. Maintenance technicians set up, adjust, service, and repair electronic broadcasting equipment. Audio control engineers regulate volume and sound quality of television broadcasts, while video control engineers regulate their fidelity, brightness, and contrast. Recording engineers operate and maintain video and sound recording equipment. Sound mixers produce the sound track of a movie, television, or radio program. Field technicians set up and operate broadcasting portable field transmission equipment outside the studio. Chief engineers, transmission engineers, and broadcast field supervisors supervise the technicians who operate and maintain broadcasting equipment.

Most Audiovisual and Broadcast Technicians work indoors under acceptable conditions. Those who broadcast from locations outside the studio may work outdoors in all types of weather. Technicians doing maintenance may climb poles or antenna towers, while those setting up equipment do heavy lifting.

Technicians in large stations and the networks usually work a 40 hour week with only occasional overtime, but they do so under tremendous pressure to meet deadlines. Technicians in small stations usually work in excess of 40 hours a week. Evening, weekend, and holiday work is usual, because most stations are on the air 18 to 24 hours a day, seven days a week.

Civilian Salaries

In 2000, the average yearly salary for Broadcast Technicians was $26,950. The middle 50 percent earned between $18,060 and $44,410. The lowest 10 percent earned less than $13,860. The highest 10 percent earned more than $63,340.

In 2000, the average yearly salary for sound engineering technicians was $39,480. The middle 50 percent earned between $24,730 and $73,720. The lowest 10 percent earned less than $17,560. The highest 10 percent earned more than $119,400.

In 2000, the average yearly salary for audio and video equipment technicians was $30,310. The middle 50 percent earned between $21,980 and $44,970. The lowest 10 percent earned less than $16,630. The highest 10 percent earned more than $68,720.

In 2000, the average yearly salary for radio operators was $29,260. The middle 50 percent earned between $23,090 and $39,830. The lowest 10 percent earned less than $17,570. The highest 10 percent earned more than $54,590.

Civilian Employment Prospects

In 2000, broadcast and sound engineering technicians and radio operators held nearly 88,000 jobs. About one-third worked in radio and television broadcasting. Almost 15 percent worked in the motion picture industry. Some 4 percent worked for cable and other pay television services. A few were self-employed. Technician jobs in television exist in nearly all cities, whereas jobs in radio are also found in many small towns.

Through 2010, opportunities for broadcast and sound engineering technicians and radio operators are expected to grow about as fast as the average for all occupations. An increase in the number of programming hours and new cable networks should require additional technicians. Those who know how to install transmitters will be in demand as television stations replace existing analog transmitters with digital transmitters.

Through 2010, opportunities for audio and video equipment technicians also are expected to grow about as fast as average. Not only will these workers have to set up audio and video equipment, but it will be necessary for them to maintain and repair this machinery. Employment of radio operators, on the other hand, will grow more slowly than other areas in this field of work. Automation will negatively impact these workers as many stations now operate transmitters and control programming remotely. Employment of broadcast and sound engineering technicians and radio operators in the cable industry should grow rapidly because of new products coming to market.

Those seeking entry-level jobs will face strong competition in major metropolitan areas. Prospects for entry-level positions generally are better in small cities and towns for beginners with appropriate training.

Civilian Advancement Prospects

Experienced technicians should have little trouble becoming supervisory technicians or chief engineers. A college degree in engineering, however, is needed to become chief engineer at most large television stations.

Education and Training

In the military, those interested in this career receive two to 12 months of classroom instruction, depending on their specialty. Classes usually contain courses in motion picture equipment operation, audio recording, scripting, special effects techniques, and maintenance of public address sound equipment. Further training occurs on the job and through advanced courses.

Outside the military, broadcast and sound engineering technicians and radio operators generally complete specialized postsecondary programs at technical schools or community colleges, or at colleges offering training in broadcast technology, engineering, or electronics. Beginners learn on the job from experienced technicians and supervisors. They often look for experience in small stations, then move on to larger ones. Large stations generally only hire experienced technicians. Many employers will pay tuition and expenses for courses or seminars to help their technicians keep abreast of developments in the field. Audio and video equipment technicians generally need a high school diploma. Many recent entrants have some form of post-secondary degree. Radio operators do not usually require any formal training.

Special Requirements

Certification by the Society of Broadcast Engineers is a mark of competence and experience. The certificate is issued to experienced technicians who pass an examination.

Experience, Special Skills, and Personality Traits

Broadcast and sound engineering technicians and radio operators must have manual dexterity and an aptitude for working with electrical, electronic, and mechanical systems and equipment. They also need an interest in creative and artistic work, a preference for working as part of a team, normal color vision, and the ability to speak clearly.

Unions and Associations

For information on careers for broadcast and sound engineering technicians and radio operators, contact the National Association of Broadcasters. For information on certification, contact the Society of Broadcast Engineers and for information on careers in the motion picture and television industry, contact the Society of Motion Picture and Television Engineers.

BROADCAST JOURNALIST/NEWSWRITER

CAREER PROFILE

Duties: Gather information for military news programs and publications; write radio and TV scripts; develop ideas for news articles; arrange and conduct interviews; collect information for commercial media use; select photographs and write captions for news articles; write news releases, feature articles, and editorials

Alternate Title(s): News Analyst; Reporter; Correspondent; Newscaster; Disc Jockey; Writer; Director; Producer; Editor

Availability: All branches

Military Salary: See How to Use This Book

Civilian Salary: $16,540 to $83,400

Civilian Employment Prospects: Fair

Civilian Advancement Prospects: Fair

Prerequisites:
  Rank—Enlisted
  Education and Training—Bachelor's degree in journalism; on-the-job training
  Experience—Any training and work experience obtained in the armed services
  Special Skills and Personality Traits—Persistence; initiative; poise; resourcefulness; a good memory; physical stamina; emotional stability; comfortable in front of a camera; comfortable in unfamiliar places and with a variety of people; detail-oriented and accurate; an interest in researching facts and issues for news stories; excellent writing skills; a strong, clear speaking voice

CAREER LADDER

```
┌─────────────────────────────────┐
│             Editor              │
└─────────────────────────────────┘

┌─────────────────────────────────┐
│   Columnist or Correspondent    │
└─────────────────────────────────┘

┌─────────────────────────────────┐
│            Reporter             │
└─────────────────────────────────┘
```

Position Description

The modern military deals in information like any other large organization in this day and age. It both publishes newspapers and broadcasts television and radio programs for its personnel and the public. Broadcast Journalists and Newswriters in the military gather information for military news programs and publications, write radio and TV scripts, develop ideas for news articles and arrange and conduct interviews. They may work in broadcasting studios, on land, aboard ships, or sometimes outdoors, depending upon the research needed for their articles. They also collect information for commercial media use, select photographs and write captions for news articles, and write news releases, feature articles, and editorials.

In the civilian world, Broadcast Journalists and Newswriters work for newspapers, magazines, wire services, and radio and television stations. Their duties are similar to those performed by military journalists and newswriters. They may be employed as newscasters, disc jockeys, writers, directors, producers, editors, or correspondents.

News analysts, reporters, and correspondents gather information, prepare stories, and make broadcasts that inform the public about local, state, national, and international events. They examine, interpret, and broadcast news received from various sources. News anchors present news stories and introduce videotaped news or live transmissions from on-the-scene reporters. Weathercasters report current and forecasted weather conditions. Sportscasters select, write, and deliver sports news.

Reporters investigate leads and news tips, look at documents, observe events at the scene, interview people, take notes and sometimes take photographs or shoot videos. Afterward they organize their material, choose a focus, write their stories, and edit accompanying video material. Commentators, or columnists, interpret the news or offer opinions to readers, viewers, or listeners. General assignment reporters write news—such as stories about an accident, a political rally, the visit of a celebrity, or a company going out of business—as assigned. Some reporters specialize in fields such as health, politics, foreign affairs, sports, theater, consumer affairs, social events, science, business, and religion. Investigative reporters cover stories that take many days or weeks of information gathering. News correspondents report on news occurring in the large U.S. and foreign cities where they are stationed. Reporters on small publications cover all aspects of the news. They take photographs, write headlines, lay out pages, edit wire service copy, write editorials, solicit advertisements, sell subscriptions, and perform general office work.

News analysts, reporters, and correspondents are usually under great pressure to meet deadlines and broadcasts sometimes are made with little time for preparation. Some work in comfortable, private offices; others in large rooms filled with the sound of keyboards and computer printers, as well as the voices of other reporters. Curious onlookers, police, or other emergency workers can distract those reporting from the scene for radio and television. Covering wars, political uprisings, fires, floods, and similar events often is dangerous.

Reporters on morning papers often work from late afternoon until midnight. Those on afternoon or evening papers generally work from early morning until early afternoon or midafternoon. Radio and television reporters usually are assigned to a day or evening shift. Magazine reporters usually work during the day. Reporters sometimes have to change their work hours to meet a deadline, or to follow late-breaking developments. Their work demands long hours, irregular schedules, and some travel.

Civilian Salaries

In 2000, the average yearly salary for news analysts, reporters, and correspondents was $29,110. The middle 50 percent earned between $21,320 and $45,540. The lowest 10 percent earned less than $16,540. The highest 10 percent earned more than $69,300.

In 1999, the National Association of Broadcasters and the Broadcast Cable Financial Management Association announced that the average yearly salary, including bonuses, was $83,400 for weekday anchors and $44,200 for those working on weekends. Television news reporters earned on average $33,700. Weekday sportscasters typically earned $68,900, while weekend sportscasters earned $37,200. Weathercasters averaged $68,500 during the week and $36,500 on weekends.

Civilian Employment Prospects

In 2000, news analysts, reporters, and correspondents held roughly 78,000 jobs. Nearly 50 percent worked for either large city dailies or suburban and small town dailies or weeklies. About 28 percent worked in radio and television broadcasting, and others worked for magazines and wire services. Some 12,000 were self-employed.

Through 2010, opportunities for news analysts, reporters, and correspondents are expected to grow more slowly than the average for all occupations. This will be the result of mergers, consolidations, and closures of newspapers; decreased circulation; increased expenses; and a decline in advertising profits. Some job growth is expected in radio and television stations, and even more rapid growth is expected in new media areas, such as online newspapers and magazines.

Competition will be keen for jobs at large metropolitan newspapers and broadcast stations and on national magazines with most entry-level openings arising on small publications. Opportunities will be best for talented writers who can handle highly specialized subjects.

Civilian Advancement Prospects

Most journalists start at small publications or broadcast stations as general assignment reporters or copy editors. With experience some news analysts and reporters can advance by moving to large newspapers or stations. A few experienced reporters become columnists, correspondents, writers, announcers, or public relations specialists. Others become editors in print journalism or program managers in broadcast journalism, who supervise reporters. Some newswriters go on to write books.

Education and Training

In the military, those interested in this career receive two to three months of classroom instruction, depending on specialty. Classes usually cover newswriting and research, newspaper format and layout, photojournalism, and radio and television programming and production.

Most civilian employers prefer individuals with a bachelor's degree in journalism as well as some kind of experience. That experience can come in the form of a part-time or summer job; an internship with a news organization; work on high school and college newspapers, at broadcasting stations, or on community papers, or U.S. Armed Forces publications; journalism scholarships, fellowships, and assistantships awarded to college journalism students by universities, newspapers, foundations, and professional organizations; work as a stringer (a part-time reporter who is paid only for stories printed). However, some will hire graduates with other majors and little to no experience. Large city newspapers and stations often prefer candidates with a degree in a subject-matter specialty such as economics, political science, or business as well as a minimum of three to five years of experience as a reporter.

In 2000, bachelor's degree programs in journalism were available at more than 400 colleges or universities. Many community and junior colleges offered journalism courses or programs. About 120 schools offered a master's degree in journalism; about 35 schools offered a Ph.D. program.

Experience, Special Skills, and Personality Traits

Those looking to enter this field should be dedicated to providing accurate and impartial news. They should also have persistence, initiative, poise, resourcefulness, a good memory, physical stamina, and emotional stability. They must be comfortable on camera, as well as traveling to unfamiliar places and working with strangers. Also important, the ability to keep detailed and accurate records, an interest in researching facts and issues for news stories, the ability to write clearly and concisely, and a strong, clear speaking voice.

Unions and Associations

For information on careers in broadcast news and related scholarships and internships, contact the Radio and Television News Directors Foundation, the National Association of Broadcasters, and the Newspaper Association of America.

For information on careers in journalism, colleges and universities offering degree programs in journalism or communications, and journalism scholarships and internships contact the Dow Jones Newspaper Fund, Inc. or the American Society of Journalists and Authors.

For information on union wage rates for newspaper and magazine reporters contact the Newspaper Guild, Research and Information Department.

For a list of schools with accredited programs in journalism, contact the Accrediting Council on Education in Journalism and Mass Communications. For information on newspaper careers and community newspapers contact the National Newspaper Association.

GRAPHIC DESIGNER AND ILLUSTRATOR

CAREER PROFILE

Duties: Produce computer-generated graphics; draw graphs and charts; develop visual ideas; design posters and signs; help instructors design artwork; draw illustrations and cartoons; make silk-screen prints; work with TV and film producers

Alternate Title(s): Commercial Artist; Graphic Arts Technician

Availability: Army, Navy Air Force, Marine Corps

Military Salary: See How to Use This Book

Civilian Salary: $14,900 to $150,000 +

Civilian Employment Prospects: Good

Civilian Advancement Prospects: Good

Prerequisites:
   Rank—Enlisted
   Education and Training—Requirements vary by specialty
   Experience—Any training and work experience obtained in the armed services or Job Corps
   Special Skills and Personality Traits—Manual dexterity; good hand-eye coordination; normal color vision; the ability to convert ideas into visual presentations; neatness; an eye for detail; creativity; imagination; persistence; a varied background; the ability to work independently and under pressure; self-discipline
   Licensure/Certification—License required for interior designers in some states

CAREER LADDER

```
┌─────────────────────────────────┐
│      Art Director or Design      │
│        Department Head           │
└─────────────────────────────────┘

┌─────────────────────────────────┐
│      Designer or Illustrator     │
└─────────────────────────────────┘

┌─────────────────────────────────┐
│ Graphic Artist or Artist's Assistant │
└─────────────────────────────────┘
```

Position Description

Most would be surprised to hear there is a need in the military for artists, but the fact is the modern military produces training manuals, newspapers, reports, promotional materials, and more, all of which incorporate numerous visual components. Working in offices on land or aboard ships, military Graphic Designers and Illustrators produce computer-generated graphics; draw graphs and charts to represent budgets, numbers of troops, supply levels, and office organization; develop visual ideas; and design posters and signs. They help instructors design artwork for training courses, draw illustrations of parts of the human body for

medical training, and create cartoons for filmstrips and animation for films. They also make silk-screen prints for clothing and other purposes and work with TV and film producers to design backdrops and props for film sets.

In the civilian world, these artists work for government agencies, advertising agencies, print shops, and engineering firms, and for large organizations that have their own graphics departments.

Artists fall into one of three categories: art directors, who formulate design concepts and presentation approaches for visual communications media; fine artists, including painters, sculptors, and Illustrators; and multi-media artists and animators, who create special effects, animation, or other visual images using film, video, computers, or other electronic media.

Art directors, animators, and fine artists are members of easily classified occupations. Among Illustrators, however, there are numerous subcategories. There are broad based Illustrators who typically create pictures for books and magazines, textiles, wrapping paper, stationery, greeting cards, calendars, etc. There are also medical and scientific illustrators who combine drawing skills with knowledge of the biological sciences; and cartoonists, who create political, advertising, social, or sports cartoons; sketch artists who create likenesses of subjects using pencil, charcoal, or pastels. Sculptors, printmakers, and painting restorers are all classified as Illustrators as well.

Most artists work in clean, well-lighted fine or commercial art studios or in private studios. Some share studio space. Artists can be exposed to fumes from their materials, and may also experience back pain, eyestrain, or fatigue due to long hours. Salaried artists usually work a regular 40-hour week.

Graphic Designers combine practical knowledge with artistic ability to turn abstract ideas into formal designs for merchandise, publications, and other items. They generally specialize in a particular area, such as automobiles, industrial or medical equipment, home appliances, clothing and textiles, floral arrangements, publications, logos, movie or television credits, interiors of homes or office buildings, merchandise displays, movie, television and theater sets, etc.

Once Graphic Designers have determined the needs of their client, they prepare sketches, then consult with the client, after which they create detailed designs using drawings, a structural model, computer simulations, or a full-scale prototype.

Like Illustrators, Graphic Designers tend to specialize in a particular area of design (although it is not uncommon for a designer to work in more than one area). These include commercial and industrial designers, designers of commercial products and equipment, fashion designers, floral designers, interior designers, merchandise displayers, and set and exhibit designers.

Graphic Designers working in manufacturing establishments, large corporations, or design firms generally work 40-hour weeks in well-lighted, comfortable settings. Self-employed designers tend to work longer hours. All designers, however, must work additional hours to meet deadlines on occasion. In addition, some Graphic Designers can find travel to production sites, film locations, manufacturing sites, etc., to be a part of their duties.

Civilian Salaries

In 2000, the average yearly salary for salaried art directors was $56,880. The middle 50 percent earned between $41,290 and $80,350. The lowest 10 percent earned less than $30,130. The highest 10 percent earned more than $109,440.

In 2000, the average yearly salary for salaried fine artists, including painters, sculptors, and illustrators was $31,190. The middle 50 percent earned between $20,460 and $42,720. The lowest 10 percent earned less than $14,690. The highest 10 percent earned more than $58,580.

In 2000, the average yearly salary for salaried multimedia artists and animators was $41,130. The middle 50 percent earned between $30,700 and $54,040. The lowest 10 percent earned less than $23,740. The highest 10 percent earned more than $70,560.

Self-employed artists yearly earnings vary widely. While some well-established freelancers can earn far more than the average salaried artist most find it impossible to rely solely on income generated from their artwork. Well-established freelance artists who are in demand might earn $150,000 or more annually.

In 2000, the average yearly salary for commercial and industrial designers was $48,780. The middle 50 percent earned between $36,460 and $64,120. The lowest 10 percent earned less than $27,290. The highest 10 percent earned more than $77,790.

In 2000, the average yearly salary for fashion designers was $48,530. The middle 50 percent earned between $34,800 and $73,780. The lowest 10 percent earned less than $24,710. The highest 10 percent earned more than $103,970.

In 2000, the average yearly salary for floral designers was $18,360. The middle 50 percent earned between $14,900 and $22,110. The lowest 10 percent earned less than $12,570. The highest 10 percent earned more than $27,860.

In 2000, the average yearly salary for graphic designers was $34,570. The middle 50 percent earned between $26,560 and $45,130. The lowest 10 percent earned less than $20,480. The highest 10 percent earned more than $58,400.

In 2000, the average yearly salary for interior designers was $36,540. The middle 50 percent earned between $26,800 and $51,140. The lowest 10 percent earned less than $19,840. The highest 10 percent earned more than $66,470.

In 2000, the average yearly salary for merchandise displayers and window dressers was $20,930. The middle 50 percent earned between $16,770 and $26,840. The lowest 10 percent earned less than $13,790. The highest 10 percent earned more than $31,130.

In 2000, the average yearly salary for set and exhibit designers was $31,440. The middle 50 percent earned between $21,460 and $42,800. The lowest 10 percent earned less than $13,820. The highest 10 percent earned more than $57,400.

Civilian Employment Prospects

In 2000, artists held close to 148,000 jobs. More than half were self-employed. Through 2010 opportunities for artists are expected to grow as fast as the average for all occupations. Despite an expanding number of opportunities, art directors will experience keen competition for available openings. Only the most successful fine artists will be able to support themselves from their talent, as has always been the case. Expected growth in all branches of the entertainment industry, however, should provide new job opportunities for Illustrators, cartoonists, and animators. Competition will be strong for these spots, however, because job opportunities are relatively few and the number of people interested in these positions usually exceeds the number of available openings.

In 2000, Graphic Designers held just under 493,000 jobs. Roughly one-third were self-employed. Through 2010, opportunities for Graphic Designers are expected to grow faster than the average for all occupations. Increased demand for industrial designers will stem from the continued emphasis on product quality and safety; easy-to-use products; the development of high-technology products; and growing global competition among businesses. Demand for Graphic Designers should also increase much faster than the average due to the rapidly increasing demand for Web-based graphics and the expansion of the video entertainment market.

Civilian Advancement Prospects

Freelance and fine artists work to develop a set of clients who regularly contract for work. They advance professionally as their work circulates and they establish a demand for a particular style.

Graphic Designers usually need several years of training before they can advance to higher-level positions. Those with the proper experience may advance to chief designer, design department head, art director, or other supervisory positions. Some teach in design schools, colleges and universities, consulting privately, or operate small design studios to complement their classroom activities. Some experienced designers open their own firms.

Education and Training

In the military, those interested in this career generally receive three months of classroom instruction including practice in preparing graphic designs and illustrations. Courses usually include such topics as introduction to graphics; lettering, drawing, and layout techniques; illustration and television graphic techniques; and theory and use of color.

The army, navy, and marine corps offer certified apprenticeship programs for some specialties in this occupation.

Illustrators usually develop their skills through a bachelor's degree program or other postsecondary training in art or design. Many colleges and universities offer degree programs leading to the Bachelor in Fine Arts and Master in Fine Arts degrees. Independent schools of art and design offer postsecondary studio training leading to an Associate in Art or Bachelor in Fine Arts degree. Typically, these programs focus more intensively on studio work than the academic programs in a university setting. Formal educational programs in art also provide training in computer techniques. Computers are used widely in the visual arts, and knowledge and training in them are critical for many jobs in these fields.

Graphic Designers need a minimum of a bachelor's degree. Those with a master's degree hold an advantage. Only floral design and visual merchandising entry-level design positions do not always require a bachelor's degree. Interior design is the only design field subject to government regulation.

The National Association of Schools of Art and Design currently accredits about 200 postsecondary institutions with programs in art and design; most of these schools award a degree in art; some award degrees in industrial, interior, textile, graphic, or fashion design.

Special Requirements

Nineteen states and the District of Columbia require interior designers to be licensed or registered. Passing the National Council for Interior Design qualification examination is required for licensure.

Experience, Special Skills, and Personality Traits

Illustrators and other artists require coordination of eyes, hands, and fingers, as well as normal color vision. Also useful are an interest in artwork or lettering, the ability to convert ideas into visual presentations, neatness, and an eye for detail.

Graphic Designers should have creativity, imagination, persistence, and the ability to communicate ideas visually and verbally. A varied background, openness to new ideas and influences, and problem-solving skills will also be helpful.

Both Graphic Designers and Illustrators should have the self-discipline to work independently and under deadline pressure.

Unions and Associations

For general information about art and design and a list of accredited college-level programs contact the National Association of Schools of Art and Design. For information on careers in medical illustration contact the Association of Medical Illustrators. Also helpful are the Graphic Artists Guild and the Society of Illustrators.

For information on industrial design careers and a list of academic programs in industrial design contact the Industrial Designers Society of America. For information about graphic design careers contact the American Institute of

Graphic Arts. For information on degree, continuing education, and licensure programs in interior design and interior design research contact the American Society for Interior Designers and the International Interior Design Association.

For a list of schools with accredited programs in interior design contact the Foundation for Interior Design Education Research. For information about careers in floral design contact the Society of American Florists.

INTERPRETER AND TRANSLATOR

CAREER PROFILE

Duties: Translate written and spoken foreign language material to and from English; interrogate prisoners of war, enemy deserters, and civilian informers; record foreign radio transmissions; prepare written reports about the information obtained; translate foreign documents; translate foreign books and articles

Alternate Title(s): None

Availability: Army, Navy, Air Force, Marine Corps

Military Salary: See How to Use This Book

Civilian Salary: $60.00/hour

Civilian Employment Prospects: Good

Civilian Advancement Prospects: Good

Prerequisites:
　Rank—Enlisted
　Education and Training—An undergraduate degree in the arts or languages
　Experience—Any training and work experience obtained in the armed services or Job Corps
　Special Skills and Personality Traits—Experience making translations, an excellent grasp of English, normal hearing, the ability to speak clearly and distinctly, fluency in a foreign language, a talent for foreign languages, an interest both in working with people and in reading and writing

CAREER LADDER

> **Varies by position**

Position Description

In today's ever-shrinking world, conflicts can come upon a nation in a breathtakingly short period of time. Preparation is essential for any military organization, and today, a large part of that preparation is spent in studying the world for signs of potential trouble. Information from foreign language newspapers, magazines, and radio broadcasts must be reviewed, analyzed, and understood. It is important to the nation's defense that forces within the military be able to understand the many languages of the world. Interpreters and Translators, usually specializing in a particular foreign language, convert written or spoken foreign languages into English or other languages.

Working on military bases, aboard ships, or in airplanes, interpreters and translators in the military translate written and spoken foreign language material to and from English, making sure to preserve the original meaning. They interrogate prisoners of war, enemy deserters, and civilian informers in their native languages, record foreign radio transmissions using sensitive communications equipment and prepare written reports about the information obtained. They also translate foreign documents, such as battle plans and personnel records and foreign books and articles describing foreign equipment and construction techniques. They must also be ready to translate or interpret written, oral, or sign language text into another language for others.

In the civilian world, Interpreters and Translators work for government agencies, embassies, universities, and companies that conduct business here and overseas. Their work is similar to the work of military Interpreters and Translators. Because of the nature of the skill these individuals learn, there are an amazingly wide range of jobs they can enter. Below is a close up of just one of these fields which will be used to illustrate this career.

Most people are aware of Interpreters and what they do. The first image that appears in the majority of people's heads when the occupation is mention is that of a United Nations translator, or diplomatic functionary. But schools and banks, doctor's offices and police stations, among many others are all finding themselves in need of Interpreters these days, often times due to the mandates of government polices.

There are positions outside these realms, however. One is that of the art journalist. Within the art world, the tendency has been leaning toward the international scene, increasing the pressure on American art magazines to include significant coverage of work that is happening not only in Europe, as one might imagine, but in many other parts of the world, particularly in South America. Often, however, it is difficult or impossible to find an English-speaking critic who knows enough about the work in these areas to write about them with any measure of authority. For this reason most art magazines find it impossible to get along without the services of a part-time translator. Although it is unlikely one could work as an art magazine translator full time, it is a viable way for a multilingual critic to supplement his or her income.

It must be noted here that a Translator can not merely understand another language. They must be able to more than simply speak and write it with textbook proficiency. They must understand it thoroughly, its nuances, slang expressions, and metaphors. Indeed, they must understand their second language better than the majority of Americans understand English.

As in all types of translation, an art magazine Translator must have a good general knowledge of, and sensitivity to, the language of the articles he or she is translating. Only a critic who has a good knowledge of another culture and an expert grasp of its language fills this position.

When an article or review needs translation an editor at the art magazine contacts the Translator, who then must read it, make a draft translation which is sent to the author for comments, and then deliver the finished copy to the magazine. Because deadlines are always tight in a periodical, the Translator will probably have to complete his or her job quickly without sacrificing accuracy.

Although any one art magazine may have only a small volume of translation to do per issue, the number of people with sufficient language skills and knowledge of the arts to perform this function well is extremely small, so a translator may be able to establish a good reputation and receive work from several sources. Working on an art magazine as a Translator may lead to other projects, such as foreign art book translation, doing editorial work for the magazine, especially with foreign authors, writing reviews in English

for the magazine or doing special research in areas of foreign art for the magazine.

Such opportunities exist in many fields for those with top-notch foreign language skills. Other career possibilities include entering the international business world, signing on for the government's foreign service, becoming a social worker, translating books for publishing houses, and teaching foreign language classes.

Civilian Salaries

In 2000, hourly rates for Interpreters and Translators ranged from $20 to $100 per hour, or even more. Interpreters and Translators are sometimes also paid by the word. Compensation varies widely due to the broad range of jobs skilled foreign language Translators may hold. Candidates should check into salaries in their specific field of interest.

Employment Prospects After Military Service

In 2000, nearly 22,000 workers earned their livings as Interpreters and Translators. Through 2010 opportunities for employment in this field are expected to grow faster than the average for all jobs. While it is true that there are only limited opportunities for translators in all fields, work is always available for highly qualified candidates. Those who combine an excellent knowledge of the subject (medicine for a hospital translator, art with an art magazine, etc.) along with expert knowledge of at least one foreign language will always be able to find work.

As with all freelance positions, however, it is up to the translator to make their qualifications and potential services known to potential employers, perhaps even working on a trial basis before being formally hired.

Some people may choose other fields such as teaching where they can apply their language skills.

Civilian Advancement Prospects

Like most freelance positions, advancement prospects are not plentiful. The Translator or Interpreter is more of a craftsman offering a service. Although it is possible that one who shows a unique understanding of a certain venue's needs might advance to a permanent position from their freelance status. Improvement most often comes from securing regular clients and taking on more high-profile projects.

Education and Training

In the military, those interested in this career receive two to five months of classroom instruction, including practice in interpretation, depending on specialty. Classes usually consist of courses such as interrogation methods, use and care of communications equipment and procedures for preparing reports. Longer training is necessary for specialties that do not require foreign language fluency prior to entry, with the addition of foreign language training (six to 12 months).

Those interested in pursuing such a career in the military would be wise to take such high school subjects as speech, communications, and foreign languages. In the civilian world, an undergraduate degree in the arts or languages is necessary, and a graduate degree in the study of a foreign language may also be required.

Experience, Special Skills, and Personality Traits

An Interpreter or Translator must have experience making translations, have an excellent grasp of English, normal hearing, the ability to speak clearly and distinctly, be fluent in a foreign language, have a talent for foreign languages, and an interest both in working with people and in reading and writing.

Unions and Associations

Candidates seeking more information may contact the American Translators Association, American Literary Translators Association, or the National Association of Judiciary Interpreters and Translators.

TRANSPORTATION AND VEHICLE MAINTENANCE

AIRCRAFT MECHANIC

CAREER PROFILE

Duties: Servicing, inspecting, and repairing fixed- and rotary-wing aircraft

Alternate Title(s): Avionics Mechanic; Airframe Mechanic; Powerplant Mechanic; A&P Mechanic; Aircraft Service Technician

Availability: All branches

Military Salary: See How to Use This Book

Civilian Salary: $11.92 to $24.40/hour

Civilian Employment Prospects: Good

Civilian Advancement Prospects: Good

Prerequisites:
    Rank—Enlisted
    Education and Training—High school diploma; FAA certification for civilian employment
    Experience—Aircraft mechanic trade school; on-the-job training
    Special Skills and Personality Traits—Analytical; focused; self-starter; problem-solver

CAREER LADDER

```
┌─────────────────────────┐
│     Shop Supervisor     │
└─────────────────────────┘

┌─────────────────────────┐
│        Inspector        │
└─────────────────────────┘

┌─────────────────────────┐
│      Lead Mechanic      │
└─────────────────────────┘

┌─────────────────────────┐
│    Aircraft Mechanic    │
└─────────────────────────┘
```

Position Description

Aircraft Mechanics are responsible for servicing, inspecting and repairing fixed- and rotary-wing aircraft. Aircraft must be kept in peak operating condition at all times, so a great deal of the work performed by aircraft mechanics consists of testing, scheduled preventative maintenance, and routine inspections.

Inspections are scheduled on a combination of factors— the number of hours the aircraft has flown, the calendar days, and cycles of operations. Engines are accessed through specifically designed openings and are removed, when necessary, with hoists or lifts. Precision instruments are used to test parts for wear. X rays and magnetic inspection equipment are utilized to check for invisible cracks. Corrosion, distortion, and stress damages must be located and repaired. Sheet metal and composite surfaces may be replaced or repaired. Control cables must be checked for wear and to ensure proper tension. Upon completion of the repairs, mechanics must then test all equipment.

Mechanics specializing in repair work rely on pilot descriptions and onboard aircraft monitoring systems to locate and repair faulty equipment. Mechanics must work as quickly as safety permits, so the aircraft can return to service in a timely manner.

While they may work on more than one type of aircraft, many Aircraft Mechanics choose to specialize. They may decide to focus on a single type of craft, such as jet transport, small propeller driven airplanes or helicopters, or on one section of a craft, such as the power plant, the avionics system or the airframe, which includes the hydraulic system and the electrical system.

Military Aircraft Mechanics service and repair propeller-driven, jet and helicopter aircraft engines. They must inspect and repair aircraft wings, tail assemblies, and fuselages as well as landing gear. Common duties include the replacing or repairing of batteries and wiring, lights, starters, and various other electrical parts.

Powerplant Mechanics are qualified to work on the engines and can perform some work on propellers. Airframe Mechanics work on all parts of an aircraft except the engines, propellers, and instruments. Combination airframe and powerplant Mechanics (A&P mechanics) work on all parts of an aircraft except the instruments (most of the mechanics working on civilian aircraft today are A&P mechanics).

Avionics Mechanics specialize in the maintenance and repair of radio instrumentation and navigation units of aircraft. They fabricate, troubleshoot, test, analyze, and assemble these units as well as read and write blueprints, technical manuals, and wiring diagrams.

Some of the equipment under their care includes automatic pilots, automatic flight stabilizers, compasses, altimeters, reference systems, airborne communication systems, radar systems, navigational displays, cockpit instruments, onboard computers, auxiliary power supplies, and voice and flight data recorders.

Many Mechanics specialize in scheduled maintenance required by the FAA. Following a schedule based on the number of hours flown, calendar days, cycles of operation, or a combination of these factors, mechanics inspect the engines, landing gear, instruments, and other parts of aircraft and perform necessary maintenance and repairs.

Mechanics work in hangars or other indoor areas most of the time (on land or aboard aircraft carriers), but outdoor work—sometimes in bad weather—can be necessary when hangars are full or time is pressing. The time pressures of the job (maintaining flight schedules, etc.) combined with the enormous responsibility to maintain safety can cause stress.

Mechanics can be based at an airline's home office/hangar or at maintenance facilities in other locations where aircraft are repaired or maintained "on-line" (during a stopover before continuing a flight). Airline Mechanics generally work at large airports near major cities. Civilian Mechanics employed by the Armed Forces work at military installations. Many Mechanics employed by aircraft assembly firms are located in California or Washington State. FAA employed Mechanics may be located at facilities in Oklahoma City, Atlantic City, or Washington, D.C.

Civilian Salaries

Civilian Aircraft Mechanics and service technicians earned a median wage of $18.30 per hour in 1998. The lowest 10 percent earned less than $11.92 and the top 10 percent earned more than $24.40 per hour.

Median hourly earnings in the industries employing the largest number of Aircraft Mechanics and service technicians in 1997 were:

Air transportation, scheduled	$20.80
Federal government	$17.40
Air transportation, nonscheduled	$15.40
Aircraft and parts	$15.20
Airports, flying fields, and services	$14.60

Civilian Employment Prospects

Aircraft Mechanics and service technicians held approximately 133,000 jobs in 1998. While about one in eight

worked for the Federal Government and about one in seven worked for aircraft assembly firms, approximately two-thirds were employed by commercial airlines, airports, or flying fields. General Aircraft Mechanics accounted for most of the remainder, the majority of whom were employed at independent repair shops or companies that operate their own aircraft for transporting executives or cargo.

The outlook for Aircraft Mechanics should remain favorable for the rest of the decade. Employment of Aircraft Mechanics is expected to keep pace with the growth for all occupations through 2008.

Job opportunities are likely to be best at smaller regional commuter airlines since their pay scale is lower and competition for these positions is not as strong. Mechanics who keep abreast of technological advances will have the best chance at larger airlines, where higher pay and extensive travel benefits attract more applicants.

Most openings for aircraft mechanics through 2008 will stem from replacement needs. Because their skills are transferable to other fields, several thousand mechanics will move on to other jobs each year, in addition to those who retire.

Civilian Advancement Prospects

Most mechanics remain in the maintenance field, but experienced Aircraft Mechanics can advance to positions of lead mechanic (crew chief), inspector, lead inspector, or shop supervisor. Mechanics with an aircraft inspector's certification have the best opportunities for advancement. In airlines, supervisors can advance to executive positions. Those with a broad experience in maintenance and overhaul can become inspectors for the Federal Aviation Administration (FAA). Those who possess business and management skills might open their own aircraft maintenance facilities. Still others take their skills and apply them to other repair positions or electronics technician jobs.

Education and Training

At least a high school education is required for most jobs. Most workers in ground occupations learn their jobs through a combination of company classroom and on-the-job training. Training consists of a minimum of three (but up to 17) weeks of classroom instruction. This includes much hands-on inspection and repair of aircraft engines and related systems and equipment. Length of courses as well as their content depends on the specialty for which an individual is being trained.

The majority of Mechanics who work on civilian aircraft hold certification from the FAA as "airframe mechanic," "powerplant mechanic," or "avionics repair specialist." Uncertified mechanics work under the supervision of those with certificates. An inspector's authorization is required for mechanics to be able to certify work by other mechanics and to perform inspections.

The FAA requires at least 18 months of work experience for an airframe, powerplant, or avionics repair certificate. For the combined airframe and powerplant certification a minimum of 30 months is required. Mechanics can substitute work experience with the completion of a program at a school certified by the FAA. Applicants for all certificates must also pass written and oral tests and demonstrate their ability to perform the work authorized by the certificate. To obtain inspectors authorization, a mechanic must have held an A&P certificate for at least three years. Most airlines require applicants to have a high school diploma and an A&P certificate.

While a few Mechanics have learned their trade on the job, most learn in one of about 200 FAA certified trade schools.

FAA requirements mandate a minimum of 1900 actual class hours. Courses in these trade schools typically run 24–30 months and provide training with the tools and equipment used on the job. There is an increased focus on skills and knowledge relating to newer technologies such as turbine engines, composite materials (fiberglass, graphite, and boron), and aviation electronics, while older technologies, such as woodworking and welding, are being downplayed. Most employers prefer mechanics with a wider range of skills.

NOTE: While Armed Forces Mechanics can acquire enough work experience to satisfy FAA certification requirements, most military jobs are too specialized to provide the broad experience needed to pass the FAA tests. Additional study is often necessary and, in many cases, the entire training program at a trade school must be completed. However, military experience does increase an applicant's chances with many employers.

FAA regulations require current experience to keep the A&P certificate valid. Mechanics must maintain a total of at least 1,000 hours of work experience in the previous two years or they must take a refresher course. In addition, Mechanics are required to take at least 16 hours of training every 24 months to keep them current on industry developments.

Experience, Skills, and Personality Traits

When hiring Aircraft Mechanics, employers prefer graduates of aircraft mechanic trade schools who are in good physical condition. Mechanics often must lift and pull large heavy objects, stand, lie, or kneel in awkward positions and, on occasion, must work on scaffolds or ladders. Noise and vibration are common, particularly when testing engines. Aircraft Mechanics must perform careful and thorough work that requires a high degree of mechanical aptitude. Employers seek individuals who are self-motivated and hard-working with excellent problem-solving skills.

Unions and Associations

Almost one half of all Aircraft Mechanics, including those employed by some major airlines, are covered by union agreements. The principal unions are the International Association of Machinists and Aerospace Workers and the Transport Workers Union of America. Some Mechanics are represented by the International Brotherhood of Teamsters.

The Aircraft Mechanics Fraternal Association is a craft-oriented, independent aviation union. It is not an industrial union. The AMFA is committed to elevating the professional standing of Aviation Maintenance Technicians and to achieving continual improvements in the wages, benefits, and working conditions of the skilled craftsmen it represents.

AIRPLANE PILOT

CAREER PROFILE

Duties: Check weather reports; develop flight plans; contact air traffic controllers to obtain takeoff and landing instructions; fly airplanes; monitor cockpit panel gauges and dials; perform combat maneuvers; take photographs; transport equipment; patrol airspace to carry out flight missions

Alternate Title(s): None

Availability: All branches

Military Salary: See How to Use This Book

Civilian Salary: $24,290 to $110,940

Civilian Employment Prospects: Fair

Civilian Advancement Prospects: Fair

Prerequisites:

Rank—Officer

Education and Training—Four-year college degree

Experience—Any training and work experience obtained in the armed services

Special Skills and Personality Traits—Top physical shape; 20/20 vision; excellent eye-hand coordination; quick reaction time; a strong desire to fly airplanes; self-confidence; ability to remain calm in stressful situations

Licensure/Certification—Federal Aviation Administration license; health certification

CAREER LADDER

```
┌─────────────────────────────┐
│  Chief Pilot or Instructor  │
└─────────────────────────────┘

┌─────────────────────────────┐
│            Pilot            │
└─────────────────────────────┘

┌─────────────────────────────┐
│           Copilot           │
└─────────────────────────────┘
```

Position Description

Every branch of the modern military needs pilots. America's armed forces control the largest fleet of specialized airplanes in the world. Supersonic fighters and bombers fly combat missions. Large transports carry troops and equipment. Intelligence gathering airplanes take photographs from high altitudes. Stationed at air bases or aboard aircraft carriers anywhere in the world, military pilots fly in all types of weather conditions, taking off and landing on airport runways and aircraft carrier landing decks.

These pilots must check weather reports to learn about flying conditions, develop flight plans showing air routes and schedules, contact air traffic controllers to obtain takeoff and landing instructions, fly airplanes by controlling engines, rudders, elevators, and other controls, and monitor gauges and dials located on cockpit control panels as well as perform combat maneuvers, take photographs, transport equipment, and patrol areas to carry out flight missions.

In the civilian world, pilots working for passenger airlines and air cargo businesses are called commercial pilots. Other civilian pilots work as flight instructors at local airports, as crop dusters, or as pilots transporting business executives in company planes. They also spread seed for reforestation, test aircraft, fly passengers and cargo to areas not serviced by regular airlines, direct firefighting efforts, track criminals, monitor traffic for news teams, and rescue and evacuate injured persons.

Except on small aircraft, two pilots usually make up the cockpit crew. Generally, the most experienced pilot, the captain, is in command and supervises all other crewmembers.

The pilot and copilot share flying and other duties, such as communicating with air traffic controllers and monitoring the instruments. Before departure, pilots plan their flights, thoroughly check their aircraft, make sure that baggage or cargo has been loaded correctly and confer with flight dispatchers and aviation weather forecasters on weather conditions en route and at their destination.

Takeoff and landing are the most difficult parts of the flight, and require close coordination between the pilot and first officer. Unless the weather is bad, however, the actual flight is relatively easy. Airplane Pilots, with the assistance of autopilot and the flight management computer, steer the plane along their planned route and are monitored by the air traffic control stations they pass along the way. All pilots must monitor warning devices designed to help detect sudden shifts in wind conditions that can cause crashes. They must also rely completely on their instruments when visibility is poor.

Airline pilots, with large support staffs at their disposal, perform few nonflying duties. Pilots employed by organizations such as charter operators or businesses may be required to load the aircraft, handle all passenger luggage to ensure a balanced load, supervise refueling, keep records, schedule flights, arrange for major maintenance, and even perform minor aircraft maintenance and repair work. Some military pilots become instructors. A few specially trained pilots work as "examiners" or "check pilots," periodically flying with other pilots or pilot's license applicants to make certain that they are proficient.

Airline pilots cannot fly more than 100 hours a month or more than 1,000 hours a year by law. Most fly roughly 75 hours a month, working 75 more hours a month performing nonflying duties. Airlines operate flights at all hours of the day and night, so work schedules are irregular, with assignments based on seniority.

Nonairline pilots have irregular schedules as well; sometimes flying 30 hours one month, 90 the next. Except for business pilots, most do not remain away from home overnight. They may work odd hours. Flight instructors may have irregular and seasonal work schedules, depending on their students' available time and the weather. Instructors frequently work at night or on weekends.

The work of test pilots, who check the flight performance of new and experimental planes, may be dangerous. Pilots who are crop dusters may be exposed to toxic chemicals and seldom have the benefit of a regular landing strip. Helicopter pilots involved in police work may be subject to personal injury. Although flying does not involve much physical effort, it can be quite stressful. Pilots must be alert and quick to react if something goes wrong, particularly during takeoff and landing.

Civilian Salaries

In 2000, the average yearly salary for airline pilots, copilots, and flight engineers was $110,940. The lowest 10 percent earned less than $36,110. Over 25 percent earned more than $145,000. In 2000, the average yearly salary for commercial pilots was $43,300. The middle 50 percent earned between $31,500 and $61,230. The lowest 10 percent earned less than $24,290. The highest 10 percent earned more than $92,000.

The amount of an aircraft pilot or flight engineer salary depends on whether they work as airline or commercial pilots. Airline pilots' salaries are among the highest in the country, as opposed to commercial pilot salaries, which are far more modest.

Civilian Employment Prospects

In 2000, civilian aircraft pilots and flight engineers held close to 118,000 jobs. Just below 85 percent worked as airline pilots, copilots, and flight engineers. The remainder were commercial pilots who worked as flight instructors at local airports or for large businesses that fly company cargo and executives in their own airplanes or helicopters. Some commercial pilots flew small planes for air taxi companies, usually to or from lightly traveled airports not served by major airlines. Others worked for a variety of businesses, performing tasks such as crop dusting, inspecting pipelines, or conducting sight-seeing trips. Federal, state, and local governments also employed pilots. A few pilots were self-employed. Pilots tend to concentrate in major travel centers or hubs such as California, New York, Illinois, Washington, or Michigan.

Most pilots traditionally have learned to fly in the military, but growing numbers have college degrees with flight training from civilian flying schools certified by the Federal Aviation Administration. They usually start with smaller commuter and regional airlines to acquire the experience needed to qualify for higher paying jobs with national airlines.

Through 2010, opportunities for pilots are expected to increase about as fast as the average for all occupations. However, computerized flight management systems on new aircraft eliminate the need for flight engineers on those planes, thus restricting growth of pilot employment. In addition, the trend toward using larger planes in the airline industry will increase pilot productivity. Employment of business pilots is expected to grow more slowly than in the past as more businesses opt to fly with regional and smaller airlines serving their area rather than to buy and operate their own aircraft. Job seekers with the most FAA licenses also will have a competitive advantage. Opportunities for pilots in the regional commuter airlines and international service are expected to be more favorable, as these segments are expected to grow faster than other segments of the industry.

Civilian Advancement Prospects

Outside the airlines, many pilots start as flight instructors, increasing their flying hours while earning money teaching. As they gain experience, they might fly charter planes, get jobs with small air transportation firms, or advance to business flying jobs. A few find flight engineer jobs with the airlines.

In the airlines, advancement depends on seniority provisions of union contracts. After one to five years, flight engineers advance according to seniority to first officer and, after five to 15 years, to captain. Seniority also determines which pilots get the more desirable routes. In a nonairline job, a first officer may advance to pilot and, in large companies, to chief pilot or director of aviation in charge of aircraft scheduling, maintenance, and flight procedures.

Education and Training

In the military, those interested in this career receive two years of instruction, one year in initial training, a second in advanced training. Initial training includes time spent in flight simulators, officer training, basic flight training, and classroom training. Course content typically includes aircraft aerodynamics, jet and propeller engine operation, operation of aircraft navigation systems, foul weather flying, and the study of Federal Aviation Administration regulations.

Advanced training begins once a pilot successfully completes initial training and is awarded his "wings." Advanced training consists of instruction in flying a particular type of aircraft.

A four-year college degree is normally required to enter this occupation. Excellent preparatory fields of study include physics and aerospace, electrical, or mechanical engineering.

The armed forces have always been an important source of trained pilots for civilian jobs. Military pilots gain valuable experience on jet aircraft and helicopters, and persons with this experience usually are preferred for civilian pilot jobs. This primarily reflects the extensive flying time military pilots receive.

Civilians may become pilots by attending flight schools. The FAA has certified some 600 civilian flying schools. Although some small airlines will hire high school graduates, most airlines require at least two years of college and prefer to hire college graduates.

Special Requirements

All pilots who are paid to transport passengers or cargo must have a commercial pilot's license with an instrument rating issued by the FAA. Applicants must be at least 18 years old and have a minimum of 250 hours flight experience. They must pass both written tests and physical examinations. They must also be rated by the FAA to fly by instruments.

Airline pilots must also have an airline transport pilot's license. Applicants must be at least 23 years old and have a minimum of 1,500 hours flight experience, including night and instrument flying, and must pass FAA written and flight examinations. All licenses are valid so long as a pilot can pass the periodic physical examinations and tests of flying skills required by federal government and company regulations.

A pilot license may have a Class I, II, and III Medical certificate. Class I Medical Certificate requires the highest standards for vision, hearing, equilibrium, and general physical condition. Class II Medical Certificate requirements are less rigid, but still require a high degree of physical health and an excellent medical history. The Class III Medical Certificate has the least stringent physical requirements. All three classes of medical certificates allow the pilot to wear glasses provided the correction is within the prescribed limits of vision.

Experience, Special Skills, and Personality Traits

Airplane Pilots must be in top physical shape, have 20/20 vision, excellent eye-hand coordination, quick reaction times, a strong desire to fly airplanes, self-confidence as well as ability to remain calm in stressful situations. They must be in excellent health.

Unions and Associations

For information on airline pilots, contact the Airline Pilots Association and the Air Transport Association of America, Inc. For a copy of the List of Certificated Pilot Schools, contact the Superintendent of Documents.

AIR TRAFFIC CONTROLLER

CAREER PROFILE

Duties: Operate radio equipment, relay weather reports, airfield conditions, and safety information; use radar equipment, plot airplane locations, compute speed, direction, and altitude of aircraft; maintain air traffic control records and communication logs

Alternate Title(s): None

Availability: Army, Navy, Air Force, Marine Corps

Military Salary: See How to Use This Book

Civilian Salary: $44,760 to $111,150

Civilian Employment Prospects: Fair

Civilian Advancement Prospects: Fair

Prerequisites:
 Rank—Enlisted
 Education and Training—Certification by the Federal Aviation Administration
 Experience—Any training and work experience obtained in the armed services
 Special Skills and Personality Traits—High school English skills; general mathematics and typing; clear speaking; intelligence; a good memory; decisiveness; the ability to concentrate, work under stress, and remain alert while performing repetitive tasks; normal color vision; normal hearing; a clear speaking voice

CAREER LADDER

```
┌─────────────────────────────┐
│    Air Traffic Supervisor    │
└─────────────────────────────┘

┌─────────────────────────────┐
│    Air Traffic Controller    │
└─────────────────────────────┘

┌─────────────────────────────┐
│          Trainee             │
└─────────────────────────────┘
```

Position Description

The military has planes and helicopters of every type in the air at all times. Air Traffic Controllers direct their movements to make certain their flight paths are clear. Working in land-based and shipboard control centers, these controllers track aircraft by radar, giving voice instructions by radio and issuing takeoff, flight, and landing instructions to pilots. Using radar to track aircraft in flight, they relay weather reports, airfield conditions, and safety information to pilots; plot airplane locations on charts and maps; compute speed, direction, and altitude of aircraft; and maintain air traffic control records and communication logs.

In the civilian world Air Traffic Controllers work for the FAA in airports and control centers. Most specialize in specific areas, such as aircraft arrivals, departures, ground control, or en route flights. As a team, they coordinate the movement of air traffic to make certain planes stay a safe distance apart. They must keep planes safe, direct them efficiently to minimize delays, and regulate both airport traffic and traffic between airports. They must watch over all planes traveling through the airport's airspace and organize the flow of aircraft in and out of the airport.

Using both radar and visual observation, Controllers closely monitor each plane to ensure a safe distance between all aircraft and to guide pilots between the hangar or ramp and the end of the airport's airspace. They also keep pilots informed about changes in weather conditions that could affect a pilot's control of an aircraft.

Controllers direct every plane that approaches or leaves an airport. They route planes to runways or, if the airport is busy, they fit them into a traffic pattern with other aircraft. Planes that have landed are sent to their assigned gate. Departing planes are handed off to the next en route Controller who will take charge.

Radar Controllers warn pilots about nearby planes, bad weather conditions, and other potential hazards. They guide planes around each other and control all aspects of a pilot's flight path. Both airport tower and en route controllers usually control several planes at a time; often, they have to make quick decisions about completely different activities.

Air Traffic Controllers also work in flight service stations. These flight service specialists provide pilots with information on a station's particular area, including terrain, preflight and in-flight weather information, suggested routes, and other information important to flight safety. They also help pilots in emergency situations and initiate and coordinate searches for missing or overdue aircraft.

Since most control towers and centers operate every moment of every day, Controllers rotate night and weekend shifts. During busy times, Controllers must work rapidly and efficiently with total concentration to keep track of several planes at the same time, and to make certain all pilots receive correct instructions. The mental stress of being responsible for the safety of several aircraft and their passengers can be exhausting.

Civilian Salaries

In 2000, the average yearly salary for air traffic controllers was $82,520. The middle 50 percent earned between $62,250 and $101,570. The lowest 10 percent earned less than $44,760 and the highest 10 percent earned more than $111,150.

Air Traffic Controllers earn relatively high pay and have good benefits. In 2000, the average annual salary, excluding overtime earnings, for Air Traffic Controllers in the federal government (which employs 89 percent of the total) was $53,313. Controllers who work at the FAA's busiest air traffic control facilities earn higher pay.

Controllers can retire at an earlier age and with fewer years of service than other federal employees. There is a mandatory retirement age of 56 for Controllers who manage air traffic.

Civilian Employment Prospects

In 2000, Air Traffic Controllers held fewer than 28,000 jobs. Most worked for the FAA. Some conduct research at the FAA's national experimental center near Atlantic City, New Jersey, or work as instructors at the FAA Academy in Oklahoma City, Oklahoma. A small number worked for the Defense Department. Outside the FAA, some worked for private air traffic control companies providing service to non-FAA towers.

Keen competition is expected for the few job openings in this occupation, due to the relatively high pay and liberal retirement benefits. Through 2010, opportunities for Air Traffic Controllers are not expected to keep pace with growth in the number of aircraft flying because of the implementation of a new air traffic control system. This computerized system will assist the controller by automatically making many of the routine decisions. Automation will allow controllers to handle more traffic, thus increasing their productivity.

Air Traffic Controllers who meet proficiency and medical requirements enjoy a higher degree of job security than most other workers. The demand for air travel and the workloads of Air Traffic Controllers decline during recessions, but Controllers are seldom laid off.

Civilian Advancement Prospects

Controllers can transfer to jobs at different locations or advance to supervisory positions, including management or staff jobs in air traffic control and top administrative jobs in the FAA. However, there are only limited opportunities for a Controller to switch from a position in an en route center to a tower.

Education and Training

Nearly all Air Traffic Controllers are employed and trained by the Federal Government. Trainees are selected through the competitive Federal Civil Service system. Applicants must pass a written test that measures their ability to learn the Controller's duties. Applicants with experience as a pilot, navigator or military Controller can improve their rating by scoring well on the occupational knowledge portion of the examination. Abstract reasoning and three-dimensional spatial visualization are among the aptitudes the exam measures. In addition, applicants usually must have three years of general work experience or four years of college, or a combination of both. Applicants also must survive a week of screening at the FAA Academy in Oklahoma City, which includes aptitude tests using computer simulators and physical and psychological examinations.

Job training consists of two to three months of classroom instruction. Typical training courses are air traffic control fundamentals, visual and instrument flight procedures, and radar and other landing approach procedures. FAA certification must be obtained during training.

Trainees receive seven months of intensive training in FAA regulations, Controller equipment, aircraft performance characteristics, accurately recognizing and correctly solving air traffic control problems, and judging spatial relationships.

Controllers must pass a physical examination each year and a job performance examination twice each year.

Experience, Special Skills, and Personality Traits

High school English, general mathematics, and typing are some of the basic skills required. Controllers must also be articulate, intelligent, and possess a good memory. Decisiveness and the ability to concentrate are important, as well as the ability to work under stress and to remain alert while performing repetitive tasks. Normal color vision, normal hearing, and a clear speaking voice are required.

Unions and Associations

Air Traffic Controllers may join the National Air Traffic Controllers Association. For information go to http://www. natca.org. Information on acquiring an air traffic controller position may be obtained from the Office of Personnel Management. Consult your telephone directory under "U.S. Government" for a local number or call (912) 757-3000. Information also is available on the Internet: http://www.usajobs. opm.gov.

AUTOMOTIVE AND HEAVY EQUIPMENT MECHANIC

CAREER PROFILE

Duties: Attend to problems in vehicles; tune and repair engines; replace or repair damaged parts; establish and follow schedules for maintaining vehicles

Alternate Title(s): Diesel Service Technician and Mechanic; Small Engine Mechanic; Automotive Service Technician and Mechanic; Heavy Vehicle and Mobile Equipment Service Technician; Garage Mechanic; Carburetor Mechanic; Transmission Mechanic; Radiator Mechanic; Construction Equipment Mechanic; Endless Track Vehicle Mechanic

Availability: All branches

Military Salary: See How to Use This Book

Civilian Salary: $7.59 to $23.67/hour

Civilian Employment Prospects: Good

Civilian Advancement Prospects: Good

Prerequisites:

　Rank—Enlisted

　Education and Training—High school diploma

　Experience—Any training and work experience obtained in the armed services

　Special Skills and Personality Traits—Strong communication and analytical skills; good reading, mathematics, and computer skills; mechanical aptitude; knowledge of how automobiles work; normal color vision; a preference for physical work; an interest in troubleshooting and repairing mechanical problems

　Licensure/Certification—May be required

CAREER LADDER

```
┌─────────────────────────────────────────┐
│  Shop Supervisor or Service Manager      │
└─────────────────────────────────────────┘

┌─────────────────────────────────────────┐
│              Technician                   │
└─────────────────────────────────────────┘

┌─────────────────────────────────────────┐
│               Trainee                     │
└─────────────────────────────────────────┘
```

Position Description

The modern military runs on automotive and heavy equipment. Keeping it in good working condition is vital to the success of military missions. Automotive and Heavy Equipment Mechanics maintain and repair vehicles such as jeeps, cars, trucks, tanks, self-propelled missile launchers, and other combat vehicles. They also repair bulldozers, power shovels, and other construction equipment.

Working inside large repair garages or outdoors when making emergency repairs in the field, Automotive and Heavy Equipment Mechanics troubleshoot problems in vehicle engines, electrical systems, steering, brakes, and suspensions. They also tune and repair engines; replace or repair damaged body parts, hydraulic arms or shovels, and grader blades; and establish and follow schedules for maintaining vehicles.

In the civilian world, these mechanics may work for service stations, auto and construction equipment dealers, farm equipment companies, and state highway agencies. Today, the work of automotive service technicians and mechanics has evolved from simple mechanics to high technology. Contemporary workers must have an increasingly broad base of knowledge about how vehicles' complex components work and interact, as well as the ability to work with electronic diagnostic equipment and computer-based technical reference materials.

Automotive service technicians and mechanics use these high-tech skills to inspect, maintain, and repair automobiles and light trucks. When mechanical or electrical troubles occur, technicians use a diagnostic approach, testing to see if components and systems are proper and secure, then isolating those components or systems that could not logically be the cause of the problem. Service technicians use a variety of tools in their work, including power tools such as pneumatic wrenches, lathes, and grinding machines as well as common hand tools like screwdrivers, pliers, and wrenches. Those working in large shops often become specialists, such as transmission technicians and rebuilders, tune-up technicians, air-conditioning repairers, those who specialize in both brake and front-end work, etc.

Nearly half of all automotive service technicians work a standard 40-hour week. Many self-employed technicians work far longer. Some service shops do offer evening and weekend service. Generally, service technicians work indoors in well-ventilated and well-lighted repair shops. However, they also work with dirty and greasy parts, often in awkward positions. They often lift heavy parts and tools. Minor cuts, burns, and bruises are common, but technicians usually avoid serious accidents when the shop is kept clean and orderly and safety practices are observed.

Diesel service technicians and mechanics repair and maintain diesel engines (heavy trucks, buses, locomotives, bulldozers, cranes, road graders, etc.). Many spend most of their time doing preventive maintenance, to ensure that equipment will operate safely. These workers also eliminate unnecessary wear on and damage to parts that could result in costly breakdowns. It must be noted that diesel maintenance is becoming increasingly complex, as more electronic components are used to control engine operation. In modern shops, diesel service technicians use hand-held computers to diagnose problems and adjust engine functions.

Like automotive service technicians, diesel service technicians use a variety of tools, both power tools and common hand tools, in their work. They usually work indoors, although they occasionally make repairs to vehicles on the road. Diesel technicians also share the same working and safety conditions as automotive service technicians.

Heavy vehicle and mobile equipment service technicians and mechanics repair and maintain engines and hydraulic, transmission, and electrical systems powering farm equipment, cranes, bulldozers, and railcars. They perform routine maintenance checks often using hand-held diagnostic computers that they plug into onboard computers to diagnose any component needing adjustment or repair. They also per-

form a variety of other repairs, such as diagnosing electrical problems, adjusting or replacing defective components, or disassembling and repairing undercarriages and track assemblies. Like automotive service technicians, it is common for service technicians in large shops to specialize in one or two types of repair. They also use a variety of power and hand tools in their work.

Mobile Heavy Equipment Mechanics and service technicians keep construction and surface mining equipment such as bulldozer, cranes, crawlers, draglines, graders, excavators, and other equipment in working order. Farm equipment mechanics service, maintain, and repair farm equipment as well as smaller lawn and garden tractors sold to suburban homeowners. Railcar repairers specialize in servicing railroad locomotives and other rolling stock, streetcars and subway cars, or mine cars.

Civilian Salaries

In 2000, the average hourly salary for automotive service technicians and mechanics, including commission, was $13.70. The middle 50 percent earned between $9.86 and $18.67 an hour. The lowest 10 percent earned less than $7.59. The highest 10 percent earned more than $23.67 an hour.

In 2000, the average hourly salary for bus and truck mechanics and diesel engine specialists, including incentive pay, was $15.55. The middle 50 percent earned between $12.33 and $19.30 an hour. The lowest 10 percent earned less than $9.88. The highest 10 percent earned more than $22.63 an hour.

In 2000, the average hourly salary for mobile heavy equipment mechanics was $16.32. The middle 50 percent earned between $13.32 and $19.86. The lowest 10 percent earned less than $10.93. The highest 10 percent earned more than $23.29.

In 2000, the average hourly salary for farm equipment mechanics was $12.38. The middle 50 percent earned between $9.99 and $15.29. The lowest 10 percent earned less than $8.15. The highest 10 percent earned more than $18.23.

In 2000, the average hourly salary for railcar repairers was $16.19. The middle 50 percent earned between $12.31 and $19.34. The lowest 10 percent earned less than $9.78. The highest 10 percent earned more than $21.19.

Civilian Employment Prospects

In 2000, automotive service technicians and mechanics held nearly 850,000 jobs. The majority worked for retail and wholesale automotive dealers, independent automotive repair shops, or automotive service facilities at department, automotive, and home supply stores.

Opportunities are expected to be very good for those who complete automotive training programs, those with good diagnostic and problem-solving skills, and those with basic electronics skills. Through 2010, opportunities for automotive service technicians and mechanics are expected to increase about as fast as the average. This growth will be concentrated in motor vehicle dealerships and independent automotive repair shops. Many new jobs will also be created in small retail operations that offer after-warranty repairs, such as oil changes, brake repair, air conditioner service, etc.

In 2000, diesel service technicians and mechanics held nearly 285,000 jobs. Some 25 percent serviced buses, trucks, and other diesel-powered equipment for customers of vehicle and equipment dealers, automotive rental and leasing agencies, or independent automotive repair shops. Another 20 percent worked for local and long-distance trucking companies.

Through 2010, opportunities for diesel service technicians and mechanics are expected to increase about as fast as the average for all occupations as freight transportation by truck increases. These opportunities will be best for those who complete formal training in diesel mechanics at community and junior colleges and vocational and technical schools.

In 2000, heavy vehicle and mobile equipment service technicians and mechanics held roughly 185,000 jobs. Some 130,000 were mobile heavy equipment mechanics; 41,000 were farm equipment mechanics; and 14,000 were railcar repairers. More than 40 percent were employed by heavy and mobile equipment dealers and distributors.

Opportunities for heavy vehicle and mobile equipment service technicians and mechanics should be good for persons who have completed formal training programs in diesel or heavy equipment mechanics. Through 2010, opportunities for heavy vehicle and mobile equipment service technicians and mechanics are expected to grow as fast as the average for all occupations. Increasing numbers of service technicians will be required to support growth in the construction industry, equipment dealers, and rental and leasing companies. Also, as equipment becomes more complex, repairs increasingly must be made by specially trained technicians.

Civilian Advancement Prospects

Experienced technicians and mechanics with leadership ability may advance to shop supervisor or service manager. Those who work well with customers may become automotive repair service estimators. Technicians and mechanics with sales ability sometimes become sales representatives. Some open their own repair shops.

Education and Training

In the military, those interested in this career receive two to eight months of classroom instruction, depending on specialty. Classes usually include such courses as engine repair and tune-up; troubleshooting mechanical and electrical problems; and repairing and replacing body panels, fenders, and radiators. Further training occurs on the job and through advanced courses. The army, navy, and marine corps offer certified apprenticeship programs for some specialties in this occupation.

Due to the increasing complexity of automotive technology, most persons seeking automotive service technician and mechanic jobs complete a formal training program in high school or in a postsecondary vocational school. The better high school programs, such as the Automotive Youth Education Service, with 150 participating schools and more than 300 participating dealers, conclude with the students receiving their technician's certification and high school diploma. Other programs offer only an introduction to automotive technology and service for the future consumer or hobbyist. Still others aim to equip graduates with enough skills to get a job as a mechanic's helper or trainee mechanic.

Some trade and technical school programs provide concentrated training for six months to a year, community college programs normally spread the training over two years; supplement the automotive training with instruction in English, basic mathematics, computers, and other subjects; and award an associate degree or certificate.

The various automobile manufacturers and their participating dealers sponsor two-year associate degree programs at postsecondary schools across the nation. The Accrediting Commission of Career Schools and Colleges of Technology currently certifies a number of automotive and diesel technology schools. The National Automotive Technicians Education Foundation, an affiliate of the National Institute for Automotive Service Excellence, establishes the standards by which training facilities become certified. In mid 2000, 1,491 high school and postsecondary automotive service technician training programs had been certified by ASE, of which 1,200 trained automobile service technicians, 224 instructed collision specialists, and 62 trained diesel and medium/heavy truck specialists.

Completion of an automotive training program in high school, vocational, or trade school, or community or junior college may be substituted for one year of experience. In some cases, graduates of ASE-certified programs achieve certification in up to three specialties. For certification as a master automotive mechanic, technicians must be certified in all eight areas. Mechanics and technicians must retake each examination at least every five years to maintain their certifications.

Many community colleges and trade and vocational schools offer programs in diesel repair lasting six months to two years, which lead to a certificate of completion or an associate degree. Technicians may be certified as Master Heavy-Duty Truck technicians or in specific areas of heavy-duty truck repair. For certification a technician must pass one or more of the ASE-administered exams and present proof of two years of relevant hands-on work experience. Two years of relevant formal training from a high school, vocational or trade school, or community or junior college program may be substituted for up to one year of the work experience requirement. To remain certified, technicians must retest every five years.

Many employers send trainee technicians to training sessions conducted by heavy equipment manufacturers. Typically lasting up to one week, these sessions provide intensive instruction in the repair of a manufacturer's equipment. Some sessions focus on particular components found in the manufacturer's equipment, others focus on particular types of equipment.

Voluntary certification by the National Institute for ASE is recognized as the standard of achievement for heavy and mobile equipment diesel service technicians. Technicians may be certified as a Master Heavy-Duty Diesel Technician or in one or more of six different areas of heavy-duty equipment repair. For certification in each area, technicians must pass a written examination and have at least two years experience. High school, vocational or trade school, or community or junior college training in gasoline or diesel engine repair may substitute for up to one year's experience. To remain certified, technicians must retest every five years.

Experience, Special Skills, and Personality Traits

Those hoping to become Automotive or Heavy Equipment Mechanics or technicians need strong communication and analytical skills; good reading, mathematics, and computer skills; mechanical aptitude and knowledge of how automobiles work; normal color vision; a preference for physical work; and an interest in troubleshooting and repairing mechanical problems and in automotive engines and how they work.

Unions and Associations

For a list of certified automotive technician training programs, contact the National Automotive Technicians Education Foundation. For a directory of accredited private trade and technical schools that offer programs in automotive technician training, contact the Accrediting Commission of Career Schools and Colleges of Technology. For a list of public automotive technician training programs, contact SkillsUSA-VICA.

For information on automobile manufacturer-sponsored programs in automotive service technology, contact the Automotive Youth Educational Systems. For information on how to become a certified automotive service technician, a certified medium/heavy-duty diesel technician or bus technician, contact the ASE. For general information about the work of automotive service technicians and mechanics, contact the National Automobile Dealers Association.

For general information about a career as a diesel service technician or mechanic, contact Detroit Diesel, Personnel Director, MS B39. For a directory of accredited private trade and technical schools with training programs for diesel service technicians and mechanics, contact the Accrediting Commission of Career Schools and Colleges of Technology or the National Automotive Technicians Education Foundation.

For general information about a career as a heavy vehicle and mobile equipment service technician or mechanic, contact the Equipment Maintenance Counsel, the Specialized Carriers and Rigging Association and the AED Foundation. For a list of certified diesel service technician training programs, contact the National Automotive Technician Education Foundation.

FLIGHT OPERATIONS SPECIALIST

CAREER PROFILE

Duties: Help plan flight schedules and air crew assignments; keep flight logs, air crew flying records and flight operations records; receive and post weather information and flight plan data; coordinate air crew needs; plan aircraft equipment needs for air evacuation and dangerous cargo flights; check military flight plans with civilian agencies

Alternate Title(s): Air Traffic Controllers; Radar Controllers

Availability: All branches

Military Salary: See How to Use This Book

Civilian Salary: $44,760 to $111,150

Civilian Employment Prospects: Good

Civilian Advancement Prospects: Good

Prerequisites:
  Rank—Enlisted
  Education and Training—Certification by the Federal Aviation Administration (FAA) normally must be obtained during training
  Experience—Any training and work experience obtained in the armed services
  Special Skills and Personality Traits—Intelligence; good memory; decisiveness; the ability to concentrate and work under stress; able to remain alert while performing repetitive tasks; normal color vision; normal hearing; a clear speaking voice

CAREER LADDER

```
┌─────────────────────────┐
│        Trainee          │
└─────────────────────────┘

┌─────────────────────────┐
│       Controller        │
└─────────────────────────┘

┌─────────────────────────┐
│       Supervisor        │
└─────────────────────────┘
```

Position Description

The modern military maintains the largest fleet of aircraft in the world sending literally hundreds of transport, passenger, and combat airplanes and helicopters aloft every day. Accurate flight information keeps operations safe and efficient. Working in flight control centers or air terminals, Flight Operations Specialists prepare and provide flight information for air and ground crews. They also help plan flight schedules and air crew assignments, keep flight logs on incoming and outgoing flights as well as air crew flying records and flight operations records.

They receive and post weather information and flight plan data, such as air routes and arrival and departure times, coordinate air crew needs, such as ground transportation, plan aircraft equipment needs for air evacuation and danger-ous cargo flights, and check military flight plans with civilian agencies.

In the civilian world Flight Operations Specialists work for commercial and private airlines and air transport companies. Although some few can find jobs where they can perform duties similar to military Flight Operations Specialists, due to the ground support system of radar and other features set up to guide commercial air traffic, most become involved in the direction and control of traffic in air transportation.

Air traffic controllers work for the FAA in airports and control centers. Most specialize in specific areas, such as aircraft arrivals, departures, ground control, or en route flights. As a team, they coordinate the movement of air traffic to make certain planes stay a safe distance apart. They must keep planes safe, direct them efficiently, and minimize delays. They must also watch over all planes traveling through the airport's airspace and organize the flow of aircraft in and out of the airport.

Using both radar and visual observation, they closely monitor each plane to ensure a safe distance between all aircraft and to guide pilots between the hangar and ramp or the end of the airport's airspace. They also keep pilots informed about changes in weather conditions that could cause pilots to lose control of aircraft.

Controllers direct every plane that approaches or leaves an airport. They direct planes to runways or, if the airport is busy, they fit them into a traffic pattern with other aircraft. Planes that have landed are directed to their assigned gate. Departing planes are handed off to the next en route controller who will take charge.

Radar controllers warn pilots about nearby planes, bad weather conditions, and other potential hazards. They direct planes around each other and control all aspects of a pilot's flight path. Both airport tower and en route controllers usually control several planes at a time; often, they have to make quick decisions about completely different activities.

Air traffic controllers also work in flight service stations. These flight service specialists provide pilots with information on a station's particular area, including terrain, preflight and inflight weather information, suggested routes, and other information important to flight safety. They also help pilots in emergency situations and initiate and coordinate searches for missing or overdue aircraft.

Since most control towers and centers operate every moment of every day, controllers rotate night and weekend shifts. During busy times, controllers must work rapidly and efficiently with total concentration to keep track of several planes at the same time, and to make certain all pilots receive correct instructions. The mental stress of being responsible for the safety of several aircraft and their passengers can be exhausting.

Civilian Salaries

In 2000, the average yearly salary for air traffic controllers was $82,520. The middle 50 percent earned between $62,250 and $101,570. The lowest 10 percent earned less than $44,760 and the highest 10 percent earned more than $111,150. Aircraft controllers earn relatively high pay and have good benefits. In 2000, the average annual salary, excluding overtime earnings, for air traffic controllers in the federal government (which employs 89 percent of the total) was $53,313. Controllers who work at the FAA's busiest air traffic control facilities earn higher pay.

Controllers can retire at an earlier age and with fewer years of service than other federal employees can. There is a mandatory retirement age of 56 for air traffic controllers.

Civilian Employment Prospects

In 2000, air traffic controllers held less than 28,000 jobs. Most worked for the FAA. Some conduct research at the FAA's national experimental center near Atlantic City, New Jersey, or work as instructors at the FAA Academy in Oklahoma City, Oklahoma. A small number worked for the Defense Department. Outside the FAA, some worked for private air traffic control companies providing service to non-FAA towers.

Keen competition is expected for the few job openings in this occupation, due to the relatively high pay and liberal retirement benefits. Through 2010, opportunities for air traffic controllers are not expected to keep pace with growth in the number of aircraft flying because of the implementation of a new air traffic control system. This computerized system will assist the controller by automatically making many routine decisions. Automation will allow controllers to handle more traffic, thus increasing their productivity.

Air traffic controllers who meet proficiency and medical requirements enjoy more job security than most workers do. The demand for air travel and the workloads of air traffic controllers decline during recessions, but controllers are seldom laid off.

Civilian Advancement Prospects

Beginning controllers supply pilots with basic flight data and airport information. Advancement goes through stages: ground controller, local controller, departure controller, arrival controller. At traffic control center, advancement goes through the stages of trainee, radar associate controller, then radar controller.

Controllers can transfer to jobs at different locations or advance to supervisory positions, including management or staff jobs in air traffic control and top administrative jobs in the FAA. However, there are only limited opportunities for a controller to switch from a position in an en route center to a tower. Controllers can transfer to jobs at different locations or advance to supervisory positions, including management or staff jobs in air traffic control and top administrative jobs in the FAA. However, there are only limited opportunities for a controller to switch from a position in an en route center to a tower.

Education and Training

In the military, those interested in becoming Flight Operations Specialists receive two to four months of classroom instruction, depending on specialty. Classes usually include such courses as Introduction to Aviation Operations, Procedures for Scheduling Aircraft and Assigning Air Crews, Flight Planning and Airfield Operations, and Preparing Flight Operations Reports and Records. Additional training occurs on the job as well as through advanced courses.

Nearly all air traffic controllers are employed and trained by the federal government. Trainees are selected through the competitive federal Civil Service system. Applicants must pass a written test that measures their ability to learn the controller's duties. Applicants with experience as a pilot, navigator, or military controller can improve their rating by scoring well on the occupational knowledge portion of the examination. Abstract reasoning and three-dimensional spatial visualization are among the aptitudes the exam measures. In addition, applicants usually must have three years of general work experience or four years of college, or a combination of both. Applicants also must survive a week of screening at the FAA Academy in Oklahoma City, which includes aptitude tests using computer simulators and physical and psychological examinations.

Job training consists of two to three months of classroom instruction. Typical training courses are: Air Traffic Control Fundamentals, Visual and Instrument Flight Procedures, Radar and Other Landing Approach Procedures. FAA certification must be obtained during training.

Trainees receive seven months of intensive training in FAA regulations, controller equipment, aircraft performance characteristics, accurately recognizing and correctly solving air traffic control problems, and judging spatial relationships.

Controllers must pass a physical examination each year and a job performance examination twice each year.

Experience, Special Skills, and Personality Traits

Air traffic controllers must be articulate, intelligent, and possess a good memory. Decisiveness and the ability to concentrate are important, as well as the ability to work under stress and to remain alert while performing repetitive tasks. Normal color vision, normal hearing, and a clear speaking voice are required.

Unions and Associations

Air traffic controllers may join the National Air Traffic Controllers Association. For information go to http://www.natca.org. Information on acquiring an air traffic controller position may be obtained from the Office of Personnel Management. Consult your telephone directory under "U.S. Government" for a local number or call (912) 757-3000. Information also is available on the Internet: http://www.usajobs.opm.gov.

HELICOPTER PILOT

CAREER PROFILE

Duties: Prepare flight plans; fly helicopters; monitor cockpit control panel gauges and dials; perform combat maneuvers; spot and observe enemy positions; transport troops and equipment; evacuate wounded troops; check weather reports to learn about flying conditions

Alternate Title(s): None

Availability: All branches

Military Salary: See How to Use This Book

Civilian Salary: $110,940

Civilian Employment Prospects: Fair

Civilian Advancement Prospects: Fair

Prerequisites:

   Rank—Officer

   Education and Training—Four-year college degree

   Experience—Any training and work experience obtained in the armed services

   Special Skills and Personality Traits—Top physical shape; 20/20 vision; excellent eye-hand coordination; quick reaction time; a strong desire to fly helicopters; self-confidence; the ability to remain calm in stressful situations; good sense of direction and balance

CAREER LADDER

```
┌─────────────────────────────────┐
│     Chief Pilot or Instructor   │
└─────────────────────────────────┘

┌─────────────────────────────────┐
│              Pilot              │
└─────────────────────────────────┘

┌─────────────────────────────────┐
│            Copilot              │
└─────────────────────────────────┘
```

Position Description

The most versatile weapon in the air forces of the modern military is the helicopter. They can take off from and land on small areas. They can also hover in one spot in the air. The military uses these versatile aircraft to transport troops and cargo, perform search and rescue missions, and provide close combat support for ground troops. Stationed at military bases or aboard aircraft carriers around the world, Helicopter Pilots in the military fly in all types of weather conditions. They take off and land from airports, forward landing areas, and ship landing decks. They also prepare flight plans showing air routes and schedules; fly helicopters by controlling engines, flight controls, and other systems; monitor gauges and dials located on cockpit control panels; perform combat maneuvers; and spot and observe enemy positions. They also transport troops and equipment, evacuate wounded troops, and check weather reports to learn about flying conditions.

In the civilian world, Helicopter Pilots work for police forces, local commuter services, and private businesses. They also work as crop dusters, fire fighters, traffic spotters, and helicopter flight instructors. Military Helicopter Pilots can also work for passenger airlines and air cargo businesses as commercial pilots. Other civilian pilots work as flight instructors at local airports, as crop dusters, or as pilots transporting business executives in company planes. They also spread seed for reforestation, test aircraft, fly passengers and cargo to areas not serviced by regular airlines, direct fire-fighting efforts, track criminals, monitor traffic for news teams, and rescue and evacuate injured persons.

Before departure, pilots plan their flights, thoroughly check their aircraft, make sure that baggage or cargo has been loaded correctly, and confer with flight dispatchers and aviation weather forecasters on weather conditions en route and at their destination. Takeoff and landing are the most difficult parts of the flight. However, helicopters are used for short trips at relatively low altitude, so pilots must be constantly on the lookout for trees, bridges, power lines, transmission towers, and other dangerous obstacles. They must also monitor warning devices designed to help detect sudden shifts in wind conditions that can cause crashes. They must also rely completely on their instruments when visibility is poor.

Helicopter Pilots can have irregular schedules, sometimes flying 30 hours one month, 90 the next. They may work odd hours. Flight instructors may have irregular and seasonal work schedules, depending on their students' available time and the weather. Instructors frequently work at night or on weekends.

Helicopter Pilots involved in police work may be subject to personal injury.

Although flying does not involve much physical effort, it can be quite stressful. Pilots must be alert and quick to react if something goes wrong, particularly during takeoff and landing.

Civilian Salaries

In 2000, the average yearly salary for airline pilots, copilots, and flight engineers was $110,940. The lowest 10 percent earned less than $36,110. Over 25 percent earned more than $145,000. In 2000, the average yearly salary for commercial pilots was $43,300. The middle 50 percent earned between $31,500 and $61,230. The lowest 10 percent earned less than $24,290. The highest 10 percent earned more than $92,000. Salaries for Helicopter Pilots may deviate from this because their work is more specialized and involves smaller aircraft.

Civilian Employment Prospects

In 2000, civilian aircraft pilots and flight engineers held close to 118,000 jobs. Just below 85 percent worked as airline pilots, copilots, and flight engineers. The remainder were commercial pilots who worked as flight instructors at local airports or for large businesses that fly company cargo and executives in their own airplanes or helicopters. Some commercial pilots flew small planes for air taxi companies, usually to or from lightly traveled airports not served by major airlines. Others worked for a variety of businesses, performing tasks such as crop dusting, inspecting pipelines, or conducting sight-seeing trips. Federal, state, and local governments also employed pilots. A few pilots were self-employed. Pilots tend to concentrate in major travel centers or population centers such as California, New York, Illinois, Washington, or Michigan.

Most pilots traditionally have learned to fly in the military, but growing numbers have college degrees with flight training from civilian flying schools certified by the Federal Aviation Administration. They usually start with smaller commuter and regional airlines or commuter services to acquire the experience needed to qualify for higher paying jobs with national airlines.

Through 2010, opportunities for pilots are expected to increase about as fast as the average for all occupations. Employment of business pilots is expected to grow more slowly than in the past as more businesses opt to fly with regional and smaller airlines serving their area rather than to buy and operate their own aircraft. Job seekers with the most FAA licenses also will have a competitive advantage. Opportunities for pilots in the regional commuter airlines and international service are expected to be more favorable, as these segments are expected to grow faster than other segments of the industry.

Civilian Advancement Prospects

Outside the airlines, many pilots start as flight instructors, increasing their flying hours while earning money teaching. As they gain experience, they might fly charter trips, get jobs with small air transportation firms, or advance to business flying jobs. A few find flight engineer jobs with the airlines.

In the airlines, advancement depends on seniority provisions of union contracts. After one to five years, flight engineers advance according to seniority to first officer and, after five to 15 years, to captain. Seniority also determines which pilots get the more desirable routes. In a nonairline job, a first officer may advance to pilot and, in large companies, to chief pilot or director of aviation in charge of aircraft scheduling, maintenance, and flight procedures.

Education and Training

In the military, those interested in this career receive two years of instruction, one year in initial training, a second in advanced training. Initial training includes time spent in flight simulators, officer training, basic flight training, and classroom training. Course content typically includes aircraft aerodynamics, jet and propeller engine operation, operation of aircraft navigation systems, foul weather flying, and the study of Federal Aviation Administration regulations.

Advanced training begins once a pilot successfully completes initial training and is awarded his "wings." Advanced training consists of instruction in flying a particular type of aircraft.

A four-year college degree is normally required to enter this occupation. Excellent preparatory fields of study include physics and aerospace, electrical, or mechanical engineering.

The armed forces have always been an important source of trained pilots for civilian jobs. Military pilots gain valuable experience on jet aircraft and helicopters, and persons with this experience usually are preferred for civilian pilot jobs. This primarily reflects the extensive flying time military pilots receive.

Civilians may become pilots by attending flight schools. The FAA has certified some 600 civilian flying schools.

Although some small airlines will hire high school graduates, most airlines require at least two years of college and prefer to hire college graduates.

Special Requirements

All pilots who are paid to transport passengers or cargo must have a commercial pilot's license with an instrument rating issued by the FAA. Applicants must be at least 18 years old and have a minimum of 250 hours flight experience. They must pass both written tests and physical examinations. They must also be rated by the FAA to fly by instruments.

Airline pilots must also have an airline transport pilot's license. Applicants must be at least 23 years old and have a minimum of 1,500 hours flight experience, including night and instrument flying, and must pass FAA written and flight examinations. All licenses are valid so long as a pilot can pass the periodic physical examinations and tests of flying skills required by federal government and company regulations.

A pilot license may have a Class I, II, and III Medical certificate. Class I Medical Certificate requires the highest standards for vision, hearing, equilibrium, and general phys-ical condition. Class II Medical Certificate requirements are less rigid, but still require a high degree of physical health and an excellent medical history. The Class III Medical Certificate has the least stringent physical requirements. All three classes of medical certificates allow the pilot to wear glasses provided the correction is within the prescribed limits of vision.

Experience, Special Skills, and Personality Traits

Airplane pilots must be in top physical shape, have 20/20 vision, excellent eye-hand coordination, quick reaction times, a strong desire to fly airplanes, self-confidence as well as ability to remain calm in stressful situations. They must be in excellent health.

Unions and Associations

For information on Helicopter Pilots, contact the Helicopter Association International. For a copy of the List of Certificated Pilot Schools, contact the Superintendent of Documents.

PILOT AND FLIGHT ENGINEER

CAREER PROFILE

Duties: Inspect aircraft; plan and monitor passengers, cargo, and fueling; assist pilots in engine start-up and shut-down; compute aircraft load weights and fuel distribution; compute fuel consumption; monitor engine instruments; adjust engine controls; check fuel, pressure, electrical, and other aircraft systems; inform pilot of aircraft performance problems and recommend corrective action; navigate and fly aircraft, through takeoff, flight, and landing

Alternate Title(s): Copilot

Availability: Navy, Air Force, Marine Corps, Coast Guard

Military Salary: See How to Use This Book

Civilian Salary: $24,290 to $145,000

Civilian Employment Prospects: Fair

Civilian Advancement Prospects: Fair

Prerequisites:

 Rank—Enlisted

 Education and Training—Four-year college degree

 Experience—Any training and work experience obtained in the armed services

 Special Skills and Personality Traits—Ability to make quick decisions and accurate judgments under pressure; mental alertness; physical strength; skill in using wiring diagrams and maintenance manuals; interest in working with mechanical systems and equipment; a strong desire to fly; the ability to work as a member of a team

CAREER LADDER

Captain

First Officer

Flight Engineer

Position Description

Those who control the skies often dictate victory in modern warfare. Our armed forces maintain thousands of jets, planes, and helicopters at all times. Pilots and aircrew members must depend upon trained personnel to keep their aircraft ready to fly at any time of the day or night. Flight Engineers live and work on air bases or aboard ships in all climates and types of weather. There they inspect airplanes and helicopters before, during, and after flights to ensure safe and efficient operations. They also serve as crew members aboard military aircraft; plan and monitor the loading of passengers, cargo, and fuel; assist pilots in engine start-up and shut-down, and compute air-

craft load weights and fuel distribution. They also compute fuel consumption using airspeed data, charts, and calculators, monitor engine instruments and adjust engine controls following pilot orders, check fuel, pressure, electrical, and other aircraft systems during flight and inform pilots of aircraft performance problems and recommend corrective action.

In the civilian world, pilots fly airplanes and helicopters to carry out a wide variety of tasks such as transporting passengers and cargo, dusting crops, spreading seed for reforestation, testing aircraft, directing fire-fighting efforts, tracking criminals, monitoring traffic, and rescuing and evacuating injured persons.

Although some small planes require only one pilot and some older models will carry three, the standard number of pilots for most flights made today is two. Before leaving the ground pilots plan their flights carefully. They check their aircraft to make sure the engines, controls, instruments, and other systems are functioning properly and that baggage or cargo has been loaded correctly, and consult flight dispatchers and aviation weather forecasters regarding weather conditions en route and at their destination. Based on this information, they choose a route, altitude, and speed that will provide the fastest, safest, and smoothest flight.

Unlike most airplane flights, helicopters are used for short trips at relatively low altitude, so pilots must be constantly on the lookout for trees, bridges, power lines, transmission towers, and other dangerous obstacles. Regardless of the type of aircraft, all pilots must monitor warning devices designed to help detect sudden shifts in wind conditions that can cause crashes.

Airline pilots, with large support staffs at their disposal, perform few nonflying duties. Pilots employed by organizations such as charter operators or businesses may be required to load the aircraft, handle all passenger luggage to ensure a balanced load, supervise refueling, keep records, schedule flights, arrange for major maintenance, and even perform minor aircraft maintenance and repair work. Some military pilots become instructors. A few specially trained pilots work as "examiners" or "check pilots," periodically flying with other pilots or pilot's license applicants to make certain that they are proficient.

Airline pilots cannot fly more than 100 hours a month or more than 1,000 hours a year by law. Most fly roughly 75 hours a month, working 75 more hours a month performing nonflying duties. Airlines operate flights at all hours of the day and night, and so work schedules are irregular, with assignments based on seniority.

Nonairline pilots have irregular schedules as well; sometimes flying 30 hours one month, 90 the next. Except for business pilots, most do not remain away from home overnight. They may work odd hours. Flight instructors may have irregular and seasonal work schedules, depending on their students' available time and the weather. Instructors frequently work at night or on weekends.

The work of test pilots, who check the flight performance of new and experimental planes, may be dangerous. Pilots who are crop dusters may be exposed to toxic chemicals and seldom have the benefit of a regular landing strip. Helicopter pilots involved in police work may be subject to personal injury. Although flying does not involve much physical effort, it can be quite stressful. Pilots must be alert and quick to react if something goes wrong, particularly during takeoff and landing.

Civilian Salaries

In 2000, the average yearly salary for airline Pilots, copilots, and Flight Engineers was $110,940. The lowest 10 percent earned less than $36,110. More than 25 percent earned more than $145,000. In 2000, the average yearly salary for commercial Pilots was $43,300. The middle 50 percent earned between $31,500 and $61,230. The lowest 10 percent earned less than $24,290. The highest 10 percent earned more than $92,000.

Civilian Employment Prospects

In 2000, civilian aircraft Pilots and Flight Engineers held just under 118,000 jobs. Nearly 85 percent worked as airline Pilots, copilots, and Flight Engineers. The remainder were commercial pilots who worked as flight instructors. Some flew small planes for air taxi companies. Others performed tasks such as crop dusting, inspecting pipelines, or conducting sight-seeing trips. Opportunities for Pilots are more concentrated in California, New York, Illinois, Washington, Michigan, Georgia, New Jersey, Florida, the District of Columbia, and Texas, locations which have a high amount of flying activity relative to their population.

Through 2010 Pilots are expected to face strong competition for jobs, even though employment is expected to increase about as fast as the average for all occupations. Expected growth in domestic and international airline passenger and cargo traffic will create a need for more airliners, Pilots, and flight instructors. Computerized flight management systems on new aircraft will continue to take over human responsibilities, reducing the need for extra Pilots on flights. Also, the new larger planes will increase Pilot productivity. And, future business travel could also be affected by the growing use of teleconferencing, facsimile mail, and electronic communications. Companies are also opting to use regional and smaller airlines serving their area rather than maintaining their own aircraft.

Pilots who have logged the greatest number of flying hours on the more sophisticated equipment typically have the best prospects. For this reason, military Pilots often have an advantage over other applicants. Those with the most FAA licenses also have a competitive advantage.

Civilian Advancement Prospects

Many Pilots start as flight instructors, building up their flying hours while they earn money teaching. These Pilots occasionally fly charter planes or perhaps get jobs with small air transportation firms. Some advance to flying jobs for businesses. A small number get Flight Engineer jobs with the airlines.

After one to five years Flight Engineers in the airlines advance according to seniority to first officer and, after five to 15 years, to captain. In a nonairline job, a first officer may advance to Pilot and, in large companies, to chief Pilot or director of aviation in charge of aircraft scheduling, maintenance, and flight procedures.

Education and Training

In the military, those interested in this career receive five-and-a-half to eight months of classroom instruction, depending on specialty. Classes usually contain courses such as operation of electronic, pressure, and fuel systems, inspection of aircraft engines, structures, and systems, operation of aircraft engine instrument controls, and preparation of aircraft performance records and logs. Further training occurs on the job during flight operations.

The armed forces have always been an important source of trained Pilots for civilian jobs. Military pilots gain valuable experience on jet aircraft and helicopters. Persons with this experience usually are preferred for civilian pilot jobs.

Initial training for airline pilots includes a week of company indoctrination, three to six weeks of ground school and simulator training, and 25 hours of initial operating experience, including a check-ride with an FAA aviation safety inspector. Once trained and "on the line," Pilots are required to attend recurrent training and simulator checks twice a year throughout their career.

Special Requirements

Outside the military, all Pilots who are paid to transport passengers or cargo must have a commercial pilot's license with an instrument rating issued by the FAA. Helicopter Pilots must hold a commercial pilot's certificate with a helicopter rating. To qualify for these licenses, applicants must be at least 18 years old and have at least 250 hours of flight experience. The experience required can be reduced through participation in certain flight school curricula approved by the FAA. Applicants also must pass a strict physical examination to make sure that they are in good health and have 20/20 vision with or without glasses, good hearing, and no physical handicaps that could impair their performance. They must pass a written test that includes questions on the principles of safe flight, navigation techniques, and FAA

regulations and must demonstrate their flying ability to FAA or designated examiners.

Airline pilots must have an airline transport Pilot's license. Applicants for this license must be at least 23 years old and have a minimum of 1,500 hours of flying experience, including night and instrument flying, and must pass FAA written and flight examinations. Usually, they also have one or more advanced ratings, such as multiengine aircraft or aircraft type ratings dependent upon the requirements of their particular flying jobs.

Experience, Special Skills, and Personality Traits

Flight Engineers must be able to make quick decisions and accurate judgments under pressure. They have to be mentally alert and physically sound, skilled in using wiring diagrams and maintenance manuals, interested in working with mechanical systems and equipment, have a strong desire to fly, and the ability to work as a member of a team.

Unions and Associations

For information about job opportunities in companies other than airlines, consult the classified section of aviation trade magazines and apply to companies that operate aircraft at local airports. For information about job opportunities, salaries for a particular airline, or qualifications requirements, contact the personnel manager of that particular airline. For information on airline pilots, contact the Airline Pilots Association and the Air Transport Association of America, Inc. For information on helicopter pilots, contact the Helicopter Association International. For a copy of the List of Certificated Pilot Schools, contact the Superintendent of Documents at the U.S. Government Printing Office, Washington, D.C. 20402.

MARINE ENGINE MECHANIC

CAREER PROFILE

Duties: Repair and maintain shipboard engines; locate and repair machinery parts and ship propulsion machinery; repair and service hoisting machinery and ship elevators; repair refrigeration and air conditioning equipment on ships; repair engine-related electrical systems

Alternate Title(s): Motorboat Mechanic; Motorcycle Mechanic; Outdoor Power Equipment and Other Small Engine Mechanic

Availability: All branches

Military Salary: See How to Use This Book

Civilian Salary: $18,930 to $41,490

Civilian Employment Prospects: Fair

Civilian Advancement Prospects: Fair

Prerequisites:

Rank—Enlisted

Education and Training—High school diploma

Experience—Any training and work experience obtained in the armed services or Job Corps

Special Skills and Personality Traits—Knowledge of basic electronics; an interest in fixing engines and machinery; the ability to use hand and power tools; a preference for doing physical work; normal color vision

CAREER LADDER

Mechanic

Shop Supervisor or Service Manager

Sales Representative

Position Description

The modern military uses a wide variety of water-going vessels, from small motor launches to massive aircraft carriers. Many of these watercraft are powered by gasoline or diesel engines. Marine Engine Mechanics usually work aboard ships, normally in the engine or power rooms, or sometimes in land-based repair centers to repair and maintain gasoline and diesel engines on ships, boats, and other watercraft. They also tend to shipboard mechanical and electrical equipment, locate and repair machinery parts, including valves and piping systems and ship propulsion machinery. They also fix and service hoisting machinery and ship elevators, refrigeration and air-conditioning equipment and systems, and engine-related electrical systems.

In the civilian world, Marine Engine Mechanics work in marine transportation, commercial fishing, and oil explo-

ration and drilling. They can even move into small engine repair, since smaller engines, ranging from racing motorcycles to chain saws to outdoor power equipment, share many characteristics with their larger counterparts.

All engines require periodic service to minimize the chance of breakdowns and to keep them operating at peak performance. During routine maintenance Mechanics follow an inspection and cleaning checklist. Afterward they replace, repair, or adjust parts that are not working properly. The mark of a skilled Mechanic is the ability to diagnose mechanical, fuel, and electrical problems, and to make repairs in a minimal amount of time. Some shops use special computerized diagnostic testing equipment that provides a systematic performance report of various components.

Motorcycle Mechanics repair and overhaul motorcycles, motor scooters, mopeds, dirt bikes, and all-terrain vehicles.

They work on engines, transmissions, brakes, and ignition systems, and make minor body repairs. Motorboat Mechanics repair and adjust the electrical and mechanical equipment of inboard and outboard boat engines. They may also work on propellers, steering mechanisms, marine plumbing, etc. Outdoor power equipment and other small engine Mechanics service and repair lawnmowers, garden tractors, edge trimmers, chain saws, portable generators, etc.

Small engine Mechanics usually work in repair shops that are well-lighted and ventilated. Motorboat Mechanics may work outdoors at docks or marinas, as well as in all weather conditions when making repairs aboard boats. They may work in cramped or awkward positions to reach a boat's engine.

Much small engine repair work is seasonal—spring brings in the lawnmowers, motorboats, and motorcycles; winter the snowmobiles and snowblowers, etc. Small engine Mechanics need to know the seasons where they set up shop and plan accordingly if they are to maintain a normal 40-hour week.

Civilian Salaries

In 2000, the average yearly salary for motorboat Mechanics was $26,660. The middle 50 percent earned between $20,760 and $33,680. The lowest 10 percent earned less than $17,320. The highest 10 percent earned more than $41,490. The same year the average yearly salary for motorboat Mechanics in boat dealerships, the industry employing the largest numbers of motorboat Mechanics, was $26,350.

In 2000, the average yearly salary for motorcycle Mechanics was $25,100. The middle 50 percent earned between $19,660 and $32,490. The lowest 10 percent earned less than $15,980. The highest 10 percent earned more than $41,180. Also, in 2000, the average yearly salary for motorcycle Mechanics in motorcycle dealerships, the industry employing the largest numbers of motorcycle Mechanics, was $25,650.

For outdoor power equipment and other small engine Mechanics the average yearly salary in 2000 was $23,780. The middle 50 percent earned between $18,930 and $29,370. The lowest 10 percent earned less than $14,830. The highest 10 percent earned more than $35,250.

Civilian Employment Prospects

In 2000, small engine Mechanics held nearly 73,000 jobs. Motorcycle Mechanics held roughly 14,000 jobs; motorboat Mechanics just under 25,000; and outdoor power equipment and other small engine Mechanics held almost 33,000. About one-third worked for retail hardware and garden stores, or retail dealers of motorboats, motorcycles, and miscellaneous vehicles. Nearly 25 percent of all small engine Mechanics were self-employed.

Through 2010, opportunities for small engine Mechanics are expected to grow slower than the average for all occupations. Opportunities will be better for those who complete Mechanic training programs. On the other hand, opportunities for motorcycle Mechanics should increase slowly as the popularity of motorcycles rebounds.

Civilian Advancement Prospects

The skills used as a small engine Mechanic generally transfer to other occupations such as automobile, diesel, or heavy vehicle and mobile equipment Mechanics. Experienced Mechanics with leadership ability may advance to shop supervisor or service manager jobs. Mechanics with sales ability sometimes become sales representatives or open their own repair shops.

Education and Training

In the military, those interested in this career receive two to six months of classroom instruction, depending on specialty. Classes, including practice in marine engine maintenance and repair, usually consist of courses such as internal combustion engine theory, repair of shipboard electronic and electrical machinery systems, service and repair of fuel injection systems and the use and care of hand and power tools. Further training occurs on the job and through advanced courses. The Army offers a certified apprenticeship program for one specialty in this occupation.

Most employers prefer to hire graduates from formal training programs for small engine Mechanics. Because the number of these specialized postsecondary programs is limited, most Mechanics learn their skills on the job or while working in related occupations. For trainee jobs, employers hire persons with Mechanical aptitude who are knowledgeable about the fundamentals of small two- and four-stroke engines. Trainees learn routine service tasks under the guidance of experienced Mechanics. As trainees gain experience and proficiency, they progress to more difficult tasks. Such on-the-job training can take up to three years to complete. Employers will also often send Mechanics and trainees to special training courses conducted by small engine manufacturers or distributors. These courses upgrade worker skills and are usually a prerequisite for the performing of warranty work for manufacturers or insurance companies.

Most employers prefer to hire high school graduates for trainee Mechanic positions, but will accept applicants with less education if they possess adequate reading, writing, and arithmetic skills.

Experience, Special Skills, and Personality Traits

Knowledge of basic electronics is essential for small engine Mechanics. Also essential are an interest in fixing engines and machinery, the ability to use hand and power tools, a preference for doing physical work, and normal color vision.

NOTE: The most important physical possessions of Mechanics are their hand tools. Mechanics usually provide their own tools and many experienced Mechanics have invested thousands of dollars in them. Employers typically furnish expensive power tools, computerized engine analyzers, and other diagnostic equipment, but Mechanics accumulate hand tools with experience.

Unions and Associations

For further information about work opportunities contact local motorcycle, motorboat, and lawn and garden equip-
ment dealers, boatyards, and marinas. Local offices of the state employment service may also have information about employment and training opportunities.

General information about motorboat Mechanic careers is available from the American Marine Institute, the American Watercraft Institute, and the Marine Mechanics Institute. General information about motorcycle Mechanic careers may be obtained from the American Motorcycle Institute and the Motorcycle Mechanics Institute.

APPENDIXES

APPENDIX I
ASSOCIATIONS, ORGANIZATIONS, AND SOURCES OF FURTHER INFORMATION

Listed here are the addresses and Web addresses of the various associations and organizations mentioned in this book. Contact them for more information about a specific job or industry. They are organized by the same subject areas by which the different jobs profiles are grouped. Web addresses often change, and if a particular association doesn't appear at the listed URL, try a search using the group name or related key words. Keep in mind that with the proper military background, one may qualify for positions in any number of industries. If you don't see an organization that suits your interests in this directory, search online. Chances are you'll find one in your field.

ADMINISTRATION AND MANAGEMENT

American Institute of Constructors
AIC Constructor Certification
    Commission
466 94th Avenue North
St. Petersburg, FL 33702
Phone: (727) 578-0317
Fax: (727) 578-9982
http://www.aicnet.org

American Bankers Association
1120 Connecticut Avenue NW
Washington, DC 20036
Phone: (800) BANKERS
http://www.aba.com

American Management Association
1601 Broadway
New York, NY 10019
Phone: (212) 586-8100
Fax: (212) 903-8168
http://www.amanet.org

American Purchasing Society
430 W. Downer Place
Aurora, IL 60506
http://www.american-purchasing.com

Association for Financial Professionals
7315 Wisconsin Avenue
Suite 600 West
Bethesda, MD 20814
Phone: (301) 907-2862
Fax: (301) 907-2864
http://www.afponline.org

Association for Government Accountants
2208 Mount Vernon Avenue
Alexandria, VA 22301-1314
Phone: (703) 684-6931
Fax: (703) 548-9367
http://www.agacgfm.org

Association for Investment Management and Research
P.O. Box 3668
Charlottesville, VA 22903
Phone: (434) 951-5499 or (800) 247-8132
Fax: (434) 951-5262
http://www.aimr.org

The Association of Management Consulting Firms
3580 Lexington Avenue
Suite 1700
New York, NY 10168
Phone: (212) 551-7887
Fax: (212) 551-7934
http://www.amcf.org

Communications Workers of America
501 3rd Street NW
Washington, DC 20001
Phone: (202) 434-1100
Fax: (202) 434-1279
http://www.cwa-union.org

The Council of State Governments
2760 Research Park Drive
P.O. Box 11910
Lexington, KY 40578-1910
Phone: (859) 244-8000
Fax: (859) 244-8001
http://www.statesnews.org

Federal Acquisition Institute (MVI)
Office of Acquisition Policy
General Services Administration
1800 F Street NW, Room 4017
Washington, DC 20405
http://www.gsa.gov/staff/v/training.htm

Financial Executives Institute
10 Madison Avenue
P.O. Box 1938
Morristown, NJ 07962-1938
Phone: (973) 898-4600
Fax: (973) 898-4649
http://www.fei.org

Financial Management Association International
University of South Florida
College of Business Administration
Tampa, FL 33620-5500
Phone: (813) 974-2084
Fax: (813) 974-3318
http://www.fma.org

The Institute of Management Consultants
2025 M Street NW
Suite 800
Washington DC 20036
Phone: (202) 367-1134 or (800) 221-2557
Fax: (202) 369-2134
http://www.imcusa.org

International Brotherhood of Electrical Workers
Telecommunication Department
1125 15th Street NW
Washington, DC 20005

Phone: (202) 833-7000
Fax: (202) 728-7664
http://www.ibew.org/telecommunications.
  htm

**International City Management
  Association (ICMA)**
777 North Capital NE
Suite 500
Washington, DC 20002
Phone: (202) 289-4262
Fax: (202) 962-3500
http://www.icma.org

**The International Council on Hotel,
  Restaurant, and Institutional
  Education**
2613 North Parham Road
2nd Floor
Richmond, VA 23294
Phone: (804) 346-4800
Fax: (804) 346-5009
http://www.chrie.org

**International Personnel Management
  Association**
1617 Duke Street
Alexandria, VA 22314
Phone: (703) 549-7100
Fax: (703) 684-0948
http://www.ipma-hr.org

National Association of Counties
440 First Street NW
Suite 800
Washington, DC 20001
Phone: (202) 393-6226
Fax: (202) 393-2630
http://www.naco.org

**National Association of Credit
  Management**
Credit Research Foundation
8840 Columbia 100 Parkway
Columbia, MD 21045-2158
Phone: (410) 740-5560
Fax: (410) 740-5574
http://www.nacm.org

**National Association of Purchasing
  Management**
P.O. Box 22160
Tempe, AZ 85285-2169
Phone: (480) 752-6276
  or (800) 888-6276
Fax: (480) 752-7890
http://www.napm.org

**National Association of Schools of
  Public Affairs and Administration**
1120 G Street NW
Suite 730
Washington, DC 20005
Phone: (202) 628-8965
Fax: (202) 626-4978
http://www.naspaa.org

**National Association of State Personnel
  Executives**
2760 Research Park Drive
P.O. Box 11910
Lexington, KY 40578-1910
Phone: (859) 244-8182
Fax: (859) 244-8015
http://www.naspe.net

**National Institute of Governmental
  Purchasing, Inc.**
151 Spring Street
Herndon, VA 20170
Phone: (703) 736-8900
  or (800) FOR-NIPG
Fax: (703) 736-9644
http://www.nigp.org

National League of Cities
1301 Pennsylvania Avenue NW
Washington, DC 20004
Phone: (202) 626-3000
http://www.nlc.org

National Management Association
2210 Arbor Boulevard
Dayton, OH 45439
Phone: (937) 294-0421
http://www.nmal.org

**National Restaurant Association
  Education Foundation**
175 West Jackson Boulevard
Suite 1500
Chicago, IL 60604-2702
Phone: (312) 715-1010 or (800) 765-2122
http://www.nraef.org

United States Telecom Association
1401 H Street NW
Suite 600
Washington, DC 20005-2164
Phone: (202) 326-7300
Fax: (202) 326-7333
http://www.usta.org

COMBAT

Army Public Affairs Center
8607 6th ACR Road
Fort Meade, MD 20755-5650

Phone: (301) 677-7272
Fax: (301) 677-7280
http://www.dtic.mil/armylink/apac/
  welcome.htm

Center of Military History
Fort Lesley J. McNair
103 Third Avenue
Washington, DC 20319-5058
http://www.army.mil/cmh-pg

CONSTRUCTION AND MACHINE OPERATIONS

American Water Works Association
6666 West Quincy Avenue
Denver, CO 80235
Phone: (303) 794-7711
Fax: (303) 794-3951
http://www.awwa.org

American Welding Society
550 NW Lejeune Road
Miami, FL 33126-5699
Phone: (305) 443-9353 or (800) 443-9353
http://www.aws.org

Associated Builders and Contractors
1300 N 17th Street
Suite 800
Arlington, VA 22209
Phone: (703) 812-2000
http://www.abc.org

**Associated General Contractors
  of America**
333 John Carlyle Street
Suite 200
Alexandria, VA 22314
Phone: (703) 548-3118
Fax: (703) 548-3119
http://www.agc.org

Association of Boards of Certification
208 Fifth Street
Ames, IA 50010-6259
Phone: (515) 232-3623
Fax: (515) 232-3778
http://www.abccert.org

**Bindery Industries Association,
  International**
70 East Lake Street, #300
Chicago, IL 60601
Phone: (312) 372-7606
Fax: (312) 704-5025
http://www.bindingindustries.org

Brick Industry Association
11490 Commerce Park Drive
Reston, VA 22091-1525
Phone: (703) 620-0010
Fax: (703) 620-3928
http://www.brickinfo.org

Graphic Arts Technical Foundation
200 Deer Run Road
Sewickley, PA 15143
Phone: (412) 741-6860
Fax: (412) 741-2311
http://www.gain.org/servlet/gateway/

Graphic Communications Council
1899 Preston White Drive
Reston, VA 20191
Phone: (703) 264-7200
Fax: (703) 620-0994
http://www.npes.org/edcouncil/index.html

**Graphic Communications
International Union**
1900 L Street NW
Washington, DC 20036
Phone: (202) 462-1400
Fax: (202) 721-0600
http://www.gciu.org

**International Brotherhood
of Electrical Workers**
1125 15th Street NW
Washington, DC 20005
Phone: (202) 833-7002
Fax: (202) 728-7664
http://www.ibew.org

International Masonry Institute
Apprenticeship and Training
837 Buena Vista Avenue
Cascade, MD 21719
Phone: (301) 241-5505 or (800) 562-7464
Fax: (301) 241-3571
http://www.imiweb.org/apprenticeship_
    and_training/training.htm

**International Union of Bricklayers
and Allied Craftsworkers**
1776 I Street NW
Washington, DC 20006
Phone: (202) 783-3788
http://www.bacweb.org

**International Union of Operating
Engineers**
1125 17th Street NW
Washington, DC 20036
Phone: (202) 429-9100
http://www.iuoe.org

National Association of Home Builders
1201 15th Street NW
Washington, DC 20005
Phone: (202) 266-8200 or (800) 368-5242
http://www.nahb.com

National Concrete Masonry Association
2302 Horse Pen Road
Herndon, VA 20171-3499
Phone: (703) 713-1900
Fax: (703) 713-1910
http://www.ncma.org

**National Terrazzo and Mosaic
Association**
101 E. Market Street
Suite 200 A
Leesburg, VA 20176-3122
http://www.ncma.org

**The National Tooling and Machining
Association**
9300 Livingston Road
Fort Washington, MD 20744
Phone: (301) 248-6200 or (800) 248-6862
Fax: (301) 248-7104
http://www.ntma.org

**Operative Plasterers' and Cement
Masons' International Association
of the United States and Canada**
14405 Laurel Place
Suite 300
Laurel, MD 20707
Phone: (301) 470-4200
Fax: (301) 470-2502
http://www.opcmia.org

**Photo Marketing Association
International**
3000 Picture Place
Jackson, MI 49201
Phone: (517) 788-8100
Fax: (517) 788-8371
http://www.pmai.org

Portland Cement Association
5420 Old Orchard Road
Skokie, IL 60077
Phone: (847) 966-6200
Fax: (847) 966-8389
http://www.portcement.org/index.asp

**The Precision Machined Products
Association**
6700 West Snowville Road
Brecksville, OH 44141

Phone: (440) 526-0300
Fax: (440) 526-5803
http://www.pmpa.org

Printing Industries of America
100 Daingerfield Road
Alexandria, VA 22314
Phone: (703) 519-8100
Fax: (703) 548-3227
http://www.gain.org/servlet/gateway/
    PIA_GATF/non_index.html

**United Brotherhood of Carpenters
and Joiners of America**
101 Constitution Avenue NW
Washington, DC 20001
http://www.ubcyes.com

Utility Workers Union of America
815 16th Street NW
Washington, DC 20006
http://www.uwua.org

Water Environment Federation
601 Wythe Street
Alexandria, VA 22314-1994
Phone: (800) 666-0206
Fax: (703) 684-2492
http://www.wef.org

ELECTRICAL AND
ELECTRONIC REPAIRS

**Accreditation Board for Engineering
and Technology, Inc.**
111 Market Place
Suite 1050
Baltimore, MD 21202-4012
Phone: (410) 347-7700
http://www.abet.org

**American Society for Engineering
Education**
1818 N Street NW
Suite 600
Washington, DC 20036-2479
Phone: (202) 331-3500
Fax: (202) 265-8504
http://www.asee.org

**American Watchmakers-Clockmakers
Institute (AWI)**
701 Enterprise Drive
Harrison, OH 45030-1696
http://www.awi-net.org

Associated Builders and Contractors
1300 N 17th Street
Rosslyn, VA 22209

Phone: (703) 812-2000
http://www.abc.org

Communications Workers of America
501 3rd Street NW
Washington, DC 20001
Phone: (202) 434-1100
Fax: (202) 434-1279
http://www.cwa-union.org

Computing Technology Industry
    Association
450 East 22nd Street
Suite 230
Lombard, IL 60148-6158
http://www.comptia.org

Electronics Technicians
    Association – International
5 Depot Street
Greencastle, IN 46135
Phone: (800) 288-3824
Fax: (765) 653-4287
http://www.eta-sda.com

Independent Electrical Contractors, Inc.
2010-A Eisenhower Avenue
Alexandria, VA 22314
Phone: (703) 549-7351
Fax: (703) 549-7448
http://www.ieci.org

Institute of Electrical
    and Electronics Engineers
445 Hoes Lane
Piscataway, NJ 08855-1331
Phone: (732) 981-0060
Fax: (732) 981-1721
http://www.ieee.org

Instrumentation, Systems,
    and Automation Society (ISA)
67 Alexander Drive
P.O. Box 12277
Research Triangle Park, NC 27709
Phone: (919) 549-8411
Fax: (919) 549-8288
http://www.isa.org

International Brotherhood
    of Electrical Workers (IBEW)
1125 15th Street NW
Washington, DC 20005
http://www.ibew.org

International Brotherhood
    of Electrical Workers
Telecommunications Department
1125 15th Street NW

Washington, DC 20005
Phone: (202) 833-7000
Fax: (202) 728-7664
http://www.ibew.org

International Society of Certified
    Electronics Technicians
3608 Pershing Avenue
Fort Worth, TX 76107
Phone: (817) 921-9101
Fax: (817) 921-3741
http://www.iscet.org

Junior Engineering Technical Society
    (JETS)-Guidance
1420 King Street
Suite 405
Alexandria, VA 22314-2794
Phone: (703) 548-5387
Fax: (703) 548-0769
http://www.jets.org

National Association of Photo
    Equipment Technicians (NAPET)
3000 Picture Place
Jackson, MI 49201

National Association of Professional
    Band Instrument Repair
    Technicians (NAPBIRT)
P.O. Box 51
Normal, IL 61761
Phone: (309) 452-4257
Fax: (309) 452-4825
http://www.napbirt.org

National Association of Radio and
    Telecommunications Engineers, Inc.
167 Village Street
Medway, MA 02053
Phone: (508) 533-8333
    or (800) 89-NARTE
Fax: (508) 533-3815
http://www.narte.org

National Council of Examiners
    for Engineers and Surveying
P.O. Box 1686
Clemson, SC 29633-1686
Phone: (864) 654-6824 or (800) 250-3196
Fax: (864) 654-6033
http://www.ncees.org

National Electrical Contractors
    Association (NECA)
3 Metro Center
Suite 1100
Bethesda, MD 20814

Phone: (301) 657-3110
Fax: (301) 215-4500
http://www.necanet.org

National Society of Professional
    Engineers
1420 King Street
Alexandria, VA 22314-2794
Phone: (703) 684-2800
http://www.nspe.org

Piano Technicians Guild
3930 Washington Street
Kansas City, MO 64111-2963
Phone: (816) 753-7747
Fax: (816) 531-0070
http://www.ptg.org

ENGINEERING, SCIENCE, AND TECHNICAL

American Academy of Forensic Sciences
P.O. Box 669
Colorado Springs, CO 80901
Phone: (800) 701-AAFS
Fax: (719) 636-1993
http://www.aafs.org

American Association of Geodetic
    Surveying (AAGS)
6 Montgomery Village Avenue
Suite 403
Gaithersburg, MD 20879
Phone: (240) 632-9716
Fax: (240) 632-1321
http://www.acsm.net

American Association of Petroleum
    Geologists
P.O. Box 979
Tulsa, OK 74101
Phone: (918) 584-2555
Fax: (918) 560-2665
http://www.aapg.org

American Astronautical Society
6352 Rolling Mill Place
Suite 102
Springfield, VA 22152-2354
Phone: (703) 866-0020
Fax: (703) 866-3526
E-mail: info@astronautical.org
http://www.astronautical.org/

American Board of Industrial Hygiene
6015 West St. Joseph
Suite 102
Lansing, MI 48917

Phone: (517) 321-2638
Fax: (517) 321-4624
http://www.abih.org

American Chemical Society
Education Division, Career Publications
1155 16th Street NW
Washington, DC 20036
Phone: (202) 872-4600 or (800) 227-5558
Fax: (202) 872-4615
http://www.acs.org

American Geological Institute
4220 King Street
Alexandria, VA 22302-1502
http://www.agiweb.org

American Geophysical Union
2000 Florida Avenue NW
Washington, DC 20009
Phone: (202) 777-7512
http://www.agu.org

**American Industrial Hygiene
    Association**
2700 Prosperity Avenue
Suite 250
Fairfax, VA 22031
Phone: (703) 849-8888
Fax: (703) 207-3561
http://www.aiha.org

**American Institute of Aeronautics
    and Astronautics**
1801 Alexander Bell Drive
Suite 500
Reston, VA 20191-4344
Phone: (703) 264-7500
    or (800) NEW-AIAA
Fax: (703) 264-7551
http://www.aiaa.org/

American Institute of Physics
Career Services Division and Education
    and Employment Division
One Physics Ellipse
College Park, MD 20740-3843
Phone: (301) 209-3100
Fax: (301) 209-0843
http://www.aip.org

American Meteorological Society
45 Beacon Street
Boston, MA 02108
Phone: (617) 227-2425
Fax: (617) 742-8718
http://www.ametsoc.org/AMS

American Nuclear Society
555 North Kensington Avenue
LaGrange Park, IL 60526
Phone: (708) 352-6611
Fax: (708) 352-0499
http://www.ans.org/contact/

American Physical Society
One Physics Ellipse
College Park, MD 20740-3844
Phone: (301) 209-3200
Fax: (301) 209-0865
http://www.aps.org

**American Society for Engineering
    Education**
ASEE Nuclear and Radiological
    Engineering Division
1818 N Street NW
Suite 600
Washington, DC 20036-2479
Phone: (202) 331-3500
Fax: (202) 265-8504
E-mail: membership@asee.org
http://www.uidaho.edu/~woodall/ASEE/

American Society of Civil Engineers
ASCE World Headquarters
1801 Alexander Bell Drive
Reston, VA 20191-4400
Phone: (703) 295-6300 or (800) 548-2723
http://www.asce.org/

**American Society of Mechanical
    Engineers**
ASME International
Three Park Avenue
New York, NY 10016-5990
Phone: (800) THE-ASME (U.S/Canada)
    or 95-800-843-2763 (Mexico)
    or 973-882-1167 (outside North
    America)
E-mail: infocentral@asme.org
http://www.asme.org/

American Society of Safety Engineers
1800 E. Oakton Street
Des Plaines, IL 60018
Phone: (847) 699-2929
Fax: (847) 768-3434
http://www.asse.org

**ASPRS: The Imaging and Geospatial
    Information Society**
5410 Grosvenor Lane
Suite 210
Bethesda, MD 20814-2160

Phone: (301) 493-0290
Fax: (301) 493-0290
http://www.asprs.org

**Association for Computing Machinery
    (ACM)**
1515 Broadway
New York, NY 10036
Phone: (212) 869-7440
Fax: (212) 944-1318
http://www.acm.org

Board of Certified Safety Professionals
208 Burwash Avenue
Savoy, IL 61874
Phone: (217) 359-9263
Fax: (217) 359-0055
http://www.bcsp.org

**Council on Certification of Health,
    Environmental, and Safety
    Technologists**
208 Burwash Avenue
Savoy, IL 61874
Phone: (217) 359-2686
Fax: (217) 359-0055
http://www.cchest.org

Geological Society of America
P.O. Box 9140
Boulder, CO 80301-9140
Phone: (303) 447-2020 or (888) 443-4472
Fax: (303) 357-1071
http://www.geosociety.org

**IEEE Computer Society, Headquarters
    Office**
1730 Massachusetts Avenue NW
Washington, DC 20036-1992
Phone: (202) 371-0101
Fax: (202) 728-9614
http://www.computer.org

**Institute for Certification of
    Computing Professionals (ICCP)**
2350 East Devon Avenue
Suite 115
Des Plaines, IL 60018
Phone: (847) 299-4227 or (800) 843-8227
Fax: (847) 299-4280
http://www.iccp.org

Marine Technology Society
1828 L Street NW
Suite 906
Washington, DC 20036
Phone: (410) 884-5330
Fax: (410) 884-9060
http://www.mtsociety.org

Materials Research Society (MRS)
506 Keystone Drive
Warrendale, PA 15086-7573
Phone: (724) 779-3003
Fax: (724) 779-8313
http://www.mrs.org

National Society of Professional Engineers
NSPE Headquarters
1420 King Street
Alexandria, VA 22314-2794
Phone: (703) 684-2800
Fax: (703) 836-4875
http://www.nspe.org/home.asp

National Society of Professional Surveyors
Suite 403
6 Montgomery Village Avenue
Gaithersburg, MD 20879
Phone: (240) 632-9716
Fax: (240) 632-1321
http://www.acsm.net/nsps/index.html

National Workforce Center for Emerging Technologies
3000 Landerholm Circle SE
Bellevue, WA 98007
Phone: (425) 564-4215
http://www.nwcet.org

Society of American Foresters
5400 Grosvenor Lane
Bethesda, MD 20814
Phone: (301) 897-8720
Fax: (301) 897-3690
http://www.safnet.org

Society of Exploration Geophysicists
8801 South Yale
Tulsa, OK 74137
Phone: (918) 497-5500
http://www.seg.org

Society of Women Engineers
120 Wall Street, Eleventh Floor
New York, NY 10005-3902
Phone: (212) 509-9577
Fax: (212) 509-0224
E-Mail: hq@swe.org
http://www.swe.org/

U.S. Department of Health and Human Services
Center for Disease Control and Prevention
National Institute of Occupational Safety and Health
Hubert H. Humphrey Building

200 Independence Avenue SW
Room 715H
Washington, DC 20201
Phone: (513) 533-8328 or (800) 35-NIOSH (800-356-4674)
Fax: (513) 533-8573 or (888) 232-3299
http://www.cdc.gov/niosh/homepage.html

U.S. Department of Labor, Occupational Safety, and Health Administration
200 Constitution Avenue NW
Washington, DC 20210
Phone: (800) 321-OSHA (6742) or (877) 889-5627 (TTY)
http://www.osha.gov

HEALTH CARE

Accrediting Commission on Education for Health Services Administration
730 11th Street NW
Washington, DC 20001-4510
Phone: (202) 638-5131
Fax: (202) 638-3429
http://www.acehsa.org

Alliance of Cardiovascular Professionals
4456 Corporation Lane
Suite 164
Virginia Beach, VA 23462
Phone: (757) 497-1225
Fax: (757) 497-0010
http://www.acp-online.org/index.html

American Academy of Audiology
8201 Greensboro Drive
Suite 300
McLean, VA 22102
Phone: (703) 790-8466 or (800) AAA-2336
Fax: (703) 790-8631
http://www.audiology.org

American Association of Bioanalysts
917 Locust Street
Suite 1100
St. Louis, MO 63101
Phone: (314) 241-1445
Fax: (314) 241-1449
http://www.aab.org

American Association of Blood Banks
8101 Glenbrook Road
Bethesda, MD 20814-2749
Phone: (301) 907-6977
Fax: (301) 907-6895
http://www.aabb.org

American Association of Colleges of Nursing
1 Dupont Circle NW
Suite 530
Washington, DC 20036
Phone: (202) 463-6930
Fax: (202) 785-8320
http://www.aacn.nche.edu

American Association of Colleges of Osteopathic Medicine
5550 Friendship Boulevard
Suite 310
Chevy Chase, MD 20815-7321
Phone: (301) 968-4100
Fax: (301) 968-4101
http://www.aacom.org

American Association of Colleges of Pharmacy
1426 Prince Street
Alexandria, VA 22314
Phone: (703) 739-2330
Fax: (703) 836-8982
http://www.aacp.org

American College of Health Care Administrators
325 S. Patrick Street
Alexandria, VA 22314
Phone: (703) 739-7900 or (888) 88-ACHCA
Fax: (703) 739-7901
http://www.achca.org

American College of Healthcare Executives
One North Franklin Street
Suite 1700
Chicago, IL 60606
Phone: (312) 424-2800
Fax: (312) 424-0023
http://www.ache.org

American Dental Association
Commission on Dental Accreditation
211 E Chicago Avenue
Chicago, IL 60611
Phone: (312) 440-2500
Fax: (312) 440-2800
http://www.ada.org

American Dental Education Association
1625 Massachusetts Avenue NW
Suite 600
Washington, DC 20036
Phone: (202) 667-9433
Fax: (202) 667-0642
http://www.adea.org

American Dietetic Association
216 West Jackson Boulevard
Suite 800
Chicago, IL 60606-6995
Phone: (312) 899-0040
http://www.eatright.org

**American Health Information
    Management Association**
233 N Michigan Avenue
Suite 2150
Chicago, IL 60601-5800
Phone: (312) 233-1100
Fax: (312) 233-1500
http://www.ahima.org

**American Medical Association,
    Department of Communications,
    and Public Relations**
515 N State Street
Chicago, IL 60610
Phone: 312-464-5000
http://www.ama-assn.org

American Medical Technologists
710 Higgins Road
Park Ridge, IL 60068
Phone: (847) 823-5169
Fax: (847) 823-0458
http://www.amt1.com

American Nurses Association
600 Maryland Avenue SW
Washington, DC 20024-2571
Phone: (800) 274-4ANA
http://www.nursingworld.org

**American Occupational Therapy
    Association**
4720 Montgomery Lane
P.O. Box 31220
Bethesda, MD 20824-1220
Phone: (301) 652-2682
Fax: (301) 652-7711
http://www.aota.org

American Optometric Association
Educational Services
243 North Lindbergh Boulevard
St. Louis, MO 63141-7881
Phone: (314) 991-4100
Fax: (314) 991-4101
http://www.aoanet.org

**American Osteopathic Association,
    Department of Public Relations**
142 East Ontario Street
Chicago, IL 60611

Phone: (312) 202-8000 or (800) 621-1773
Fax: (312) 202-8200
http://www.aoa-net.org

American Psychological Association
Research Office and Education in
    Psychology and Accreditation Offices
750 1st Street NE
Washington, DC 20002
Phone: (202) 336-5510 or (800)374-
    2721; (202) 336-6123 (TDD/TTY)
http://www.apa.org

**American Registry of Diagnostic
    Medical Sonographers**
600 Jefferson Plaza
Suite 360
Rockville, MD 20852-1150
Phone: (301) 738-8401 or (800) 541-9754
Fax: (301) 738-0312/0313
http://www.ardms.org

**American Registry of Radiologic
    Technologists**
1255 Northland Drive
St. Paul, MN 55120-1155
Phone: (651) 687-0048
http://www.arrt.org

**American Society for Clinical
    Laboratory Science**
7910 Woodmont Avenue
Suite 530
Bethesda, MD 20814
Phone: (301) 657-2768
Fax: (301) 657-2909
http://www.ascls.org

**American Society for Clinical
    Pathology, Board of Registry**
2100 West Harrison Street
Chicago, IL 60612
Phone: (312) 738-1336
http://www.ascp.org/bor

American Society of Echocardiography
4101 Lake Boone Trail
Suite 201
Raleigh, NC 27607
Phone: (919) 787-5181
Fax: (919) 787-4916
http://www.asecho.org

**American Society of Radiologic
    Technologists**
15000 Central Avenue SE
Albuquerque, NM 87123-3917
Phone: (505) 298-4500 or (800) 444-2778

Fax: (505) 298-5063
http://www.asrt.org/asrt.htm

**American Speech-Language-Hearing
    Association**
10801 Rockville Pike
Rockville, MD 20852
Phone: (800) 498-2071
    (Professionals/Students)
    or (800) 638-8255 (Public)
http://www.professional.asha.org

**Association of American Medical
    Colleges, Section for Student
    Services**
2450 N Street NW
Washington, DC 20037-1126
Phone: (202) 828-0400
Fax: (202) 828-1125
http://www.aamc.org

**Association of Schools and Colleges
    of Optometry**
6110 Executive Boulevard
Suite 510
Rockville, MD 20852
Phone: (301) 231-5944
Fax: (301) 770-1828
http://www.opted.org

**Association of State and Provincial
    Psychology Boards**
P.O. Box 241245
Montgomery, AL 36124-1245
Phone: (334) 832-4580
Fax: (334) 269-6379
http://www.asppb.org

Association of Surgical Technologists
7108-C South Alton Way
Englewood, CO 80112
Phone: (303) 694-9130
Fax: (303) 694-9169
http://www.ast.org

**Association of University Programs
    in Health Administration**
730 11th Street NW
Washington, DC 20001-4510
Phone: (202) 638-1448
Fax: (202) 638-3429
http://www.aupha.org

**Cardiovascular Credentialing
    International**
4456 Corporation Lane
Suite 110
Virginia Beach, VA 23462

Phone: (800) 326-0268
Fax: (757) 497-3491
http://www.cci-online.org

**Joint Review Committee on Education
in Cardiovascular Technology**
3525 Ellicott Mills Drive
Suite N
Ellicott City, MD 21043-4547
Phone: (410) 418-4800
Fax: (410) 418-4805
http://www.sicp.com/jrc-cvt

**Joint Review Committee on Education
in Radiologic Technology**
20 N Wacker Drive
Suite 600
Chicago, IL 60606-2901
Phone: (312) 704-5300
Fax: (312) 704-5304
http://www.jrcert.org

**Liaison Council on Certification
for the Surgical Technologist**
7790 East Arapahoe Road
Suite 240
Englewood, CO 80112-1274
Phone: (719) 328-0800
or (800) 707-0057
Fax: (719) 328-0801
http://www.lcc-st.org/index_ie.htm

**Medical Group Management
Association**
104 Inverness Terrace East
Englewood, CO 80112
Phone: (303) 799-1111
or (877) ASK-MGMA
Fax: (303) 643-4439
http://www.mgma.com

**National Association for Practical
Nurse Education and Service, Inc.**
1400 Spring Street
Suite 330
Silver Spring, MD 20910
Phone: (301) 588-2491
Fax: (301) 588-2839
http://www.napnes.org

**National Association of Boards
of Pharmacy**
700 Busse Highway
Park Ridge, IL 60068
Phone: (847) 698-6227
Fax: (847) 698-0124
http://www.nabp.net

**National Association of Chain Drug
Stores**
413 N Lee Street
P.O. Box 1417-D49
Alexandria, VA 22313-1480
Phone: (703) 549-3001
Fax: (703) 836-4869
http://www.nacds.org

**National Association of School
Psychologists**
4030 East West Highway
Suite 402
Bethesda, MD 20814
Phone: (301) 657-0270
Fax: (301) 657-0275
http://www.nasponline.org

**National Center for Competency
Testing**
7007 College Boulevard
Suite 250
Overland Park, KS 66211-2437
Phone: (800) 875-4404
Fax: (913) 498-1243
http://www.ncctinc.com

**National Credentialing Agency
for Laboratory Personnel**
P.O. Box 15945-289
Lenexa, KS 66285-5935
Phone: (913) 438-5110, ext. 647
Fax: (913) 599-5340
http://www.nca-info.org

**National Federation of Licensed
Practical Nurses, Inc.**
893 US Highway 70 West
Suite 202
Garner, NC 27529-2597
Phone: (919) 779-0046 or (800) 948-2511
Fax: (919) 779-5642
http://www.nflpn.org

National League for Nursing
61 Broadway
New York, NY 10006
Phone: (212) 363-5555 or (800) 669-1656
http://www.nln.org

**Professional Association of Health Care
Office Managers**
461 East Ten Mile Road
Pensacola, FL 32534-9712
Phone: (800) 451-9311
Fax: (850) 474-6352
http://www.pahcom.com

Society of Vascular Technology
4601 Presidents Drive
Suite 260
Lanham, MD 20706-4365
Phone: (301) 459-7550
Fax: (301) 459-5651
http://www.svtnet.org

HUMAN RESOURCES AND SERVICES

American Counseling Association
5999 Stevenson Avenue
Alexandria, VA 22304-3300
Phone: (800) 347-6647
Fax: (800) 473-2329
http://www.counseling.org

**American Society for Healthcare
Human Resources Administration**
One North Franklin, 31st Floor
Chicago, IL 60606
Phone: (312) 422-3725
Fax: (312) 422-4577
http://www.ashhra.org

**American Society for Training
and Development**
1640 King Street Box 1443
Alexandria, VA 22313
Phone: (703) 683-8100 or (800) 628-2783
Fax: (703) 683-1523
http://www.astd.org

Association of Social Work Boards
400 South Ridge Parkway
Suite B
Culpeper, VA 22701
Phone: (540) 829-6880 or (800) 225-6880
Fax: (540) 829-0142
http://www.aswb.org

**Center for Applied Research
in the Apostolate (CARA)**
Georgetown University
2300 Wisconsin Avenue NW
Suite 400
Washington, DC 20057
Phone: (202) 687-8080
Fax: (202) 687-8083
http://www.cara.georgetown.edu

**Commission on Rehabilitation
Counselor Certification**
1835 Rohlwing Road
Suite E
Rolling Meadows, IL 60008
Phone: (847) 394-2104
http://www.crccertification.com

**Council for Accreditation of
Counseling and Related
Educational Programs**
American Counseling Association
5999 Stevenson Avenue, 4th floor
Alexandria, VA 22304
Phone: (800) 347-6647 ext. 301
http://www.counseling.org/cacrep

Council on Social Work Education
1725 Duke Street
Suite 500
Alexandria, VA 22314-3457
Phone: (703) 683-8080
Fax: (703) 683-8099
http://www.cswe.org

**Hebrew Union College-Jewish Institute
of Religion**
One West 4th Street
New York, NY 10012
Phone: (212) 647-5300
Fax: (212) 388-1720
http://www.huc.edu

**Industrial Relations Research
Association**
University of Illinois, Urbana-Champaign
121 Labor Industrial Relations Building
504 E Armory Avenue
Champaign, IL 61820
Phone: (217) 333-0072
Fax: (217) 265-5130
http://www.irra.uiuc.edu/

**International Foundation of Employee
Benefit Plans**
18700 W Bluemound Road
P.O. Box 69
Brookfield, WI 53008-0069
Phone: (262) 786-6700
Fax: (262) 786-8670
http://www.ifebp.org

**Jewish Theological Seminary of
America**
3080 Broadway
New York, NY 10027
Phone: (212) 678-8000
Fax: (212) 678-8947
http://www.jtsa.edu

National Association of Social Workers
750 First Street NE
Suite 700
Washington, DC 20002-4241
Phone: (202) 408-8600
http://www.naswdc.org

**National Board for Certified
Counselors, Inc.**
3 Terrace Way
Suite D
Greensboro, NC 27403-3660
Phone: (336) 547-0607
Fax: (336) 547-0017
http://www.nbcc.org

Rabbinical Council of America
305 7th Avenue
New York, NY 10001
Phone: (212) 807-7888
Fax: (212) 727-8452
http://www.rabbis.org

Reconstructionist Rabbinical College
1299 Church Road
Wyncote, PA 19095
Phone: (215) 576-0800
Fax: (215) 576-6143
http://www.rrc.edu

**WorldatWork (formerly the American
Compensation Association)**
14040 Northsight Boulevard
Scottsdale, AZ 85260
Phone: (877) 951-9191
Fax: (480) 483-8352 or (866) 816-2962
http://www.worldatwork.org

LAW AND PROTECTIVE
SERVICES

American Bar Association
541 N Fairbanks Court
Chicago, IL 60611
Phone: (312) 988-5522
http://www.abanet.org

American Jail Association
2053 Day Road
Suite 100
Hagerstown, MD 21740
Phone: (301) 790-3930
Fax: (301) 790-2941
http://www.corrections.com/aja/
index.html

**International Association
of Firefighters**
1750 New York Avenue NW
Washington, DC 20006
Phone: (202) 737-8484
Fax: (202) 737-8418
http://www.iaff.org/

Law School Admission Council
P.O. Box 40
Newtown, PA 18940
Phone: (215) 968-1001
http://www.lsac.org

**National Association of Legal
Investigators**
6109 Meadowwood
Grand Blanc, MI 48439
Phone: (800) 266-6254
Fax: (810) 694-7109
http://www.nali.com/index.html

National Fire Academy
Degrees at a Distance Program
16825 South Seton Avenue
Emmitsburg, MD 21727
Phone: (301) 447-1000
Fax: (301) 447-1052
http://www.usfa.fema.gov/nfa/index.htm

U.S. Border Patrol
Chester A. Arthur Building
425 I Street NW
Washington DC 20536
http://www.ins.usdoj.gov/graphics/
workfor/careers/bpcareer/index.htm

**U.S. Bureau of Alcohol, Tobacco
and Firearms**
Personnel Division
650 Massachusetts Avenue NW
Room 4100
Washington, DC 20226
http://www.atf.treas.gov

U.S. Fire Administration
16825 South Seton Avenue
Emmitsburg, MD 21727
Phone: (301) 447-1000
Fax: (301) 447-1052
http://www.usfa.fema.gov

United States Marshals Service
Employment and Compensation Division,
Field Staffing Branch
600 Army Navy Drive
Arlington, VA 22202
http://www.usdoj.gov/marshals

U.S. Secret Service
Personnel Division
Suite 912
950 H Street NW
Washington, DC 20223
Phone: (202) 406-5800
http://www.secretservice.gov

MEDIA AND PUBLIC AFFAIRS

Accrediting Council on Education in Journalism and Mass Communications
University of Kansas School of Journalism
and Mass Communications
Stauffer-Flint Hall
Lawrence, KS 66045
Phone: (785) 864-3973
Fax: (785) 864-5225
http://www.ukans.edu/~acejmc

Actors Equity Association
165 West 46th Street
New York, NY 10036
Phone: (212) 869-8530
Fax: (212) 719-9815
http://www.actorsequity.org

American Federation of Television and Radio Artists-Screen Actors Guild
4340 East-West Hwy.
Suite 204
Bethesda, MD 20814-4411
http://www.aftra.org or
    http://www.sag.org

American Institute of Graphic Arts
164 Fifth Avenue
New York, NY 10010
Phone: (212) 807-1990
http://www.aiga.org

American Society for Interior Designers
608 Massachusetts Avenue NE
Washington, DC 20002-6006
Phone: (202) 546-3480
Fax: (202) 546-3240
http://www.asid.org

Association of Medical Illustrators
2965 Flowers Road South
Suite 105
Atlanta, GA 30341
http://www.medical-illustrators.org

Dow Jones Newspaper Fund, Inc.
P.O. Box 300
Princeton, NJ 08543-0300
http://www.dowjones.com

Foundation for Interior Design Education Research
146 Monroe Center NW
Suite 1318
Grand Rapids, MI 49503

Phone: (616) 458-0400
Fax: (616) 458-0460
http://www.fider.org

Industrial Designers Society of America
45195 Business Court
Suite 250
Dulles, VA 20166
Phone: (703) 707-6000
Fax: (703) 787-8501
http://www.idsa.org

International Interior Design Association
13-122 Merchandise Mart
Chicago, IL 60654
Phone: (312) 467-1950
Fax: (312) 467-0779
http://www.iida.org.

National Association of Broadcasters
1771 N Street NW
Washington, DC 20036
Phone: (202) 429-5300
Fax: (202) 429-4199
http://www.nab.org

National Association of Schools of Art and Design
11250 Roger Bacon Drive
Suite 21
Reston, VA 20190
http://www.arts-accredit.org/nasad/default.htm

National Association of Schools of Theater
11250 Roger Bacon Drive
Suite 21
Reston, VA 20190
Phone: (703) 437-0700
Fax: (703) 437-6312
http://www.arts-accredit.org/nast/default.htm

National Newspaper Association
P.O. Box 7540
Columbia, MO 65205-7540
Phone: (573) 882-5800
    or (800) 829-4NNA (4662)
Fax: (573) 884-5490
http://www.nna.org

Newspaper Association of America
1921 Gallows Road
Suite 600
Vienna, VA 22182

Phone: (703) 902-1600
Fax: (703) 917-0636
http://www.naa.org

Newspaper Guild, Research and Information Department
501 3rd Street NW
Suite 250
Washington, DC 20001
Phone: (202) 434-7177
Fax: (202) 434-1472
http://www.newsguild.org

Radio and Television News Directors Foundation
1600 K Street NW
Suite 700
Washington, DC 20006-2838
Phone: (202) 659-6510
Fax: (202) 223-4007
http://www.rtndf.org

Screen Actors Guild
5757 Wilshire Blvd.
Los Angeles, CA 90036-3600
Phone: (323) 954-1600
Fax: (323) 549-6603
http://www.sag.org

Society of American Florists
1601 Duke Street
Alexandria, VA 22314
Phone: (703) 836-8700 or (800) 336-4743
http://www.safnow.org

Society of Broadcast Engineers
9247 North Meridian Street
Suite 305
Indianapolis, IN 46260
Phone: (317) 846-9000
Fax: (317) 846-9120
http://www.sbe.org

Society of Motion Picture and Television Engineers (SMPTE)
595 West Hartsdale Avenue
White Plains, NY 10607
Phone: (914) 761-1100
Fax: (914) 761-3115
http://www.smpte.org

TRANSPORTATION AND VEHICLE MAINTENANCE

Accrediting Commission of Career Schools and Colleges of Technology
2101 Wilson Boulevard
Suite 302
Arlington, VA 22201

Phone: (703) 247-4212
Fax: (703) 247-4533
http://www.accsct.org

**AED Foundation (Associated
Equipment Dealers affiliate)**
615 W 22nd Street
Oak Brook, IL 60523
Phone: (630) 574-0650
or (800) 388-0650
Fax: (630) 574-0132
http://www.aednet.org/aed_foundation

Air Line Pilots Association
1625 Massachusetts Avenue NW
Washington, DC 20036
http://www.alpa.org

**Air Transport Association
of America, Inc.**
1301 Pennsylvania Avenue NW
Suite 1100
Washington, DC 20004
Phone: (202) 626-4000
http://www.airlines.org

American Marine Institute
3042 West International Speedway
Boulevard
Daytona Beach, FL 32124
Phone: (386) 255-0295
or (800) 874-0645
Fax: (386) 252-3523
http://www.amiwrench.com

American Motorcycle Institute
3042 West International Speedway
Boulevard
Daytona Beach, FL 32124
Phone: (386) 255-0295
or (800) 874-0645
Fax: (386) 252-3523
http://www.amiwrench.com

American Watercraft Institute
3042 West International Speedway
Boulevard
Daytona Beach, FL 32124
Phone: (386) 255-0295
or (800) 874-0645
Fax: (386) 252-3523
http://www.amiwrench.com

**Automotive Service Excellence,
National Institute for**
101 Blue Seal Drive SE
Suite 101
Leesburg, VA 20175
Phone: (877) ASE-TECH
http://www.asecert.org

**Automotive Youth Educational Systems
(AYES)**
2701 Troy Center Drive
Suite 450
Troy, MI 48084
Phone: (248) 273-1200 or (888) 664-0044
Fax: (248) 273-1201
http://www.ayes.org

Detroit Diesel
Personnel Director, MS B39
13400 West Outer Drive
Detroit, MI 48239
Phone: (313) 592-5990
Fax: (313) 592-5887
http://www.detroitdiesel.com

Equipment Maintenance Counsel
P.O. Box 1368
Glenwood Springs, CO 81602
Phone: (970) 384-0510
Fax: (970) 384-0512
http://www.equipment.org

Helicopter Association International
1635 Prince Street
Alexandria, VA 22314
Phone: (703) 683-4646
http://www.rotor.com

International Brotherhood of Teamsters
25 Louisiana Avenue NW
Washington D.C. 20001
Phone: (202) 624-6800
http://www.teamster.org/

**International Transport Workers'
Federation**
49-60 Borough Road
London SE1 1DS,
Great Britain
Phone: +44 (020) 7403 2733
Fax: +44 (020) 7357 7871
E-mail: mail@itf.org.uk
http://www.itf.org.uk/index.html

Marine Mechanics Institute
9751 Delegates Drive
Orlando, FL 32827
Phone: (407) 240-2422
or (800) 342-9253
Fax: (407) 240-1318
http://www.uticorp.com/techtraining

Motorcycle Mechanics Institute
2844 West Deer Valley Road
Phoenix, AZ 85027
Phone: (602) 869-9644
or (800) 582-7995
Fax: (602) 581-2871
http://www.uticorp.com/techtraining

**National Automobile Dealers
Association**
8400 Westpark Drive
McLean, VA 22102
Phone: (703) 821-7000 or (800) 252-6232
http://www.nada.org

**National Automotive Technicians
Education Foundation**
101 Blue Seal Drive
Suite 101
Leesburg, VA 20175
Phone: (703) 669-6650
Fax: (703) 669-6125
http://www.natef.org

SkillsUSA-VICA
P.O. Box 3000
1401 James Monroe Highway
Leesburg, VA 20177-0300
Phone: (703) 777-8810
Fax: (703) 777-8999
http://www.skillsusa.org

**Specialized Carriers and Rigging
Association**
2750 Prosperity Avenue
Suite 620
Fairfax, VA 22031-4312
Phone: (703) 698-0291
Fax: (703) 698-0297
http://www.scranet.org

Superintendent of Documents
U.S. Government Printing Office
Washington, DC 20402
http://www.access.gpo.gov/su_docs/

APPENDIX II
COLLEGE AND UNIVERSITY
ROTC PROGRAMS

The following list provides contact information for schools that sponsor Reserve Officer Training Corps programs. Further information regarding ROTC may be available online. Contact information may change and updates can usually be found on a school's website.

(A; N; AF)—indicates which branch(es) of the service maintain an ROTC post on the campus of the school indicated. A=Army, N=Navy, and AF=Air Force.

(CE)—indicates a host school that offers a Crosstown Enrollment option which, typically, means a student attends regular classes at a different college or university in the area and attends ROTC classes once a week at the host college or university.

(PNE)—indicates a college or university that is a Partnership in Nursing Education school. According to the official U.S. Army ROTC website, the PNE program established "partnerships" with a number of nursing schools affiliated with Army ROTC to guarantee progression of qualified Army ROTC nurse cadets into the clinical nursing classes.

ALABAMA

Alabama A&M University (A)
Office of Admissions
Alabama A&M University
P.O. Box 908
Normal AL 35762
Phone: (205) 851-5775
http://www.aamu.edu/

Alabama State University (AF)
915 South Jackson Street
Montgomery, AL 36101-0271
Phone: (334) 229-4304
Fax: (334) 229-7485
http://www.alasu.edu/

Auburn University (A; N; AF)
Undergraduate Admissions Office
202 Mary Martin Hall
Auburn University
Auburn, AL 36849
Phone: (334) 844-4080 or (205) 844-4305
E-mail: admissions@mail.auburn.edu
http://www.auburn.edu/

Auburn University at Montgomery
    (A; AF)
P.O. Box 244023
Montgomery, AL 36124-4023
Phone: (334) 244-3000 or (205) 244-3528
    or (800) 227-2649
E-mail: chill@mickey.aum.edu
http://www.aum.edu/home

Jacksonville State University (A)
Office of Admissions
Jacksonville State University
700 Pelham Road North
Jacksonville, Alabama 36265-1602
Phone: (205) 782-5601
E-mail: info@jsucc.jsu.edu
http://www.jsu.edu

Marion Military Institute (A)
Admissions Office
1101 Washington Street
Marion, AL 36756
Phone: (334) 683-2306
    or (334) 683-2310
    or (800) MMI-1842
http://www.marion-institute.org/

Marion Military Institute
Professor of Military Science
P.O. Box 450
Marion, Alabama 36756
Phone: (800) MMI-ROTC
    or (334) 683-2332
Fax: (334) 683-2331
E-mail: mmi_rotc@zebra.net
http://www.marion-institute.org/rotc/

Samford University (AF)
800 Lakeshore Drive
Box 292247
Birmingham, AL 35202-0001
Phone: (205) 726-2859
Fax: (205) 726-2672

E-mail: afrotc@samford.edu
http://www.samford.edu/

Troy State University (AF)
Troy, Alabama 36082
Phone: (334) 670-3000
E-mail: admit@trojan.troyst.edu
    or afrotc17@trojan.troyst.edu
http://www.troyst.edu/

Tuskegee University (A; AF)
Tuskegee, AL 36088
Phone: (800) 622-6531
E-mail: Admissions@tusk.edu
http://www.tusk.edu/index.htm

University of Alabama (A)
Department of Military Science
610 Capstone Drive
Tuscaloosa, AL 35487-0260
Phone: (205) 348-1056
E-mail: bealua@knox-rotc.army.mil
    or afrotc@aalan.ua.edu
http://www.bama.ua.edu

**University of Alabama
    at Birmingham** (A)
Registrar
Hill University Center, Room 207
1400 University Boulevard
Birmingham, AL 35294-1150
Phone: (205) 934-8222
E-mail: registrar@uab.edu or
    Web.Center@vpuadv.uab.edu
http://www.students.uab.edu

University of North Alabama (A)
University of North Alabama Military
    Science Department (ROTC)
UNA Box 5024 Wesleyan Annex
Florence, AL 35632-0001
Phone: (800) TALK-UNA, x4271
Fax: (256) 765-4663
http://www2.una.edu/
http://www.unarotc.com/

University of South Alabama
    (A; AF) (CE)
USA Office of Admissions
182 Administration Building
Mobile, AL 36688-0002
Phone: (251) 460-6141
    or (800) 872-5247
Fax: (251) 460-7876
E-mail: admiss@usamail.usouthal.edu
http://www.southalabama.edu/

ALASKA

University of Alaska at Anchorage (AF)
2811 Merrill Field Drive
Anchorage, AK 99508
Phone: (907) 786-1800
E-mail: afjf@uaa.alaska.edu
http://www.uaa.alaska.edu/

University of Alaska at Fairbanks (A)
UAF Army ROTC
115 Patty Center Building
Fairbanks, AK 99775
Phone: (907) 474-7501
E-mail: rotc@uaf.edu
http://www.uaf.alaska.edu/ROTC/

ARIZONA

Arizona State University (A; AF)
Undergraduate Admissions
P.O. Box 870112
Tempe, AZ 85287-0112
Phone: (480) 965-7788;
    for ROTC (480) 965-3318
    or (800) 858-ROTC (ext. 7682)
E-mail: askasu@asu.edu
http://www.asu.edu/

Northern Arizona University (A)
Office of the Registrar
P.O. Box 4103
Flagstaff, AZ 86011-4103
Phone: (928) 523-2108
Fax: (928) 523-1414
E-mail: nau.registrar@nau.edu
http://www.nau.edu/web/index.shtml

University of Arizona (A; N; AF) (CE)
The University of Arizona
Tucson, AZ 85721
Phone: (520) 621-2211 for campus
    operator; (520) 621-3641 for
    admissions office
E-mail: appinfo@arizona.edu
http://www.arizona.edu/

ARKANSAS

Arkansas State University (A)
Office of Admissions
P.O. Box 1630
State University, AR 72467
Phone: 1-800-382-3030 or for ROTC:
    (501) 972-2064
http://www.astate.edu/

University of Arkansas (A; AF)
Fayetteville, AR 72701
Phone: (479) 575-2000
E-mail: uafadmis@uark.edu
http://www.uark.edu/

University of Arkansas—Pine Bluff (A)
University of Arkansas at Pine Bluff
1200 North University
Pine Bluff, AR 71601
Phone: (870) 575-8000; for ROTC (501)
    543-8448
http://www.uapb.edu/index.html

University of Central Arkansas (A)
201 Donaghey Avenue
Conway, AR 72035
Phone: (501) 450-5000 or (800) 243-
    8245; for ROTC (501) 450-3145
E-mail: admissions@mail.uca.edu
http://www.uca.edu/

CALIFORNIA

**California Polytechnic State
    University** (A)
1 Grand Avenue
San Luis Obispo, CA 93407
Phone: (805) 756-1111
http://www.calpoly.edu/

California State University at Fresno
    (A; AF) (CE)
5241 N Maple
Fresno, CA 93740-8027
Phone: (559) 278-2795
Fax: (559) 278-2436
http://www.csufresno.edu/

**California State University
    at Fullerton** (A)
800 N State College Boulevard
Fullerton, CA 92834-6850
Phone: (714) 278-201; Public Affairs
    Office (714) 278-2414
http://www.fullerton.edu

**California State University
    at Sacramento** (AF) (CE)
Public Service Building, Room 208
6000 J Street
Sacramento, CA 95819
Phone: (916) 278-7315
Fax: (916) 278-6777
E-mail: davisc@skymail.csus.edu
http://www.csus.edu/afrotc/index.html

**California State University
    at San Bernardino** (AF) (CE)
5500 University Parkway
San Bernardino, CA 92407
Phone: (909) 880-5000
E-mail: moreinfo@csusb.edu
http://www.csusb.edu/

Claremont-McKenna College (A) (CE)
Claremont, CA 91711-6400
Phone: (909) 621-8102
E-mail: vearl.dickson@
    claremontmckenna.edu
http://www.claremontmckenna.edu/

Loyola Marymount University (AF) (CE)
One LMU Drive
Los Angeles, CA 90045
Phone: (310) 338-2700 or (800) 568-4636
http://www.lmu.edu/pages/1.asp

Loyola Law School
Loyola Marymount University
919 S Albany Street
P.O. Box 15019
Los Angeles, CA 90015
Phone: (213) 736-1000
http://www.lmu.edu/pages/1.asp

San Diego State University
    (A; N: AF) (CE)
Bldg ENS 21, Room 451
5500 Campanile Drive
San Diego, CA 92182
Phone: (619) 594-4943
E-mail: armyrotc@mail.sdsu.edu;
    75afrotc@mail.sdsu.edu
http://www.sdsu.edu/

San Jose State University (AF) (CE)
One Washington Square
San Jose, CA 95192
Phone: (408) 924-1000
E-mail: info@soar.sjsu.edu
http://www.sjsu.edu/

Santa Clara University (A)
Undergraduate Admissions
500 El Camino Real
Santa Clara, CA 95053
Phone: (408) 554-4700
Fax: (408) 554-5255
http://www.scu.edu/SCU/Departments/
    ROTC/Army/

University of California at Berkeley
    (A; N; AF) (CE)
U.C. Berkeley Army ROTC
University of California Berkeley
171 Hearst Gym
Berkeley, CA 94720
Phone: (510) 643-7505
E-mail: armyrotc@uclink4.berkeley.edu;
    airforce@uclink4.berkeley.edu
http://www.berkeley.edu/

University of California at Davis (A)
Undergraduate Admissions
    and Outreach Services
178 Mrak Hall, One Shields Avenue
University of California
Davis, CA 95616-8507
Phone: (530) 752-3710
http://www.ucdavis.edu/index.shtml

University of California at Los Angeles
    (A; N; AF)
UCLA Undergraduates Admissions and
    Relations With Schools (UARS)
1147 Murphy Hall, Box 951436
Los Angeles, CA 90095-1436
Phone: (310) 825-3101; for campus tours
    (310) 825-8764
Fax: (310) 206-1206
E-mail: ugadm@saonet.ucla.edu
http://www.ucla.edu/

University of California at Santa
    Barbara (A) (PNE)
Santa Barbara, CA 93106
Phone: (805) 893-8000; for admissions
    (805) 893-2881
http://www.ucsb.edu/

UCSB Military Science
Bldg 451
Santa Barbara, CA 93106

Phone: (805) 893-2769
E-mail: milsci@mail.1sit.ucsb.edu
http://www.milsci.ucsb.edu/

University of San Diego (N) (CE)
5998 Alcalá Park
San Diego, CA 92110-2492
Phone: (619) 260-4600
http://www.sandiego.edu

University of Southern California
    (A; N: AF) (PNE)
Los Angeles, CA 90089
Phone: (213) 740-1111
http://www.usc.edu/

COLORADO

Colorado State University (A; AF) (CE)
Fort Collins, CO 80523
Phone: (970) 491-6909
http://www.colostate.edu/

University of Colorado—Boulder
    (A; N; AF) (CE)
Department of Military Science
University of Colorado at Boulder
370 UCB
Boulder, CO 80309-0370
Phone: (303) 492-1411
Fax: (303) 492-5560
http://www.colorado.edu

University of Colorado—Colorado
    Springs (A)
1420 Austin Bluffs Parkway
Colorado Springs, CO 80918
Phone: (719) 262-3000 or (800) 990-8227
Fax: (719) 262-3116
E-mail: admrec@mail.uccs.edu
http://www.uccs.edu/

CONNECTICUT

University of Connecticut (A; AF) (CE)
Storrs-Mansfield, CT 06269
Phone: (860) 486-2000
E-mail: beahusky@uconnvm.uconn.edu
http://www.uconn.edu/

DELAWARE

University of Delaware (A; AF) (CE)
Newark, DE 19716
Phone: (302) 831-2000
http://www.udel.edu/
http://www.udel.edu/armyrotc/

DISTRICT OF COLUMBIA

Georgetown University (A) (CE)
37th and O Streets NW
Washington, DC 20057
Phone: (202) 687-0100
http://www.georgetown.edu/

George Washington University (N) (CE)
2121 Eye Street NW
Washington, DC 20052
Phone: (202) 994-4949 or (800) 447-3765
Fax: (202) 994-0325
E-Mail: gwadm@gwu.edu
http://www.gwu.edu/

Howard University (A; AF) (CE)
2400 Sixth Street NW
Washington, DC 20059
Phone: (202) 806-6100
E-Mail: admission@howard.edu
http://www.howard.edu/

FLORIDA

Embrey-Riddle Aeronautical
    University (A; AF) (CE)
600 S. Clyde Morris Boulevard
Daytona Beach, FL 32114-3900
Phone: (386) 226-6000
    or (800) 222-3728; (386) 226-6100
    or (800) 862-2416 for admissions
E-mail: admit@db.erau.edu
http://www.embryriddle.edu/index.html

Florida A&M University (A; N) (PNE)
    (CE)
Wahnish Way and Gamble Street
Tallahassee, FL 32307
Phone: (850) 599-3796
E-mail: adm@famu.edu
http://www.famu.edu/famu.asp

Florida Institute of Technology (A)
150 W University Boulevard
Melbourne, FL 32901
Phone: (321) 674-8000
http://www.fit.edu

Florida International University (A)
University Park Campus
11200 SW 8th Street—PC140
Miami, FL 33199
Phone: (305) 348-2363
http://www.fiu.edu/choice.html
Office of Admissions
P.O. Box 659003
Miami, FL 33265-9003

Florida Southern College (A)
111 Lake Hollingsworth Drive
Lakeland, FL 33801
Phone: (863) 680-4111; (863) 680-4131
  or (800) 274-4131 for admissions
Fax: (863) 680-4120
E-mail: rotc@flsouthern.edu
http://www.flsouthern.edu/index.htm

Florida State University (A; AF) (PNE)
  (CE)
Tallahassee, FL 32306
Phone: (805) 644-2525
http://www.fsu.edu

Jacksonville University (N) (CE)
2800 University Boulevard North
Jacksonville, FL 32211
Phone: (904) 744-3950; (904) 745-7000
  or (800) 225-2027 for admissions
E-mail: admissions@ju.edu
http://www.ju.edu/

University of Central Florida (A; AF)
  (CE)
4000 Central Florida Boulevard
Orlando, FL 32816
Phone: (407) 823-2000
http://www.ucf.edu/

University of Florida (A; N; AF) (CE)
Gainesville, FL 32611
Phone: (352) 392-3261
http://www.ufl.edu/

University of Miami (AF) (CE)
Office of Admissions
P.O. Box 248025
Coral Gables, FL 33124
Phone: (305) 284-2211
E-mail: admission@miami.edu
http://www.miami.edu/UMH/CDA/
  UMH_Main/

University of South Florida (A; N; AF)
  (CE)
4202 E. Fowler Avenue
Tampa, FL 33620
Phone: (813) 974-2011; (813) 974-3350
  or (877) 873-2855 for admissions
http://www.usf.edu/

University of Tampa (A)
401 W Kennedy Boulevard
Tampa, Florida 33606-1490
Phone: (813) 253-3333
http://www.utampa.edu/

University of West Florida (A)
11000 University Parkway
Pensacola, FL 32514
Phone: (850) 474-2000
E-mail: armyrotc@uwf.edu
http://www.uwf.edu/uwfMain/

GEORGIA

Augusta State University (A)
Office of Admissions
2500 Walton Way
Augusta, GA 30904-2200
Phone: (800) 341-4373
E-mail: admissions@aug.edu
http://www.aug.edu/

Columbus State University (A)
4225 University Avenue
Columbus, GA 31907
Phone: (706) 568-2001 or (866) 264-2035
E-mail: academic_affairs@colstate.edu
http://www.colstate.edu/

Fort Valley State University (A)
Fort Valley, GA 31030
Phone: (912) 825-6307 or (800) 248-7343
E-mail: admissap@mail.fvsu.edu
http://www.FVSU.edu

Georgia Institute of Technology
  (A; N; AF) (CE)
225 North Avenue NW
Atlanta, GA 30332-0320
Phone: (404) 894-2000
Fax: (404) 894-9511
E-mail: admissions@success.gatech.edu
http://www.gatech.edu/

Georgia Military College (A) (CE)
201 East Greene Street
Milledgeville, GA 31061
Phone: (478) 445-2700 or (800) 342-0413
http://www.gmc.cc.ga.us

Georgia Southern University (A)
Admissions
GSU P.O. Box 8024, Building 805
Forest Drive
Statesboro, GA 30460
Phone: (912) 681-5391
Fax: (912) 486-7240
E-mail: admissions@gasou.edu
http://www.gasou.edu/

Georgia State University (A)
Undergraduate Admissions
P.O. Box 4009
Atlanta, GA 30302-4009

Phone: (404) 651-2365
http://www.gsu.edu/gsuhome-v1/
  enhanced.html

Morehouse College (N) (CE)
830 Westview Drive SW
Atlanta, GA 30314
Phone: (800) 851-1254
E-mail: webmaster@morehouse.edu
http://www.morehouse.edu/

North Georgia College and State
  University (A)
Dahlonega, GA 30597
Phone: (706) 864-1400
E-mail: admissions@ngcsu.edu
http://www.ngcsu.edu/

Savannah State University (N) (CE)
3219 College Street
Savannah, GA 31404
Phone: (912) 356-2186; (912) 356-2181
  for admissions
E-mail: admissions@savstate.edu
http://www.savstate.edu/

University of Georgia (A; AF) (CE)
Athens, GA 30602
Phone: (706) 542-3000
E-mail: undergrad@admissions.uga.edu
http://www.uga.edu/

Valdosta State University (AF) (CE)
1500 N Patterson Street
Valdosta, GA 31698
Phone: (229) 333-5791 or (800) 618-1878
Fax: (229) 333-5482
E-mail: admissions@valdosta.edu
http://www.valdosta.edu/

HAWAII

University of Hawaii at Hilo (A)
200 West Kawili Street
Hilo, HI 96720-4091
Phone: (808) 974-7414 or (808) 974-
  7414; (800) 897-4456
E-mail: uhhao@hawaii.edu
http://www.uhh.hawaii.edu/

University of Hawaii at Manoa (A; AF)
  (CE)
2600 Campus Road
Honolulu, HI 96822
Phone: (808) 956-8975 or (800) 823-9771
Fax: (808) 956-4148
E-mail: ar-info@hawaii.edu
http://www.uhm.hawaii.edu/

University of Hawaii—West Oahu (A)
96-043 Ala Ike
Pearl City, HI 96782
Phone: (808) 453-4700
Fax: (805) 453-6076
E-mail: jeano@uhwo.hawaii.edu
http://www.uhwo.hawaii.edu/

IDAHO

Boise State University (A)
Enrollment Services
1910 University Drive
Boise, ID 83725
Phone: (208) 426-1177
   or (800) 632-6586 (in-state);
   (800) 824-7017 (out-of-state)
E-mail: bsuinfo@boisestate.edu
http://www.boisestate.edu/

University of Idaho (A; N) (CE)
Undergraduate Admissions
P.O. Box 444264
Moscow, ID 83844-4264
Phone: (208) 885-6111
E-mail: info@uidaho.edu
http://www.uidaho.edu/

ILLINOIS

Eastern Illinois University (A)
600 Lincoln Avenue
Charleston, IL 61920-3099
Phone: (217) 581-2223 or (800) 252-5711
E-mail: admissns@www.eiu.edu
http://www.eiu.edu/

Illinois Institute of Technology (N; AF)
   (CE)
3300 South Federal Street
Chicago, IL 60616-3793
Phone: (312) 567-3000
E-mail: admission@iit.edu
http://www.iit.edu/

Illinois State University (A)
Department of Military Science
Normal, IL 61790-5160
Phone: (309) 438-5408
E-mail: arotc@ilstu.edu
http://www.cast.ilstu.edu/msc/home.htm

Northern Illinois University (A)
Office of Admissions
Northern Illinois University
DeKalb, IL 60115
Phone: (815) 753-1000 or (800) 892-3050
E-mail: admissions-info@niu.edu
http://www.niu.edu/index.html

Northwestern University (N) (CE)
633 Clark Street
Evanston, IL 60208
Phone: (847) 491-3741
E-mail: ug-admission@northwestern.edu
http://www.northwestern.edu/

Southern Illinois University—
   Carbondale (A; AF) (CE)
Carbondale, IL 62901-6899
Phone: (618) 453-2121
http://www.siu.edu/

Southern Illinois University—
   Edwardsville (A)
Edwardsville, IL 62026
Phone: (618) 650-2000
E-mail: admis@siue.edu
http://www.siue.edu/

University of Illinois Champaign—
   Urbana (A; N; AF) (CE)
Office of Admissions and Records
901 West Illinois Street
Urbana, IL 61801-3028
Phone: (217) 333-0302
E-mail: undergraduate@
   admissions.uiuc.edu
http://www.uiuc.edu/

University of Illinois—Chicago (A) (CE)
Office of Admissions and Records
University of Illinois at Chicago
Box 5220
Chicago, IL 60680-5220
Phone: (312) 996-4350
E-mail: uicadmit@uic.edu
http://www.uic.edu/index.html/

Western Illinois University (A)
1 University Circle
Macomb, IL 61455-1390
Phone: (309) 298-1414
E-mail: info@wiu.edu
http://www.wiu.edu/

Wheaton College (A) (CE)
501 College Avenue
Wheaton, IL 60187
Phone: (630) 752-5000
http://www.wheaton.edu/

INDIANA

Ball State University (A)
Muncie, IN 47306
Phone: (765) 289-1241
   or (800) 482-4BSU
http://www.bsu.edu/UP/cover.html

Indiana State University (AF) (CE)
200 North Seventh Street
Terre Haute, IN 47809-9989
Phone: (812) 237-2121
   or (800) GO-TO-ISU
   or (800) 742-0891
Fax: (812) 237-8023
E-mail: admissions@indstate.edu
http://www.web.indstate.edu/

Indiana University (A; AF) (CE)
107 S Indiana Avenue
Bloomington, IN 47405-7000
Phone: (812) 855-4848
E-mail: iuadmit@indiana.edu
http://www.indiana.edu/

Indiana University Purdue University
   Indianapolis (A) (CE)
425 University Boulevard
Indianapolis, IN 46202-5143
Phone: (317) 274 4591
Email: apply@iupui.edu
http://www.iupui.edu/index.html

Purdue University (A; N; AF) (PNE)
1080 Schleman Hall
West Lafayette, IN 47907-1080
Phone: (765) 494-1776
Fax: (765) 494-0544; (765) 496-1373
   (TDD)
E-mail: admissions@purdue.edu
http://www.purdue.edu/

Rose-Hulman Institute of Technology
   (A) (CE)
5500 Wabash Avenue
Terre Haute, IN 47803
Phone: (812) 877-1511 or (800) 248-7448
Fax: (812) 877-8941
E-mail: admis.ofc@rose-hulman.edu.
http://www.rose-hulman.edu/

University of Notre Dame (A; N; AF)
   (CE)
Notre Dame, IN 46556
Phone: (574) 631-5000
Fax: (574) 631-8865
E-mail: admissio.1@nd.edu
http://www.nd.edu/

IOWA

Iowa State University (N; AF) (CE)
Ames, IA 50011
Phone: (515) 294-4111
E-mail: admissions@iastate.edu
http://www.iastate.edu/

University of Iowa (AF) (CE)
Office of Admissions
107 Calvin Hall
Iowa City, IA 52242
Phone: (319) 335-3500
  or (800) 553-IOWA
http://www.uiowa.edu/

KANSAS

Kansas State University (A; AF) (CE)
Office of Admissions
119 Anderson Hall
Manhattan, KS 66506
Phone: (785) 532-6011
  or (800) 432-8270
Fax: (785) 532-6393
E-mail: kstate@k-state.edu
http://www.ksu.edu/

Pittsburg State University (A)
1701 S. Broadway
Pittsburg, KS 66762
Phone: (620) 231-7000
  or (800)-854-7488
Fax: (620) 235-6003
E-mail: psuadmit@pittstate.edu
http://www.pittstate.edu

University of Kansas (A; N; AF) (CE)
Lawrence, KS 66045
Phone: (785) 864-2700
E-mail: adm@ku.edu
http://www.ku.edu

KENTUCKY

Eastern Kentucky University (A)
521 Lancaster Avenue
Richmond, KY 40475
Phone: (859) 622-1000
E-mail: admissions@eku.edu
http://www.eku.edu

Morehead State University (A)
150 University Boulevard
Morehead, KY 40351
Phone: (800) 585-6781
E-mail: admissions@moreheadstate.edu
http://www.morehead-st.edu/

University of Kentucky (A; AF) (CE)
100 W.D. Funkhouser Building
Lexington, KY 40506
Phone: (859) 257-9000
E-mail: admissio@uky.edu
http://www.uky.edu

University of Louisville (A; AF) (CE)
Office of Admissions, Department AO
Houchens Building, Room 150
2211 S Brook Street
Louisville, KY 40208
Phone: (502) 852-6531 or (800) 334-8635
Fax: (502) 852-4776
http://www.louisville.edu/ns4/
  index_noflash.html

Western Kentucky University (A)
Office of Admissions
1 Big Red Way
Bowling Green, KY 42101-3576
Phone: (270) 745-2551
E-mail: Admission@wku.edu
http://www.wku.edu/

LOUISIANA

Grambling State University (A; AF)
  (CE)
Grambling, LA 71245
Phone: (800) 569-4714
Fax: (318) 274-3292
E-mail: admissions@alpha0.gram.edu
http://www.gram.edu/

Louisiana State University (A; AF) (CE)
Office of Undergraduate Admissions
110 Thomas Boyd Hall
Louisiana State University
Baton Rouge, LA 70803
Phone: (225) 578-1175
E-mail: admissions@lsu.edu
http://www.Isu.edu/index2.html

Louisiana Tech University (AF)
P.O. Box 3178
Ruston, LA 71272
Phone: (318) 257-3036 or (800)
  LATECH-1
E-mail: Bulldog@latech.edu
http://www.latech.edu/

Northwestern State University (A)
  (PNE) (CE)
Natchitoches, LA 71497
Phone: (800) 426-3754
http://www.vic/nsula.edu/

Southern University and A&M College
  (A; N) (CE)
Baton Rouge, LA 70813
Phone: (225) 771-4500 or (800) 256-1531
http://www.subr.edu/

Tulane University (A; N; AF) (CE)
Office of Undergraduate Admission
210 Gibson Hall
6823 St. Charles Avenue
New Orleans, LA 70118
Phone: (504) 865-5000
Fax: (504) 862-8715
E-mail: undergrad.admission@tulane.edu
http://www2.tulane.edu/main.cfm

MAINE

Maine Maritime Academy (N) (CE)
Castine, ME 04420
Phone: (207) 326-2206 or (800) 464-6565
  (Maine); (800) 227-8465 (out-of-state)
E-mail: admissions@mma.edu
http://www.supersloop.mma.edu/intranet/

University of Maine (A) (PNE) (CE)
Office of Admission
5713 Chadbourne Hall
Orono, ME 04469
Phone: (207) 581-1561 or (877) 486-2364
Fax: (207)581-1213
E-mail: um-admit@maine.edu
http://www.umaine.edu/

MARYLAND

Bowie State University (A)
14000 Jericho Park Road
Bowie, Maryland 20715-9465
Phone: (301) 860-4000
  or (877) 77-BOWIE
E-mail: admissions@bowiestate.edu
http://www.bowiestate.edu

The Johns Hopkins University (A)
3400 North Charles Street
Baltimore, MD 21218
Phone: (410) 516-8171
Fax: (410) 516-6025
E-mail: gotojhu@jhu.edu
http://www.jhu.edu/

Loyola College (A)
4501 North Charles Street
Baltimore, MD 21210-2699
Phone: (410) 617-2000
http://www.loyola.edu/

McDaniel College (A)
2 College Hill
Westminster, MD 21157-4390
Phone: (410) 848-7000 or (800) 638-5005
E-mail: admissio@mcdaniel.edu
http://www.wmdc.edu/

Morgan State University (A)
1700 East Cold Spring Lane
Baltimore, MD 21251
Phone: (443) 885-3333
E-mail: admissions@morgan.edu
http://www.morgan.edu/

University of Maryland (AF) (CE)
College Park, MD 20742
Phone: (301) 405-1000
http://www.umd.edu/

Western Maryland College (A)
see McDaniel College

MASSACHUSETTS

Boston University (A; N; AF) (CE)
121 Bay State Road
Boston, MA 02215
Phone: (617) 353-2300
E-mail: admissions@bu.edu
http://www.bu.edu/

College of the Holy Cross (N) (CE)
1 College Street
Worcester, MA 01610-2395
Phone: (508) 793-2011
E-mail: admissions@holycross.edu
http://www.holycross.edu/

Massachusetts Institute of Technology
    (A; N; AF) (CE)
77 Massachusetts Avenue
Cambridge, MA 02139-4307
Phone: (617) 253-1000
http://www.web.mit.edu/

Northeastern University (A) (CE)
360 Huntington Avenue
Boston, MA 02115
Phone: (617) 373-2000
http://www.northeastern.edu/

University of Massachusetts at
    Amherst (A; AF) (CE)
37 Mather Drive
Amherst, MA 01003-9291
Phone: (413) 545-0222
Fax: (413) 545-4312
http://www.umass.edu/

University of Massachusetts at Lowell
    (AF)
One University Avenue
Lowell, MA 01854
Phone: (978) 934-4000

E-mail: admissions@uml.edu
http://www.uml.edu/

Worcester Polytechnic Institute
    (A; AF) (CE)
Worcester Campus
100 Institute Road
Worcester, MA 01609-2280
Phone: (508) 831-5000
E-mail: admissions@wpi.edu
http://www.wpi.edu/

MICHIGAN

Central Michigan University (A)
Mount Pleasant, MI 48859
Phone: (989) 774-4000 or (888) 292-5366
Fax: (989) 774-7267
E-mail: cmuadmit@mail.cmich.edu
http://www.cmich.edu/default.asp

Eastern Michigan University (A) (CE)
Ypsilanti, MI 48197
Phone: (734) 487-1849
http://www.emich.edu/

Michigan State University (A; AF) (CE)
East Lansing, MI 48824
Phone: (517) 355-1855
E-mail: admis@msu.edu
http://www.msu.edu/home/

Michigan Technological University
    (A; AF) (CE)
1400 Townsend Drive
Houghton, MI 49931-1295
Phone: (906) 487-1885
    or (888) MTU-1885
E-mail: mtu4u@mtu.edu
http://www.mtu.edu/

Northern Michigan University (A)
1401 Presque Isle Avenue
Marquette, MI 49855
Phone: (800) 682-9797
E-mail: admiss@nmu.edu
http://www.nmu.edu/

University of Michigan (A; N; AF)
    (PNE) (CE)
Office of Undergraduate Admissions
1220 Student Activities Building
515 E Jefferson
Ann Arbor, MI 48109-1316
Phone: (734) 764-7433
Fax: (734) 936-0740
E-mail: ugadmiss@umich.edu
http://www.umich.edu/

Western Michigan University (A) (CE)
1903 W Michigan Avenue
Kalamazoo, MI 49008-5201
Phone: (269) 387-1000
E-mail: ask-wmu@wmich.edu
http://www.wmich.edu/

MINNESOTA

Minnesota State University at Mankato
    (A) (CE)
Mankato, MN 56001
Phone: (800) 722-0544
Fax: (507) 389-1511
http://www.mankato.msus.edu/

Saint John's University (A) (CE)
P.O. Box 7155
Collegeville, MN 56321
Phone: (320) 363-2196 or (800) 245-6467
Fax: (320) 363-3206
E-mail: admissions@csbsju.edu
http://www.csbsju.edu/

University of Minnesota (A; N; AF) (CE)
Office of Admissions
240 Williamson Hall
231 Pillsbury Drive SE
Minneapolis, MN 55455-0213
Phone: (612) 625-2008 or (800) 752-1000
Fax: (612) 626-1693
E-mail: admissions@tc.umn.edu
http://www1.umn.edu/

University of Minnesota at Duluth
    (AF) (CE)
1049 University Drive
Duluth, MN 55812
Phone: (218) 726-8000
E-mail: umdadmis@d.umn.edu
http://www.d.umn.edu/

University of Saint Thomas (AF) (CE)
Office of Admissions
Mail # 32F-1
2115 Summit Avenue
St. Paul, MN 55105-1096
Phone: (651) 962-6150 or (800) 328-
    6819, Ext. 2-6150
E-mail: admissions@stthomas.edu
http://www.stthomas.edu

MISSISSIPPI

Alcorn State University (A)
1000 ASU Drive #300
Alcorn State, MS 39096-9900
Phone: (601) 877-6147 or (800) 222-6790
Fax: (601) 877-6347

E-mail: ebarnes@lorman.alcorn.edu
http://www.alcorn.edu/

Jackson State University (A)
P.O. Box 17330
Jackson, MS 39217
Phone: (601) 979-2100 or (800) 848-6817
E-mail: gblakley@maill.jsums.edu
http://www.jsums.edu/

Mississippi State University (A; AF)
  (CE)
Mississippi State, MS 39762
Phone: (662) 325-2323
E-mail: msuinfo@ur.msstate.edu
http://www.msstate.edu/

Mississippi Valley State University (AF)
  (CE)
Office of Admissions and Recruitment
14000 Highway 82 W #7222
Itta Bena, MS 38941-1400
Phone: (662) 254-3347 or (800) 844-
  6885 (in-state)
Fax: (662) 254-3759
E-mail: admsn@mvsu.edu
http://www.mvsu.edu

University of Mississippi (A; N; AF)
  (CE)
University, MS 38677
Phone: (662) 915-7211
Fax: (662) 915-5869
E-mail: admissions@olemiss.edu
http://www.olemiss.edu/

University of Southern Mississippi
  (A; AF) (CE)
Office of Admissions
Box 5166
Hattiesburg, MS 39406-5166
Phone: (601) 266-5000
http://www.usm.edu/

MISSOURI

Central Missouri State University (A)
Office of Admission
1401 Ward Edwards
Warrensburg, MO 64093
Phone: (660) 543-4111
E-mail: christiansen@cmsul.cmsu.edu
http://www.cmsu.edu

Lincoln University (A)
820 Chestnut Street
Jefferson City, MO 65101

Phone: (800) 521-5052
E-mail: enroll@lincolnu.edu
http://www.lincolnu.edu/

Missouri Western State College (A) (CE)
4525 Downs Drive
St. Joseph, MO 64507
Phone: (816) 271-4200
E-mail: admissn@mwsc.edu
http://www.mwsc.edu/

Saint Louis University (AF) (CE)
221 North Grand Boulevard
St. Louis, MO 63103
Phone: (800) SLU-FORU
E-mail: admitme@slu.edu
http://www.slu.edu/

Southwest Missouri State University (A)
901 South National Avenue
Springfield, MO 65804
Phone: (417) 836-5000
E-mail: admissions@smsu.edu
http://www.smsu.edu/

Truman State University (A)
100 East Normal Street
Kirksville, MO 63501
Phone: (660) 785-4000
E-mail: admissions@truman.edu
http://www.truman.edu/

University of Missouri at Columbia
  (A; N; AF) (CE)
Office of Admissions
230 Jesse Hall
Columbia, MO 65211
Phone: (573) 882-2121
E-mail: mu4u@missouri.edu
http://www.missouri.edu/index.cfm

University of Missouri at Rolla (A; AF)
1870 Miner Circle
Rolla, MO 65409-1060
Phone: (573) 341-4111 or (800) 522-0938
E-mail: admissions@umr.edu
http://www.campus.umr.edu/index.html

Washington University (A) (CE)
One Brookings Drive
St. Louis, MO 63130
Phone: (314) 935-6000
Fax: (314) 935-4290
E-mail: admissions@wustl.edu
http://www.wustl.edu/

Wentworth Military Academy (A)
1880 Washington Avenue
Lexington, Missouri 64067
Phone: (660) 259-2221 or (800) 962-7682
Fax: 660-259-2677
http://www.wmal880.org/

MONTANA

Montana State University (A; AF)
  (PNE) (CE)
Admissions and New Student Services
120 Hamilton Hall
P.O. Box 172190
Bozeman, MT 59717-2190
E-mail: admissions@montana.edu
http://www.montana.edu

University of Montana (A)
Missoula, MT 59812
Phone: (406) 243-6266 or (800) 462-8636
E-mail: admiss@selway.umt.edu
http://www.umt.edu/

NEBRASKA

Creighton University (A) (PNE)
2500 California Plaza
Omaha, NE 68178
Phone: (402) 280-2700
E-mail: admissions@creighton.edu
http://www.creighton.edu/

University of Nebraska at Lincoln (A; N)
Office of Admissions
1410 Q Street
Lincoln, NE 68588-0417
Phone: (402) 472-7211
http://www.unl.edu/unlpub/index.shtml

University of Nebraska at Omaha
  (AF) (CE)
6001 Dodge Street
Eppley Administration Building,
  Room 103
Omaha, NE 68182-0286
Phone: (402) 554-2393
Fax: (402) 554-3472
E-mail: unoadm@unomaha.edu
http://www.unomaha.edu/home.html

NEVADA

University of Nevada at Reno (A) (CE)
1664 North Virginia Street
Reno, NV 89557-0042
Phone: (775) 784-1100
E-mail: asknevada@unr.edu
http://www.unr.edu/content/

NEW HAMPSHIRE

University of New Hampshire (A; AF) (CE)
Office of Undergraduate Admissions
Grant House
4 Garrison Avenue
Durham, NH 03824
Phone: (603) 862-1360
Fax: (603) 862-0077
http://www.unh.edu/

NEW JERSEY

New Jersey Institute of Technology (AF) (CE)
University Heights
Newark, NJ 07102-9895
Phone: (973) 596-3000
E-mail: admissions@njit.edu
http://www.njit.edu/

Princeton University (A) (CE)
Admission Office
110 West College, Box 430
Princeton, NJ 08544-0430
Phone: (609) 258-3060
Fax: (609) 258-6743
http://www.princeton.edu/index.shtml

Rutgers University (A; AF) (CE)
Office of University Undergraduate
  Admissions
Room 202
65 Davidson Road
Piscataway, NJ 08854-8097
Phone: (732) 932-INFO
http://www.rutgers.edu/

Seton Hall University (A) (PNE)
400 South Orange Avenue
South Orange, NJ 07079
Phone: (973) 761-9000
E-mail: thehall@shu.edu
http://www.shu.edu/

NEW MEXICO

New Mexico Military Institute (A)
101 W College Boulevard
Roswell, NM 88201-5173
Phone: (800) 421-5376
E-mail: admissions@nmmi.edu
http://www.nmmi.cc.nm.us/

New Mexico State University (A; AF)
MSC 3A
P.O. Box 30001
Las Cruces, NM 88003-8001

Phone: (505) 646-0111
E-mail: admissions@nmsu.edu
http://www.nmsu.edu/

University of New Mexico (N; AF) (CE)
Office of Admissions
Student Services Center 140
Albuquerque, NM 87131
Phone: (505) 277-2446
Fax: (505) 277-6686
E-mail: apply@unm.edu
http://www.unm.edu

NEW YORK

Canisius College (A) (CE)
2001 Main Street
Buffalo, NY 14208-1098
Phone: (716) 883-7000
Fax: (716) 888-2525
E-mail: inquiry@canisius.edu
http://www.canisius.edu/

Clarkson University (A; AF)
Undergraduate Admission
Holcroft House
P.O. Box 5605
Potsdam, NY 13699-5605
Phone: (315) 268-6479
Fax: (315) 268-7647
E-mail: admission@clarkson.edu
http://www.clarkson.edu/

Cornell University (A; N; AF) (CE)
Undergraduate Admissions Office
410 Thurston Avenue
Ithaca, NY 14850-2488
Phone: (607) 255-5241
Fax: (607) 254-5175
http://www.cornell.edu/

Fordham University (A) (CE)
Office of Undergraduate Admission
Thebaud Hall
441 East Fordham Road
New York, NY 10458-5191
Phone: (800) FORDHAM
E-mail: enroll@fordham.edu
http://www.fordham.edu/

Hofstra University (A)
Hempstead, NY 11549-1000
Phone: (516) 463-6600
http://www.hofstra.edu/home/index.html

Manhattan College (AF) (CE)
Manhattan College Parkway
Riverdale, NY 10471

Phone: (718) 862-8000
  or (800) MC2-XCEL
Fax: (718) 862-8019
E-mail: admit@manhattan.edu
http://www.manhattan.edu/

Niagara University (A)
The Office of Undergraduate Admissions
Bailo Hall
PO Box 2011
Niagara University, NY 14109-2011
Phone: (716) 285-1212 or (800) 462-2111
Fax: (716) 286-8710
E-mail: admissions@niagara.edu
http://www.niagara.edu/index.php

Rensselaer Polytechnic Institute
  (N; AF) (CE)
110 8th Street
Troy, NY 12180
Phone: (518) 276-6000
E-mail: admissions@rpi.edu
http://www.rpi.edu/

Rochester Institute of Technology
  (A; AF) (CE)
One Lomb Memorial Drive
Rochester, NY 14623-5603
Phone: (585) 475-2411
http://www.rit.edu/index1.php3

Saint Bonaventure University (A) (CE)
St. Bonaventure, NY 14778
Phone: (716) 375-2000
http://www.sbu.edu/index.html

Saint John's University (A)
8000 Utopia Parkway
Jamaica, NY 11439
Phone: (718) 990-2000 or (888) 978-5646
E-mail: admhelp@stjohns.edu;
http://www.stjohns.edu/pls/portal30/
  sjudev.school.adminhome

Siena College (A) (CE)
515 Loudon Road
Loudonville, NY 12211-1462
Phone: (518) 783-2300
E-mail: admissions@siena.edu
http://www.siena.edu/

**State University of New York at
  Brockport** (A)
350 New Campus Drive
Brockport, NY 14420
Phone: (585) 395-2211 or 2751
Fax: (585) 395-5452
E-mail: admit@brockport.edu
http://www.brockport.edu/

State University of New York Maritime College (N) (CE)
6 Pennyfield Road
Throggs Neck, NY 10465
Phone: (718) 409-7200
    or (800) 654-1874 (in-state);
    (800) 642-1874 (out-of-state)
E-mail: admissions@sunymaritime.edu
http://www.sunymaritime.edu/core.makka

Syracuse University (A; AF) (PNE) (CE)
Office of Admissions
201 Tolley Administration Building
Syracuse, NY 13244
Phone: (315) 443-3611
Fax: (315) 443-4226
E-mail: orange@syr.edu
http://www.syr.edu/

University of Rochester (N) (CE)
Office of Undergraduate Admissions
P.O. Box 270251
Rochester, NY 14627-0251
Phone: (585) 275-3221
    or (888) 822-2256
Fax: (585) 461-4595
http://www.rochester.edu/

NORTH CAROLINA

Appalachian State University (A)
Office of Admissions
Box 32004
Boone, NC 28608-2004
Phone: (828) 262-2000
Fax: (828) 262-3296
E-mail: admission@appstate.edu
http://www.appstate.edu/

Campbell University (A) (CE)
Office of Admissions
P.O. Box 546
Buies Creek, NC 27506
Phone: (910) 893-1300
    or (800) 334-4111 ext. 1290
Fax: (910) 893-1288
Email: adm@mailcenter.campbell.edu
http://www.campbell.edu/

Duke University (A; N; AF) (CE)
Office of Undergraduate Admissions
2138 Campus Drive
Box 90586
Durham, NC 27708-0586
Phone: (919) 684-3214
Fax: (919) 681-8941
E-mail: askduke@admiss.duke.edu
http://www.duke.edu/main/welcome.html

East Carolina University (A; AF)
East Fifth Street
Greenville, NC 27858-4353
Phone: (252) 328-6131
E-mail: admis@mail.ecu.edu
http://www.ecu.edu/

Elizabeth City State University (A)
1704 Weeksville Road
Elizabeth City, NC 27909
Phone: (252) 335-3400
E-mail: damoore@mail.ecsu.edu
http://www.ecsu.edu/

Fayetteville State University (AF)
1200 Murchison Road
Fayetteville, NC 28301-4298
Phone: (910) 672-1111
    or (800) 222-2594
Fax: (910) 672-1414
E-mail: admissions@uncfsu.edu
http://www.uncfsu.edu/

North Carolina A&T State University
    (A; AF) (PNE)
1601 East Market Street
Greensboro, NC 27411
Phone: (336) 334-7500
    or (800) 443-8964
E-mail: uadmit@ncat.edu
http://www.ncat.edu/

North Carolina State University
    (A; N; AF)
Office of Undergraduate Admissions
Campus Box 7103
Raleigh, NC 27695-7103
Phone: (919) 515-2011
E-mail: undergrad_admissions@
    ncsu.edu
http://www.ncsu.edu/

Saint Augustine's College (A)
1315 Oakwood Avenue
Raleigh, NC 27604
Phone: (919) 516-4000
E-mail: admissions@st-aug.edu
http://www.st-aug.edu/

University of North Carolina at Chapel Hill (A; N; AF)
Office of Undergraduate Admissions
CB #2200, Jackson Hall
Chapel Hill, NC 27599-2200
Phone: (919) 966-3621
Fax: (919) 962-3045
E-mail: uadm@email.unc.edu
http://www.unc.edu/

University of North Carolina at Charlotte (A; AF) (CE)
9201 University City Boulevard
Charlotte, NC 28223-0001
Phone: (704) 687-2000
http://www.uncc.edu/

Wake Forest University (A) (CE)
1834 Wake Forest Road
Winston-Salem, NC 27106
Phone: (336) 758-5255
E-mail: admissions@wfu.edu
http://www.wfu.edu/

NORTH DAKOTA

North Dakota State University (A; AF)
Office of Admission
Ceres 124
P.O. Box 5454
Fargo, ND 58105-5454
Phone: (701) 231-8643
    or (800) 488-NDSU
E-mail: NDSU.Admission@
    ndsu.nodak.edu
http://www.ndsu.nodak.edu/

University of North Dakota (A; AF) (CE)
University Station
Grand Forks, ND 58202
Phone: (701) 777-2011
    or (800) CALL-UND
E-mail: enrollment_services@
    mail.und.nodak.edu
http://www.und.edu/

OHIO

Bowling Green State University (A; AF)
    (CE)
Bowling Green, OH 43403
Phone: (419) 372-BGSU
    or (866) CHOOSEBGSU
E-mail: choosebgsu@bgnet.bgsu.edu
http://www.bgsu.edu/

Capital University (A) (PNE)
2199 E Main Street
Columbus, OH 43209-2394
Phone: (614) 236-6011 or (800) 289-6289
Fax: (614) 236-6926
E-mail: admissions@capital.edu
http://www.capital.edu

Central State University (A)
P.O. Box 1004
Wilberforce, OH 45384
Phone: (937) 376-6011

E-mail: Info@csu.ces.edu
http://www.centralstate.edu/

John Caroll University (A)
20700 North Park Boulevard
University Heights, OH 44118
Phone: (216) 397-1886
http://www.jcu.edu/

Kent State University (A; AF) (CE)
Kent, OH 44242
Phone: (330) 672-2444
E-mail: info@kent.edu
http://www.kent.edu/

Miami University (N; AF)
Oxford, OH 45056
Phone: (513) 529-1809
E-mail: admission@muohio.edu
http://www.miami.muohio.edu/

Ohio University (A; AF) (CE)
Office of Admissions
120 Chubb Hall
Athens, OH 45701-2979
Phone: (740) 593-4100
Fax: (740) 593-0560
E-mail: admissions@ohio.edu
http://www.ohiou.edu/

Ohio State University (A; N; AF) (CE)
Undergraduate Admissions
Enarson Hall
154 West 12th Avenue
Columbus, OH 43210
Phone: (614) 292-3980
E-mail: askabuckeye@osu.edu
http://www.acs.ohio-state.edu/index.php

University of Akron (A; AF) (CE) (PNE)
302 Buchtel Mall
Akron, OH 44325
Phone: (330) 972-7111
http://www.uakron.edu/

University of Cincinnati (A; AF) (CE)
2624 Clifton Avenue
Cincinnati, OH 45221
Phone: (513) 556-6000
http://www.uc.edu/

University of Dayton (A)
Office of Admission
300 College Park
Dayton, OH 45469-1300
Phone: (937) 229-4411 or (800) 837-7433
E-mail: info@udayton.edu
http://www.udayton.edu/

University of Toledo (A)
Toledo, OH 43606-3390
Phone: (419) 530-4636
E-mail: enroll@utnet.utoledo.edu
http://www.utoledo.edu/

Wright State University (A; AF) (CE)
3640 Colonel Glenn Highway
Dayton, OH 45435-0001
Phone: (937) 775-3333 or (800) 247-1770
E-mail: admissions@wright.edu
http://www.wright.edu/

Xavier University (A) (CE)
3800 Victory Parkway
Cincinnati, OH 45207
Phone: (513) 745-3000 or (800) 344-4698
http://www.home.xu.edu/

OKLAHOMA

Cameron University (A)
2800 West Gore Boulevard
Lawton, OK 73505-6377
Phone: (580) 581-2200
E-mail: admissions@cameron.edu
http://www.cameron.edu/index.php

Oklahoma State University (A; AF) (CE)
Office of Admissions
324 Student Union
Stillwater, OK 74078-1012
Phone: (800) 233-5019 (in-state) or (405)
    744-6858 (out-of-state)
Fax: (405) 744-5285
E-mail: admit@okstate.edu
http://osu.okstate.edu/

University of Central Oklahoma (A)
100 North University Drive
Edmond, OK 73034
Phone: (405) 974-2000
E-mail: 4ucoinfo@ucok.edu
http://www.ucok.edu/

University of Oklahoma (A; N; AF) (CE)
550 Parrington Oval, L-1
Norman, OK 73019-3032
Phone: (405) 325-2151 or (800) 234-6868
E-mail: ou-pss@ou.edu
http://www.go2.ou.edu/

OREGON

Oregon State University (A; N; AF) (CE)
Office of Admissions
104 Kerr Administration Building
Corvallis, OR 97331-2106

Phone: (800) 291-4192
E-mail: osuadmit@orst.edu
http://www.orst.edu/

University of Oregon (A)
Office of Admissions
240 Oregon Hall
1217 University of Oregon
Eugene, OR 97403-1217
Phone: (541) 346-1000 or (800) 232-3825
Fax: (541) 346-5815
E-mail: uoadmit@oregon.uoregon.edu
http://www.uoregon.edu/

University of Portland (A; AF) (CE)
    (PNE)
5000 N. Willamette Boulevard
Portland, OR 97203-5798
Phone: (503) 943-7911
E-mail: admissio@up.edu
http://www.up.edu/

PENNSYLVANIA

Bucknell University (A) (CE)
Moore Avenue
Lewisburg, PA 17837
Phone: (570) 577-2000
Fax: (570) 577-3760
E-mail: admissions@bucknell.edu
http://www.bucknell.edu

Carnegie-Mellon University (N) (CE)
5000 Forbes Avenue
Pittsburgh, PA 15213
Phone: (412) 268-2000
E-mail: undergraduate-admissions@
    andrew.cmu.edu
http://www.cmu.edu/

Dickinson College (A) (CE)
P.O. Box 1773
Carlisle, PA 17013
Phone: (717) 243-5121
E-mail: admit@dickinson.edu
http://www.dickinson.edu/

Drexel University (A) (CE)
Philadelphia, PA 19104
Phone: (215) 895-6731
E-mail: admissions@drexel.edu
http://www.drexel.edu/

Edinboro University of Pennsylvania (A)
Edinboro, PA 16444
Phone: (814) 732-2000
    or (888) 8GO-BORO
http://www.IIsl.edinboro.edu/home/
    welcome.asp

Gannon University (A) (CE)
109 University Square
Erie, PA 16541-0001
Phone: (800) GANNON-U
E-mail: admissions@gannon.edu
http://www.gannon.edu/

Indiana University of Pennsylvania (A)
    (PNE)
1011 South Drive
Indiana, PA 15705-1085
Phone: (724) 357-2100
http://www.iup.edu

Lehigh University (A) (CE)
27 Memorial Drive West
Bethlehem, PA 18015
Phone: (610) 758-3000
http://www3.lehigh.edu/default.asp

Lock Haven University of Pennsylvania
    (A)
Lock Haven, PA 17745
Phone: (800) 332-8900 (in-state)
    or (800) 233-8978 (out-of-state)
http://www.lhup.edu/

Saint Joseph's State University (AF)
    (CE)
Office of Undergraduate Admissions
Bronstein Hall
5600 City Avenue
Philadelphia, PA 19131
Phone: (610) 660-1000
Fax: (610) 660-1314
E-mail: admit@sju.edu
http://www.sju.edu/

Shippensburg University (A)
1871 Old Main Drive
Shippensburg, PA 17257
Phone: (717) 477-7447
E-mail: admiss@ship.edu
http://www.ship.edu/

Slippery Rock University (A)
1 Morrow Way
Slippery Rock, PA 16507
Phone: (800) SRU-9111
Fax: (724) 738-2913
http://www.sru.edu/

Temple University (A)
1801 North Board Street
Philadelphia, PA 19122
Phone: (215) 204-7000
E-mail: tuadm@vm.temple.edu
http://www.temple.edu/

The Pennsylvania State University (A;
    N; AF) (CE)
Undergraduate Admissions Office
201 Shields Building, Box 3000
University Park, PA 16804-3000
Phone: (814) 865-5471
Fax: (814) 863-7590
http://www.psu.edu/

University of Pennsylvania (N) (CE)
The Office of Undergraduate Admissions
1 College Hall
Philadelphia, PA 19104-6376
Phone: (215) 898-7507
http://www.upenn.edu/

University of Pittsburgh (A; AF) (CE)
Office of Admissions and Financial Aid
4227 Fifth Avenue (Alumni Hall)
Pittsburgh, PA 15260
Phone: (412) 624-PITT
http://www.pitt.edu/

University of Scranton (A) (PNE) (CE)
Scranton, PA 18510
Phone: (570) 941-7400
E-mail: admissions@scranton.edu
http://www.matrix.scranton.edu/

Valley Forge Military Academy
    and College (A) (CE)
1001 Eagle Road
Wayne, PA 19087-3695
Phone: (610) 989-1200 or (800) 234-8362
Fax: (610) 688-1545
E-mail: admissions@vfmac.edu
http://www.vfmac.edu/index_flash.shtml

Villanova University (N)
Office of University Admission
800 Lancaster Avenue
Villanova, PA 19085-1672
Phone: (610) 519-4000
E-mail: gotovu@villanova.edu
http://www.wi03.villanova.edu/web2000/
    external?

Widener University (A) (PNE)
One University Place
Chester, PA 19013
Phone: (610) 499-4126
E-mail: Admissions.Office@widener.edu
http://www.widener.edu/

Wilkes University (AF) (CE)
P.O. Box 111
Wilkes-Barre, PA 18766

Phone: (570) 408-5000
E-mail: admissions@wilkes.edu
http://www.wilkes.edu/

RHODE ISLAND

Providence College (A)
549 River Avenue
Providence, RI 02918-0001
Phone: (401) 865-1000
http://www.providence.edu/

University of Rhode Island (A)
Undergraduate Admissions Office
14 Upper College Road
Kingston, RI 02881
Phone: (401) 874-7100
E-mail: uriadmit@uriacc.uri.edu
http://www.uri.edu/

SOUTH CAROLINA

Charleston Southern University (AF)
    (CE)
P.O. Box 118087
Charleston, SC 29423-8087
9200 University Boulevard
Charleston, SC 29406
Phone: (843) 863-7050
    or (800) 947-7474
http://www.csuniv.edu/

The Citadel (A; N; AF) (CE)
171 Moultrie Street
Charleston, SC 29409
Phone: (843) 953-5000
    or (800) 868-1842
Fax: (843) 953-7036
E-mail: admissions@citadel.edu
http://www.citadel.edu/

Clemson University (A; AF) (CE)
    (PNE)
Office of Undergraduate Admissions
Clemson University
105 Sikes Hall
Box 345124
Clemson, SC 29634-5124
Phone: (864) 656-3311
E-mail: cuadmissions@clemson.edu
http://www.clemson.edu/home.htm

Furman University (A)
3300 Poinsett Highway
Greenville, SC 29613
Phone: (864) 294-2000
E-mail: admissions@furman.edu
http://www.furman.edu

Presbyterian College (A)
503 South Broad Street
Clinton, SC 29325
Phone: (864) 833-2820
E-mail: admissions@presby.edu
http://www.presby.edu/

South Carolina State University (A)
300 College Street NE
Orangeburg, SC 29117
Phone: (803) 536-7000
E-mail: admissions@scsu.edu
http://www.scsu.edu/

University of South Carolina
(A; N; AF) (CE)
Columbia, SC 29208
Phone: (803) 777-7000 or (800) 868-5872
Fax: (803) 777-0101
E-mail: admissions-ugrad@sc.edu
http://www.sc.edu/

Wolford College (A)
429 North Church Street
Spartanburg, SC 29303-3663
Phone: (864) 597-4000
E-mail: admissions@wofford.edu
http://www.wofford.edu/

SOUTH DAKOTA

South Dakota School of Mines (A)
501 East Saint Joseph Street
Rapid City, SD 57701
Phone: (605) 394-2400 or (800) 544-8162
Fax: (605) 394-6131
E-mail: info@sdsmt.edu
http://www.hpcnet.org/cgi-
    bin/global/a_bus_card.cgi?SiteID=21

South Dakota State University (A; AF)
(CE)
Admissions Office
Box 2201
Brookings, SD 57007
Phone: (605) 688-4121 or (800) 952-3541
Fax: (605) 688-6384
E-mail: SDSU_Admissions@sdstate.edu
http://www.sdstate.org/

University of South Dakota (A)
14 East Clark Street
Vermillion, SD 57069
Phone: (605) 677-6287
    or (877) COYOTES
Fax: (605) 677-5202
http://www.usd.edu/

TENNESSEE

Austin-Peay State University (A) (CE)
P.O. Box 4548
Clarksville, TN 37044
Phone: (931) 221-7011
Fax: (931) 221-6168
E-mail: admissions@apsu.edu
http://www.apsu.edu/

Carson-Newman College (A) (PNE)
Admissions Office
Jefferson City, TN 37760
Phone: (865) 471-2000
Fax: (865) 471-3502
E-mail: sgray@cn.edu
http://www.cn.edu/

East Tennessee State University (A)
Office of Admissions
Box 70731
Johnson City, TN 37614-0054
Phone: (423) 439-1000
E-mail: stevew@etsu.edu
http://www.etsu.edu/

Middle Tennessee State University (A)
1301 East Main Street
Murfreesboro, TN 37132-0001
Phone: (615) 898-2300
E-mail: admissions@mtsu.edu
http://www.mtsu.edu/

Tennessee State University (AF) (CE)
3500 John A. Merritt Boulevard
Nashville, TN 37209
Phone: (615) 963-5000
E-mail: ctaylor@picard.tnstate.edu
http://www.tnstate.edu/

Tennessee Tech University (A)
Office of Admissions
P.O. Box 5006
Cookeville, TN 38505-0001
Phone: (931) 372-3888
    or (800) 255-5881
Fax: (931) 372-6250
E-mail: admissions@tntech.edu
http://www.tntech.edu/

University of Memphis (A; N; AF) (CE)
Office of Admissions
229 Administration Building
Memphis, TN 38152
Phone: (901) 678-2111
E-mail: recruitment@cc.memphis.edu
http://www.memphis.edu/

University of Tennessee (A; AF) (CE)
Knoxville, TN 37996
Phone: (865) 974-1000
E-mail: admissions@utk.edu
http://www.utk.edu/

University of Tennessee at Martin (A)
Office of Admissions
544 University Street
Martin, TN 38238
Phone: (731) 587-7000
    or (800) 829-UTM1
E-mail: admitme@utm.edu
http://www.utm.edu/

Vanderbilt University (A; N) (CE)
Office of Undergraduate Admissions
2305 West End Avenue
Nashville, TN 37235
Phone: (615) 322-2561 or (800) 288-0432
E-mail: admissions@vanderbilt.edu
http://www.vanderbilt.edu/

TEXAS

Angelo State University (AF)
2601 West Avenue N
San Angelo, TX 76909
Phone: (915) 942-2041
E-mail: admissions@angelo.edu
http://www.angelo.edu/

Baylor University (AF)
Waco, TX 76798
Phone: (800) BAYLOR-U
http://www.baylor.edu/

Prairie View A&M University (A; N)
P.O. Box 3089
Prairie View, TX 77446-3089
Phone: (936) 857-2626
E-mail: admissions@pvamu.edu
http://www.pvamu.edu/

Rice University (N) (CE)
6100 Main Street
Houston, TX 77005
Phone: (713) 348-7423
E-mail: info@rice.edu
http://www.rice.edu/

Saint Mary's University (A) (CE)
One Camino Santa Maria
San Antonio, TX 78228-8503
Phone: (800) FOR-STMU
E-mail: uadm@stmarytx.edu
http://www.stmarytx.edu/

Southwest Texas State University
   (A; AF)
1803 Avenue I
Huntsville, TX 77341
Phone: (936)294-1111
E-mail: admissions@shsu.edu
http://www.shsu.edu/

Stephen F. Austin State University (A)
SFA Station
Nacogdoches, TX 75962
Phone: (936) 468-2011
E-mail: admissions@sfasu.edu
http://www.sfasu.edu/index2.html

Tarleton State University (A)
Box T-0030
Stephenville, TX 76401
Phone: (254) 968-9125
   or (800) 687-4878
Fax: (254) 968-9951
E-mail: info@tarleton.edu
http://www.tarleton.edu/

Texas A&M University (A; N; AF) (CE)
Office of Admissions
P.O. Box 30014
College Station, TX 77843
Phone: (979) 845-3211
http://www.tamu.edu/

Texas A&M University – Kingsville (A)
700 University Boulevard MSC 114
Kingsville, TX 78363
Phone: (361) 593-2111
   or (800) 687-6000
E-mail: tamukrequest@tamuk.edu
http://www.tamuk.edu/

Texas Christian University (A; AF)
2800 S University Drive
Fort Worth, TX 76129
Phone: (817) 257-7000
   or (800) 828-3764
E-mail: frogmail@tcu.edu
http://www.tcu.edu/

Texas Tech University (A; AF)
Office of Admissions and School
   Relations
West Hall
P.O. Box 45005
Lubbock, TX 79409-5005
Phone: (806) 742-1480
Fax: (806) 742-0062
E-mail: nsr@ttu.edu
http://www.ttu.edu/

University of Houston (A) (CE)
Office of Admissions
122 E Cullen Building
Houston, TX 77204-2023
Phone: (713) 743-2255
E-mail: admissions@uh.edu
http://www.uh.edu/

University of North Texas (AF)
P.O. Box 311277
Denton, TX 76203
Phone: (940) 565-2000
E-mail: undergrad@unt.edu
http://www.unt.edu/

University of Texas at Austin (A; N; AF)
   (CE)
Office of Admissions
1 University Station DO700
Austin, TX 78712
Phone: (512) 475-7348
http://www.utexas.edu/

University of Texas at El Paso (A)
   (PNE)
Undergraduate Admissions
Academic Services Building, Room 104
500 W University Avenue
El Paso, TX 79968
Phone: (915) 747-5576
   or (877) 746-4637
Fax: (915) 747-5848
E-mail: futureminer@utep.edu.
http://www.utep.edu

University of Texas—Pan American (A)
1201 West University Drive
Edinburg, TX 78539-2999
Phone: (956) 381-3522
Fax: (956) 381-2606
E-mail: admissions@panam.edu
http://www.panam.edu/

University of Texas at San Antonio
   (A; AF)
6900 N Loop 1604 W
San Antonio, TX 78249-0619
Phone: (210) 458-4011
E-mail: Prospects@utsa.edu
http://www.utsa.edu/

UTAH

Brigham Young University (A; AF)
   (CE)
Admissions Office
A-153 ASB
Provo, UT 84602
Phone: (801) 378-2507
E-mail: admissions@byu.edu
http://www.byu.edu/index.html

University of Utah (A; N; AF) (CE)
201 S 1460 E
Room 250 S
Salt Lake City, UT 84112
Phone: (801) 581-7281
E-mail: admissweb@sa.utah.edu
http://www.utah.edu/

Utah State University (AF)
Logan, UT 84322
Phone: (435) 797-1000
E-mail: recruit@cc.usu.edu
http://www.usu.edu/

Weber State University (A) (CE)
Ogden, UT 84408
Phone: (801) 626-6000
http://www.weber.edu/ns.asp

VERMONT

Norwich University (A; N; AF) (PNE)
   (CE)
158 Harmon Drive
Northfield, VT 05663
Phone: (800) 468-6679
E-mail: nuadm@norwich.edu
http://www.norwich.edu/index.html

University of Vermont (A) (CE)
Office of Undergraduate Admissions
194 South Prospect Street
Burlington, VT 05401
Phone: (802) 656-3370
Fax: (802) 656-8611
E-mail: admissions@uvm.edu
http://www.uvm.edu/

VIRGINIA

The College of William and Mary (A)
   (CE)
P.O. Box 8795
Williamsburg, VA 23187-8795
Phone: (757) 221-4000
http://www.wm.edu/

George Mason University (A)
Office of Undergraduate Admissions
MSN 3A4
4400 University Drive
Fairfax, VA 22030-4444
Phone: (703) 993-1000
Fax: (703) 993-2392
http://www.gmu.edu/

Hampton University (A; N) (PNE)
Hampton, VA 23668
Phone: (800) 624-3328
E-mail: admissions@hamptonu.edu
http://www.hamptonu.edu/

James Madison University (A)
800 S Main Street
Harrisonburg, VA 22807
Phone: (540) 568-6211
E-mail: gotojmu@jmu.edu
http://www.jmu.edu/

Norfolk State University (A; N) (PNE)
700 Park Avenue
Norfolk, VA 23504
Phone: (757) 823-8600
http://www.nsu.edu/index.htm

Old Dominion University (A; N)
Hampton Boulevard
Norfolk, VA 23529
Phone: (757) 683-3000
E-mail: admit@odu.edu
http://www.web.odu.edu/

University of Richmond (A) (CE)
28 Westhampton Way
Richmond, VA 23173
Phone: (800) 700-1662
http://www.richmond.edu/alt_index.htm

University of Virginia (A; N; AF) (CE)
P.O. Box 400160
Charlottesville, VA 22904-4160
Phone: (434) 982-3200
Fax: (434) 924-3587
E-mail: undergradadmission@virginia.edu
http://www.virginia.edu

Virginia Military Institute (A; N; AF)
   (CE)
Lexington, VA 24450
Phone: (540) 464-7000
E-mail: Admissions@vmi.edu
http://www.vmi.edu/

**Virginia Polytechnic Institute
   and State University** (A; N; AF) (CE)
Undergraduate Admissions
201 Burruss Hall
Blacksburg, VA 24061
Phone: (540) 231-6000
Fax: (540) 231-3242
E-mail: vtadmiss@vt.edu
http://www.vt.edu/

Virginia State University (A)
Petersburg, VA 23806
Phone: (804) 524-5000
E-mail: admiss@vsu.edu
http://www.vsu.edu/

WASHINGTON

Central Washington University (A; AF)
400 E 8th Avenue
Ellensburg, WA 98926
Phone: (509) 963-2461
   or (866) 298-4968
E-mail: cwuadmis@cwu.edu.
http://www.cwu.edu

Eastern Washington University (A)
101 Sutton Hall
Cheney, WA 99004-2447
Phone: (509) 359-2397
   or (888) 740-1914
Fax: (509) 359-6692
E-mail: admissions@mail.ewu.edu
http://www.ewu.edu/

Gonzaga University (A)
Office of Admission
502 East Boone Avenue
Spokane, WA 99258-0102
Phone: (800) 322-2584
   or (509) 323-6572
Fax: (509) 323-5780
E-mail: ballinger@gu.gonzaga.edu
http://www.gonzaga.edu

Seattle University (A) (CE) (PNE)
900 Broadway
Seattle, WA 98122-4340
Phone: (206) 296-6000
E-mail: admissions@seattleu.edu
http://www.seattleu.edu/

University of Washington (A; N; AF)
   (CE)
Schmitz Hall—Admissions
Box 355852
Seattle, WA 98195-5852
Phone: (206) 543-9686
Fax: (206) 685-3655
http://www.washington.edu/

Washington State University (A; AF)
   (CE)
Office of Admissions
370 Lighty Student Services Bldg
P.O. Box 641067
Pullman, WA 99164-1067

Phone: (888) 468-6978
E-mail: admiss2@wsu.edu
http://www.wsu.edu/

WEST VIRGINIA

Marshall University (A)
Marshall University Admissions
One John Marshall Drive
Huntington, WV 25755
Phone: (304) 696-3160
   or (800) 642-3499
Fax: (304) 696-3135
E-mail: admissions@marshall.edu
http://www.marshall.edu

West Virginia State College (A)
P.O. Box 1000
Institute, WV 25112-1000
Phone: (800) 987-2112
E-mail: ruhnkeam@mail.wvsc.edu
http://www.wvsc.edu/

West Virginia University (A; AF)
P.O. Box 6201
Morgantown, WV 26506
Phone: (304) 293-0111
E-mail: go2wvu@mail.wvu.edu
http://www.wvu.edu/indexflash.html

WISCONSIN

Marquette University (A; N; AF) (CE)
   (PNE)
P.O. Box 1881
Milwaukee, WI 53201-1881
Phone: (414) 288-7302
   or (800) 222-6544
http://www.marquette.edu/index.html

University of Wisconsin at La Crosse
   (A) (CE)
1725 State Street
La Crosse, WI 54601
Phone: (608) 785-8000
http://www.uwlax.edu/

University of Wisconsin at Madison
   (A; N; AF) (CE)
Office of Admissions
716 Langdon Street
Madison, WI 53706-1481
Phone: (608) 262-3961
E-mail: onwisconsin@
   admissions.wisc.edu
http://www.wisc.edu/

University of Wisconsin at Oshkosh
   (A) (CE)
P.O. Box 2423
Oshkosh, WI 54903-2423
Phone: (920) 424-0202
E-mail: mckinney@uwosh.edu
http://www.uwosh.edu/

**University of Wisconsin at Stevens
   Point** (A)
2100 Main Street
Stevens Point, WI 54481-3897
Phone: (715) 346-0123
E-mail: admiss@uwsp.edu
http://www.uwsp.edu/

WYOMING

University of Wyoming (A; AF) (CE)
P.O. Box 3435
Laramie, WY 82071
Phone: (307) 766-1121
http://www.uwyo.edu/

PUERTO RICO

University of Puerto Rico at Mayaguez
   (A; AF) (CE)
P.O. Box 5000
Mayaguez, PR 00681-5000
Phone: (787) 265-3811
http://www.uprm.edu/

**University of Puerto Rico
   at Rio Piedras** (A; AF) (CE)
P.O. Box 23344
San Juan, PR 00931-3344
Phone: (787) 764-0000
http://www.rrp.upr.edu/

GUAM

University of Guam (A)
UOG Station
Mangilao, Guam 96923
Phone: (671) 735-2207
Fax: (671) 734-4245
E-mail: bcdungca@uog9.uog.edu
http://www.uog.edu

APPENDIX III
UNITED STATES SERVICE ACADEMIES

Acceptance to three of the four U.S. Service Academies requires nomination by a member of Congress. The Coast Guard Academy is the only academy that does not require a congressional nomination.

United States Military Academy (A)
West Point, NY 10996
Phone: (845) 938-4011
E-mail: admissions@www.usma.edu
http://www.usma.edu/

United States Naval Academy
(N; MC)
Candidate Guidance Office
117 Decatur Road
Annapolis, MD 21402-5018
Phone: (410) 293-4361
http://www.usna.edu

U.S. Air Force Academy (AF)
HQ USAFA/RRS
2304 Cadet Drive
Suite 200
USAF Academy, CO 80840
Phone: (800) 443-9266
Fax: (719) 333-3647
E-mail: rr_webmail@usafa.af.mil
http://www.usafa.af.mil/flash/index.html

U.S. Coast Guard Academy (CG)
31 Mohegan Avenue
New London, CT 06320-8103
Phone: (860) 444-8501
    or (800) 883-USCG (8724)
E-mail: admissions@cga.uscg.mil
http://www.cga.edu/

APPENDIX IV
BIBLIOGRAPHY

A. BOOKS

Bonn, Keith E. *Army Officer's Guide, 49th Edition.* Mechanicsburg, Pa.: Stackpole Books, 2002.

Budahn, P.J. *What to Expect from the Military: A Practical Guide for Young People, Parents, and Counselors.* Westport, Conn.: Greenwood Publishing Group, 2000.

Editors of VGM Career Books. *Résumés for Former Military Personnel.* Lincolnwood, Ill.: VGM Career Horizons, 2001.

Farley, Janet I. *Jobs and the Military Spouse: Married, Mobile and Motivated for the New Job Market.* Waupaca, Wisc.: Impact Publications, 1997.

Harris, Bill. *The Complete Idiot's Guide to Careers in the U.S. Military.* Indianapolis, Ind.: Alpha Books, 2002.

Henderson, David G. *Job Search: Marketing Your Military Experience.* Mechanicsburg, Pa.: Stackpole Books, 1999.

Hurwitz, Sue. *Careers Inside the World of the Government.* New York, N.Y.: Rosen Publishing Group, 1998.

Hutton, Donald B. *A Guide to Military Careers.* Hauppauge, N.Y.: Barron's Educational Series, 1998.

Jacobsen, K.C. *Retiring from Military Service: A Commonsense Guide.* Annapolis, Md.: Naval Institute Press, 1995.

JIST. *America's Top Military Careers: The Official Guide to Occupations in the Armed Forces.* Indianapolis, Ind.: JIST, 2000.

Lewis, Audie G. *Career Progression Guide for Soldiers: A Practical, Complete Guide for Getting Ahead in Today's Competitive Army.* Mechanicsburg, Pa.: Stackpole Books, 1998.

Macdonald, Robert W. *Transitions: Military Pathways to Civilian Careers.* New York, N.Y.: Rosen Publishing Group, 1988.

———*Exploring Careers in the Military Services.* New York, N.Y.: Rosen Publishing Group, 1987.

Mendlin, Ronald C. and Marc Polonsky with J. Michael Farr. *Being "Job-Ready": Identify Your Skills, Strengths, and Career Goals.* Indianapolis, Ind.: JIST, 2000.

Ostrow, Scott A. *The Insider's Guide to Joining the Military.* Lawrenceville, N.J.: Arco/Peterson's, 2000.

———and Solomon Wiener. *ASVAB.* Lawrenceville, N.J.: Arco/Peterson's, 2001.

Paradis, Adrian A. *Opportunities in Military Careers.* Lincolnwood, Ill.: VGM Career Horizons, 1999.

Rafferty, Robert. *Careers in the Military: Good Training for Civilian Life.* New York: Elsevier/Nelson Books, 1980.

Roza, Greg. *Careers in the Military.* New York, N.Y.: Rosen Publishing Group, 2000.

Rush, Robert S. *Enlisted Soldier's Guide 5th Edition.* Mechanicsburg, Pa.: Stackpole Books, 2002.

Savino, Carl S. and Ronald L. Krannich. *Military Resumes and Cover Letters.* Indianapolis, Ind.: Impact Publications, 2001.

———and Ronald L. Krannich. *From Army Green to Corporate Gray: A Career Transition Guide for Army Personnel.* Indianapolis, Ind.: Impact Publications, 2001.

———and Ronald L. Krannich. *From Air Force Blue to Corporate Gray: A Career Transition Guide for Air Force Personnel.* Indianapolis, Ind.: Impact Publications, 1996.

———and Ronald L. Krannich. *From Navy Blue to Corporate Gray: A Career Transition Guide for Navy, Marine Corps and Coast Guard Personnel.* Indianapolis, Ind.: Impact Publications, 2001.

Schwager, Tina and Michele Schuerger. *Cool Women, Hot Jobs ... and How You Can Go For It, Too!* Minneapolis, Minn.: Free Spirit Pub., 2002.

Slappy, Mary McGowan. *Exploring Military Service for Women.* New York, N.Y.: Rosen Publishing Group, 1989.

Stiehm, Judith Hicks. *The U.S. Army War College: Military Education in a Democracy.* Philadelphia, Pa.: Temple University Press, 2002.

U.S. Department of Defense. *Military Careers: A Guide to Military Occupations and Selected Military Career Paths, 1992–1994.* Washington, D.C.: U.S. Department of Defense, 1992.

Vincent, Lynn. *The Military Advantage: Your Path to an Education and a Great Civilian Career.* Ayer, Mass.: Learning Express, 2001.

Wiener, Solomon and E.P. Steinberg. *ASVAB.* New York, N.Y.: Macmillan General Reference, 1999.

B. WEBSITES

Air Force ROTC Online
http://www.afrotc.com/home.htm

Army ROTC Online
http://www-rotc.monroe.army.mil/Information/index2.html

Department of Defense
http://www.defenselink.mil/

Military Career Guide Online
http://www.militarycareers.com/

Military Careers
http://www.military.com/Careers/Home/1,13373,,00.html

Navy and Marine Corps ROTC Online
http://www.nrotc.navy.mil/

The Occupational Outlook Handbook Online
http://www.bls.gov/oco/

Today's Military
http://www.todaysmilitary.com/index.php

U.S. Air Force
http://www.af.mil/
http://www.airforce.com/index_fr.htm

U.S.A. Jobs
http://www.usajobs.opm.gov/

U.S. Army
http://www.army.mil/
http://www.goarmy.com/index02.htm
http://www.army-military.org/

U.S. Coast Guard
http://www.uscg.mil/

U.S. Marines
http://www.usmc.mil/
http://marines.com/

U.S. Military
http://www.usmilitary.com/

U.S. Military Armed Forces Careers
http://www.armedforcescareers.com/

U.S. Navy
http://www.navy.mil/
http://www.navy.com/index.jsp

INDEX

Boldface page numbers denote main entries.